Pragmatics & Language Learning

Pragmatics & Language Learning
Series Editor
Gabriele Kasper

Pragmatics & Language Learning ("PLL"), a refereed series sponsored by the National Foreign Language Resource Center at the University of Hawai'i, publishes selected papers from the biennial International Conference on Pragmatics & Language Learning under the editorship of the conference hosts and the series editor. Check the NFLRC website (nflrc.hawaii.edu) for upcoming PLL conferences and PLL volumes.

Pragmatics and language learning (Vol. 11)
Kathleen Bardovi-Harlig, César Félix-Brasdefer, & Alwiya S. Omar (Eds.), 2006
ISBN 978-0-8248313-7-0

Pragmatics & Language Learning

volume 12, 2010

editors
Gabriele Kasper
Hanh thi Nguyen
Dina Rudolph Yoshimi
Jim K. Yoshioka

NATIONAL FOREIGN LANGUAGE RESOURCE CENTER
University of Hawai'i at Mānoa

© 2010 Gabriele Kasper
Some rights reserved. See: http://creativecommons.org/licenses/by-nc-nd/2.5/
Manufactured in the United States of America.

The contents of this publication were developed in part under a grant from the U.S. Department of Education (CFDA 84.229, P229A060002). However, the contents do not necessarily represent the policy of the Department of Education, and one should not assume endorsement by the Federal Government.

ISBN 978-0-9800459-6-3
ISSN 1943-6947

∞ The paper used in this publication meets the minimum requirements of the American National Standard for Information Sciences—Permanence of Paper for Printed Library Materials.
ANSI Z39.48-1984

book design by Deborah Masterson

distributed by
National Foreign Language Resource Center
University of Hawai'i
1859 East-West Road #106
Honolulu HI 96822-2322
nflrc.hawaii.edu

contents

vii   Acknowledgements

1   Introduction
Gabriele Kasper
Hanh thi Nguyen
Dina Rudolph Yoshimi

Part I: Sequences and Resources in Second Language and Multilingual Talk

15   Learning Language in Real Time:
A Case Study of the Japanese Demonstrative Pronoun
Are in Word-Search Sequences
Junko Mori

43   Switching Languages, Juggling Identities:
A Sequence of Multilingual, Multiparty Talk
Tim Greer

67   A Pragmatic Study of the Hawai'i Creole Discourse
Marker *Daswai* in Second-Generation Okinawan
American Speech
Toshiaki Furukawa

91   The Socialization of Leave-Taking in Indonesian
Margaret A. DuFon

113   Dinkas Down Under:
Request Performance in Simulated Workplace Interaction
Lynda Yates

	141	Recognition of Conventional Expressions in L2 Pragmatics *Kathleen Bardovi-Harlig*
	163	The Use of Conventional Expressions and Utterance Length in L2 Pragmatics *Kathleen Bardovi-Harlig* *Maria-Thereza Bastos* *Beatrix Burghardt* *Eric Chappetto* *Edelmira Nickels* *Marda Rose*
	187	Effects of Cultural Background in a Test of ESL Pragmalinguistics: A DIF Approach *Carsten Roever*

Part II: Second Language Interaction in Pedagogical Settings

	215	Achieving Distinction Through Mock ESL: A Critical Pragmatics Analysis of Classroom Talk in a High School *Steven Talmy*
	255	Teacher Deployment of Applause in Interactional Assessments of L2 Learners *Yuri Hosoda* *David Aline*
	277	Other-Correction of Language Form Following a Repair Sequence *Eric Hauser*
	297	Agreements and Disagreements: The Small Group Discussion in a Foreign Language Classroom *Donna Fujimoto*
	327	I Can Be With! A Novice Kindergartner's Successes and Challenges in Play Participation and the Development of Communicative Skills *Martha Sif Karrebæk*
	361	About the Contributors

acknowledgements

This volume has greatly benefited from helpful commentaries at different stages of the editorial process. The editors gratefully acknowledge the following reviewers:

Karin Aijmer, *Göteborg University*
Polly Björk-Willén, *Linköping University*
Cade Bushnell, *University of Tsukuba*
Donald Carroll, *Shikoku Gakuin University*
Asta Thunqvist Čekaite, *Linköping University*
Haruko M. Cook, *University of Hawai'i at Mānoa*
Diana Eades, *University of New England*
Juliane Edenstrom, *University of Illinois at Urbana-Champaign*
César Félix-Brasdefer, *Indiana University*
Michael Forman, *University of Hawai'i at Mānoa*
Marta González-Lloret, *University of Hawai'i at Mānoa*
Timothy Hassall, *Australian National University*
Michael Haugh, *Griffith University*
Christina M. Higgins, *University of Hawai'i at Mānoa*
Thorsten Huth, *Southern Illinois University at Carbondale*
Midori Ishida, *University of Hawai'i at Mānoa*
Younhee Kim, *Kyung Hee University*
Irene Koshik, *University of Illinois at Urbana-Champaign*
Li Duanduan, *University of British Columbia*
Anthony Liddicoat, *University of South Australia*
Liu Jianda, *Guangdong University of Foreign Studies*
Numa Markee, *University of Illinois at Urbana-Champaign*
Munehiko Miyata, *University of Hawai'i at Mānoa*
Emi Morita, *National University of Singapore*
Makoto Omori, *University of Hawai'i at Mānoa*

David Olsher, *San Francisco State University*
Tae-Il Pae, *Yeungnam University*
Lynn Pearson, *Bowling Green State University*
Kenneth R. Rose, *City University of Hong Kong*
Scott Saft, *University of Hawai'i at Hilo*
Fritjof Sahlström, *Uppsala University*
Mi-suk Seo, *Sacramento State University*
Carol Spöttl, *University of Innsbruck*
Marina Terkourafi, *University of Illinois at Urbana-Champaign*
Hansun Z. Waring, *Teachers College, Columbia University*
Regina Weinert, *University of Sheffield*
Jean Wong, *College of New Jersey*

Introduction

Gabriele Kasper
University of Hawai'i at Mānoa

Hanh thi Nguyen
Hawai'i Pacific University

Dina Rudolph Yoshimi
University of Hawai'i at Mānoa

Pragmatics & Language Learning (PLL) *Vol. 12* marks the 20th anniversary of the series. This occasion invites us to reflect on the developments in the field over the past two decades as they are documented in the PLL volumes. *Pragmatics & Language Learning, Monograph Series Vol. 1*, was published in 1990 under the coeditorship of Professors Lawrence Bouton and Yamuna Kachru. A comparative look at the inaugural volume and the current collection makes visible continuing research traditions and innovative trends that have only recently entered the agenda of pragmatics as a subdiscipline in second language (L2) studies. What are the theories, research styles, modalities of language use, and topics that engaged L2 pragmaticians 20 years ago, and what are the dominant and emerging research themes and strategies in the present landscape of L2 pragmatics? What disciplines in the social sciences and humanities have supplied theoretical and methodological resources to the field? This introduction cannot do more than offer short answers to these complex questions, yet they will still outline a historical perspective on the chapters in this volume.

Although the earliest studies in L2 pragmatics had begun to appear a decade before *PLL 1*, the first volume in the series still bears the signs of a field under construction. Of its 14 chapters, eight report original data-based research, predominantly on some aspect of L2 pragmatics. Five of the empirical studies investigated aspects of L2 writing, focusing on politeness, rhetorical questions, tense and aspect, negative constructions, and narrative style, operationalized as sets of variable grammatical features that differentiate between written and spoken narratives. The remaining three empirical chapters report on diverse topics in sociolinguistics, psycholinguistics, and L2 classroom research with equally diverse empirical methods: a study of inversion in reported questions in a New Jersey dialect, based on data collected through informant consultations; a protocol analysis of students' monitoring during a peer activity in French as a foreign language, grounded in Vygotskyan theory; and a discourse analysis of EFL classroom interaction from the perspective of Sinclair and Coulthard's (1975) systemic-functional discourse model. The styles of data analysis are evenly split between statistical methods and qualitative analyses of patterns or rules at sentence or discourse level. The nonempirical six chapters run the gamut from historical sociolinguistics, sketching the development of vernacular literacy in Eastern Christianity, to personal anecdotes of the use of English by first language (L1) speakers of Japanese as a motivation for developing a textbook on authentic communication in English as a second language (ESL). As a counterpoint to these widely varying disciplinary and topical orientations, two related theories dominate the volume, Grice's theory of conversational implicature and Brown and Levinson's politeness theory. Contributors appealed to Gricean pragmatics in particular to explicate how utterances are understood from theoretical and cross-cultural perspectives. The Gricean maxims also furnish the theoretical background for a pedagogical proposal on how to teach implicature comprehension to ESL students. Finally, the chapters drew on several social sciences as donor disciplines for theories and methodologies: ordinary language philosophy, linguistics, linguistic anthropology, discourse analysis, sociolinguistics, social and developmental psychology, and L2 acquisition and pedagogy.

The striking diversity of the chapters in *PLL 1* is attributable in part to the very broad scope of topics and objects that registered under pragmatics at the time, and this makes it difficult to discern common ground among them. As the field matured, such research strands as historical and variationist sociolinguistics and L2 writing research with a focus on grammatical resources faded out of the purview of L2 pragmatics, as did theoretical and descriptive concerns without a cross-cultural or L2 perspective. But several of the topics and approaches represented in the series' first volume have developed into continuing lines of research. Bouton's (1990) recommendation for the teaching of implicature comprehension in an ESL context was partly motivated by his longitudinal study on the topic and foreshadowed a later empirical study on the effectiveness of teaching different types of implicature (Bouton, 1999). Bouton's early work continues to serve as a template for the teaching and testing of implicature, as can be seen in Roever's chapter in this volume. Johnson and Yang's (1990) study on ESL students' politeness in written peer reviews built on work on positive politeness that had emerged in the mid 1980s and was followed up in immediately subsequent work (e.g., He, 1993; Johnson, 1992) and research on the pragmatics of L2 academic writing more broadly (e.g., Hyland, 2002). Donato and Lantolf's (1990) proposal to reconceptualize the intrapsychological notion of 'monitoring' in light of Vygotskyan sociocultural theory resonates both with different lines of Vygotskyan research on L2 learning and alternative approaches that also see social interaction as constitutive of learning and development. Lastly, although Sinclair and Coulthard's (1975) structuralist discourse-analytical model has been superseded by approaches that view interaction as social practice and consequently emphasize the mutually enabling and constraining forces of interactional structures and participants' agency, classroom interaction has been a focus of convergence for research on education, institutional discourse, socialization and development, (second) language acquisition, and discourse and pragmatics. In *PLL 12*, studies of classroom interaction make up five of the 13 chapters, enough to warrant a section of their own.

In the current volume, a first observation is that the scope of the contributions is more circumscribed and coherent. All chapters report on empirical studies addressing topics in L2 or multilingual pragmatics. Although the chapters examine a wide variety of objects from diverse theoretical and methodological perspectives, they share an understanding of pragmatics as the study of language-mediated social action. Furthermore, they predominantly scrutinize not only bilingual and multilingual speakers' language use and the competencies underlying it, but also L2 learning and development. This volume, then, fulfils what the series title promises: to investigate the relation between pragmatics and language learning. Needless to say, this more firmly contoured field of research did not emerge overnight. The ten volumes between *PLL1* and *PLL 12* were progressively shaped by developments in the emerging domain of L2 pragmatics and in turn helped the field come into its own. The present volume reaps the fruits of this process.

The chapters in Part I examine speakers' use and knowledge of linguistic resources in one or more languages and their interactional and pragmatic functions. The predominant theme of these studies is L2 learners' pragmatic development, evident both in everyday language use (DuFon; Mori) and in instrument-based production and comprehension (Bardovi-Harlig; Bardovi-Harlig et al.; Roever; Yates). In addition, two chapters (Furukawa; Greer) explore how speakers engage their multilingual competencies through language alternation and discourse markers in different interactional settings.

In her conversation analytic study of learner initiation of word-search sequences, Mori draws on interactional linguistics to explore the ways in which a learner's syntactic competence combined with experience with word search as a regular practice in everyday talk-in-interaction may underlie the effective use of a common pragmatic resource in initiating a word-search activity. Mori demonstrates that more advanced L2 learners of Japanese with experience living in Japan conducted word-search activities using the distal demonstrative pronoun *are* as a placeholder for the missing word without disrupting the flow of their talk, whereas less proficient classroom learners of Japanese as a foreign language turned to their L1 lexicon to initiate a word search on the gap in their L2 lexicon, thereby disrupting the flow of talk. Mori argues for the need to recognize grammar as an important resource of talk-in-interaction and for a more effective integration of grammar and pragmatics in L2 classroom instruction.

Greer's conversation analytic study of multiparty talk among bilingual teenagers at an international school in Japan highlights how language alternation is implicated in the construction of simultaneous activities and situated identities. The episode in question shows how one of the participants managed two groups of recipients that cast him as an incumbent of different categories, that of an entertainer and a seller of cakes (for fundraising). In addition to Japanese and English, the focal participant also talks in the voice of Yoda, a character from the *Star Wars* series. For the most part, he conducts the business transaction of selling cakes in Japanese with some Japanese-English code-mixing while performing his Yoda impersonation in (a Yoda variety of) English. The language choices and shifts, initiated at times by group members other than the focal participant, not only index and reflexively constitute multiple activities and identities in the setting but also accomplish humor and social affiliation through a richer repertoire of resources than what is available in monolingual interaction. At the same time, the analysis underscores that the students' diverse language repertoires enable style shifts that are available to monolingual speakers as well.

Continuing the theme of multilingual interaction, Furukawa's chapter zooms in on one common resource in Hawai'i Creole, the discourse marker *daswai*. Although the marker is ubiquitously used in Hawai'i Creole and has been commented on in the literature, Furukawa is the first to examine empirically how *daswai* is used in interaction. His study is contextualized in the ethnography of communication and conducted in the classic format of multiple sociolinguistic interviews. The interview participant is a second-generation Okinawan American woman. Like other members of this community, the participant is a multilingual speaker of varieties of English, Japanese, Ryukyuan (Okinawan), and Hawai'i Creole (Pidgin). Examining the pragmatic meanings and interactional functions of *daswai* in its sequential contexts, Furukawa finds that the item accomplishes two key functions, that is, closing an active topic and marking the beginning of an explanation. A comparison with the Japanese connective *dakara* indicates some shared properties, suggesting discourse-pragmatic transfer from the Japanese substratum into Hawai'i Creole (Siegel, 2003).

Moving from competent pragmatic usage to the development of pragmatic competencies, DuFon's chapter documents how three learners of L2 Indonesian developed their use of leave-taking routines during an extended in-country stay. Adopting a language socialization framework, she demonstrates how the learners' observations of and participation in everyday interaction in their host families and government offices, including explicit guidance from expert community members, contributed to the learners' growing awareness of leave-taking practices and the cultural values underlying them, and their increasingly proficient use (and nonuse) of these pragmatic routines in their own talk.

In order to identify areas where L2 learners require pragmatics-focused instruction to facilitate their participation at the workplace, Yates used simulated workplace interactions, eliciting acts of requesting from native speakers of Australian English and L2 English-speaking Dinka migrants to Australia. Differences in patterns of use of a range of pragmatic resources associated with stance marking led Yates to explore the ways the participants in the two groups conceptualized workplace relationships, particularly between an employee and boss. Her findings reveal that the stance-marking devices used by the Dinka migrants in the role-play tasks are informed both by sociopragmatic expectations derived from previous workplace experiences in their home country and by a general lack of experience with a workplace environment. She promotes the introduction of model dialogs to raise awareness of these pragmatic differences and to establish a starting place from which to bridge the cross-cultural gap.

The final three chapters in this section examine ESL speakers' knowledge and use of pragmalinguistic resources. It has often been noted that L2 speakers tend to underuse formulaic expressions or use such phrases incorrectly. This problem is the topic of two companion studies conducted by Bardovi-Harlig and her collaborators. Bardovi-Harlig investigated ESL users' recognition of conventional expressions with the goal of developing a clearer understanding of how and why such expressions pose challenges to learners, especially with respect to their pragmalinguistic development. Building on her previous research on the topic (Bardovi-Harlig, 2008), the cross-sectional study reveals that with increasing L2 proficiency, learners become more capable in recognizing modified forms of conventional expressions but do not always mark authentic expressions as acceptable, suggesting a more central role for exposure than for proficiency. Bardovi-Harlig also raises the possibilities that learner development in this area of pragmatics may not be uniform across learners and that differences in learning styles may be underlying differences in learners' accuracy of recognition.

Complementing Bardovi-Harlig's chapter, Bardovi-Harlig, Bastos, Burghardt, Chappetto, Nichols, and Rose turn to the production of formulaic phrases, with a focus on the relationship between utterance length and use of conventional expressions among L1 speakers of English and ESL speakers across a broad range of scenarios. Previous research had suggested that learners' verbosity in their speech-act production may be an artifact of using written discourse completion tasks as the elicitation instrument. In an effort to circumvent this potential instrument effect, the authors developed an innovative computer-based oral production task representing a wide variety of scenarios that encouraged the use of conventional expressions. Their analysis of the cross-sectional dataset revealed that the L2 learners did not display a tendency towards greater verbosity than the participants in the native-speaker comparison groups. At the same time, the L2 speakers' use of conventional expressions showed a developmental pattern: Beginning with a lexical core, the learners' production of the target form increasingly approximated the production of the conventional expression by the native speakers. The authors note a corresponding development of learners' production of semantic formulae; however, evidence in their study suggests that the use and development of semantic formulae must be explored separately from the production of conventional expressions.

Turning from L2 pragmatic use and learning to the assessment of pragmalinguistic knowledge, Roever's investigation of differential item functioning (DIF) in a pragmalinguistics test for ESL speakers highlights the challenges of creating an assessment instrument that can measure L2 pragmatic competence without privileging or disadvantaging test takers from particular language and cultural backgrounds. Two groups of ESL users, one with Asian language and cultural backgrounds, the other with European backgrounds, took Roever's (2005) web-delivered test of pragmalinguistic knowledge. This multitrait, multimethod instrument was designed to evaluate ESL speakers' comprehension of implicatures, knowledge of routines, and production of speech acts. Through two standard DIF procedures, the Mantel-Haenszel Odds Ratio and logistic regression, Roever found that 25% of the total test items showed a large DIF effect. Further analysis of these items revealed two kinds of DIF, one related to construct-relevant factors and thus legitimate, the other attributable to construct-irrelevant variance and thus posing a threat to validity. However, more often than not, distinguishing one from the other is a judgment call, strongly indicating further the need for qualitative and statistical research on valid and reliable tests of L2 pragmatics.

Although the chapters in this section have a distinct investigative focus in common—the association of specific linguistic resources with pragmatic and interactional meanings—they also show considerable theoretical and methodological diversity. One salient point of divergence is the implicit understanding of pragmatic and interactional competence that informs the studies. Instrument-based research on L2 pragmatics derives its rationale from the view that it is possible to identify a person's individual pragmatic competence separate from and underlying their language use in situated interactional activities. This view is perhaps most salient in the studies that used participants' responses to (variably contextualized) pragmatic stimuli as evidence of pragmalinguistic and sociopragmatic knowledge (Bardovi-Harlig; Bardovi-Harlig et al.; Roever; Yates). The position that pragmatic competence forms a component of a broader communicative competence that is distinct from language use (*performance*) has been one of the most powerful and enduring ontological perspectives in the field, as a cursory look at the background sections to interlanguage pragmatics studies over the past 30 years reveals (see Roever, this volume). But it is no longer uncontested. Indeed, the majority of chapters in this collection take an alternative stance. For them, social actions and the resources through which they are implemented cannot be separated from the interactional environments in which they are located. Nor are social actions, mediated through language and other semiotic resources, seen to originate in individual speakers' minds: Rather, social actions are understood as the joint and contingent interactional accomplishments of all participants. From this perspective, explicating competence remains a central research concern, but consistent with the shift from individual action to the social level of interaction, the relevant locus of the competences that enable speakers to participate in talk exchanges is interaction itself. Whether referred to as sociolinguistic, communicative, pragmatic, or indeed interactional competence, the critical point, as Mehan (1979) noted, is that we are concerned with "a competence that is available in the interaction" (p. 129).

The discipline dedicated to explicating how interactional competence is organized and how it operates is conversation analysis (CA). For the past decade, L2 researchers have increasingly used CA to study L2 and multilingual talk in a wide range of social settings. More recently, a growing body of research has drawn on CA for the analysis of L2 learning and development. For instance, Mori shows in her chapter how L2 speakers in ordinary conversation accomplish language learning as a contingently arising social activity. The second section in this volume features CA studies that examine interaction, learning, and development in L2 classrooms and out-of-class activities arranged for language learning.

Of the chapters in Part II, Talmy's study of classroom interaction in a public high school in Hawai'i takes the broadest perspective. Starting from the well attested observation that ESL is often a stigmatized identity category in North American public schools, Talmy examines how senior ESL students deployed a stylized language practice called "Mock ESL" and what the speakers accomplished through its use. The study integrates an "ethnographically informed, socially constituted critical pragmatics" with microanalyses of Mock ESL episodes in the classroom interaction. While the senior students in the classroom community resort to Mock ESL as a device to parodically claim incompetence and thereby refuse to cooperate with the teacher's pedagogical agenda, both teachers and senior students simultaneously collude in stratifying the students into those who fit the stigmatized category of the inept "fresh off the boat" novice and the senior students who distinguish themselves as Local by using English and Pidgin (Hawai'i Creole). Talmy's study shows how the reproduction of ESL as an undesirable identity category is bound up with language ideologies and educational practices that reflexively reinforce and reproduce linguistic prejudice and social inequality. On a wider theoretical and methodological scale, this research also shows how microscopic language practices in classroom interaction and macroscopic educational and language policies are mutually constitutive, thereby calling into question the micro-macro dichotomy altogether.

The next three chapters examine classroom practices associated with the organized learning of L2 English, predominantly in formal educational settings in Japan. Hosoda and Aline focus attention on the ways in which assessment practices and their contingent delivery reflexively constitute the students' performance as according with or diverging from the teacher's expectations. In the elementary school English as a foreign language (EFL) classes observed for this study, the teachers would frequently ratify the students' responses using positive verbal assessments combined with applause. The analyses reveal how the joint production of verbal assessment and applause, delayed applause, and withheld applause had differential consequences for the subsequent action or activity and that the students oriented to the teachers' modes of assessment by adjusting their task performance in accordance with the required format.

Other-correction of language form, typically but not exclusively done by the teacher, is a pervasive and often constitutive practice in language instruction. In his chapter, Hauser focuses on a particular sequential environment for exposed other-corrections of language form, namely the turn(s) following the completion of a repair sequence. Based on an analysis of three such sequences in EFL classes and an ESL conversation club, Hauser discusses why such exposed postrepair corrections are rare and what their interactional import is when they do occur. In all three cases, the correction was sequentially displaced from the correctable item and therefore required extra interactional work to recover the error. Furthermore, because the participants made the error correction their joint interactional business, these correction sequences offered opportunities for L2 learning. Besides these similarities, the sequences also reveal differences that Hauser relates to the institutional settings in which the interactions occurred.

Fujimoto's study examines a common activity in peer-group discussions, students agreeing or disagreeing with a previous speaker's proposal, assessment, or stance towards some topical matter. Consistent with previous work on talk among novice L2 speakers (e.g., Carroll, 2004; Hauser, 2009), Fujimoto demonstrates that the novice EFL speakers in her study were sequentially competent participants who drew on a range of vocal and nonvocal resources to accomplish agreements and disagreements. The organization of their assessment, agreement, and disagreement sequences fundamentally corresponds to the organization of such sequences described in the CA literature for adult L1 speakers. It shows the novice speakers' sensitivity to the moment-to-moment unfolding of the talk and their ongoing analysis of each other's turns to enable orderly turn-taking and sequentially relevant actions that propel the activity forward. One key finding of the study is that the participants did not structure their disagreements as dispreferred responses, in accordance with the preference for agreement (Sacks, 1987) postulated for ordinary conversation (a preference that needs qualification because it is demonstrably subject to cultural variation). Instead, they oriented to their oppositional alignments as preferred actions in the discussion activity, consonant with research showing that participants treat dissenting actions as preferred in a range of institutional activities.

The final chapter in this volume takes us from grade school and university settings (mostly) in Japan to a kindergarten in Denmark and from language learning activities to the achievement of participation. In a longitudinal case study conducted over a 6-month period, Karrebæk traces a minority child's growing interactional competence in using a range of semiotic resources to gain entry to peer play groups. Although the child became ultimately more successful in his endeavors to join the other children's activities, or "be with" (være med), Karrebæk shows through microanalysis of multiparty sequences that in the kindergartners' community of practice, the better established members controlled access to the central positions in play activities. The child's achievement of participation thus was not exclusively conditional on his own resources but depended on the participation opportunities afforded by the senior group members.

The chapters in *Pragmatics and Language Learning 12* point to promising future directions as the series enters its third decade. The well-established traditions of experimental and quasi-experimental work in empirical L1 and L2 pragmatics will be able to benefit from new developments in their cognitive-psychological and linguistic foundations, experimentation, and technology. Concurrently, a contrasting and expanding research trajectory is visible from several chapters in this volume: the project to conceptualize and analyze pragmatic competence as interactional competence, as participants' ability to utilize a range of interactional resources to accomplish social actions contingently and as co-constructed achievements in natural settings. Building on the view of interactional competence as an enabling condition for learning, teaching, and development (Lee, 2006), developmental pragmatics can be expected to increasingly examine how changes in pragmatic competence are situated in specific social activities and sequential environments. As one biproduct of this research direction, the notion of context, one of the enduring theoretical and empirical concerns in pragmatics, may need further respecification. Investigating the interactions of multilingual and multicompetent participants requires researchers to reexamine how conventionality and indexicality are implicated in creating, maintaining, and changing context. Such a perspective also connects with critical pragmatics, aiming to explicate how identities, ideologies, and power are locally invoked and constituted through semiotic resources and categorization in action formation and sequence organization. Critical pragmatics (Talmy, this volume, cf. Mey, 2001) establishes important links with research on institutional interaction, among them the policies and practices of language education and their relation to wider sociopolitical ecologies. As a resource for transformative agendas, the potential of critical pragmatics remains to be explored.

References

Bardovi-Harlig, K. (2008). Recognition and production of formulas in L2 pragmatics. In Z.-H. Han (Ed.), *Understanding second language process* (pp. 205–222). Clevedon, England: Multilingual Matters.

Bouton, L. F. (1990). The effective use of implicature in English: Why and how it should be taught in the ESL classroom. In L. F. Bouton & Y. Kachru (Eds.), *Pragmatics and language learning monograph series* (Vol. 1, pp. 43–51). Urbana-Champaign: University of Illinois, Division of English as an International Language.

Bouton, L. F. (1999). Developing nonnative speaker skills in interpreting conversational implicatures in English: Explicit teaching can ease the process. In E. Hinkel (Ed.), *Culture in second language teaching and learning* (pp. 47–70). Cambridge, England: Cambridge University Press.

Bouton, L. F., & Kachru, Y. (Eds.). (1990). *Pragmatics and language learning monograph series* (Vol. 1). Urbana-Champaign: University of Illinois, Division of English as an International Language.

Carroll, D. (2004). Restarts in novice turn beginnings: Disfluencies or interactional achievements? In R. Gardner & J. Wagner (Eds.), *Second language conversations* (pp. 201–220). London: Continuum.

Donato, R., & Lantolf, J. (1990). The dialogic origins of L2 monitoring. In L. F. Bouton & Y. Kachru (Eds.), *Pragmatics and language learning monograph series* (Vol. 1, pp. 83–98). Urbana-Champaign: University of Illinois, Division of English as an International Language.

Hauser, E. (2009). Turn-taking and primary speakership during a student discussion. In H. t. Nguyen & G. Kasper (Eds.), *Talk-in-interaction: Multilingual perspectives* (pp. 215–244). Honolulu: University of Hawai'i, National Foreign Language Resource Center.

He, A. W. (1993). Language use in peer review texts. *Language in Society, 22,* 403–420.

Hyland, K. (2002). Authority and invisibility: Authorial identity in academic writing. *Journal of Pragmatics, 34,* 1091–1112.

Johnson, D. M. (1992). Compliments and politeness in peer-review texts. *Applied Linguistics, 13,* 51–71.

Johnson, D. M., & Yang, A. W. (1990). Politeness strategies in peer-review texts. In L. F. Bouton & Y. Kachru (Eds.), *Pragmatics and language learning monograph series*

(Vol. 1, pp. 99–114). Urbana-Champaign: University of Illinois, Division of English as an International Language.

Lee, Y. A. (2006). Towards respecification of communicative competence: Condition of L2 instruction or its objective? *Applied Linguistics, 27,* 349–376.

Mehan, H. (1979). *Learning lessons.* Cambridge, MA: Harvard University Press.

Mey, J. L. (2001). *Pragmatics: An introduction* (2nd ed.). Malden, MA: Blackwell.

Roever, C. (2005). *Testing ESL pragmatics.* Frankfurt, Germany: Peter Lang.

Sacks, H. (1987). On the preferences for agreement and contiguity in sequences in conversation. In G. Button & J. Lee (Eds.), *Talk and social organization* (pp. 54–69). Clevedon, England: Multilingual Matters.

Siegel, J. (2003). Substrate influence in Creoles and the role of transfer in second language acquisition. *Studies in Second Language Acquisition, 25,* 185–209.

Part I

**Sequences and Resources
in Second Language
and Multilingual Talk**

Learning Language in Real Time: A Case Study of the Japanese Demonstrative Pronoun *Are* in Word-Search Sequences

Junko Mori
University of Wisconsin-Madison

In recent discussions of the reconceptualization of language learning, C. E. Brouwer and J. Wagner (2004) proposed that learning should be described in terms of the learners' development of "interactional skills" and "interactional resources." To further articulate this developmental process, however, the investigation of a variety of interactional resources is necessary; and for this, interactional linguistics (e.g., E. Ochs, E. A. Schegloff, & S. A. Thompson, 1996; M. Selting & E. Couper-Kuhlen, 2001), a research paradigm that combines discourse functional linguistics and conversation analysis, presents a promising direction. The study reported in this chapter uses interactional linguistics to examine word-search sequences with a focus on what kinds of resources, linguistic or nonlinguistic, language specific or seemingly universal, are available for a speaker of Japanese who encounters trouble producing a word in the midst of a turn. In particular, the study focuses on the use of the distal demonstrative pronoun are as a placeholder (M. Hayashi, 2003a, 2003b, 2004a) and demonstrates how the ability to draw upon this device might indicate the speaker's advanced proficiency in the language and how such an ability might be fostered through exposure to and participation in interactions unfolding in real time.

Recent debates on the conceptualization of language learning pose two distinct models: cognitive, knowledge-based understanding of learning on one hand and social, participation-based understanding of learning on the other. Although Hall (1997), Pavlenko and Lantolf (2000), Sfard (1998), and Thorne (2000), among others, have suggested that these differing views of learning are not supposed to defeat or supplant each other, in reality, one or the other tends to be emphasized in each study. For instance, in her commentary in the 2004 special issue of *The Modern Language Journal* titled "Classroom Talks," Larsen-Freeman attempted to classify the studies featured in the volume based on whether the object of learning was "a priori target rules and structures being assimilated by the individual mind" or an "evolving bond between the individual and others—becoming a member of a community," or based on whether learning was discussed in terms of "having or gaining some knowledge" or in terms of "doing or becoming able to do something with the language" (p. 606).

Contributing to this ongoing discussion concerning learning, Brouwer and Wagner (2004) proposed that language learning should be conceptualized as "the development of interactional skills and interactional resources" (p. 32) or "increasing interactional complexity in language encounters" (p. 44). These descriptions of language learning underscore the importance of participation in interactions conducted in a second language (L2) and "learning as a social process" traced over the course of an individual's history rather than "learning as a social practice" incidentally observed (p. 32); but at the same time, they refer to "skills" and "resources," including those that are transportable from one situation to another. As an example, Brouwer and Wagner reported a case of a novice learner of Danish who "employ[ed] a growing set of repair initiating techniques, and engag[ed] in longer sequences for indicating and clarifying trouble in talk" (pp. 43–44) as her residence in Denmark extended.

To further articulate the developmental process concerning such fundamental actions as repair initiation, however, one needs to explore what constitutes a set of potential "interactional resources" that speakers can draw on. They can include not only linguistic but also various nonlinguistic, multimodal resources; some of them can be seen as potentially universal features of human interaction commonly available across languages, whereas others can be seen as specific features tightly correlated with the structures of a particular language. To put it differently, interactional resources include what learners transport from their first language (L1) speaking experience to their L2 learning experience and what they need to acquire through the L2 learning experience (i.e., "competences as resources for learning" vs. "competences as objectives of learning," discussed by Kasper, 2006; Lee, 2006; Mondada & Pekarek Doehler, 2004; and Mori & Hayashi, 2006; among others).

This chapter explores this complex web of interactional resources by referring to recent developments in interactional linguistics, research that combines the approaches and perspectives of discourse functional linguistics and conversation analysis (CA; e.g., Couper-Kuhlen & Selting, 1996; Ford, Fox, & Thompson, 2002; Ford & Wagner, 1996; Ochs et al. 1996; Selting & Couper-Kuhlen, 2001); it does so by closely examining *word-search* sequences in Japanese talk-in-interaction, and more specifically, the use of the distal demonstrative pronoun *are* as a placeholder in such sequences (Hayashi, 2003a, 2003b, 2004a; Hayashi & Yoon, 2006). The primary aim of this chapter is to illustrate (a) how the linguistic resources of a given language and the organizations of social interaction are tightly interrelated and inseparable and (b) how the learning of certain interactional resources specific to the L2 can be accomplished only through extensive participation in situated, real-time interaction taking place outside of the classroom.

This chapter starts with a brief summary of the development of interactional linguistics and studies of word-search sequences conducted within this framework. Subsequently, it reviews how the grammatical practice involving the distal demonstrative pronoun *are* as a placeholder operates as an interactional resource. The examination of L2 data follows, first providing a brief overview and then introducing close analysis of selected excerpts. Concluding remarks reflect on the analysis of the excerpts and discuss some implications for language pedagogy and suggestions for future research.

Interactional linguistics

As the following quote from the introduction of *Interaction and Grammar*, edited by Ochs et al. (1996), indicates, the emerging research paradigm of interactional linguistics conceptualizes grammar in a way quite different from the commonly held view of grammar that assumes a priori rules and structures of a given language:

> A grammar is part of a broader range of resources—organization of practices, if you will—which underlie the organization of social life, and in particular the way in which language figures in everyday interaction and cognition....Grammar's integrity and efficacy are bound up with its place in larger schemes of organization of human conduct, and with social interaction in particular. (pp. 2–3)

The idea that grammar should be viewed as the recurrence of forms and structures in language use sharply contrasts with the dominant perspective in traditional linguistics that views grammar as an autonomous system. This alternative view of grammar, dubbed *emergent grammar* by Hopper (1988), has been promoted in the broader field of discourse functional linguistics (e.g., Bybee, 2006; Bybee & Hopper, 2001; Chafe, 1994; Givón, 1979, 1995; Haiman, 1998; Halliday, 1985, 2002). For discourse functional linguists, however, written discourse and spoken narratives can constitute their data, and cognitive processing and information packaging aspects of language use tend to be the target of their analysis. In contrast, interactional linguistics, empowered by CA, explores how fundamental interactional necessities such as initiating, maintaining, or yielding turns at talk; addressing troubles in speaking, hearing, or understanding in the midst of interaction; securing the recipients' attention; and designing talk according to the recipients' backgrounds shape the ways in which grammar is realized in talk-in-interaction. Recent studies in interactional linguistics have examined a wide range of languages including not only English and other European languages but also East Asian languages (e.g., Wu, 2004, 2005 on Mandarin Chinese; Hayashi, 2003a, 2003b, 2004a, 2004b, 2005; Lerner & Takagi, 1999; Mori, 1999, 2006; Morita, 2005; Tanaka, 1999, 2001a, 2001b, 2005 on Japanese; Kim, 1999a, 1999b, 2001; Kim & Suh, 2002; Park, 1998, 1999, 2002; Suh & Kim, 2001 on Korean); these studies demonstrate how typological differences among varying languages may or may not affect the ways in which the speakers of each language accomplish seemingly universal, fundamental actions in social interaction. Their findings provide us with clues for investigating what kinds of linguistic resources L2 learners need to acquire through their engagement in L2 interactions. In short, studies in interactional linguistics can offer fresh insights into the reconceptualization of grammar as interactional resources and consequently, the understanding of some aspects of L2 speakers' proficiency.

Word-search sequences

To illustrate how interactional linguistics can inform our understanding of language proficiency, this chapter examines cases of word search observed in second language conversations in Japanese. Whereas repair-initiation techniques discussed by Brouwer and Wagner (2004) are associated with cases in which L2 speakers encounter trouble understanding the coparticipants' talk, word search refers to cases in which speakers encounter trouble producing a next item due in the ongoing development of the current turn. This is a ubiquitous phenomenon recurrently observed in not only L2 but also L1 talk conducted in (perhaps) all languages. Word-search sequences in English and Japanese, the two languages relevant to the current data, are extensively documented in previous CA studies (e.g., M. H. Goodwin & C. Goodwin, 1986; Hayashi, 2003a, 2003b, 2004a; Hosoda, 2000, 2002, 2006; Schegloff, Jefferson, & Sacks, 1977).[1]

The following vocal and nonvocal behaviors have been reported as features typically associated with the initiation of word search. These features can be viewed as indications of the speaker's experience of cognitive difficulty, but they also serve as resources for conveying to the interlocutors whether the speaker is engaging in a solitary search or is inviting the interlocutors to participate in a collaborative search (e.g., M. H. Goodwin & C. Goodwin, 1986; Hayashi, 2003a, 2003b; Olsher, 2004):

- orientational shift (e.g., eye gaze, posture, head tilts);
- manual and facial gestures (e.g., iconic gestures, "thinking face");
- intraturn pauses, word cut-offs, sound stretches, rising intonation;
- interjective delaying devices (L1 or L2) such as "uhm," "ah" in English or *ano, eeto* in Japanese;

- self-addressed questions for recollection (L1 or L2) such as "what'you ma call it" in English, or *nante iu no* in Japanese;
- direct appeal for a word (L1 or L2).

The first two nonvocal resources listed above appear to be used by speakers of any language. The third, prosodic resources, also appears to be common in various languages. The remaining linguistic resources listed above take forms specific to each language, but it is relatively easy to locate their functional equivalents in various languages.

In addition to these nonvocal and vocal resources often utilized for the initiation of a word search, recent studies by Hayashi (2003a, 2003b, 2004a), Hosoda (2000, 2002), and Kitano (1999) have discussed the use of the distal demonstrative pronoun *are* as a device available for Japanese speakers experiencing trouble producing or remembering a word or a descriptor in the midst of talk (see the next section for a detailed explanation of this practice).[2] In fact, Hosoda (2000, 2002) reported that although L1 speakers in her data frequently used this device, no L2 speakers did so. Unlike Hosoda's data, however, my L2 data include cases in which L2 speakers successfully used *are* in their word searches. Nevertheless, what is notable is that this grammatical practice is only performed by L2 speakers who have lived in Japan for more than a year and have attained a certain level of proficiency that enables them to participate in daily activities conducted in Japanese with relative ease.[3] In fact, the use of the distal demonstrative pronoun *are* as a placeholder is not a type of grammatical practice usually taught in the classroom; rather, it appears to be something that L2 speakers acquire through their exposure to and engagement in naturally occurring, real-time talk-in-interaction taking place outside of the classroom.

The distal demonstrative pronoun *are* as a placeholder

How exactly does the focal practice work in word-search sequences, and why could it be considered evidence of advanced L2 proficiency in Japanese? An example provided by Hayashi (2004a) and reproduced below exemplifies how the pronoun *are* serves as a substitute for a missing item while the speaker continues with his intended action (see Appendix for transcription conventions and abbreviations). Hayashi refers to such a use of *are* as a "placeholder," emphasizing its realization as a syntactic constituent of a sentential unit that forms a turn. In this sense, the use of *are* is quite different from the use of other interjective delaying devices such as *ano::* in Japanese or "uhm" in English, which are not treated as a part of a syntactic unit.

For the reader who is unfamiliar with the Japanese language, it is important to note the difference in basic word order between the original Japanese provided on the left (below) and its approximate English translation on the right. Namely, Japanese is an SOV language, whereas English is an SVO language. That is, sentential turn-constructional units (Sacks, Schegloff, & Jefferson, 1974; Schegloff, 1996, 2007) in Japanese typically complete with a verb, adjective, or copula, which is often followed by various sentence-final expressions that convey social or emotive meanings. This formulation of Japanese turns, viewed from their temporal development, also influences the projectability of imminent action, compared to English, in which modals and predicates appear relatively early on in the construction of turns (e.g., Fox, Hayashi, & Jasperson, 1996; Tanaka, 1999).[4]

Excerpt 1 (Hayashi, 2004a, p. 1357)

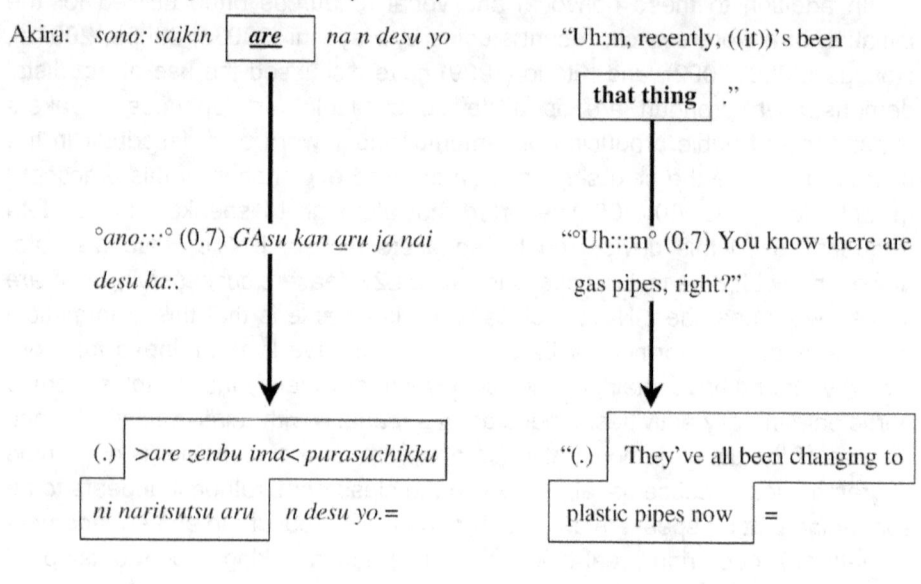

In this example, the beginning part of the first utterance, *sono* ("uh:m") *saikin* ("recently"), develops in a parallel fashion in the original Japanese and the English translation. The construction of the rest of the turn, however, takes quite different shapes in the two versions. In Japanese, the distal demonstrative pronoun *are* ("that thing") in line 1, whose referent is not yet unveiled, comes first, followed by the copula, *na*, and the final expression, *n desu yo*, which characterizes the preceding utterance as providing some kind of explanation. That is, the speaker, Akira, who encounters trouble producing or remembering a particular noun or descriptor, uses *are* as a placeholder for the searched-for item for the time being and continues to complete the turn-constructional unit indicating his intended action.[5] This temporal development of the turn is not fully represented in the English translation in which the copula comes before the pronoun or the blank item in search, and therefore, the basic formulation of the turn shape has been revealed by the time the turn reaches the pronoun.

After performing the intended action once using *are*, Akira attempts to specify the referent of the demonstrative. In this case, Akira reformulates what he meant to say earlier; and notably, the second version is also marked by the same sentence-final expression, *n desu yo*, indicating that this is a redoing of the first unit in which *are* was used as a placeholder.

To sum up, from an interactional point of view, this format enables the speaker to complete an intended action first despite the existence of a problematic vocabulary item. Further, by completing the action first and specifying the context in which the searched-for item occurs, the speaker can also increase the possibility that the coparticipants can figure out what the missing item is. Thus, among the various ways of approaching word-search situations, the use of *are*, which is tightly connected to the basic clausal structure of the Japanese language and enables the speaker to continue with an intended action in a timely fashion, can be seen as a highly sophisticated maneuver that demonstrates the speaker's advanced competence.

L2 speakers' use of *are* as a placeholder

As mentioned earlier, Hosoda (2000, 2002, 2006) reported that the participants in her L2 data never performed this grammatical practice involving the use of *are* as a placeholder. However, our small-scale exploratory study identifying characteristics of word searches performed by L2 speakers yielded several cases in which L2 speakers did this.[6] The following table summarizes the data examined in this study, which consist of four groups of learners with different lengths and types of learning experiences. All of the interactions were casual multiparty conversations video-recorded outside of the classroom. Approximately 1 hour from each dataset was analyzed for this exploratory study.

Table 1. Summary of data

dataset	background of L2 speakers	context of interaction
A	2 speakers who had received 350–400 hours of college-level classroom instruction in the US	chatting with L1 Japanese speakers
B	3 speakers who had received 650–700 hours of college-level classroom instruction in the US	chatting among L2 classmates
C	3 speakers who had received 480 hours of college-level classroom instruction in the US and attended 1 academic year study abroad program in Japan	chatting among L2 classmates
D	2 speakers who had attended a language school for a few months, lived and worked in Japan for a few years, and were married to Japanese	dinner table conversation among the two L2 speakers and one L1 speaker

As expected, the general tendency is that the more experienced the L2 speakers were, the more resources (especially those associated with L2 forms) they utilized in conducting word searches and the more quickly they returned to their main activities. The use of nonvocal and prosodic resources, for instance, can be observed across all of the levels. Delaying devices produced in L2 forms are also observed in all four datasets, but self-addressed questions and direct appeals tend to be produced in the L1 by the L2 speakers in Dataset A. On the other hand, the three L2 speakers chatting in Dataset C, who participated in an academic-year study abroad program after completing approximately 480 hours of classroom instruction in the US, all produced self-addressed questions or direct appeals in Japanese. And finally, the grammatical practice involving the distal demonstrative pronoun *are* is performed by one of the participants in Dataset C and by the two L2 participants in Dataset D. In the following, we examine cases in which three different L2 speakers used *are* as a placeholder as they produced turns accomplishing different social actions.

Excerpt 2 demonstrates a case in which Lili, one of L2 speakers in Dataset C, uses *are* as a placeholder.[7] Prior to the focal turn, Karen mentions that, in her opinion, lacrosse is more dangerous than football (lines 1, 6). In response to Lili's request for further elaboration (lines 8, 10), Karen points out that lacrosse players do not wear helmets (line 12) and tries to continue her explanation (line 13). In an overlap with Karen's production of the connective expressions that project further explanation, *shi, sorekara* ("and moreover"), Lili initiates her turn with *demo* ("but") and produces the first turn-constructional unit starting with *are* in line 14.

Excerpt 2 Initiating a challenge to the prior speaker's opinion

```
1   Karen:  demo rakurosu no hoo ga abunai   to omoimasu yo.
            but            LK side S dangerous QT think    FP
```
"But I think lacrosse is more dangerous."

```
2           (0.7)

3   Lili:   kura:[su?
            class
```
"class?"

```
4   Karen:       [foot- rakurosu
                  foot  lacrosse
```
"foot- lacrosse"

```
5   Lili:   aa[::::::::
            oh
```
"Oh:::"

```
 6  Karen:   [football yori.
              football more.than
             "than football"

 7           (0.9)

 8  Lili:    hontoni?
             really
             "Really?"

 9           (0.1)

10  Lili:    nande?
             why
             "Why?"

11           (0.5)

12  Karen:   herumetto o: (0.4) tsuka-  zenzen  tsukatte  nai
             helmet   O                 at.all  use       Neg

13           shi:[:,°(sorekara)°
             and      moreover
```

"(We) don't use helmets at all, and moreover"

```
14→Lili:        [demo: are deshoo::? (0.6) are (0.2) are
                 but   that Cop.Tag         that      that
```
"But, isn't it are? (0.6) are (0.2) are"

```
15→          su- (0.2) nan- nandakke?
                       what what.PST
```
"su- (0.2) What was it?"

```
16  Ron:     stikku:?
             stick
```
"Stikku?"
((a possible Japanese pronunciation of the loan word))

```
17  Lili:    s:[tikku.
              stick
```
"Stikku."

```
18  Ron:       [hahaha sto(h)kku. hh
                       stock
```
"hahaha stokku. hh" ((another possible loan word))[8]

19 Karen: [stikku o: tsukatteru kedo::, honto<u>ni</u>::
              stick O   using   but   really

20   abunai yo.
             dangerous FP

"(we) are using sticks, but it is really dangerous."

    The turn-initial component *demo* ("but"), along with the copula, *desho::?*, with rising intonation that follows *are*, frames Lili's turn to be a question that (at least partially) challenges Karen's stated opinion,[9] even though the critical item in her question is not in place. At the time that she utters *are*, Lili also starts producing an iconic gesture indicating the shape of a long slender object (Figure 1) and repeatedly produces this gesture during the following component of the turn that includes a self-addressed question in Japanese (line 15).

    By looking at Lili's gestures juxtaposed with her talk, Ron assigns a meaning to this gesture and supplies a candidate item, *stikku* ("stick"), which constitutes an important component of Lili's disagreeing turn originally delivered with the placeholder *are*. Lili immediately confirms that *stikku* indeed is the item that she was in search of (line 17), although Ron, with laughter, provides another possible way of verbalizing the gesture (line 18).[10] Karen, in the meantime, initiates her defending turn by starting it with the term provided by Ron, *stikku* (line 19). Karen's turn in lines 19–20, which acknowledges Lili's point but reasserts her original statement, indicates that Karen has indeed interpreted Lili's turn in line 14 to be a challenge or disagreement. Further, she verbalizes her interpretation of Lili's point (i.e., lacrosse uses sticks), which was expressed only through the unelaborated turn with the accompanying gesture.

Figure 1. Gesture (lines 14, 15).

This excerpt demonstrates Lili's ability to perform a disagreement in a timely manner by using this grammatical practice; she effectively moves forward with the action indication while delaying referential specification and appealing to the coparticipants' understanding through the use of gesture embedded in this specific sequential and syntactic context. Further, the excerpt also demonstrates Ron and Karen's understanding of Lili's intents, both in terms of her contribution to the ongoing discussion as well as her initiation of the word search.

The two L2 speakers in Dataset D also managed the use of *are* as a placeholder. Hao, a native speaker of Chinese, and Neal, a native speaker of American English, both had had only a few months of classroom language instruction in Japan, but lived and worked in Japan for a few years and were married to Japanese with whom they regularly spoke Japanese. Both of these married couples moved to the US a few years prior to this recording, but they continued to use Japanese in the US on a daily basis. This recording was made when Neal visited Hao's house and had dinner there. The participants in this interaction were Neal, Hao, and Hao's wife, Saki.

Prior to the segment shown in Excerpt 3, Neal was explaining a Korean dish that he had brought to the dinner. Lines 1, 2, and 5 show the tail end of his explanation that one can use the same soup for one's next meal by adding other items such as rice cake or vegetables, and therefore, it is best to use plenty of water at the beginning. The use of *are* as a placeholder is observed in Hao's turn in line 13, in which he demonstrates his understanding of Neal's explanation by saying that this Korean dish is essentially the same as *are*.

Excerpt 3 Demonstrating understanding of the prior speaker's explanation

```
1   Neal:   mochi      toka  ano:   mata   negi       iretemo      ii.
            rice.cake  or    uhm    again  scallion   put.in.if    good
```
"You can put in rice cake or scallion again."

```
2                      dakara (.) [mizu    takusan-=
                       so          water   a.lot
```
"So, (use) a lot of water"

```
3   Saki:                          [u:::n
                                    uh huh
```
"uh huh"

```
4   Saki:   =a naruhodo   ne.
            oh I.see      FP
```
"Oh I see."

```
5   Neal:   tsukatte    don°don              tsukuru(    )°
            use         one-after-another    make
```
"and keep making (by adding) one item after another."

6 Saki: aa haa   haa [haa °haa   haa°
             oh uhhuh uhhuh uhhuh uhhuh uhhuh
            "Oh uh huh uh huh uh huh °uh huh uh huh°"

7 Neal: [yoku wakan nai n   da kedo::,
                          well know Neg Nom Cop but
                         "I don't know well, but"

8   jitsuwa- [ah ha ha
            actually
            "actually ah ha ha"

9 Hao: [ano::::::
                        uhm
                       "Uh:::::m"

10 Neal: jitsuwa wakan nai kedo sore [kiita. ahahahaha
            actually know Neg but that heard
            "Actually I don't know but I heard so. ahahahaha."

11 Saki: [u::n
                                           uhhuh
                                          "uh huh"

12 Saki: °hu:[:n°
             hmm
            "°hmm°"

13→Hao: [yoowa   are to   onaji da °yo.°
                essentially that with same Cop FP
               "Essentially it's the same as are."

14   (0.6)

15   a:no: nanda-
            uhm   what.Cop
            "uhm what"

16 Saki: onabe   desho   nihon no.
            hot.pot   Cop.Tag Japan LK
            "hot pot, right? Japanese."

17 Hao: sss. so::   maa   chu- chuukanabe   demo onaji da
                        right well China.hot.pot also same Cop

18	mon na.
	Nom FP

> *"sss. Right. Well, chi- Chinese hot pot is the same way, too."*

In lines 4 and 6, Saki claims her understanding of Neal's explanation and indicates her interpretation that this explanation sequence is coming to a possible closure. Neal, however, adds statements that qualify his knowledge about the Korean dish (lines 7–8, 10). While providing his explanation, Neal essentially faces Saki, who is heating up the dish (Figure 2).

Hao's initial attempt to join this exchange takes the form of *ano:::::* ("uh:::m"), a delaying device typically used as one initiates a word search (line 9). From a cognitive point of view, this token may be considered to indicate that Hao has started the search of the unknown item, for which he will eventually substitute *are* in his following turn in line 13. From an interactional point of view, Hao's prolonged delaying device does not stop Neal's continuation of his self-qualifying statement, but it does succeed in getting his coparticipants' attention (Figure 3).

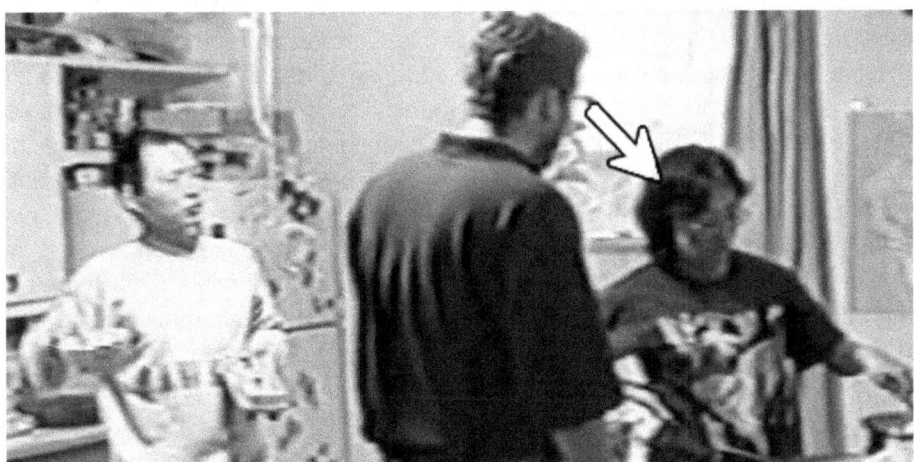

Figure 2. Gaze (line 9).

After securing both Neal's and Saki's gaze towards him, Hao produces his response to Neal's explanation. The initial component of the turn, *yoowa* ("essentially"), projects that this turn delivers a summary of the prior talk. Despite the missing key item in this summary, Hao uses *are* as a placeholder and completes his turn that points out the similarity between this Korean dish and some other item. In his delivery of this summary statement, Hao gazes at Saki, his wife and a fellow recipient of Neal's explanation, and thereby invites her to participate in the collaborative search. He then extends his word-search sequence by producing a delaying device and a self-addressed question (line 15). Subsequently, Saki supplies a candidate item, "Japanese hot pot" (line 16), and Hao partially accepts the item, although he asserts that China also has a similar dish (lines 17–18).

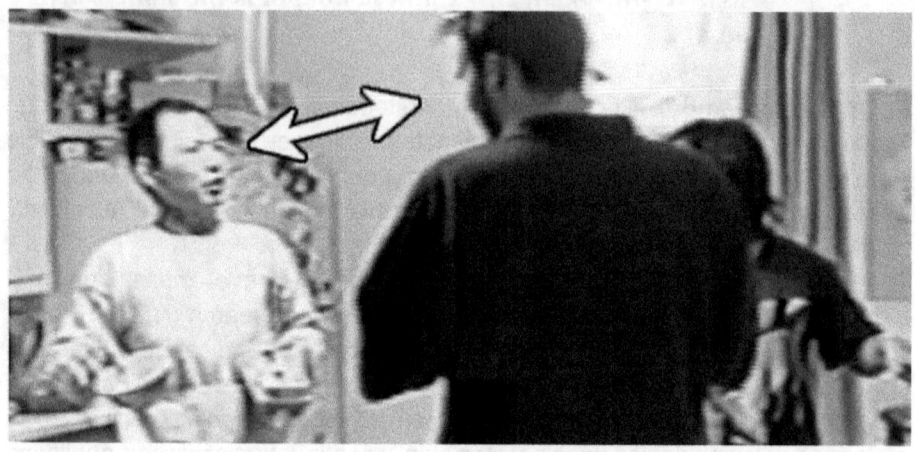

Figure 3. Gaze (beginning of line 13).

To demonstrate his active listening to and understanding of Neal's explanation, it is critical for Hao to produce this summary statement at the moment that he does because the explanation sequence is nearing its completion and at the stage of winding down with self-qualifying remarks. If Hao had waited until he could come up with the name of a dish comparable to this Korean dish, he might have missed the opportunity to make a relevant contribution to this exchange because the talk might have shifted its topical focus, and if it did, his demonstration of understanding would no longer have been relevant.

In the next example, Neal uses *are* as a placeholder while explaining the ingredients of the Korean dish. In line 15, Neal mentions an alternative ingredient that can be used in place of chicken broth cooked from scratch or ready-made liquid chicken broth. Namely, one can simply use *are,* which is later specified as Chinese bouillon granules.

Excerpt 4 Introducing an alternative ingredient

```
1   Neal:    sorede, (0.3)   torigara       (0.3) shio  koshoo.
             and.then        chicken.bones        salt  pepper
```
"And then (0.3) chicken bones (0.3) salt pepper."

```
2            (0.7)
```

```
3   Hao:     torigara: ss [sore    (to yuute sore)
             chichen.bones that    QT  say   that
```
"Chicken bones ss that, (you mean that)"

```
4   Saki:             [torigara       suupu.
                      chicken.bone    soup
                   "chicken bone soup"

5             (0.5)

6   Hao:    sooyuu dashi wa aru?
            such   broth Top exist
            "Is there such broth?"

7             (0.4)

8   Neal:   da[shi
            broth
            "broth"

9   Saki:     [uttoru.  chanto.
               sold     readily
            "It's available. Readily."

10  Hao:    aa:: torigara      dashi?
            oh   chicken.bones broth
            "Oh:: chicken broth?"

11  Neal:   n de- a[no::
            and   uhm
            "and uhm::"

12  Saki:             [kore morau yo.
                       this take  FP
                    "I'll take this."
                    ((Saki directs this talk to Hao while pouring
                      beer in her glass.))

13            (0.6)

14  Hao:    u:n
            uhhuh
            "uh huh"

15→ Neal:   a[no:::::::::  are  demo ii kedo.
             uhm           that even OK but
            "uh:::::m are would do, too."
```

```
16  Hao:      [>doozo doozo<
              go.ahead go.ahead
              "go ahead go ahead"
              ((Hao directs this talk to Saki, responding to her turn
              in line 12.))

17            (0.7)

18  Saki:     are tte?
              that QT
              "What do you mean by are?"

19            (1.3)

20  Neal:     chuuka: aji    no moto.  aji=
              Chinese taste  LK base   taste
              "Chinese bouillon granules."

21  Saki:     =>sonnan       demo<  ii no?
              such.kind      even   OK Q
              "Such a thing would do?"

22  Neal:     hun      demo ii kedo.
              uhhuh    even OK  but
              "uh huh it's good/it works, too."
```

Unlike the previous two cases, in which the turns containing *are* as a placeholder constitute responses to the prior speaker's talk (whether making a challenge or demonstrating an understanding), Neal's turn in line 15 offers new information to the coparticipants. That is, like Excerpt 1, in which Akira, an engineer, is explaining his work to his unknowledgeable coparticipants, Neal is a knowledgeable participant explaining the recipe of the dish he cooked for Saki and Hao. Such a participation structure makes it difficult for the coparticipants to figure out the referent of *are,* as indicated by Saki's repair initiator in line 18. But Neal eventually succeeds in his search for the expression in line 20.

Like Excerpt 3, the timely execution of the turn involving *are* as a placeholder is critical at this interactional juncture where the imminent closure of the current sequence has been insinuated. Namely, Saki seems to indicate that this sequence concerning the recipe has come to a possible closure by informing Hao that she is going to drink beer and then starting to pour beer into her glass (cf. C. Goodwin, 1987), while Neal attempts to continue with his explanation. The prolongation of the delaying device *ano:::::* does not make it clear to his coparticipants what kind of search is underway and how the search is relevant to the preceding talk. Instead, Neal indicates that he is continuing with his explanation by making a suggestion for an alternative ingredient, "*are demo ii kedo*" ("*are* would do, too"), even though he does not name what the possible alternative is. By doing so, he can retain the coparticipants' orientation as unknowing recipients of this new information rather than risking their initiation of a new sequence on a different matter.

In the three excerpts introduced so far, the L2 speakers use the demonstrative pronoun *are* to manage their troubles with words while accomplishing varying types of actions. The inability to instantaneously produce a next item due does not prevent these speakers from performing their intended actions at the precise moments that they are relevant and making contributions to the ongoing sequence of talk. In contrast, Excerpt 5, extracted from Dataset A, presents a case in which the speaker, who had studied Japanese only through classroom instruction in the US, with few occasions to participate in interactions taking place outside of the classroom, handles a word search in a very different manner. The examination of this last case, I hope, further illustrates the significance of the use of the placeholder *are*.

As shown in Table 1, the L2 speakers, Alan and David, had received approximately 350–400 hours of classroom instruction in the US by the time of recording, but they had not stayed in Japan for an extended period of time. The following interaction took place at a weekly extracurricular conversation hour where these students met the Japanese participants, Toru, Yoshi, and Koji, for the first time.[11] The segment shown in Excerpt 5 occurred shortly after Toru expressed his bewilderment at the driving direction in the US (i.e., driving on the right), which is different from the Japanese system (i.e., driving on the left). In an attempt to contribute to this topical talk on driving, Alan initiates a question about the difficulty of obtaining a driver's license in Japan (line 1). However, soon after he initiates this turn, he encounters trouble producing the Japanese term for "driver's license." The fact that he is experiencing the trouble is indicated by pauses and the interjective delaying device *ano:::*. Unlike the cases shown in Excerpts 2–4, however, Alan does not use the placeholder and therefore, cannot complete the action he initiated. Instead, in the midst of the turn, he switches to English and gazes at David, his classmate, asking for his assistance in the search for the Japanese word (line 2). As a result, a collaborative word search dealing with the trouble starts without Alan's indication of his intended action in which the searched-for item should be embedded.

Excerpt 5 Introducing the English equivalent of the searched-for item

```
1  Alan:    ee::: nihon de wa: (0.2) ano:::
            well  Japan in Top         uhm
            "we::ll in Japan (0.2) uh::m"

2→          (1.5) °driver's license?° unten::
                                      driving
            "°Driver's license°? driving"¹²

3  David:   un unten menkyoshoo
            uh driving license
            "uh driver's license."

4           (0.6)

5  Alan:    unten men°kyo°- (.)
            driving licen-
            "driver's licen-"

6  Toru:    driver's [license?
            "driver's license?"

7  Yoshi:           [driver's [driver's [license
                    "driver's driver's license"

8  Koji:                                [aa::::::::
                                        oh
                                        "oh::::::"

9  Toru:                                [driver's license
                                        "driver's license"

10 Alan:    o::: morau    no ga (0.5) ano:: (0.8)
            O    receive  LK S        uhm
            "receiving (it) (0.5) uh::m (0.8)

11          mora- morai nikui     desu ka?
                  receive difficult Cop Q
            "Is it difficult to receive?"
```

In line 2, Alan produces the English equivalent of the searched-for item in a soft voice while gazing at David. Subsequently, he produces the first half of the item, *unten* ("driving"), and by stretching the end of this word while keeping his gaze on David, invites David's supplying of the second half of the item that corresponds to the English word "license." In line 3, David indeed responds to this call and provides Alan with the Japanese term for "driver's license," *unten menkyoshoo*. After a short pause, Alan attempts to repeat the term supplied by David, but he cannot completely reproduce the word uttered by David (line 5). Following Alan's unsuccessful repetition of *unten menkyoshoo*, the Japanese coparticipants claim their understanding of the English term "driver's license" (lines 6–9). By the end of line 9, the participants have established an understanding that Alan is going to talk about drivers' licenses, but they still do not know what exact aspect of them Alan is going to address. In line 10, Alan finally completes the utterance that he initiated at the beginning of this excerpt.

Comparing this case to the previous three cases, we can see that this is a situation where the distal demonstrative pronoun *are* could have been used as a placeholder. Hypothetically speaking, given that the talk so far had developed around the topic of driving, he could have possibly gotten by with filling the object slot of the sentence with *are* as in *nihon de wa are o morai nikui desu ka?* ("Is it difficult to receive *are* in Japan?"). The indication of the action to be accomplished in relation to the preceding talk and the verb to be used with the searched-for item all could have provided the coparticipants with clues for conjecturing about the referent of *are*. Producing some kind of gesture indicating the rectangular shape of a driver's license[13] along with the talk could have further helped the coparticipants figure out the referent of *are*.

As observed in Excerpt 5, without the ability to manage *are* as a placeholder, speakers who encounter trouble producing a next item due in the midst of a turn are likely to end up going into an "exposed" (cf. Jefferson, 1987) and possibly extensive word-search sequence without completing or projecting the intended action that contributes to the main activity in progress. In fact, while trying to manage the trouble with a word on their own before initiating their contributions that include the problematic word, some individuals might miss opportunities to perform actions that are only relevant to particular moments in an ongoing interaction, although this possibility cannot be empirically studied. The use of *are* as a placeholder, on the other hand, enables them to minimize, or at least reduce, possibly negative consequences of the momentary lapse in managing the production of a next item due and increases the chance of being understood by coparticipants with regard to their projected action. Thus, such "fluent disfluency" demonstrated in their language use appears to constitute a critical element of their advanced L2 competence.

The excerpts introduced here also attest to different ways in which L2 speakers construct their identities as they participate in talk-in-interaction. Recent CA-informed studies of L2 talk have questioned researchers' categorical judgments concerning the participants' identities, such as natives versus nonnatives or novices versus experts (cf. Carroll, 2000, 2006; Firth & Wagner, 1997; Hosoda, 2006; Kasper, 2004; Kurhila, 2001, 2005; Wong, 2005). Brouwer

(2003) examined the architecture of word-search sequences from this point of view. Namely, Brouwer challenged a taken-for-granted assumption that these types of sequences "constitute crucial moments in the learner's acquisition of target language structure" (Hammarberg, 1998, p. 178, quoted by Brouwer, p. 535) and demonstrated how a detailed analysis of interactional practices enables us to differentiate those that can and cannot be identified as learning opportunities. The most important feature that differentiates the two types of word searches is whether the participants "demonstrate an orientation to language expertise, with one participant being a novice and the other being an expert" (Brouwer, p. 542). To put it differently, in those cases that can be identified as learning opportunities, the participants themselves make the L2 participants' identities as learners prominent in interaction.

Viewed from this perspective, Excerpts 2–4 do not exhibit this characteristic of learning opportunities as stated by Brouwer (2003). Even though a few nonnativelike features (in regard to pronunciation, word choice, and morphosyntax) might be observed in their speech, the L2 speakers in those excerpts do not make these features particularly relevant to or problematic for the ongoing interaction. The use of *are* as a placeholder also contributes to this effect. In these cases, those speakers, who happen to be L2 speakers, are participating in those segments of interaction merely as users of Japanese language and handle the lexical problems not as those specific to L2 learners, but as those that are common to any speaker of Japanese. On the other hand, Alan in Excerpt 5 appeals to David's expertise in searching for the Japanese word,[14] and the coparticipants also treat Alan as a less-than-fully-competent speaker of Japanese by establishing a mutual understanding of the referent through the use of English. We cannot tell whether Alan learned the vocabulary item *unten menkyoshoo* after this incident, but we can observe how Alan's identity as a learner in need of assistance is made salient by Alan himself as well as his coparticipants in this word-search sequence.

Concluding remarks

This chapter demonstrated how interactional linguistics that investigates linguistic forms vis-à-vis their workings in interactive processes contributes to our understanding of L2 speakers' proficiency. In particular, the chapter discussed how the Japanese distal demonstrative pronoun *are* works as a placeholder when the speaker encounters trouble producing a word or descriptor and why its use can be seen as an indicator of advanced L2 proficiency.

For second language acquisition researchers who are concerned with learners' states of knowledge with regard to the rules and structures of an L2, cases of word search may appear as simply more evidence of the L2 learners' deficient or incomplete lexicon. However, upon close examination of word-search sequences occurring in talk-in-interaction, we can learn much more than that.[15]

The analysis of how L2 speakers attend to lexical problems that they contingently and unexpectedly encounter in the midst of interaction provides us with a renewed appreciation of their competence. The cases observed in this chapter specifically attest to how L2 speakers with intensive experience participating in naturally occurring interactions can effectively manipulate a grammatical practice, the consequence of which is tightly related to the linguistic structures of Japanese and their effect in turn-taking practices. Grammar, as discussed in this chapter and in interactional linguistics in general, does not stand for rules and structures that constitute an autonomous system independent of their use. Rather, it forms the core of interactional resources that are consequential for achieving social actions. The grammatical practice demonstrated in this chapter traditionally has not been taught in the language classroom. Because the opportunity to perform such a practice emerges contingently in an ongoing talk-in-interaction, such opportunities are not easily simulated in the classroom. Instead, learners need to acquire this practice through observing how it works in an actual interaction and then trying it out at an opportune moment as they participate in interaction. The process of learners' repeated experience of L2 forms as grammatical practices in emerging talk-in-interaction, or learning language in real time, thus constitutes a critical step for learners to advance their L2 competence.

As indicated by the recent publication of the American Association of University Supervisors and Coordinators, Volume 2008, titled *Conceptions of L2 Grammar: Theoretical Approaches and Their Application in the L2 Classroom*, there is a growing interest in reviewing the role of grammar in the language classroom. Such a movement towards usage-based conceptualizations of grammar, I think, fosters the integration of pragmatics and grammar, neither one of which can exist without the other. And this endeavor can be informed by conversation analysis and interactional linguistics. At the same time, however, language educators need to keep in mind that talk-in-interaction, an important part of L2 learners' lived experience, is not the only genre of discourse that they need to acquire to be an active member of L2 communities of practice. Byrnes (2006) and Swaffar and Arens (2005), among others, highlighted the importance of taking the notion of multiple literacies and genre-specific lexico-grammars into consideration for foreign language curriculum design. How to blend and juxtapose different grammars coexisting in a given language in classroom instruction, how to encourage L2 learners to seek out opportunities to experience their L2 as action, and how to capture the exact process through which L2 learners acquire this sort of grammatical practice are questions that need to be further explored in the future.

Acknowledgements

I would like to thank Cecilia E. Ford and Makoto Hayashi, who read earlier versions of this chapter and gave me constructive suggestions. The comments from anonymous reviewers and the editors of this volume were also invaluable for refining this chapter. Research for this chapter was funded in part by a grant from the United States Department of Education (CFDA 84.229, P229A020010–03). However, the content does not necessarily represent the policy of the Department of Education, and one should not assume endorsement by the federal government.

Notes

1. English is a native or fluent second language of the speakers examined, and Japanese is an L2 that these speakers had acquired to varying degrees by the time these interactions were recorded.
2. Hayashi and Yoon (2006) reported that the use of demonstrative pronouns as a placeholder is observed in languages such as Korean, Mandarin Chinese, Indonesian, Ilocano, Russian, Romani, and Maliseet-Passamaquoddy as well, although their realization may differ based on the basic word orders of the languages.
3. It is not my intention to claim that L2 speakers never master this practice unless they live in Japan. Those who live outside of Japan but have extensive experience interacting with Japanese speakers in naturalistic settings may be able to perform this practice. The statement here is limited to the set of data examined in this study.
4. Of course, not all turn-constructional units consist of sentential units. In certain sequential environments, a word or phrase alone can serve as a complete turn.
5. Hayashi (2004a) also reported that not every case of *are* used as a placeholder in his native-speaker data involved a word search. There were cases in which the speakers did not necessarily display that they were searching for a word or descriptor. In such cases, the speakers appeared to be oriented to securing some turn space to accomplish extended talk thereafter. He calls this "action-projecting" use of *are*.
6. I thank Kanae Nakamura and Yumiko Matsunaga for their assistance in the examination of these datasets.
7. All of the participants' names are pseudonyms.
8. In Japanese, *stikku* (from English) is used to refer to the equipment used for hockey, ice hockey, and so on, whereas *stokku* (from German) is used to refer to the poles used for skiing.
9. See Mori's (1999) study for the use of the connective *demo* in opinion-negotiation sequences.
10. In fact, the netted stick used for lacrosse is called *kurosu,* although not many Japanese (including the author) are familiar with lacrosse nor do many know the exact name of the equipment. Figuring out the correct name of this equipment is not the main issue here. As long as the participants can accomplish an understanding that Lili is referring to the equipment used for lacrosse, they can proceed with their opinion negotiation.
11. See Mori's (2003) study for further details concerning this setting and the kinds of interactions taking place there.
12. Wavy lines in the approximate English translations in the third line indicate that those words are actually uttered in English.

13 In another recording made during the same conversation-table event, for instance, a speaker can be observed using his thumb and index figure to indicate the shape of the license and moving the hand quickly out of the other hand, which appeared to represent his wallet.
14 Brouwer (2003, p. 542) emphasized that a language expert need not be a native speaker.
15 Word-search sequences involving elements of "private speech" can also be investigated from sociocognitive perspectives (Antón & DiCamilla, 1998; Buckwalter, 2001; DiCamilla & Antón, 2004; Lantolf & Thorne, 2006; McCafferty, 2004).

References

Antón, M., & DiCamilla, F. (1998). Socio-cognitive functions of L1 collaborative interaction in the L2 classroom. *The Canadian Modern Language Journal,, 54*, 314–342.

Brouwer, C. E. (2003). Word searches in NNS-NS interaction: Opportunities for language learning? *The Modern Language Journal, 83*, 534–545.

Brouwer, C. E., & Wagner, J. (2004). Developmental issues in second language conversation. *Journal of Applied Linguistics, 1*, 29–47.

Buckwalter, P. (2001). Repair sequences in Spanish L2 dyadic discourse: A descriptive study. *The Modern Language Journal, 85*, 380–397.

Bybee, J. (2006). *Frequency of use and the organization of language.* Oxford, England: Oxford University Press.

Bybee, J., & Hopper, P. (2001). *Frequency and the emergence of linguistic structure.* Amsterdam: John Benjamins.

Byrnes, H. (2006). A semiotic perspective on culture and foreign language teaching: Implications for collegiate materials development. In V. Galloway & B. Cothran (Eds.), *Language and culture out of bounds: Discipline-blurred perspectives on the foreign language classroom* (pp. 37–66). Boston: Heinle Thomson.

Chafe, W. (1994). *Discourse, consciousness, and time: The flow and displacement of conscious experience in speaking and writing.* Chicago: University of Chicago Press.

Carroll, D. (2000). Precision timing in novice-to-novice L2 conversations. *Issues in Applied Linguistics, 11*, 67–110.

Carroll, D. (2006). Co-constructing competence: Turn construction and repair in novice-to-novice second language interaction. Unpublished doctoral dissertation, University of York, England.

Couper-Kuhlen, E., & Selting, M. (Eds.). (1996). *Prosody in conversation: Interactional studies.* Cambridge, England: Cambridge University Press.

DiCamilla, F., & Antón, M. (2004). Private speech: A study of language for thought in the collaborative interaction of language learners. *International Journal of Applied Linguistics, 14*, 36–68.

Firth, A., & Wagner, J. (1997). On discourse, communication, and (some) fundamental concepts in SLA research. *The Modern Language Journal, 81*, 237–259.

Ford, C. E., Fox, B. A., & Thompson, S. A. (Eds.). (2002). *The language of turn and sequence.* Oxford, England: Oxford University Press.

Ford, C. E., & Wagner, J. (Eds.). (1996). Interaction-based studies of language [Special issue]. *Pragmatics, 6*(3).

Fox, B. A., Hayashi, M., & Jasperson, R. (1996). Resources and repair: A cross-linguistic study of syntax and repair. In E. Ochs, E. A. Schegloff, & S. A. Thompson (Eds.), *Interaction and grammar* (pp. 185–237). Cambridge, England: Cambridge University Press.

Givón, T. (1979). *On understanding grammar.* New York: Academic Press.

Givón, T. (1995). *Functionalism and grammar.* Amsterdam: John Benjamins.

Goodwin, C. (1987). Unilateral departure. In G. Button & J. R. Lee (Eds.), *Talk and social organisation* (pp. 206–216). Clevedon, England: Multilingual Matters.

Goodwin, M. H, & Goodwin, C. (1986). Gesture and coparticipation in the activity of searching for a word. *Semiotica, 62*, 51–75.

Haiman, J. (1998). *Talk is cheap: Sarcasm, alienation, and the evolution of language.* Oxford, England: Oxford University Press.

Hall, J. K. (1997). A consideration of SLA as a theory of practice: A response to Firth and Wagner. *The Modern Language Journal, 81*, 301–306.

Halliday, M. A. K. (1985). *Introduction to functional grammar.* London: Edward Arnold.

Halliday, M. A. K. (2002). *On grammar.* London: Continuum.

Hammarberg, B. (1998). The learner's word acquisition attempts in conversation. In D. Albrechtsen, B. Henriksen, I. M. Mees, & E. Poulsen (Eds.), *Perspectives on foreign and second language pedagogy* (pp. 177–190). Odense, Denmark: Odense University Press.

Hayashi, M. (2003a). *Joint utterance construction in Japanese conversation.* Amsterdam: John Benjamins.

Hayashi, M. (2003b). Language and the body as resources for collaborative action: A study of word searches in Japanese conversation. *Research on Language and Social Interaction, 36*, 109–141.

Hayashi, M. (2004a). Projection and grammar: Notes on the 'action-projecting' use of the distal demonstrative *are* in Japanese. *Journal of Pragmatics, 36*, 1337–1374.

Hayashi, M. (2004b). Discourse within a sentence: An exploration of postpositions in Japanese as an interactional resource. *Language in Society, 33*, 343–376.

Hayashi, M. (2005). Reference problems and turn construction: An exploration of an intersection between grammar and interaction. *Text, 25*, 437–468.

Hayashi, M., & Yoon, K. (2006). A cross-linguistic exploration of demonstratives in interaction: With particular reference to the context of word-formulation trouble. *Studies in Language, 30*, 485–540.

Hopper, P. J. (1988). Emergent grammar and the a priori grammar constraint. In D. Tannen (Ed.), *Linguistics in context: Connecting observation and understanding* (pp. 117–134). Norwood, NJ: Ablex.

Hosoda, Y. (2000). Other-repair in Japanese conversations between nonnative and native speakers. *Issues in Applied Linguistics, 11*, 39–65.

Hosoda, Y. (2002). *Analyzing Japanese native-nonnative speaker conversation: Categories, other-repair, and production delay.* Unpublished doctoral dissertation, Temple University, Tokyo.

Hosoda, Y. (2006). Repair and relevance of differential language expertise in second language conversations. *Applied Linguistics, 27,* 25–50.

Jefferson, G. (1987). On exposed and embedded correction in conversation. In G. Button & J. R. E. Lee (Eds.), *Talk and social organisation* (pp. 86–100). Clevedon, England: Multilingual Matters.

Kasper, G. (2004). Participant orientation in conversation-for-learning. *The Modern Language Journal, 88,* 551–567.

Kasper, G. (2006). Beyond repair: Conversation analysis as an approach to SLA. *AILA Review, 19,* 83–99.

Kim, K. H. (1999a). Other-initiated repair sequences in Korean conversation: Types and functions. *Discourse and Cognition, 6,* 141–168.

Kim, K. H. (1999b). Phrasal unit boundaries and organization of turns and sequences in Korean conversation. *Human Studies, 22,* 425–446.

Kim, K. H. (2001). Confirming intersubjectivity through retroactive elaboration: Organization of phrasal units in other-initiated repair sequences in Korean conversation. In M. Selting & E. Couper-Kuhlen (Eds.), *Studies in interactional linguistics* (pp. 345–372). Amsterdam: John Benjamins.

Kim, K. H., & Suh, K. H. (2002). Demonstratives as prospective indexicals: *Ku* and *ce* in Korean conversation. In N. M. Akatsuka & S. Strauss (Eds.), *Japanese/Korean Linguistics* (Vol. 10, pp. 192–205). Stanford, CA: CSLI.

Kitano, H. (1999). On interaction and grammar: Evidence from one use of the Japanese demonstrative *are* ('that'). *Pragmatics, 9,* 383–400.

Kurhila, S. (2001). Correction in talk between native and non-native speakers. *Journal of Pragmatics, 33,* 1083–1110.

Kurhila, S. (2005). Different orientations to grammatical corrections. In K. Richards & P. Seedhouse (Eds.), *Applying conversation analysis* (pp. 143–158). London: Palgrave-Macmillan.

Lantolf, J. P., & Thorne, S. L. (2006). *Sociocultural theory and the genesis of second language development.* Oxford, England: Oxford University Press.

Larsen-Freeman, D. (2004). CA for SLA? It all depends... *The Modern Language Journal, 88,* 603–607.

Lee, Y. (2006). Towards respecification of communicative competence: Condition of L2 instruction or its objective? *Applied Linguistics, 27,* 349–376.

Lerner, G. H,. & Takagi, T. (1999). On the place of linguistic resources in the organization of talk-in-interaction: A co-investigation of English and Japanese grammatical practices. *Journal of Pragmatics, 31,* 49–75.

McCafferty, S. G. (2004). Space for cognition: Gesture and second language learning. *International Journal of Applied Linguistics, 14,* 148–165.

Mondada, L., & Pekarek Doehler, S. (2004). Second language acquisition as situated practice: Task accomplishment in the French second language classroom. *The Modern Language Journal, 88,* 501–518.

Mori, J. (1999). *Negotiating agreement and disagreement in Japanese: Connective expressions and turn construction.* Amsterdam: John Benjamins.

Mori, J. (2003). The construction of interculturality: A study of initial encounters between Japanese and American students. *Research on Language and Social Interaction, 36,* 143–184.

Mori, J. (2006). The workings of the Japanese token *hee* in informing sequence: An analysis of sequential context, turn shape, and prosody. *Journal of Pragmatics, 38,* 1175–1205.

Mori, J., & Hayashi, M. (2006). The achievement of intersubjectivity through embodied completion: A study of interactions between first and second language speakers. *Applied Linguistics, 27,* 195-219.

Morita, E. (2005). *Negotiation of contingent talk: The Japanese interactional particles ne and sa.* Amsterdam: John Benjamins.

Ochs, E., Schegloff, E. A., & Thompson, S. A. (Eds.). (1996). *Interaction and grammar.* Cambridge, England: Cambridge University Press.

Olsher, D. (2004). Talk and gesture: The embodied completion of sequential actions in spoken interaction. In R. Gardner & J. Wagner (Eds.), *Second language conversations* (pp. 221–245). London: Continuum.

Park, Y. Y. (1998). A discourse analysis of contrastive connectives in English, Korean, and Japanese conversation: With special reference to the context of dispreferred responses. In A. Jucker & Y. Ziv (Eds.), *Discourse markers: Descriptions and theory* (pp. 277–300). Amsterdam: John Benjamins.

Park, Y. Y. (1999). The Korean connective *nuntey* in conversational discourse. *Journal of Pragmatics, 31,* 191–218.

Park, Y. Y. (2002). Recognition and identification in Japanese and Korean telephone conversation openings. In K. K. Luke & T. S. Pavlidou (Eds.), *Telephone calls: Unity and diversity in conversational structure across languages and cultures* (pp. 25–47). Amsterdam: John Benjamins.

Pavlenko, A., & Lantolf, J. P. (2000). Second language learning as participation and the (re)construction of selves. In J. P. Lantolf (Ed.), *Sociocultural theory and second language learning* (pp. 155–177). Oxford, England: Oxford University Press.

Sacks, H., Schegloff, E. A., & Jefferson, G. (1974). A simplest systematics for the organization of turn taking for conversation. *Language, 50,* 696–735.

Schegloff, E. A. (1996). Turn organization: One intersection of grammar and interaction. In E. Ochs, E. A. Schegloff, & S. A. Thompson (Eds.), *Interaction and grammar* (pp. 52–133). Cambridge, England: Cambridge University Press.

Schegloff, E. A. (2007). *Sequence organization in interaction: A primer in conversation analysis* (Vol. 1). Cambridge, England: Cambridge University Press.

Schegloff, E. A., Jefferson, G., & Sacks, H. (1977). The preference for self-correction in the organization of repair in conversation. *Language, 53,* 361–382.

Selting, M., & Couper-Kuhlen, E. (Eds.). (2001). *Studies in interactional linguistics.* Amsterdam: John Benjamins.

Sfard, A. (1998). On two metaphors for learning and the dangers of choosing just one. *Educational Researcher, 27,* 4–13.

Suh, K. H., & Kim, K. H. (2001). The Korean modal marker *keyss* revisited: A marker of achieved state of intersubjectivity. *Berkeley Linguistic Society, 26,* 271–282.

Swaffar, J., & Arens, L. (2005). *Remapping the foreign language curriculum: An approach through multiple literacies.* New York: Modern Language Association of America.

Tanaka, H. (1999). *Turn-taking in Japanese conversation: A study in grammar and interaction.* Amsterdam: John Benjamins.

Tanaka, H. (2001a). Adverbials for turn projection in Japanese: Toward a demystification of the "telepathic" mode of communication. *Language in Society, 30,* 559–587.

Tanaka, H. (2001b). The implementation of possible cognitive shifts in Japanese conversation: Complementizers as pivotal devices. In M. Selting & E. Couper-Kuhlen (Eds.), *Studies in interactional linguistics* (pp. 81–109). Amsterdam: John Benjamins.

Tanaka, H. (2005). Grammar and the timing of social action: Word order and preference organization in Japanese. *Language in Society, 34,* 389–430.

Thorne, S. L. (2000). Second language acquisition theory and the truth(s) about relativity. In J. P. Lantolf (Ed.), *Sociocultural theory and second language learning* (pp. 219–243). Oxford, England: Oxford University Press.

Watzinger-Tharp, J., & Katz, S. (Eds.) (2009). *AAUSC 2008: Conceptions of L2 grammar: theoretical approaches and their application in the L2 classroom.* Boston: Heinle Cengage Learning.

Wong, J. (2005). Sidestepping grammar. In K. Richards & P. Seedhouse (Eds.), *Applying conversation analysis* (pp. 159–173). London: Palgrave-Macmillan.

Wu, R.-J. R. (2004). *Stance in talk: A conversation analysis of Mandarin final particles.* Amsterdam: John Benjamins.

Wu, R.-J. R. (2005). There is more here than meets the eye!: The use of final *ou* in two sequential positions in Mandarin Chinese conversation. *Journal of Pragmatics, 37,* 967–995.

Appendix: Transcription conventions and abbreviations

Transcript symbols

[	point where overlapping talk starts
(0.0)	length of silence in tenths of a second
(.)	micropause of less than 2/10 of a second
underline	relatively high pitch
CAPS	relatively high volume
::	lengthened syllable
-	cut-off; self-interruption
=	"latched" utterances
?/./,	rising/falling/continuing intonation
!	animated tone, not necessarily an exclamation
( )	unintelligible stretch
(word)	word transcriber is unsure of
(( ))	transcriber's descriptions of events, including nonvocal conduct
hh	audible outbreath
.hh	audible inbreath
(hh)	laughter within a word
> <	increase in tempo, as in a rush-through
° °	passage of talk quieter than the surrounding talk

Abbreviations used in the interlinear glosses

Cop	various forms of copula verb *be*
FP	final particle
Neg	negative morpheme
PST	past-tense morpheme
QT	quotative particle
Tag	tag-like expression
LK	mominal linking particle
Nom	nominalizer
O	object particle
Q	question particle
S	subject particle
Top	topic particle

Switching Languages, Juggling Identities: A Sequence of Multilingual, Multiparty Talk

Tim Greer
Kobe University, Japan

Speakers are sometimes put in positions in which they are asked to perform 2 or more aspects of their identities at the same time. This chapter documents one such episode through a single case analysis of multiparty, multilingual interaction in which the focal participant, Peter, is called upon to simultaneously complete 2 distinct action sequences for 2 separate groups of people. While he is initiating a sales transaction with 1 interactant in Japanese, a larger group of coparticipants urges Peter to perform an impersonation, invoking his situated identity as "entertainer." He manages this interactional dilemma by responding to each of these groups in a preferred medium, combining not only Japanese and English, but also drawing on other elements of his language repertoire such as Yoda-speak and Japanese/English mixed phonological code. The analysis examines individual instances of codeswitching in their sequential contexts to highlight the ways in which microidentities are invoked and occasioned by other participants through their choices of languages and language varieties. The sequence is taken from a corpus of naturally occurring conversations video-recorded among bilingual teenagers at an international school in Japan.

People regularly orient to a variety of social identities in everyday conversation, including such macrosocial categories as ethnicity or gender. However, within the sequential context of particular instances of interaction, identities are used to accomplish temporary roles, interactionally specific stances, and locally emergent positions (Benwell & Stokoe, 2006; Bucholtz & Hall, 2005). Speakers and recipients may, on occasion, align to each other as "male" or "Japanese," but they simultaneously co-construct identity at its most elemental level within the turn-taking organization of talk by demonstrating an understanding of each other as next speaker, self-selected speaker, and the like. Studies conducted from the perspectives of conversation analysis (CA) and membership categorization analysis (MCA) have examined such turn-generated microidentity categories as caller/called in telephone conversations (Schegloff, 1979), questioner/answerer in adjacency pairs (C. Goodwin & Heritage, 1990); Heritage, 1984a) and speaker/audience in storytelling (C. Goodwin, 1986). Zimmerman (1998) called these moment-by-moment intersubjective positionings *discourse identities* and differentiated them from *situated identities* and *transportable identities*.

By the way they choose to formulate any particular utterance, "speakers commit themselves to a range of beliefs about themselves, their coparticipants and their relationships" (Heritage, 1984b, p. 270). This notion is parallel to Goffman's (1981) concept of footing, which refers to "the alignment we take up to ourselves and the others present as expressed in the way we manage the production or reception of an utterance" (p. 128). Goffman saw bilingual interaction as one of the most obvious displays of footing, referring to Blom and Gumperz's (1972) work on situational and metaphorical codeswitching. Thus, the organization of a turn can orient to membership categories, making relevant certain attributes of the speaker and his or her audience. In that sense, "footing invokes a broad range of phenomena in that it concerns not only speakers, but both speakers and recipients, and, perhaps most importantly, *recipient design* and participants' mutual adjustments, that is, the participation framework" (Cromdal & Aronsson, 2000, p. 436, emphasis added). Recipient design in particular refers to the way that each turn displays the speaker's "orientation and sensitivity" to another participant (Sacks, Schegloff, & Jefferson, 1974, p. 42). For example, C. Goodwin (1986) demonstrated that members of an audience can be separated into relevant subsets by the way the speaker frames his or her talk, which can serve to differentiate recipients from each other without explicitly stating identity membership categories. In his analysis, Goodwin examined such elements as profanity and depictions of violent actions in the way a story is constructed by a male speaker to direct it primarily to the males in a mixed group of listeners. At the same time, the recipients' responses help to shape the way a story is told when an interpretation other than that intended by the storyteller is proffered.

If speakers design their utterances for intended audiences, and this reflects their understanding of the listeners' personal characteristics and background knowledge, recipient design and footing must therefore be some of the key concepts for an understanding of identity construction in bilingual interaction. In a mixed-preference multiparty conversation, alternating the language (or "medium") can serve to select certain coparticipants as the primary recipients of a given segment of talk.

This chapter adopts an ethnographically informed CA/MCA perspective (Bilmes, 1992; M. Goodwin, 1990; Have, 2007; Moerman, 1988). It carries out a single case analysis to offer a glimpse into the way students at an international high school accomplish identity in everyday bilingual interaction. By focusing in detail on one episode of multiparty, multilingual talk-in-interaction, the study examines the ways in which bilingual interactants can design an utterance for a particular recipient by alternating between languages and linguistic styles. While the act of codeswitching may ultimately index aspects of transportable identities (Zimmerman, 1998), such as "multiethnic Japanese,"[1] the speakers also simultaneously accomplish both discursive identities, which can be used as turn-allocating resources in the ongoing talk, and temporary situated identities, such as vendor/customer, that are locally emergent within the sequential context of the talk. Through a detailed examination of the locally occasioned use of membership categories (Antaki & Widdicombe, 1998; Sacks, 1979; Schegloff, 2007; Silverman, 1998), the analysis focuses on the way bilingual speakers can use linguistic resources and discourse/situated identities to position themselves in moment-to-moment participation frameworks.

Data and background

The present study considers one sequence of naturally occurring bilingual talk that was video-recorded among Japanese/English bilingual teenagers at an international school in Japan. In the segment examined, a single speaker manages two situated identities, largely by switching between his languages. The analysis centers on the way he uses each language with two distinct recipient subsets to manage separate but simultaneous actions.

The participants in this conversation were all bilingual in Japanese and English; they communicated in both of these languages on a daily basis, although naturally, some were more competent in one language than the other. A brief summary of the participants' ethnolinguistic backgrounds is provided in Table 1. This information, including the language preferences indicated, was self-reported by means of a questionnaire during the broader study (Greer, 2007).

Table 1. Ethnolinguistic backgrounds of the key participants[2]

pseudonym	age	grade	years in Japan	parents' nationalities: mother/father	preferred language (self-reported)
Ryan	17	12	14	USA/USA	English
Peter	15	10	14	Japan/UK	Japanese
Nina	17	12	16	Japan/UK	Japanese (spoken)
Yumi	17	12	17	Japan/USA	Japanese
Ulliani	17	12	17	Japan/USA	Japanese
Anja	17	12	17	USA/Japan	English

The sequence examined is typical of the multiparty, multilingual conversations that took place around the lunch table at this high school. The "lunch table" was actually two large desks in a corridor that the senior students claimed as their own. Unspoken, but implicitly acknowledged through their everyday practice, the lunch table was a focal feature of the social territory for the group that included most of the key participants in my broader study (see Greer, 2003, 2005, 2007). Because the senior high school department had a small student body (only around 40 students in total), all of the 12th graders as well as certain 11th graders regularly gathered around this table when they were not in class. It was rare to see non-Japanese Asian students at the table, but otherwise, it was frequently populated by a mix of American, Japanese, and multiethnic Japanese students. Consequently, it was one of the most fertile sites for gathering codeswitching data and became one of the key locations for my video recordings. In the conversation analyzed in this chapter, the participants had arranged themselves according to the seating pattern shown in Figure 1.

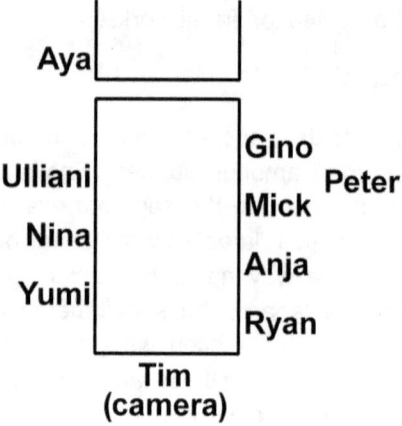

Figure 1. Diagram of seating arrangement in the Yoda sequence.

Prior to this episode, the group had been discussing Peter, a 10th-grade multiethnic Japanese boy, and commenting in particular on his ability to do impersonations. A few minutes later, Peter came past, carrying a basket of cakes to sell.[3] Figure 2 shows a frame grab of Peter's position relative to the group of 12th graders at the start of the conversation.

The sequence begins when the group makes relevant Peter's situated identity as a comedian by soliciting him to give an impromptu performance, including his impression of the *Star Wars* character Yoda.[4] The talk is carried out primarily in English, but Peter's imitations themselves constitute a kind of style shift in which Peter alternates between his own voice and his Yoda voice. At the same time, one of the members (Yumi) orients instead to Peter's initial purpose and attempts to negotiate the sale of a cake in Japanese.

Figure 2. Some key participants. Yumi and Nina are seated to the left, just out of the shot.

Yoda

```
01 Ryan:      next time you come up here come up
02            with a yoda voice
03            [           (0.5)            ]
04            [((Peter walks toward Ryan))]
05 Peter:     ((grunts in a Yoda voice)) ooh
06 Tim:       hhh
07 Anja:      [>yatte<?]=
              do-IMP
              Do (it).
08            [((bang))]
09 Peter:     =(te-h)
10 Ulliani:   >to[tally totally]<
11 Peter:        [tenth graders]=
12 Ryan:      =be like say we:ll
13            ((switches to his version of Yoda))
14            mgmm (0.2) [how ya doin']
15 Yumi:                 [(          )]
16            (0.2)
17 Anja:      eh totally
18 Peter:     well i[t's like  ]totally is
```

```
19                  ((in Yoda voice)) totally mgm
20  Yumi:           [tabe    tai ]
                     eat     want
                    (I) want to eat (some).
21                  ((takes cake))
22  Others:    he [ heh  ] ha [ha ha h hha ha::::::=
23  Yumi:          [ikura?] =
                    how much
                   How much (are they)?
24  Nina:                    =[yoda voisu de [ne   ]
                               yoda voice in  IP
                              Hey, in a Yoda voice, huh…
25  Peter:                                   [one.]
26             hundred yen nan desu kedo
                                NR   COP  POL
               That'll be one hundred yen please.
27  Anja?:    =heh ha   ha   .hhh
28  Mick:     heh he
29  Anja:     .hhh
30           °ukeru    n [na]°
              receive NR IP
             (He) gets a laugh, doesn't he?
31  Nina:              [ne]
                        IP
32           *yoda   voice de   totaru rifohmu=
              Yoda voice   in   total  reform
32  Yumi:    *((takes out a 500 yen coin))
33  Nina:    =[    itte    kureru?       ]
                   say     for us
             (Can you) do Total Reform in
             a Yoda voice for us?
34  Yumi:    [((passes coin to Peter))  ]
35  Tim:     hh HA
36  Peter:   ((in Yoda voice)) like totally
37          ((accepts coin)) mgm
38          ((gives "hang loose" sign))
```

```
39 All:         hehh [      heh        ] [heh heh  ]
40 Peter:            [((returns coin))] [  oh (.) ]=
41 All:         [    ha:    ha    ha ]
42 Peter:       [=a   soh         da ]
                oh   that way    COP     (.)
                Oh, that's right.
43                   (0.2)
44              matte  cheinji
                wait   change
                Hold on, the change.
45              [        (0.5)           ]
46 Peter:       [((turns to Mr. S.))]
47 Peter:       um do you have change?
48              °I've got five hundred yen.°
49                   (1.5)
50 Mr. S:       I might. ((looks in wallet))
```

While filming, I originally noted the sequence because it includes a striking example of participant-related codeswitching (Auer, 1984) in lines 42–47, in which Peter switches from Japanese to English to address Mr. S, his teacher. After examining the interaction that surrounds this switch, we return to the start of the sequence to explore the ways in which Peter uses bilingual resources and footing (Goffman, 1981) to partition his audience into relevant subsets (C. Goodwin, 1986), orienting differently to the various recipients to conduct serious business with one member while simultaneously entertaining the others.

Polyvalent local meanings of codeswitching

Obviously, the participants are speaking in Japanese and English, but Peter's Yoda impression constitutes a third kind of "code" that is relevant throughout the sequence. Yoda, a diminutive, sage-like alien mystic from the *Star Wars* series, speaks in a rather particular way. In the original English versions of these films, Yoda speaks a "dialect" of English that features an OSV word order (Gross, 2009), resulting in lines such as, "A visitor we have," and "Impossible to see the future is." It is likely that these are the sorts of archetypical Yoda-isms that the group is expecting Peter to perform, but possibly due to the sudden nature of the request, the first and perhaps most minimal way for Peter to perform a Yoda voice is by delivering a rather nasal grunt (line 5), the sort of sound that Yoda often uses between sentences. A subsequent request from Ulliani in line

10, "totally," is not the sort of thing that Yoda would say,[5] but Peter delivers it in a Yoda voice in line 19 by switching from his own British English to a somewhat raspy, nasal American accent that is immediately recognizable to the group as Yoda's voice.

By line 36, Peter is engaged in his Yoda impression, performing for the audience in English (and the English variant that indexes Yoda). At the same time, he has been serving his customer, Yumi, and realizes that he does not have the correct change to carry out the transaction (lines 40–44). This leads to a moment during which Peter is required to both switch languages and conduct a completely different action sequence within a very short space of time.

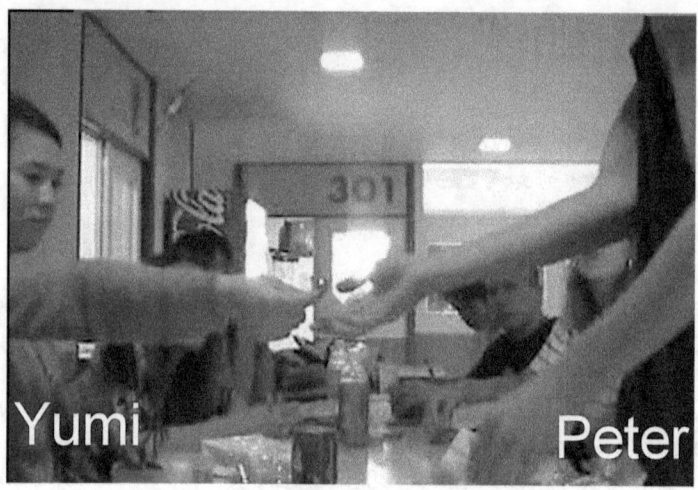

Figure 3. Line 37. Peter receives the coin.

When Peter accepts the 500-yen coin from Yumi in line 37, he has received strong uptake of his Yoda routine, through affiliative laughter (Jefferson, Sacks, & Schegloff, 1987) from the group (line 22) as well as specific appreciations (line 30). However, the jointly developed and ongoing sequence of talk with Yumi necessitates a serious response to conduct the business for which he came. During the confusion that arises from these coinciding actions, Peter drops Yumi's coin (line 40). At first, he receives it successfully in his right hand (Figure 3) but follows this immediately with a dual-handed "hang loose" sign, in which the thumb and index finger are extended. Facial expressions, a Yoda-like grunt, and a slight bobbing motion denote this gesture as a continuance of Peter's comic performance. The coin is grasped in his three middle fingers as he performs the gesture, as depicted in Figure 4.

Figure 4. Line 38. Peter's double-handed "hang loose" sign.

He continues to grasp the coin while he gives a further short Yoda grunt in line 37 and then immediately attempts to place it back in Yumi's hand amid the burst of laughter in line 39. Yumi's outstretched hand (see Figure 4) may have been her signal to Peter that she required change, but perhaps because he has been focused on his impersonation, he simply returns the coin that she gave him (Figure 5, line 40). In line with her situated identity as customer, Yumi does not close her hand around the coin, and it falls to the table.

Figure 5. Line 40. Peter returns the coin.

This complicated sequence of gestures occurs at the overlap between two points where Peter's duties as both comedian and vendor coincide. A possible next relevant action for Peter at this point is to notice his mistake and undertake some sort of interactional work to rectify it. He accomplishes this by codeswitching between lines 40 and 47. Peter completes his turn in line 40 in his own voice, not the Yoda voice, and along with the obvious prosodic difference between this and his natural speech, the switch to Japanese occurs at a point where Peter abandons his Yoda impersonations. From this turn to the end of the sequence, he is noticeably occupied with the business of serving his customer.

From lines 40 to 47, Peter produces three turn constructional unit (TCUs) that together constitute the codeswitch in question. Simplified, the switch is, "oh, *a soh da. Matte cheinji.* Um, do you have change?" Taking into consideration the action that each part of the utterance performs, I maintain that each utterance is directed at a particular recipient, and thus that Peter's codeswitching illustrates his knowledge of a preferred[6] language to be used for each specific recipient.

The first part of the utterance effectively contains two "ohs": the first produced in English and the second in Japanese. Clearly, there is a switch between the first and second "oh," and each refers to a different source of trouble. The English "oh" in line 40 is hearable as a response cry (Goffman, 1981), providing a reactive token to the dropped coin, while the Japanese "*a*" in line 42 is similar to the change of state token "oh" in English (Heritage, 1984a; Ikeda, 2007), which indicates that Peter has achieved a new knowledge state, as he realizes that he needs to provide his customer with money as well as the cake.[7]

The first "oh" seems to be Peter's display of his recognition of his mistake in dropping the coin. The consequent codeswitch into Japanese is part of the recipient design, which suggests that the sound "*a*" ("oh") as well as the rest of this turn is tailored either to fit Yumi's individual language preference, or to be heard as part of the vending exchange,[8] or indeed both. In either case, the language choice, together with the function of the utterance, makes the turn demonstrably directed towards Yumi.

Consider also the action that Peter is performing in uttering "*a, soh da.*" There is a recognizable organization of such business transactions such that if a customer pays for goods with too large a bill or coin, he or she is entitled to some change back. Clearly, the participants all know this. Further, Yumi realizes Peter's mistake in returning the original coin, rather than giving change back, as evidenced by the fact that she does not close her hand around the coin to accept it. This apparent lack of action is in itself an action: By not accepting the coin, Yumi shows that something has gone wrong because not accepting change back is a marked response. The first part of Peter's turn in line 42 ("oh, that's right") then, is a receipt and recognition of Yumi's action as an orientation to the trouble source.

The form of the second part of the utterance, "*matte cheinji*" ("hold on, the change"), is typical of bilingual Japanese-English speakers in my corpus (see Auer, 1999, on fused lects). In "standard" Japanese, Peter would probably have said "*matte, otsuri.*" The English word "change" does exist as a loanword in Japanese (*chenji*), but its lexical scope is limited to the substitution of one thing for another, such as in the expression *chenji suru*, which is used when two sporting teams change sides. At present, it cannot be used in the wider Japanese-speaking community to refer to the balance of money that is due to a customer who has given more than the required amount. In other words, Peter's utterance, "*matte cheinji*," is hearable as a turn-internal codeswitch, albeit one that has been somewhat altered phonologically. Such phonological codeswitches were a common element of bilingual interaction at this school.[9] We can therefore view the two mediums that Peter uses here as Standard Japanese and Phonologically Japanese English (see Hosoda, 2001, for a related discussion of "katakana English" in interaction). However, a closer look at how the participants themselves view this turn may establish a case for it as an instance of interactional otherness (Gafaranga & Torras, 2002).

Peter produces "*matte cheinji*" ("hold on, the change") for Yumi, to whom change is due, to show that he has not got any change at the moment but that he is dealing with it. In other words, this is a specification of the trouble source acknowledged immediately prior that was initiated nonverbally by Yumi by refusing to accept her own coin back. Even though Yumi does not actually accompany this action with any words because Peter delivers his response to it in localized Japanese-English, we can see that he is addressing her by continuing the conversation in what he orients to as an appropriate medium. However, this part of the conversation is also probably overheard by Mr. S., who is standing a short distance away. In line 46, immediately after he says "*matte cheinji*," Peter turns to where Mr. S. is standing and shifts his gaze towards him (Figure 6). This effectively serves to exclude any of those sitting at the table as the incumbent next speaker.

Figure 6. Line 46. Peter turns to Mr. S.

Peter drops the Yoda-speak and produces his next TCU in standard English. Here, Peter seems to be conforming to the social expectation of addressing a teacher in English, a strict convention within this particular linguistic community. However, Mr. S. also happens to be one of the few faculty members at this school who is Japanese. While he very rarely speaks it in front of the students, his accent and appearance are available to the participants in such a way that everyone is aware that he is a native speaker of Japanese. At this time, his physical location in relation to the conversation has not ratified him as an active participant, but Peter's codeswitch in line 47, together with his eye gaze and other actions described below, clearly slates him as the intended recipient.[10]

Bani-Shoraka (2005) observed that codeswitching in reported speech can also serve as an imitation. In her study, she analyzed Azerbaijani/Persian talk in which two coparticipants imitated their nonpresent aunt by switching languages along with a change of pitch, tone, and quality of voice—the kinds of paralinguistic features we would expect to see in a monolingual impersonation. Peter's Yoda impression is likewise not achieved by codeswitching alone. His switch in lines 40–47 is noticeably different from the preceding talk. It is accompanied by an explicit reference (the proterm *you*), prosodic features (amplitude, tone), and bodily conduct (gaze, the cessation of the previous jocular gestures, a directional turn) that all work in conjunction with the medium switch to determine the next speaker, a discourse-related purpose of codeswitching. Note that it is not only Peter who orients to Mr. S. as next speaker. We can also see that Mr. S. himself realizes that he has been selected (because he responds), and the other students demonstrate that they have not been selected because they stop laughing and do not respond.

At the same time, this switch is participant-related because even though Mr. S. is Japanese, in this situation, his identity as a teacher is shown to be relevant to the coparticipants. Speaking Japanese to a teacher would be unusual in this particular context. In other words, Mr. S.'s entrance into the conversation has altered the group's language preference, where preference is taken in the CA sense to refer to expectedness or unmarkedness. Up until this point, language alternation itself was the medium (Gafaranga & Torras, 2002), but by selecting Mr. S. as the next speaker, the language that the coparticipants are expected to speak becomes English. Peter's switch here accommodates the preferred medium for a certain recipient. In this sense, the motivation behind this switch can be understood to be polyvalent, both discourse and participant related. As Cromdal and Aronsson (2000) argued, it is uncommon to find clear-cut cases of participant-related codeswitching that are not relevant for the ongoing organization of talk because any action, including medium shift, is procedurally consequential for the ongoing talk-in-interaction.

Here, the institutional identities (teacher/student) are more relevant to language/medium choice than language competence or visually available facial characteristics. Clearly, codeswitching does not occur simply to accommodate a person's stronger language but according to the most appropriate language in a given situation. Throughout my observations at the school, I noted that the students routinely spoke to Mr. S. in English only, although it was clear from his accent that he was a "nonnative speaker." While this could no doubt easily be accounted for in reference to the school's language policy, which specified that only English should be spoken during school hours, only by both parties choosing to accept this policy throughout their everyday interaction did a habitual medium choice arise. Clearly, the students chose to ignore the policy among themselves, but adhered to it for teachers (whether they understood Japanese or not), which made language choice an indicator of not only ethnic but also institutional identities within the bounds of this school.

Institutional and mundane identities in bilingual interaction

Let us now return to the beginning of the sequence to establish how Peter utilizes codeswitching as a resource for managing the simultaneous presence of two distinct recipients: a potential customer and a multiparty audience with a somewhat frivolous agenda. He seems to be directing each of his two languages at a different kind of participant. With some exceptions, the comical Yoda persona is carried out mostly in English, while the business transaction is conducted largely in Japanese, together with the use of fused lects.

At first, Ryan's request for a Yoda impression (line 1) meets with only a minimal response from Peter. First, because the request is specifically for a character from a well-known American film, it can be assumed that the impersonation should occur in English. In addition, this initial request has come from a speaker whose preferred language Peter knows to be English, further implying that the language of the impression should be English. The short grunt in line 5 is hearable as a minimal response that works more to Peter's advantage than to that of the recipients: It satisfies the request for a Yoda impression without committing to either language, and Peter continues to move toward Yumi, offering her the cakes he is selling and thus maintaining his primary objective.

So in one sense, the grunt can be seen as a convenient means of managing the issue of language choice. However, in fact, there are a variety of codes at play in this interaction: In addition to "standard" forms of Japanese and English, we have noted that the participants use a phonologically Japanese form of English (*cheinji, voisu*), turns that combine both English and Japanese, and a stylized mock-language, Yoda-speak (codes such as these are not equatable with established linguistic systems).[11] In line with the conversation analytic perspective (Alvarez-Caccamo, 1998; Auer, 1984, 1998, 2005; Gafaranga, 1999, 2000, 2001; Gafaranga & Torras, 2002), I view codeswitching as an instance of socially and interactionally meaningful action and as a matter of local recontextualization of talk and action. The Yoda-speak comprises a code for the participants and is indeed very much relevant to their conduct in organizing the discourse. Hence, as part of my interaction-oriented analysis, that is how I treat it.

While Yoda-speak could be said to have its own syntax, Peter's impressions in this instance are not long enough to demonstrate the extent of his familiarity with the Yoda-like word order. Instead, he indexes Yoda through paralinguistic elements such as the grunts in lines 5, 18, and 36 and by using a raspy American accent that contrasts significantly with his usual (British-English) pronunciation. In fact, the only word that Peter uses in the Yoda voice—"totally" (lines 18, 36)—is not actually something that Yoda would normally say. Instead, it seems to index some other pop-culture reference that is available to the participants,[12] effectively adding to the humor by having Peter giving an impression of Yoda doing an impression. Quotations and reported speech have been well documented in the literature as frequent environments in which codeswitching occurs (Alfonzetti, 1998; Nishimura, 1997; Sebba & Wooffitt, 1998). Peter's Yoda impression can be seen as hypothetical reported speech or "virtual quotation" (Alfonzetti, 1998, p.202) in that he is not quoting something that Yoda did say but rather something Yoda could say. In Goffman's (1981) terms, Peter is the *animator* because he is producing the sounds, but Ryan, Ulliani, and Nina are the *authors* because they are coming up with the words for Peter to produce in Yoda's voice.[13]

Peter is not the only one that uses Yoda-speak: Ryan also attempts an impression of Yoda in line 13, but it is not ratified with laughter from the rest of the group in the same way that Peter's impersonations are. Instead, Ryan switches to Yoda-speak as a form of quoted speech, a well-documented discourse-related function of codeswitching (Alfonzetti, 1998; Auer, 1984). There is nothing particularly Yoda-like about the quote that Ryan suggests ("How ya' doin'?") in either its form or its content, but sequentially, we can see that what this turn achieves is to offer an assessment of Peter's initial Yoda impression (a grunt) as insufficient, and consequently, it acts as a request for a more elaborate impersonation, similar to those being made by Anja, Nina, and Ulliani in their own voices. The video recording provides evidence that Ryan is directing lines 12 and 13 primarily at Peter because Ryan shifts his gaze and moves his head and upper body to follow Peter while he moves behind Ryan throughout this turn. When Peter takes up the Yoda voice midway through line 18, the turn-internal codeswitch from standard English to Yoda-speak is integral to Peter's performance.

Peter and the rest of the group jointly accomplish Peter's situated identity as "performer." First, by requesting an impression, the group casts him with associated attributes that belong to the identity category "entertainer." Such requests occasion Peter's Yoda impersonation and make his identity as "entertainer" relevant and consequential to the ongoing interaction (Schegloff,

1992). Second, Peter himself indexes the identity category "entertainer" in accepting the group's attempts to position him that way and demonstrating the ability to switch from English to Yoda-speak, which in turn is ratified by the coparticipants and becomes procedurally consequential. Conversely, we can see that Ryan is not attributed with an entertainer identity because his attempts at Yoda-speak are structured as a request to Peter and do not receive ratification from the group in the way that Peter's do.

On the other hand, Yumi makes a bid to cast Peter in a second identity category, that of "vendor." She introduces Japanese as the medium of institutional business (vending) in this conversation by responding to his inferred offer of cakes ("tenth graders," line 11)[14] with an acceptance ("*tabetai*" ["I want to eat some"], line 20). Yumi's utterances to Peter are consistently in Japanese, with the possible exception of the unsure transcription in line 15, which is hearable as directed to the researcher. During my fieldwork, I noted that Yumi demonstrated a definite preference for Japanese, and this was regularly accommodated by the other participants. In this case, this presents Peter with the dilemma of how to simultaneously conduct two conversations in two different languages.

As noted earlier, his overlapped English turn in line 11 is an account directed at Yumi because it was the 10th-grade class that was selling the cakes. It is not clear from the video footage why Peter begins walking toward Yumi, but it is possible that she signaled him with some kind of gesture or made eye contact off camera. It is likewise uncertain whether Peter heard Yumi's Japanese turn in line 20 ("*tabetai*" ["I want to eat some"]) because it occurs in overlap with his own Yoda impression. However, he does display receipt of her Japanese inquiry in line 23 ("*ikura?*" ["how much?"]) and responds in mixed code in lines 25–26 with "one hundred yen *nan desu kedo.*"

One possible explanation for this turn-internal switch might be its proximity to Peter's earlier English turns (lines 11, 18) and the predominant use of English by the other participants in the sequence up until that point. In this case, lines 25–26 are hearable as an instance of self-initiated self-repair (Schegloff, Jefferson, & Sacks, 1977) where, I propose, the trouble source or "repairable" is the use of a dispreferred medium (Gafaranga, 2000). Yumi's utterance in line 23 is the first part of an adjacency pair (Schegloff & Sacks, 1973) in which an action initiated in Japanese (the question, "*ikura?*" ["how much?"]) would normatively be completed in the second pair part with a response in the same medium. Peter begins his response in line 25 in English ("one hundred yen") but completes the sentence in Japanese, providing possible evidence to suggest that he considers the medium in which he delivered the first half of his utterance repairable. The English segment of this turn constitutes a complete TCU, but due to the verb-final word order in Japanese syntax, the subsequent Japanese increment seems to acknowledge that the second pair part has been delivered in an other-medium. In this case, Peter is clearly orienting to Japanese as the established medium for the vending episode through the bilingual practice of medium repair[15] (Gafaranga, 2000).

The syntactic order of Japanese grammar (subject-object-verb) allows him to do exactly this. Although the English segment of this turn provides sufficient information to act as a complete TCU on its own, adding the Japanese increment "*nan desu kedo*" helps match the medium of the response to that of the first pair part and simultaneously upgrades the politeness level, which activates the service-encounter frame of the interaction. This phrase is typically heard in polite Japanese speech such as that used in the retail industry and therefore helps to accomplish Peter's situated identity as "purveyor of goods," which is appropriate to a specific recipient (Yumi) and contrasts with the stance as "entertainer" that he has adopted with the rest of the group.

In addition, "*nan desu kedo*" may also index the age difference between the two speakers. Japanese politeness endings are used by *kohai* ("juniors") to their *sempai* ("seniors") in a way that is difficult to convey in English. Peter is 2 years younger than Yumi and the others at the table, and he does not usually socialize with this group at lunch, having only approached them to sell cakes on this occasion. Therefore, this politeness upgrade could also be interpreted as Peter's attempt to cast himself within the *kohai/sempai* relationship, another aspect of his identity that needs to be juggled along with his languages.

Conclusion

This study has documented one episode in which bilingual teenagers interacted with each other. We have seen that they use a mix of English and Japanese, not due to a lack of competence in one or the other, but because their linguistic repertoire consists of both of these languages and because the sequential contexts in which they find themselves demand that they use both. Through a detailed microanalysis of a single instance of multiparty, multilingual interaction, we have found that various discourse and situated identities are jointly accomplished by and through mundane interaction with others.

The analysis has shown, in line with previous research on discourse identities, that *transportable* identities and macrosocial membership category devices such as gender or ethnicity are not always the most relevant aspect of their identities for these participants in any given conversation. Imbedded in the Yoda sequence, we have observed the students evoking relational pairs that index situated identities such as vendor/customer, entertainer/audience, and teacher/student.

The ability to proficiently alternate between Japanese and English firstly serves various discourse functions (Auer, 1984). Peter switched to Yoda-speak to (hypothetically) quote a well-known character for humorous effect, while Ryan's use of Yoda-speak was used to request further impressions from Peter. Nina and Yumi both switched to another medium to provide an interactional juxtaposition to grab Peter's attention (lines 20, 24). Here, codeswitching was another way to manage interaction; in monolingual interaction, these sorts of discourse-related tasks are accomplished by prosodic variations in pitch, volume, and so on. Naturally, participants in multilingual interaction have these resources at their disposal as well and regularly use them in conjunction with codeswitching to achieve various pragmatic actions.

However, language alternation in bilingual interaction is often participant-related, highlighting what the speaker knows about his or her interlocutor. Although in many cases, it is difficult to separate the two because any switch in medium is likely to have consequences for the ongoing discourse, a participant-related switch often partitions the talk, making relevant the various identities and language preferences of the speaker and recipients.

In the Yoda sequence, the participants are separated into two groups, not only on the basis of the content of the talk, but also on the medium in which it is being delivered. The Yoda impression is delivered largely in English (and Yoda-speak), while the business transaction occurs concurrently in Japanese (with some codeswitching). Because Peter responds in the medium in which he is addressed, a preferred action in bilingual interaction, the two conversations emerge according to Peter's demonstrated understanding of his coparticipants' language preferences, at least in that time and place. This does not imply that the two subgroups he is addressing consist of English speakers on the one hand and Japanese on the other. Everyone at the table has sufficient knowledge of both languages to follow what is happening in both threads of the conversation.

Taking a CA approach means suspending the analyst notion of "language" to discover the "codes" or "mediums" that the participants themselves orient to as relevant through the sequence of talk (Gafaranga & Torras, 2002). In the current analysis, this has led us to notice not only the use of Japanese and English, but also Japanized English and Yoda-speak, a form of stylized mock-language (Chun, 2004; Hill, 1998) that indexes a specific character and setting and accomplishes humor within the talk by juxtaposing that character with the current context. In addition, the hypothetical quotation voiced in Yoda-speak achieved its humor because someone who obviously does not speak that way under normal circumstances produced it, in a way that is somewhat reminiscent of Rampton's (1995, 1999) notion of *crossing*. However, Peter's use of Yoda-speak is not so much a comment on Yoda himself as it is an attempt at humor. Indeed, as we have seen, in this case, the switch to Yoda-speak was not initiated by Peter but by those around him. Again, this kind of "codeswitch" or "styleshift" could easily have been produced by monolingual speakers—a fact that is worth pointing out to monolinguals who persist in portraying bilingual interaction as somehow deficient.

From an interactional perspective, it is also worth considering how an individual deals with situations in which he or she is called on to be active in two simultaneous conversations and to perform two separate aspects of his or her identity. Of course, this kind of thing is not limited to bilingual speakers either. A monolingual speaker can be active in two simultaneous conversations as well and would probably make use of intonation, bodily conduct, and other interactional practices such as style shift and register shift to do so. In this sense, having access to another language is merely an additional communicative resource that helps the speaker achieve certain interactional goals. However, before the speaker can use such a resource, he or she must know (or assume) something of the interlocutor's linguistic proficiency, which in turn makes relevant perceptions of self and other. Discourse functions of codeswitching are a reflection of participant-related functions and in turn, shape both the ongoing interaction and the speakers' impressions of each other.

Notes

1. I use the term *multiethnic Japanese* to refer to those Japanese people who have one non-Japanese parent. In Japan, they are most commonly referred to as *haafu*, a loanword from the English "half." See Greer's (2001a, 2001b) studies for a more detailed discussion.
2. The participants' names are pseudonyms chosen by the author.
3. Each homeroom class organized various fundraising events, and charity bake sales were a regular occurrence during lunchtimes at the school.
4. *Star Wars* is a series of six science fiction movies written and produced by George Lucas. One of the recurring characters in this series, Yoda, is a short, elderly humanoid with long pointy ears and grayish-green skin. He is the leader of the Jedi council and is revered within the *Star Wars* world both for his wisdom and his fighting skills. With the possible exception of Yumi, this character was evidently known to some extent by all of those present at the table, as evidenced by their requests for Peter to give a Yoda impression.
5. Here, it is possible that Ulliani was originally requesting some other impression from Peter's repertoire, although it appears that Peter interprets it as a request to do "totally" in a Yoda voice.
6. Here "preferred" is used in the CA sense, meaning roughly "expected" or "unmarked."
7. The question of whether a response cry can provide any insight into an individual's stronger or preferred language is beyond the scope of the present study but remains a worthwhile topic for future research.
8. Japanese is not inherently part of the vending exchange per se. It is, however, indicative of this particular vending exchange in that Yumi has initiated an action sequence in Japanese, with the first pair part in line 23, "*ikura*" ("how much"), which sets the base medium for the sales thread as Japanese.
9. A further example can be found in line 24, where Nina produces "Yoda voisu *de ne*"; the phoneme /v/ in her "voisu" does not normally exist in Japanese, yet she

combines it with other Japanese elements such as the token-final /u/ to produce a "codeswitch" at the lexical level.

10 Cromdal and Aronsson (2000) found similar codeswitching behavior among bilingual speakers who were attempting to increase the number of ratified addressees, resulting in what Auer (1984) has termed *polyvalent* local meanings of codeswitching. Such switches simultaneously perform both discourse-related and participant-related functions of bilingual interaction. First, at the discourse level, it affects the ongoing interaction by signaling a change in the participation framework to deselect the group as ratified addressed recipients and effectively select Mr. S. as the next speaker. In monolingual talk, a current speaker can select a coparticipant to speak next by producing a turn that includes a sequence-initiating device and an addressing device (Sacks et al., 1974), such as when a name is used to allocate a next turn. Another way to directly select a specific recipient as next speaker is to use gaze direction in conjunction with the recipient proterm "you" (C. Goodwin, 1986; Lerner, 1993). In bilingual interaction, codeswitching can co-occur with such interactional devices as an additional means of making clear who is expected to speak next.

11 By "established linguistic systems," I mean the idealizations that traditionally are objects of linguistic theories.

12 Although as an analyst, I am unsure exactly what "totally" refers to at this point, it is apparent from the data that Peter recognizes what Ulliani means by it. It seems to index the sort of phrase that is commonly used by young people in the US. "Totally" is regularly used in movies such as "Wayne's World" to characterize and even lampoon speech, but the Yoda character does not use this word in any of the five *Star Wars* movies in which he appears.

13 And yet, the situation is even more complex because all of the participants are animating the "real" or "hypothetical" Yoda world, albeit from positions of different discourse identities.

14 Peter seems to be using this utterance as a minimal account for why he is walking around with a basket of cakes in his hands, and the others appear to accept this as unremarkable. That is, by saying "tenth graders," Peter is explaining that the money he raises from selling these cakes will go to the 10th graders' charity fundraising efforts, and for Yumi in this time and place, this is enough to infer that the cakes are for sale.

15 Although self-repair usually involves some sort of speech disruption such as pauses or hesitations markers, here, the falling intonation after "one" (line 25) seems to be the only orientation to a repairable by Peter in this turn.

References

Alfonzetti, G. (1998). The conversational dimension in code-switching between Italian and dialect in Sicily. In P. Auer (Ed.), *Code-switching in conversation: Language, interaction, and identity* (pp. 180–214). London: Routledge.

Alvarez-Caccamo, C. (1998). From "switching code" to "codeswitching": Towards a reconceptualization of communicative codes. In P. Auer (Ed.), *Codeswitching in conversation* (pp. 29–48). London: Routledge.

Antaki, C., & Widdicombe, S. (1998). Identity as an achievement and as a tool. In C. Antaki & S. Widdicombe (Eds.), *Identities in talk* (pp. 1–14). London: Sage.

Auer, P. (1984). *Bilingual conversation*. Amsterdam: Benjamins.

Auer, P. (1998). *Codeswitching in conversation: Language, interaction, and identity*. London: Routledge.

Auer, P. (1999). From code switching via language mixing to fused lects: Toward a dynamic typology of bilingual speech. *International Journal of Bilingualism, 3,* 309–332.

Auer, P. (2005). A postscript: Code-switching and social identity. *Journal of Pragmatics, 37,* 403–410.

Bani-Shoraka, H. (2005). *Language choice and code-switching in the Azerbaijani community in Tehran: A conversation analytic approach to bilingual practices.* Unpublished doctoral dissertation, Uppsala University, Sweden.

Benwell, B., & Stokoe, E. (2006). *Discourse and identity*. Edinburgh, Scotland: Edinburgh University Press.

Bilmes, J. (1992). Dividing the rice: A microanalysis of the mediator's role in a Northern Thai negotiation. *Language in Society, 21,* 569–602.

Blom, J., & Gumperz, J. (1972). Social meaning in linguistic structure: Code-switching in Norway. In J. Gumperz & D. Hymes (Eds.), *Direction in sociolinguistics* (pp. 407–434). New York: Holt, Reinhart and Winston.

Bucholtz, M., & Hall, K. (2005). Identity and interaction: A sociocultural linguistic approach. *Discourse Studies, 7,* 585–614.

Chun, E. W. (2004). Ideologies of mockery: Margaret Cho's revoicings of mock Asian. *Pragmatics, 14,* 263–290.

Cromdal, J., & Aronsson, K. (2000). Footing in bilingual play. *Journal of Sociolinguistics, 4,* 435–457.

Gafaranga, J. (1999). Language choice as a significant aspect of talk organization: The orderliness of language alternation. *Text, 19,* 201–225.

Gafaranga, J. (2000). Medium repair versus other-language repair: Telling the medium of bilingual conversation. *International Journal of Bilingualism, 4,* 327–350.

Gafaranga, J. (2001). Linguistic identities in talk-in-interaction: Order in bilingual conversation. *Journal of Pragmatics, 33,* 1901–1925.

Gafaranga, J., & Torras, M.-C. (2002). Interactional otherness: Towards a redefinition of code-switching. *International Journal of Bilingualism, 6,* 1–22.

Goffman, E. (1981). *Forms of talk*. Philadelphia: University of Pennsylvania Press.

Goodwin, C. (1986). Audience diversity, participation and interpretation. *Text, 6,* 283–316.

Goodwin, C., & Heritage, J. (1990). Conversation analysis. *Annual Review of Anthropology, 19,* 283–307.

Goodwin, M. H. (1990). *He-said-she-said: Talk as social organization among black children.* Bloomington and Indianapolis: Indiana University Press.

Greer, T. (2001a). Half, double or somewhere in-between? Multi-faceted identities among biracial Japanese. *Japan Journal of Multilingualism and Multiculturalism, 7,* 1–17.

Greer, T. (2001b). What should I call you? Self-applied and other-applied referents for biracial Japanese. *JALT Hokkaido Proceedings,* 29–36.

Greer, T. (2003). Multiethnic Japanese identity: An applied conversation analysis. *Japan Journal of Multilingualism and Multiculturalism, 9,* 1–23.

Greer, T. (2005). The multi-ethnic paradox: Towards a fluid notion of being haafu. *Japan Journal of Multilingualism and Multiculturalism, 11,* 1–18.

Greer, T. (2007). *Accomplishing identity in interaction: Codeswitching practices among a group of multiethnic Japanese teenagers.* Unpublished doctoral dissertation, University of Southern Queensland, Toowoomba, Australia.

Gross, T. (2009). Minimalist Yoda. *Aichi Daigaku Gengo to Bunka* [Aichi University Journal of Language and Culture], *20,* 3–29. Retrieved August 6, 2009, from http://leo.aichi-u.ac.jp/~goken/bulletin/pdfs/NO20/02GrossT.pdf

Have, P. t. (2007). *Doing conversation analysis: A practical guide* (2nd ed.). London: Sage.

Heritage, J. (1984a). A change-of-state token and aspects of its sequential placement. In J. M. Atkinson & J. Heritage (Eds.), *Structures of social action: Studies in conversation analysis* (pp. 299–345). New York: Cambridge University Press.

Heritage, J. (1984b). *Garfinkel and ethnomethodology.* Cambridge, England: Polity Press.

Hill, J. (1998). Language, race and white public space. *American Anthropologist, 100,* 680–689.

Hosoda, Y. (2001). Conditions for other-repair in NS/NNS conversation. *The Language Teacher, 25*(11), 29–31.

Ikeda, K. (2007). The change-of-state token *a* in Japanese language proficiency interviews. In T. Newfields, I. Gledall, P. Wanner, & M. Kawate-Mierzejewska (Eds.), *Second language acquisition—theory and pedagogy: Proceedings of the 6th Annual JALT Pan-SIG Conference* (pp. 56–64). Retrieved August 3, 2009, from http://jalt.org/pansig/2007/HTML/Ikeda.htm

Jefferson, G., Sacks, H., & Schegloff, E. (1987). Notes on laughter in the pursuit of intimacy. In G. Button & J. R. E. Lee (Eds.), *Talk and social organization* (pp. 152–188). Clevedon, England: Multilingual Matters.

Lerner, G. (1993). Collectivities in action: Establishing the relevance of conjoined participation in conversation. *Text, 13,* 213–245.

Moerman, M. (1988). *Talking culture.* Philadelphia: University of Pennsylvania Press.

Mori, J. (1999). *Negotiating agreement and disagreement in Japanese: Connective expressions and turn constructions.* Amsterdam: John Benjamins.

Nishimura, M. (1997). *Japanese/English code-switching: Syntax and pragmatics.* New York: Peter Lang.

Rampton, B. (1995). *Crossing: Language and ethnicity among adolescents.* London: Longman.

Rampton, B. (1999). Styling the other: Introduction. *Journal of Sociolinguistics, 3*, 421–427.
Sacks, H. (1979). Hotrodder: A revolutionary category. In G. Psathas (Ed.), *Everyday language: Studies in ethnomethodology* (pp. 7–14). New York: Irvington.
Sacks, H., Schegloff, E., & Jefferson, G. (1974). A simplest systematics for the organization of turn-taking in conversation. *Language, 50*, 696–735.
Schegloff, E. (1979). The relevance of repair to syntax-for-conversation. In T. Givón (Ed.), *Syntax and semantics 12: Discourse and syntax* (pp. 261–288). New York: Academic Press.
Schegloff, E. (1992). On talk and its institutional occasions. In P. Drew & J. Heritage (Eds.), *Talk at work: Interaction in institutional settings* (pp. 101–136). Cambridge, England: Cambridge University Press.
Schegloff, E. (2007). A tutorial on membership categorization. *Journal of Pragmatics, 39*, 462–482.
Schegloff, E., Jefferson, G., & Sacks, H. (1977). The preference for self-correction in the organization of repair in conversation. *Language, 53*, 361–382.
Schegloff, E., & Sacks, H. (1973). Opening up closings. *Semiotica, 7*, 289–327.
Sebba, M., & Wooffitt, T. (1998). We, they and identity: Sequential versus identity-related explanation in code-switching. In P. Auer (Ed.), *Code-switching in conversation: Language, interaction and identity* (pp. 262–289). London: Routledge.
Silverman, D. (1998). *Harvey Sacks: Social science and conversation analysis.* New York: Oxford University Press.
Tanaka, H. (1999). *Turn-taking in Japanese conversation: A study in grammar and interaction.* Amsterdam: John Benjamins.
Zimmerman, D. H. (1998). Identity, context and interaction. In C. Antaki & S. Widdicombe (Eds.), *Identities in talk* (pp. 87–106). London: Sage.

Appendix: Transcription conventions and abbreviations

Transcript symbols

[	point where overlapping talk starts
(0.0)	length of silence in tenths of a second
(.)	micropause of less than 2/10 of a second
underline	emphasis
CAPS	relatively high volume
::	lengthened syllable
word-	cut-off; self-interruption
=	"latched" utterances
?/./,	rising/falling/continuing intonation
( )	unintelligible stretch
(word)	transcriber's best guess of what is said
(( ))	transcriber's descriptions of events, including nonvocal conduct
hh	audible outbreath
.hh	audible inbreath
(hh)	laughter within a word
> <	increase in tempo, as in a rush-through
° °	passage of talk quieter than the surrounding talk

Abbreviations used in the interlinear glosses
(adapted from Tanaka (1999) and Mori (1999))

IP	interactional particle (e.g., *ne, sa, no, yo, na*).
POL	politeness marker.
NR	nominalizer (e.g., *no, n*).
COP	copula
NEG	negative morpheme.
IMP	imperative form

A Pragmatic Study of the Hawai'i Creole Discourse Marker *Daswai* in Second-Generation Okinawan American Speech[1]

Toshiaki Furukawa
University of Hawai'i at Mānoa

The present study is the first pragmatics-oriented foray into Hawai'i Creole, especially with its implications for possible Japanese contributions to it. I examine the use of daswai as part of the linguistic repertoire of a 2nd-generation Okinawan American in Hawai'i. Drawing on data from sociolinguistic interviews, this study provides a pragmatic sketch of daswai. The following questions are posed: What does the speaker do with daswai, and what are the functions of daswai? This study concludes that daswai (a) closes off an ongoing topic and (b) signals a point where relevant explanation will start. Furthermore, it appears that it shares some characteristics with the Japanese connective dakara. More data are necessary to further examine the uses of daswai and its variants in talk-in-interaction as well as to investigate Japanese contributions to the Hawai'i Creole discourse marker.

Ways of speaking

The ethnography of communication identifies a speech community with its ways of communicating. Second-generation Okinawan Americans in Hawai'i, who were born in the early 20th century and raised primarily in Hawai'i, are considered to form such a community because of their distinctive ways of using linguistic resources from English, Japanese, and Okinawan/Ryukyuan varieties. These speakers show linguistic resources that seem to be closely related to but differ significantly from those of Standard American English speakers as well as Japanese speakers. They also tactically use linguistic resources from Hawai'i Creole. Little is known about the pragmatic aspects of these linguistic resources within the second-generation Okinawan Americans' linguistic repertoire. I investigated a particular pragmatic phenomenon, the use of *daswai*, by a second-generation Okinawan American. It is "one of the most common connectors" in Hawai'i Creole (Sakoda & Siegel, 2003, p. 106).[2] I attempt, by an analysis of the contexts of its use, to determine what this linguistic resource is and how it works.

Drawing on the data obtained through sociolinguistic interviews, I provide a pragmatic sketch of the Hawai'i Creole discourse marker *daswai*. In addition, I show that this linguistic resource is used to (a) close off an ongoing topic and (b) mark a point where a relevant explanation will start.

In the next section, a sociolinguistic history of Hawai'i and Hawai'i Creole is outlined. The languages of second-generation Okinawan Americans are also discussed. Following this, several concepts are introduced that may be adopted to analyze the use of *daswai* in talk-in-interaction. The subsequent sections describe the methodology used in this study, explain the focus of the study, pose two research questions, and provide and analyze the data. The final section presents a discussion of the data in detail.

A sociolinguistic sketch of Hawai'i and Hawai'i Creole

Following contact with Europeans in 1778, Hawai'i became a stopover for whalers and traders between China and the west coast of North America. The establishment and expansion of the sugar plantation industry in the last quarter of the 19th century brought many laborers from different areas, which included China, the Pacific islands, Portugal, Norway, Germany, Japan, the Philippines, Puerto Rico, Korea, Russia, and Spain (Sakoda & Siegel, 2003). Hawaiian and Pidgin Hawaiian may have been first used as a common language among these immigrants (Da Pidgin Coup, 1999). By the turn of the century, Hawai'i Pidgin English began to emerge, becoming the primary language of many, including children acquiring it as their first language (Da Pidgin Coup). This marked the beginning of Hawai'i Creole, which is locally referred to as Pidgin.

According to Sakoda and Siegel (2003), Hawai'i Creole was established as a distinct language sometime between 1905 and 1920 and was fully established as the language of the majority of the population in Hawai'i between 1920 and 1930.

Generally speaking, Hawai'i Creole is used primarily within families and among friends in informal settings. It is considered a marker of local identity. Juxtaposed to Standard English, Hawai'i Creole is covertly prestigious among its speakers, although it has a long history of stigmatization.

The languages spoken by second-generation Okinawan Americans

To understand Okinawan Americans in Hawai'i as a speech community, it is necessary to review a history of immigration from Japan to Hawai'i. The first wave of immigrants from Japan arrived in Hawai'i in the late 19th century.

For the members of the second generation, interactions were limited to the Japanese-speaking community before going to school, and from the 1900s, the Hawai'i public school system had a major impact on the Americanization process of this second generation of Japanese immigrants (Maeda, 1997). With the introduction of Buddhism to Hawai'i, Japanese language schools were established. Many Japanese immigrants, who desired to return with their families to Japan, sent their children to these schools (Maeda). The majority of Japanese immigrants were from areas of Western Honshu such as Hiroshima and Yamaguchi Prefectures, where western dialects of Japanese were spoken.

In 1900, the first group of immigrants came from Okinawa, or the Ryukyu Islands (Kimura, 2001). Although they came from a part of the same nation-state as the Japanese immigrants, their linguistic capabilities were more multilingual and complex due to language planning in Okinawa. The dialects of the islands were significantly different from other Japanese dialects and could be classified as a separate language (Reinecke, 1969). Heinrich (2004) summarized the Japanese influence in the Ryukyu Islands as follows: It "predates the Meiji restoration of 1868, as it [Okinawa] became a vassal state in 1609. In 1872 Japan assimilated them [the Okinawans] into the Japanese nation state....In 1879 a compulsory school system was inaugurated" (p. 155). In the Meiji period (1868–1912), a contact variety emerged, and the eradication of this variety was a primary objective of language planning in the 20th century (Heinrich).

Second-generation Okinawan Americans presumably do not share the linguistic capabilities of their first-generation predecessors. They are competent, to various degrees, in only a few of the following languages and dialects: English, a Tokyo dialect of Japanese that was the language of instruction in Japanese language schools in Hawai'i, a western dialect of Japanese, a dialect of Ryukyuan (Okinawan), a contact variety (Okinawan Japanese), and Hawai'i Creole. Generally speaking, second-generation Okinawan Americans have a more solid foundation in English because of schooling.[3] Some second-generation speakers may have neither Japanese- nor Okinawan-language communicative ability. My goal, however, is not to reveal the linguistic capabilities of second-generation Okinawan Americans as a speech community or Okinawans in Hawai'i as a community of practice. The present research is a case study based on the linguistic practice of GM, a second-generation Okinawan American, who can put linguistic resources drawn from some of the above varieties to strategic use in talk-in-interaction. Her linguistic capabilities are discussed in detail in Section 4.

Conceptual framework

Discourse markers

In attempting to understand how *daswai* is used in Hawai'i Creole, it is useful to review some relevant research on discourse markers or discourse connectives. Schiffrin (1987) discussed similar, but functionally more specific, devices or discourse markers. She defined discourse markers as "*sequentially dependent* elements which bracket units of talk" (p. 31, emphasis in original). They "provide *contextual coordinates* for utterances: they index an utterance to the local contexts in which utterances are produced and in which they are to be interpreted" (p. 326, emphasis in original). Furthermore, they "allow speakers to construct and integrate multiple planes and dimensions of an emergent reality" (p. 330). Schiffrin examined the various discourse markers in English, which include "oh," "well," "and," "but," "or," "so," "because," "now," "then," "y'know," and "I mean."

Pidgin Grammar, the published grammar of Hawai'i Creole, explains that *daswai* can appear "at the beginning or at the end of a sentence" (Sakoda & Siegel, 2003, p. 106). When it appears at the beginning of a sentence, that sentence represents a fact, and the preceding sentence provides the reason for the fact. When *daswai* appears at the end of a sentence, that sentence offers the reason, and the preceding sentence describes the fact (Sakoda & Siegel, pp. 106–107).

In her discussion of discourse modality, Maynard (1993) attributed multiple functions to the Japanese connective *dakara*: It (a) "expresses the culturally shared assumption that [X] is a sufficient cause/explanation for a possible (or plausible) result/consequence [Y]," (b) "signals a point in discourse where relevant explanation will begin," and (c) "expresses that [X] is mentioned by self or by another speaker or is assumed to be understood or self-evident in the current discourse, so I add (reluctantly) an explanation related to [X]" (pp. 97–98). Interestingly, by examining the interactional function of the Japanese connective, Maynard implied its relation to the English discourse marker "that's why," which is superficially similar to *daswai*: "*dakara*... is used at the end of the turn to signal that A is willing to yield the turn. *Dakara* may be interpreted as 'that's why' in this position, giving a conclusive tone to the turn" (p. 93).

Matsui (2002), in a more recent study of the Japanese connective *dakara*, proposed that the primary function of *dakara* is to introduce a reformulation of another utterance or assumption. Based on Matsui's proposal, Sasamoto (2008) investigated the similarities and differences in meaning between two Japanese connectives, *dakara* and *sorede*, and concluded that they are not interchangeable due to the workings of contextual constraints.

Code-switching to a mixed code

Auer (1998) discussed "the emergence of a new structural division of linguistic labour between the elements originally taken from language A and those from language B" (p. 20). He stated that this structural change plays a key role in changing a juxtaposition of two languages to a mixed code. He also presented three sets of diagnostic questions that are designed to distinguish insertions from a mixed code. If the second alternative in each question proves true, it gives supportive evidence for existence of a mixed code. The questions are as follows:

1. Do the candidate insertions compete with discourse markers in the surrounding language or are they the only discourse markers available for the speaker(s)?
2. If there are competing discourse markers in the surrounding language, are they interchangeable with the candidate inserted markers without a difference in meaning apart from that which is created by the alternation, or have the markers rather specialized in function?
3. Have both the candidate insertions and the possible discourse markers of the surrounding language retained their meaning and/or function (apart from what is due to the alternation) when compared to the monolingual usage, or have they specialized in meaning? (pp. 20–21)

In line with these interests, Serra (1998) and Maschler (1998) studied the transition from code-switching to an emerging Italian/French and a Hebrew/English mixed code, respectively.

Method

The primary data collection method for this study was the sociolinguistic interview. I interviewed an elderly Okinawan American woman living in Honolulu. I refer to this participant as GM. I am the only other interactant (i.e., TF) in the data.

Three sociolinguistic interviews were conducted and audio recorded at GM's residence in 2006 for a total of 2.5 hours. The data contain 43 tokens of the Hawai'i Creole discourse marker *daswai* and are analyzed from a CA perspective. I thus adopt a sequential analysis of conversational code-switching (Li & Milroy, 1995).

GM and I had known each other since 2004 when, as an international student from Tokyo, I rented an apartment from her. Besides the three interviews used for this study, I have conducted many other sociolinguistic interviews with her.

Participant

GM was in her late 80s at the time of the data collection and considered herself a second-generation Okinawan. Regardless of her language choice, GM usually referred to herself as Okinawan. This category is, therefore, an emic term. Meanwhile, Okinawan American is the analyst's or etic term. I have chosen to refer to GM as Okinawan American due to her ethnic Okinawan heritage as well as to her American citizenship.

GM draws on various linguistic resources from the languages and dialects discussed in the previous section. She switches and mixes these resources in her linguistic repertoire, and the switching and mixing is conditioned by use in her daily interactions. GM's use of switching and mixing is part of a creative process of interaction that is enabled by the rich resources of her linguistic repertoire. Based on the ethnographic observations of GM's language use that I had the opportunity to make while I was her tenant, I can claim that GM's default language choice in talking with me was Japanese, even though she speaks predominantly in English when interacting with her third-generation daughter and others who do not speak much Japanese.

Research questions

In this study, I seek to address the issue of how to interpret the use of *daswai*. For this purpose, I present the following research questions:
1. What does the speaker do with *daswai*?
2. What are the functions of *daswai*?

In the next section, five excerpts are examined to answer these inquiries.

Data analysis

I focus on GM's use of the Hawai'i Creole discourse marker *daswai* in conversations that are predominantly Japanese and that include some Standard English as well as a little Hawai'i Creole in addition to *daswai*. It is not my goal to showcase GM's full competence as a multilingual.

To indicate for each utterance which language it is in, I transcribe Japanese utterances in plain font (e.g., Japanese), English utterances in bold font (e.g., **English**), and Hawai'i Creole utterances in a box (e.g., Hawai'i Creole). (For other transcription conventions, refer to the appendix.) Note, however, that these indications about languages in the data reflect the analyst's perspective, not the member's perspective.[4] The participants (i.e., GM and TF) do not necessarily treat every switch in code as meaningful.

Excerpt 1 GM is telling TF about her talkative son-in-law. Mary, to whom GM makes reference, is GM's friend.

```
1      GM    owar-an   no  yo     hanashi-ga.
             end-not   PAR PAR    story-NOM
             (He) never stops talking, you know.

2            hahahaha

3      TF    ((cough))

4      GM    ano:
             well
             well

5            tabemo-
             food
             food
```

```
6              tabemono-no  hanashi  shitemo  no
               food-GEN     story    do-if    PAR
               when it comes to talking about food

7              (.)

8       GM     mo:
               oh jeez
               oh jeez.

9    →         daswai.

10             (.)

11      GM     hm I tell Mary (.) no      a:sk.
                                  don't
               I tell Mary not to ask (him) questions.

12             [hahahaha

13      TF     [hahahaha
```

In line 1, GM provides a general statement, describing how talkative her son-in-law is. This draws a laugh from her in line 2. TF coughs in line 3, but there is no uptake by him until he starts laughing with GM in line 13. GM opens up the next utterance in line 4 and gives a false start in line 5. She continues to talk about her son-in-law in line 6, implying that he becomes even more talkative when he talks about food. At this point, GM, arguably, brings the topic to a closure, which is indicated by the co-occurrence of a micropause in line 7, "*mo:*" in line 8, and "*daswai*" in line 9. After the micropause in line 10, GM's talk, which is initiated with a disfluency (i.e., "*hm*" in line 11), reopens the topic, and she constructs a dialog between herself and her friend Mary, delivering her own reported speech (i.e., "*no a:sk*") with a slight change in voice quality. The reopened topic leads to a jointly organized, and perhaps more interactionally successful, closure in lines 12 and 13, which is indicated by joint laughter after the completion of line 11.

It is also noteworthy that code-switching from Japanese occurs in line 9. Both GM and TF laugh in lines 12 and 13 and treat GM's animating of her utterance in Hawai'i Creole to her friend as humorous.

In this excerpt, *daswai* co-occurs with micropauses and other features (e.g., disfluencies and "*mo:*"). This type of *daswai* is the most frequent in the data, and it seems to be responsible for closing and reopening the preceding topic.

Excerpt 2 GM has two daughters and a son. She has told TF that one of her daughters lived in Oregon. TF asks GM in English if her son also lives there. In fact, it turns out that her son lives in Vancouver, Washington (not Vancouver, British Columbia), and she talks about the two states while responding to TF's question.

```
1      TF    does your son li:ve in Oregon too?

2            (3.0)

3      GM    Oregon

4            (0.4)

5      GM    Columbia River=ga  atte. (xxx)
                          NOM  there is
             There is the Columbia River.

6            (0.6)

7      GM    (river [no muko.)
                    GEN over there
             Over the river.

8      TF    awh [he lives in] Washingt[on.

9      GM        [Washington.]          [Washington.

10           Vancouver.

11           (0.3)

12     TF    °Vancou[ver°.

13     GM           [°u=v° Van- ekchhe

14           (1.0)

15     GM    mo: ((recording noise))
             I'm telling you

16           (0.5)

17     GM    big sign=ga atte,
                      NOM there is
             There is a big sign.
```

```
18      TF     hmm.

19      GM     <wel come to: Van cou ver> iute,
                                            say
                      (It) says "Welcome to Vancouver."

20      TF     mm::::::[::.

21      GM             [are
                        that
                        That

22             (1.0)

23      GM     ichiban shi:ta.
               most    bottom
               is at the very bottom (of the state).

24             (.)

25      TF     hmm.

26             (.)

27   →  GM     daswai.

28             (1.5)

29      GM     Portland=↓°no° (.) Oregon=no air↑port
                         GEN              GEN
               The airport of Portland, of Oregon.

30      TF     mmm.

31             (0.3)

32      GM     >only five minutes↑<

33             (0.4)

34      TF     uh hu [    [Mmm.

35      GM           [Uch[i=no
                         our=GEN
                    Our (son's place)
```

36   **f<u>i</u>ve t<u>e</u>n minutes** gurai ↑ne
                                        about AFF
                      (It is) about five to ten minutes
                      (to the airport), you know.

GM produces a fairly long repair sequence to dissolve the confusion that TF has displayed about the geographical area. It may be helpful, therefore, to provide some geographical information here. The states of Oregon and Washington are located on the west coast of the mainland US. If one goes from Oregon to Washington, one will get to Vancouver, in the south of Washington State. The Columbia River runs between these states.

After TF's utterance in English, there is a 3.0-s pause in line 2. GM initiates a repair sequence, responding to TF's inquiry in Japanese and talking about the location of Oregon and the Columbia River. Following this, GM provides more information on the locations of these states. In line 7, she says, "over the river." She keeps speaking in Japanese and does not align with TF in terms of language choice. In line 8, TF does not align with GM in terms of language choice, either, and delivers an English utterance (i.e., "Awh he lives in Washington"), showing his understanding of the whereabouts of GM's son. GM overlaps with TF in line 9, repeating "Washington" twice, and in line 10, she specifically names Vancouver. In line 12, TF repeats the city name, inviting GM to provide more utterances. TF produces backchanneling, but his responses remain minimal throughout the rest of the excerpt.

GM produces a partial formulation of "Vancouver" in line 13 and an anomalous noise. This is followed by a lengthy 1.0-s pause, and then "*mo:*," a sequence that, in Excerpt 1, led to a production of "*daswai*" and a closure of the topical talk. Here, prior to the closure, a somewhat lengthy 0.5-s pause in line 16 is followed by an expansion of the topic of the preceding talk about Vancouver and by an expansion of the preceding activity of repair. More specifically, she restarts her description of Vancouver in line 17, describing a road sign in line 19 that one sees when traveling from Oregon to Washington.

In lines 21 and 23, GM specifies the location of Vancouver. The lengthy pause (1.0 s) in line 22 seems to signal an upcoming closure to the repair activity. The closure that was possibly initiated prior to the above extension is arguably completed with the micropause followed by "*daswai*" in lines 26 and 27. There is a relatively long pause (1.5 s) in line 28.

In the rest of the excerpt, GM makes reference to the Portland airport in line 29 and makes a comment about how far her son's residence is from the airport in lines 32, 35, and 36.

Note a fairly long pause in line 28. This kind of lengthy pause after *daswai* is rarely found in the data; more typically, it is followed by a micropause as in Excerpt 1. However, attention to the activities in which the participants are engaged (e.g., repair) and the use of other co-occurring linguistic resources by the participants (e.g., "*mo:*" and disfluencies), rather than to the length of pauses, would enable a more elaborated argument to be presented. This point is well attested in the next excerpt, too. In the following Excerpts 3–5, GM talks of experiences in her relatively remote past.

Excerpt 3   GM is talking about a guest couple from Wisconsin.

```
1        GM    soshitara
               and then
               And then

2              a- £ame-ga chotto futta kara    no.£
               rain-NOM little fall because PAR
               it started raining a little, so

3        TF    e:.
               yes
               Yes

4        GM    £shower£↑

5        TF    e:.
               yes
               Yes

6        GM    so they had to come in the house.

7              and £the£ ha lady said

8              (.)

9        GM    °o:h (.) they have refrigerator, °

10       TF    e:↑
               really
               Really?

11             (0.5)

12       GM    ano hito-ra:
               that person-PL
               They
```

```
13              (.)

14      GM      no
                PAR
                you know

15              (.)

16      GM      Wisconsin-no inaka-no (.) jigyo:ka      ya↑
                -GEN country-GEN entrepreneur PAR
                are entrepreneurs from rural Wisconsin,
                you see

17      TF      hm:.

18              (0.5)

19      TF      un.
                yes
                Yes.

20  →   GM      daswai.

21              (1.5)

22      GM      real

23              (.)

24      TF      un.
                yes
                Yes.

25              (.)

26      GM      real    inaka   yo. haha
                        country PAR
                Really countrified

27              soremo      mukashi     kara.
                even that long time ago from
                Even from a long time ago.

28      TF      hm:.
```

```
29      GM    ima demo so:              desyo:
              now even like that        you know
              (It is) so even now, you know.
```

From line 1 to 6, GM talks in Japanese about their guest who had to go into the house because of the rain. TF responds to her with Japanese backchanneling, "*e:*" ("yes") in lines 3 and 5. GM switches from Japanese to English in line 4. She also utters "shower" with a laughing voice, indicating what comes next in relation to the shower is humorous and meaningful. She then delivers English utterances in lines 6 and 7. She completes the buildup by saying "and £the£ ha lady said" in line 7. After a micropause in line 8, she uses a soft voice and animates the wife talking to her husband in line 9, being surprised to find a refrigerator in the house. The soft voice contrasts with GM's ordinary voice and is used to animate the wife. TF responds to this with "*e:↑*" ("really") in line 10, presenting his interpretation of the wife's comment as a surprise to him. GM then switches back to Japanese in line 12, explains the background of the couple in lines 12–16, and attributes the wife's reaction to the fact that she is from a rural area, namely, Wisconsin. After TF's backchanneling in lines 17 and 19 and a 0.5-s pause in line 18, she uses *daswai* in line 20, and it is followed by a 1.5-s pause.

Note that a micropause in line 8 seems to initiate a closure of the topic. It is followed by a relatively lengthy pause (0.5 s) in line 11 as well as by micropauses in lines 13, 15, and 16, all of which seem to be connected with disfluencies. Finally, a lengthy pause (0.5 s) in line 18 is followed by "*daswai,*" which marks the closure of the preceding topic.

In the talk that follows "*daswai,*" GM returns to and starts to expand upon the previous topic in line 22. She describes Wisconsin as "real, real *inaka yo*" ("really, really countrified"), and she adds that Wisconsin has long been that way and still is in lines 27 and 29. As in Excerpt 1, she expands the previous topic with co-occurring features such as laughter in line 26.

The use of *daswai* in this excerpt is similar to that in Excerpts 1 and 2. It constructs a closure to the preceding activity, and subsequent talk after the pause in line 21 orients to the closure signaled by *daswai.*

It should also be noted that TF is consistently using Japanese backchanneling (e.g., "*e:*" ["yes"] in lines 3 and 5 and "*un*" ["yes"] in lines 19 and 24) except for two ambiguous instances (i.e., "*hm:*") in lines 17 and 28. Meanwhile, GM responds to him in English in lines 4 and 6. She also responds in Japanese in lines 12, 26, 27, and 29. In response to TF's "*un*" ("yes") in line 19, she delivers "*daswai*" in line 20. In short, GM does not always orient to TF's language choice in his backchanneling.

Excerpt 4   GM is talking about what she ate for breakfast as a child before going to school.

```
1      GM    asa       gakko:-ni    iku no ni no
             morning   school-DAT   go GEN DAT PAR
             In the morning, to go to school, you know

2      TF    hm.

3      GM    misoshiru (.) every morning.
             miso soup
             (We ate) miso soup every morning.

4      TF    every morning.

5      GM    misoshiru ya (.)        tamago watte
             miso soup PAR           egg   crack
             Miso soup, you see? With an egg cracked
             into it.

6      TF    hmm.

7            (2.0)

8      GM    misoshiru demo
             miso soup even
             even miso soup

9      TF    hmm.

10     GM    demo areba
             even there is-if
             if there is even (miso soup)

11           (1.0)

12     GM    milk toka cereal-no kawari-ni
                  or          -GEN substitution-DAT
             instead of milk or cereal

15     GM    and we had to walk about three miles

16           to get to school.

17     TF    oh three miles.
```

```
18    GM    so-
              the-

19            (1.0)

20    GM    so:de nakattara XXXXXXXXXX
              then   if not
              Then, if (we) don't have (miso soup for
              breakfast)

21    TF    hmm.

22    GM    **hungry** ni naru     ya
                      -DAT become PAR
              (We) get hungry, you know?

23    TF    hmm.

24            miso-wa  himochi   suru kara   ne:
              miso-TOP last long do   because PAR
              Miso doesn't become bad quickly.

25            (.)

26    TF    daijo:bu      dashi.
              no problem   it is
              There is no problem

27    GM    yeah.

28  →        **so** daswai .

29            (.)

30    GM    we had little bit money  no.
                                      PAR
              we didn't have much money, you know.

31    TF    hmm.

32    GM    kimatta      yo:na.
              decided     kind of
              (Our breakfast was always) the same.
```

GM talks about eating miso soup for breakfast in lines 1–13. She mentions how many miles she had to walk to school every morning in lines 15–16. She also says that she would have become hungry if she did not eat anything for breakfast in lines 18, 20, and 22. After TF's comments in lines 24 and 26, GM acknowledges them in line 27 and produces "so *daswai*" in line 28, which is followed by a micropause along with additional information about her family's financial situation uttered almost completely in Hawai'i Creole with a Japanese sentence-final particle. In the last line, she says, "(Our breakfast was always) the same."

It should be noted that GM uses "so *daswai*," not *daswai*, in line 28. The English conjunction "so" is preceded by a cause and is followed by an effect (Schiffrin, 1987). The co-occurrence of "so" suggests that there may be a sort of hybrid code being used here. This use of *daswai* may not share all of the features pointed out in the preceding examples.

A close look shows that *mo:* does not co-occur, as opposed to Excerpts 1 and 2. Meanwhile, lengthy pauses are found in lines 7, 11, and 19. The pause in line 19 follows a false start (i.e., "*so-*") in line 18. These actions culminate in a closure of the topic (about what GM used to eat every morning) with the production of "*daswai.*" However, this is a somewhat abrupt closure, thereby leading up to an interactionally unsuccessful reopening and expansion of the preceding topic in lines 30–32. In summary, it seems that the type of *daswai* in this excerpt is not exactly the same as that in the previous excerpts due to the lack of co-occurring features that regularly appear in the surrounding talk of *daswai*.

TF responds to GM by either producing minimal backchanneling (i.e., "*hm*" and "*hmm*") or repeating part of GM's utterance (e.g., "every morning" in line 4 and "three miles" in line 17). With these responses, he invites GM to produce more utterances. The only exception is lines 24–26, where he makes a comment in Japanese. This comment is oriented to GM's reference to "*misoshiru*" ("miso soup") in lines 3, 5, and 8. GM responds to TF's comment with "yeah" in line 27 but somewhat abruptly closes the preceding topic with "so *daswai*" in line 28. She attaches a Japanese sentence-final particle in line 30 and switches back into Japanese in line 32.

Excerpt 5 GM is talking about economic difficulties she went through in her childhood.

```
1      GM    are kara mo:
              that from I'm telling you
              Since then, I'm telling you,

2             (.)

3      GM    dandan
              gradually
              gradually
```

```
4              (.)

5        GM    rakuni   nattekita        yo.
               easy     started getting  PAR
               Life started getting easier.

6        TF    n:.

7        GM    are made fukeiki.
               that until depression
               Up until then, we were in the Depression.

8              (.)

9        GM    anta-ra
               you-PL
               Your generation

10             (.)

11       GM    fukeiki     iu    koto mo
               depression  say   thing also
               Something like depression

12             (.)

13       GM    ajiwatta koto-ga          nai         kara
               experience thing-NOM      there's no  because
               has never experienced the depression,

14             wakaran.
               don't know
               so you don't know

15       TF    ((cough))

16       GM    mo- (.) **no more money**.

17             (0.5)

18   →         >daswai.<

19             (1.5)
```

```
20            kane        nai        ya↑
              money       there's no PAR
              There is no more money, you see?

21      TF    n:

22      GM    tsukutta mono taberu ya↑
              made     thing  eats   PAR
              (One) eats what (one) has grown, you see?

23            dakara       genki.
              therefore    healthy
              Therefore (one is) healthy.

24      TF    n:.

25      GM    haha £genki    da  yo  no.£
              healthy COP PAR PAR
              (One is) healthy, right?
```

In Excerpt 5, GM says, "Since then, I'm telling you, gradually, life started getting easier" in lines 1–5, "Up until then, we were in the Depression" in line 7, and "Your generation has never experienced a depression, so you don't know" in lines 9–14. Following this, she says, "*mo- (.) no more money*" in line 16. There is a 0.5-s pause in line 17, and she uses "*daswai*" in line 18, followed by a 1.5-s pause in line 19. She then switches into Japanese in line 20 and produces an utterance that repeats the content of the utterance in line 16. She says, "(One) eats what (one) has grown, you see" in line 22. Finally, she says, "Therefore, (one is) healthy" in line 23 and repeats the same adjective in line 25.

Note that the status of "*mo-*" in line 16 is at least ambiguous. It cannot be a false start for "money," which is part of the immediately following phrase "no more money," because it would have the sound *muh*. It seems to be a false start for either "more," which is part of the same phrase in line 16, or a Japanese *mo:*, which also appears in the vicinity of "*daswai*" in line 8 of Excerpt 1 as well as in line 15 of Excerpt 2. It seems to me more reasonable to assume that the latter is the case because it regularly appears in two of the previous excerpts to construct the co-occurrence of *mo:*, (micro)pause, and *daswai*, which serves to close off the preceding topic. Moreover, the restart in line 20 again picks up the topic of the immediately preceding talk. These pieces of evidence support my assumption about the status of "*mo-*" in line 16 as well as about the function of *daswai* and other co-occurring features.

It is also noteworthy that there are two contrastive discursive developments in the above excerpt. One sequence is produced as follows: GM describes economic difficulties as facts between lines 1 and 14, provides a coda that sums up the experience of living through the Depression in line 16, and closes the preceding discourse unit with "*daswai*" in line 18, along with a lengthy 1.5-s pause in line 19. The other sequence starts with her picking up the preceding topic and switching back into Japanese in line 20. She then produces a sequence that seems to consist of a cause ("One eats what one has grown" in line 22), "*dakara*" ("therefore," in line 23), and a consequence ("healthy" in line 23).

The co-occurrence of *daswai* and *dakara* here is intriguing. As indicated above, *daswai*, along with other features, marks the end of the preceding topic. In addition, the use of *daswai* allows additional information to follow; thereby, the previous topic is repeated in line 20 in a different language. It is further expanded in line 22. Both lines 20 and 22 are accompanied by a Japanese sentence-final particle with rising intonation, indicating, and raising the expectation of, the delivery of a concluding remark, which finally comes in line 23 with a falling intonation. Even after the conclusive tone of line 23, laughter occurs in line 25, and this is followed by the expansion or repetition of the immediately preceding topic and is coupled with a laughing voice.

Given the multiple functions of *dakara* discussed in Section 2, *dakara* in line 23 expresses the shared assumption that [X] is a cause for a result [Y]: That is, "(one) eats what (one) has grown, so (one is) healthy." It also signals a point where relevant explanation will start by reopening or repeating the preceding topic, here with co-occurring features such as laughter, sentence-final particles, and a laughing voice (i.e., "haha £genki da yo no.£" ["haha (one is) healthy, right?"] in line 25).

Discussion

Two recurring patterns have been observed. The first pattern is found in Excerpts 1, 2, 3, and 5, where GM initiates a closing of the current topic through (micro)pauses, disfluencies, and the Japanese lexical item *mo:*. These actions lead to the production of the Hawai'i Creole discourse marker *daswai*, which is followed by a pause. Once the closure is completed, however, GM picks up the immediately preceding topic (i.e., "a talkative son-in-law" in Excerpt 1, "Vancouver" in Excerpt 2, "Wisconsin" in Excerpt 3, and "breakfast" in Excerpt 5) or restarts the preceding activity (i.e., repair in Excerpt 2), thereby expanding the preceding topic or activity, an expansion that is usually accompanied by laughter and/or a laughing voice quality (Excerpts 1, 3, and 5) and creates an interactionally successful closure (Excerpt 1).

The second pattern is found in Excerpt 4, where GM uses "so *daswai.*" This sequence lacks some of the co-occurring features of *daswai*—such as the Japanese lexical item *mo:* and a jointly organized closure—that are observed in the other excerpts. Even though "so *daswai*" indicates a point where relevant explanation starts to develop, the point turns into an abrupt abandonment of the preceding topic because relevant explanation is not provided in an interactionally smooth manner.

As seen in all of the above excerpts but Excerpt 4, GM uses *daswai* to highlight the end of a certain discourse unit. It could be said that *daswai* and the preceding discourse unit form one unit of talk, with *daswai* having a conclusive tone. This is characteristic for GM, and presumably for other second-generation Okinawan Americans in Hawai'i and Hawai'i Creole speakers.

Sakoda and Siegel (2003), whose study is briefly discussed in Section 2, explained that *daswai* can appear at the beginning or the end of a sentence. When it appears at the beginning, that sentence is heard as stating a fact, and the preceding sentence is given as a reason for the fact, and vice versa. My study supports and adds to Sakoda and Siegel by taking a pragmatics-oriented approach towards Hawai'i Creole and demonstrating the emergence of a Hawai'i Creole discourse marker in talk-in-interaction where it appears along with co-occurring features in its two recurring patterns.

Moreover, the co-occurrence of *daswai* with the Japanese connective *dakara* in Excerpt 5 is suggestive of possible Japanese contributions to the Hawai'i Creole discourse marker. There are some similarities between my observation of *daswai* and Maynard's (1993) proposal regarding the multifunctional Japanese connective. For instance, Sakoda and Siegel's (2003) proposal to explain *daswai* as indexing a cause-fact sequence corresponds with one of the functions of *dakara* posited by Maynard (i.e., [X] is a cause for a result [Y]). In addition, both *daswai* and *dakara* in the above excerpts indicate a point where a relevant explanation of the immediately preceding topic will start. To pursue this line of argument, however, I must reexamine GM's conversational data where these discourse markers/connectives are in use.

Conclusion

A pragmatic sketch of *daswai* has been provided. The introduction gave a brief sociolinguistic history of Hawai'i and the languages spoken by second-generation Okinawan Americans. The section "Conceptual framework" reviewed several theoretical notions that are helpful in the analysis of *daswai* as a linguistic resource. Following this, the next three sections described the methods of data collection and analysis, elaborated on the participant's communicative competence, and the stated the two research questions. The section "Data analysis" commented on the main focus of the study, the Hawai'i Creole discourse marker *daswai* within predominantly Japanese conversations, and presented the data. The final section discussed the data in detail.

In conclusion, this study has examined a conversational sequence in which *daswai* closes off the preceding topic along with co-occurring features in the surrounding talk that initiate the closing. More specifically, the sequence of a pause, *mo:*, and *daswai* leads to a closure of the topical talk. *Daswai* and a (micro)pause that follows create a somewhat abrupt abandonment of the preceding topic. However, we have also observed that *daswai* has a pragmatic use as a marker that indicates a point where a relevant explanation will begin to reopen and expand the preceding topic. My study supports and adds to Sakoda and Siegel's (2003) study by demonstrating two recurring patterns in talk-in-interaction. Furthermore, based on Maynard's (1993) study and other studies on the Japanese connective *dakara*, I have pointed out possible Japanese contributions to the emergence of the Hawai'i Creole discourse marker *daswai*.

More data need to be collected from sociolinguistic interviews as well as from other interactional settings to further examine the uses of *daswai* and its variants (e.g., *aswai*, *so daswai*) and the possible Japanese contribution to the Hawai'i Creole discourse marker. The present study attempts to be a small but important landmark for adopting a pragmatics-oriented approach to the study of Hawai'i Creole.

Notes

1   I am indebted to Dina Yoshimi for her insightful comments that were extremely helpful in revising my manuscript. I would also like to thank Kent Sakoda, Laurie Durand, and two reviewers who read earlier drafts. Thanks also go to participants of the Conversation Analysis Seminar 2006 and of the Pragmatics and Language Learning Conference 2007, both of which were held at the University of Hawai'i at Mānoa. Last but not least, I am grateful to "Grandma" and her family for their support and generosity. The remaining shortcomings are, of course, my own responsibility.
2   Sakoda and Siegel (2003) provided the alternate forms of *daswai*: *aeswai* and *daeswai* (with slight orthographic variation), as two variants of this form; my data contain only the latter.
3   I exclude *Kibei*, or returnees, from this discussion of second-generation Okinawan Americans because they were born in Hawai'i, were brought up in Okinawa, and returned to Hawai'i in their late teens or early 20s. *Kibei*, therefore, have a more solid foundation in Japanese and Okinawan/Ryukyuan varieties than do second-generation Okinawan Americans who grew up primarily in Hawai'i.
4   The distinctions between languages can be obscure, as discussed in Woolard (1999),who examined simultaneity and bivalency within Catalan/Castilian bilingual conversations. I thus make supplementary comments where there is ambiguity in the data.

References

Auer, P. (1998). Introduction: Bilingual conversation revisited. In P. Auer (Ed.), *Code-switching in conversation: Language, interaction and identity* (pp. 1–24). London: Routledge.

Da Pidgin Coup. (1999). *Pidgin and education*. Retrieved February 8, 2007, from http://www.hawaii.edu/sls/pidgin.html

Heinrich, P. (2004). Language planning and language ideology in the Ryukyu Islands. *Language Policy, 3*, 153–179.

Kimura, Y. (2001). Immigrants from Okinawa-ken. In J. Y. Okamura (Ed.), *The Japanese American historical experience in Hawai'i* (pp. 13–38). Dubuque, IA: Kendall/Hunt.

Li, W., & Milroy, L. (1995). Conversational code-switching in a Chinese community in Britain: A sequential analysis. *Journal of Pragmatics, 23*, 281–299.

Maeda, C. (1997). *A study of second generation Japanese American (Nisei) speech in Hawai'i as an expression of ethnic identity.* Unpublished master's thesis, University of Hawai'i at Mānoa, Honolulu.

Maschler, Y. (1998). On the transition from code-switching to a mixed code. In P. Auer (Ed.), *Code-switching in conversation: Language, interaction and identity* (pp. 125–149). London: Routledge.

Matsui, T. (2002). Semantics and pragmatics of a Japanese discourse marker *dakara* (*so/in other words*): A unitary account. *Journal of Pragmatics, 34*, 867–891.

Maynard, S. K. (1993). *Discourse modality: Subjectivity, emotion and voice in the Japanese language.* Amsterdam: John Benjamins.

Reinecke, J. E. (1969). *Language and dialect in Hawai'i: A sociolinguistic history to 1935.* Honolulu: University of Hawai'i Press.

Sakoda, K., & Siegel, J. (2003). *Pidgin grammar: An introduction to the creole language of Hawai'i.* Honolulu, HI: Bess Press.

Sasamoto, R. (2008). Japanese discourse connectives *dakara* and *sorede*: A reassessment of procedural meaning. *Journal of Pragmatics, 40*, 127–154.

Schiffrin, D. (1987). *Discourse markers.* Cambridge, England: Cambridge University Press.

Serra, C. O. (1998). Discourse connectives in bilingual conversation: The case of an emerging Italian-French mixed code. In P. Auer (Ed.), *Code-switching in conversation: Language, interaction and identity* (pp. 101–122). London: Routledge.

Woolard, K. A. (1999). Simultaneity and bivalency as strategies in bilingualism. *Journal of Linguistic Anthropology, 8*, 3–29.

Appendix: Transcription conventions

.	falling intonation
,	continuing contour
?	questioning intonation
(.)	micropause
_	emphasis
:	sound stretching
(XXX)	cannot be transcribed
( )	unsure transcription
(( ))	other details
↑	prominent rising intonation
-	abrupt cut-off
><	quicker than surrounding talk
°°	quieter than surrounding talk
£	laughing voice
JPN	Japanese utterances (plain)
ENG	English utterances (bold)
HC	Hawai'i Creole utterances (square)

The Socialization of Leave-Taking in Indonesian

Margaret A. DuFon
California State University–Chico

Using a language-socialization perspective, this study investigates the acquisition of leave-taking in homes and government offices by three American students abroad in Indonesia. Learner diaries and field notes collected over a period of 4 semesters were analyzed to determine how the learners were socialized to use the language and socialized through the use of the language (Schieffelin & Ochs, 1986) of leave-taking during naturalistic interactions with native speakers. The data reveal that lower status persons were required to ask the higher status persons permission to leave using the words permisi *or* pamit *and seeking them out when necessary. When taking leave from persons of relatively equal or lower status, a simple announcement sufficed, and taking leave was only required if the person was already present; neither asking permission nor seeking the person out was required. Both through explicit instruction and modeling, these differences became apparent to the learners. Both the verbal and the body language helped to convey the importance of the Javanese Indonesian values of* empan papan *("proper place occupancy"),* andhap asor *("humility"), and* hormat *("respect").*

Leave-taking

Leave-taking is an important part of human interaction, and as the quote from Shakespeare's from Romeo and Juliet, "parting is such sweet sorrow," indicates, at least in Western societies, it can also be emotional, even if the emotion is low-keyed (Firth, 1972). Moreover, the mixture of emotions—sweetness and sorrow—that are often associated with saying goodbye can make the task a difficult one even for competent speakers. It can be difficult because the act of saying goodbye not only signals the end of the encounter, but also the onset of a period of decreased accessibility to the interlocutor. Depending on the nature of the relationship and the encounter, this does not necessarily signal the end of the relationship. However, because leave-taking potentially suggests not only anticipated absence but also possible rejection of the interlocutor,[1] it can be face threatening. The interlocutors therefore need to reassure each other that the contact was pleasant and that the relationship will continue even though the interlocutors might be temporarily, though possibly indefinitely, separated. Thus, in addition to sending a referential message (that the encounter is being terminated), a positive and successful leave-taking sends a relational message regarding feelings and attitudes toward the other (e.g., enjoyment of the encounter, sadness at parting, respect for the interlocutor) that is face supportive and bolsters the relationship for the time apart (Firth; Goffman, 1971; Knapp, Hart, Friedrich, & Shulman, 1973).

Because leave-taking occurs at the end of an interaction, it can serve a *summarizing function* at both the referential (recapitulating the substantive portion of the interaction) and relational (serving as an interpersonal summary) levels (Knapp et al., 1973). Even in those cases where the relationship is not expected to continue beyond the life of the encounter (e.g., when parting from one's seatmate on an airplane or when terminating a service encounter in a distant city), the leave-taking can send a referential and relational message regarding the pleasure of the contact just completed (Firth, 1972; Goffman, 1971; Ide, 1998; Knapp et al.; Laver, 1981). In those cases where the relationship is expected to continue beyond the encounter in question, the way in which a conversation is terminated can set the tone for future interactions. A leave-taking that is judged to be too abrupt (Omar, 1993; Schmidt, 1993), too prolonged (Fitch, 1990/1991; Hartford & Bardovi-Harlig, 1992), or insufficiently respectful can leave the participants feeling ill at ease with one another. This, in turn, could influence their willingness to be available for future interactions. Thus, to ensure future access to others, it is important to close the conversation successfully, that is, to say goodbye in a way that participants judge to be appropriate and respectful.

More than a speech act, leave-taking is a ritual; it follows patterned routines (Firth, 1972). These routines can be performed verbally, nonverbally, or using a combination of words and gestures that appear as preclosing and closing moves (Schegloff & Sacks, 1973). Nonverbal behavior can include head, face, arm, hand, and other body movements and may involve the use of clothing such as tipping a hat or waving a scarf (Firth). Postural shifts and other bodily signals can indicate that parting will take place, possibly how soon, and for how long (Knapp et al., 1973) as well as signal the status relationship of the interlocutors (Firth).

Verbal behavior includes the use of discourse markers that mean something like "okay," which can serve as preclosing moves (in which the user checks to see if the other party is ready to terminate the conversation) and sometimes as terminating moves (Hartford & Bardovi-Harlig, 1992; Omar, 1993; Schegloff & Sacks, 1973; Takami, 2002; Tchizmarova, 2005); illocutionary-force-indicating devices such as "goodbye"; and a wide range of other semantic formulas including an announcement of intention to terminate the encounter, reasons for terminating, phatic inquiries and responses, benedictions, well-wishing, and expressions of welcoming, encouragement, gratitude, apology, cautionary advice, or concern for the hearer. The formulas may also include regards to others or references to future meetings either generally or at specific times, which suggest continuation of the relationship (Firth, 1972; Hartford & Bardovi-Harlig; Hoffman-Hicks, 2000; Ide, 1998; Knapp et al., 1973; Laver, 1981; Omar; Schegloff & Sacks; Sukwiwat & Fieg, 1987; Tchizmarova).

Although there are many possible semantic formulas that could be included in a leave-taking ritual or routine, in any given situation, only a subset might be appropriate. The precise way in which leave-taking is carried out varies depending on the characteristics of the interlocutors such as age, gender, and social class; their relationship to each other in terms of power, social distance (including whether they are newly acquainted), and their affective stance toward one another at the time of the encounter; the nature of the situation including the emotional quality ascribed to the occasion, the length of time the interlocutors expect to be apart, the number of people involved, and whether the interaction occurs in face-to-face or distant, public or private, and formal or informal settings (Firth, 1972; Laver, 1981). Moreover, leave-taking routines vary across cultures. What is appropriate in a given context in one culture might not be in another. For example, while thanking a host at the end of the evening is common in English-speaking cultures, Fitch (1990/1991) observed that the purpose of the *salsipuede* routine between hosts and guests in Colombia "does not seem to be to thank the host. Often...no word of thanks is uttered in the course of the interaction" (p. 217). Likewise, Hoffman-Hicks (2000) noted that in contrast with English leave-taking routines, French speakers rarely acknowledge formulaic expressions of well-wishing and never with expressions of gratitude such as *merci*. Given the complexity of leave-taking routines in that they consist of several moves (preclosing, shutting down the topic, and terminating), which may be verbal, nonverbal, or some combination of the two, and accompanied by a range of possible semantic formulas, not to mention the range of lexical and syntactic options for conveying the semantic content, which vary depending upon the characteristics of the interlocutors and the situation, the acquisition of leave-taking must take place over a period of time in which many opportunities to experience and practice the routines present themselves (Hassall, 2006; Omar, 1993). Novices, whether L1 or L2 learners, acquire their ability to take leave appropriately through a process of language socialization.

Language socialization

Language socialization theory views language acquisition, whether in the first or a subsequent language, as grounded in social interaction and views the relationship between language and socialization as twofold: *socialization to use language* and *socialization through the use of language* (Schieffelin & Ochs, 1986). Socialization to use language refers to those instances when learners are taught, either explicitly or implicitly, what to say in a given context. In naturalistic contexts, parents might teach their children by telling them to "say 'goodbye'" when leaving someone's home, or the children might simply pick it up from observing their parents' modeling. Native speakers (NSs) might tell a learner how to say goodbye appropriately or correct them for inappropriate closings. For example, Hassall (2006) described an incident in which he was taking leave from two Indonesian women who had struck up a conversation with him as he passed their home. He took leave with the expression "*Pulang dulu, ya?*" ("I'm going home for now, okay?"), but one of the women corrected him by saying, "excuse me," in English and then translating it into Indonesian, "*permisi,*" thus modeling the behavior that she expected from Hassall. In foreign language classrooms, teachers socialize their students to use language by informing them of how to perform a particular speech act in a given context. In my Indonesian class, for example, we were taught to use the expression "*permisi dulu*" ("ask permission first") when taking leave from a host's home to show them proper respect (cf. Wolff, Oetomo, & Fietkiewicz, 1986, p. 12).

In contrast to socialization to use language, socialization through the use of language refers to the process by which learners acquire knowledge of the culture in question, as well as of their status and role and their associated rights and obligations as they learn the language. That is, the ways in which discourse is structured, the linguistic forms that are chosen, the functions of these forms, and the contexts in which they occur carry implicit messages regarding the values, beliefs, and attitudes of the culture toward the situation and participants in any given interaction. For example, Ide (1998) investigated the use of *sumimasen* by NSs of Japanese from a language socialization perspective. *Sumimasen,* whose English translation is "I'm sorry," is used in a variety of speech acts including apologizing, requesting, thanking, and leave-taking. Ide argued that *sumimasen* in leave-taking routines is hearer-focused and serves both a remedial function for any imposition that might have occurred and a supportive function that reassures the hearer that the interaction was pleasant and might continue. It is a sign of involvement and connectedness and socializes the participants concerning the value placed on indebtedness to the other.

Fitch (1990/1991) described what she calls the *salsipuede* ("leave if you can") ritual among native Spanish speakers in Colombia in the context of a visit to someone's home. When the guests initiate a preclosing move, the host refuses to warrant the close (cf. Schegloff & Sacks, 1973). Instead, the host asks why they are leaving and refuses to accept their reasons until they relent and stay longer. While leaving the host in Colombia can be problematic, participating in this ritual reinforces the bonds between those involved and builds their sense of community. Although Fitch does not frame her data from a language-socialization perspective, it is clear that she views the Columbian *salsipuede* as connected to the value of collectivism or group membership and that a child's or language learner's participation in the spoken routines of saying goodbye and denying the guest's reasons for departure socializes those participants into that value.

These examples demonstrate the close link between language and cultural values. Indeed, according to language socialization theory, as children acquire a language, they are simultaneously socialized into a system of values, beliefs, and attitudes. However, language socialization theory also notes that socialization is bidirectional (Garrett & Baquedano-López, 2002; Kulick & Schieffelin, 2004). While caregivers typically socialize their children, to some extent, children also socialize their caregivers. Nevertheless, by and large, caregivers pass their language and culture to the next generation.

In second language socialization, the "success rate" is not as high; that is, second language learners either unintentionally or intentionally fail to conform to the norms that the competent members try to socialize them into (Zuengler & Cole, 2005). One reason that learners might unintentionally fail to conform is because unlike first language socialization, where children have ready access to competent members of their community, second language learners frequently find themselves without ready access to competent speakers (Duff, 2003; Hoffman-Hicks, 2000; Isabelli-García, 2003, 2006; Kinginger & Farrell, 2004).

One reason they might intentionally not conform to native norms is that unlike first language socialization, where children begin from a neutral position, second language socialization is overlaid on top of the first language and its associated cultural values. Because of the close connection between language use and cultural values, second language learners sometimes discover that what natives consider appropriate language use conveys a cultural message that conflicts with their own cultural and personal values. Consequently, they resist conforming to the native norms and may even go so far as to attempt to socialize the natives (Duff, 1996, 2007, 2008b; Duff & Uchida, 1997; DuFon, 2000; Garrett & Baquedano-López, 2002; Li, 2000; Siegal, 1995a, 1995b, 1996; Zuengler & Cole, 2005).

Moreover, in second language socialization, learners are not aiming to be full-fledged monolingual members of a single target community. Rather, they are aiming to become bi- or multilingual speakers who are trying to integrate into a range of communities such that the very questions of what community they are trying to participate in, which norms they need to acquire, and who is qualified to socialize them are not as straightforward as in first language socialization (Duff, 2003, 2007, 2008a; DuFon, 2008; Garrett & Baquedano-López, 2002; House, 2003). In spite of these differences between first and second language socialization, language socialization theory has proven sufficiently flexible to be applied to the study of second and foreign language socialization (Garrett & Baquedano-López).

Cross-cultural variation and intercultural interaction

According to language socialization theory, the way language is used reflects and reinforces cultural values. Consequently, leave-taking routines vary across cultures. Cross-cultural differences in leave-taking routines can lead to miscommunication in intercultural contacts and can contribute to negative transfer for second language learners. These differences have been found on many levels including the semantic content of leave-taking expressions (Hoffman-Hicks, 2000); the pragmalinguistics of leave-taking, that is, understanding the intended meaning of formulas and knowing which formulas apply to leave-taking in the target culture (Hassall, 2006; Sukwiwat & Fieg, 1987); the sociopragmatics of leave-taking, that is, knowing which formulas apply in a particular context depending on the relationship of the interlocutors, the setting, and the nature of the situation (cf. Hassall); conversational management such as the speed at which closing the conversation occurs (Fitch, 1990/1991; Hartford & Bardovi-Harlig, 1992; Omar, 1993; Schmidt, 1993; Sukwiwat & Fieg; Tchizmarova, 2005); and the values associated with and projected by leave-taking routines (Fitch). Likewise, L2 learners have been found to violate sequential constraints on conversational organization, particularly in institutional settings, though it is not clear whether this is due to cross-cultural differences or a developmental stage in acquisition (Hartford & Bardovi-Harlig). Failure to conform to native-speaker conventions can lead to confusion (Sukwiwat & Fieg) and irritation (Hartford & Bardovi-Harlig). Therefore, it is important that second language speakers acquire knowledge of the target-language norms and their associated values so that they can have the option available to them to conform and thus ease communication.

Studies of leave-taking by nonnative speakers of a language have indicated that learning the basic leave-taking formulas in a second or foreign language is a relatively easy task, particularly when students have access to NSs who can socialize them and they pay attention to the input that they receive (Cook, 1985; Hoffman-Hicks, 2000; Schmidt, 1993); in other words, leave-taking formulas can be rapidly acquired when learners have opportunities for and open themselves up to the language socialization process. This occurs in part because leave-taking is a routine that occurs with high frequency in interactions with NSs when compared to other speech acts such as complimenting (Hoffman-Hicks). In any given culture, the ease with which one can become competent in leave-taking will depend on the number and complexity of constraints involved. For example, in Kiswahili, leave-taking is easier to acquire than greeting because while there are many possible formulas, unlike greetings, they are not compulsory, there is no strict order in which these options must occur, and either interlocutor may initiate them (Omar, 1993). Nevertheless, studies of leave-taking acquisition have demonstrated that even after considerable time, attention, and socialization resulting from interaction with NSs of the target language, learners remained confused over what was and was not required and what was and was not appropriate (Hassall, 2006; Hoffman-Hicks; Omar). Furthermore, while phrases for the terminating move in a conversational closing such as "goodbye" or *kwaheri* are relatively easy to learn, other aspects of leave-taking take longer. For example, Scarcella (1983) found that for those learning English, preclosing moves took longer to acquire than the terminating moves. Omar reported that only the advanced learners were likely to approach native norms of making phatic inquiries or expressing regards for their hearers' families, linking closings to openings, or reopening the conversation after *kwaheri* ("goodbye") had been exchanged.

Leave-taking in Indonesian

Of particular interest to this study is Hassall's (2006) diary study of his own acquisition of leave-taking in Indonesian, which he examined from a cognitive perspective. Three predominant issues surfaced with respect to leave-taking: (a) whether to use *permisi* or a *dulu* statement as his main leave-taking formula; (b) whether a preclosing was required, and later in the study, whether a closing formula was required in casual conversations; and (c) whether to preplan which formula to use when closing or to remain open and focused on the present moment to cooperatively close the conversation in an appropriate way. The use of *permisi* is most relevant to this study. Although Hassall did not focus on the sociopragmatic aspects, he initially came to the conclusion that *permisi* was required only in more formal leave-taking situations. For example, he used *permisi* with an airport official and never even considered using a *dulu* statement to take leave. However, in conversations with people of lesser status such as acquaintances he met in shops or along the streets, he concluded that a *permisi* was not needed. From a language socialization perspective, we could say that through his interactions with Indonesian NSs, Hassall was explicitly and implicitly socialized to use *permisi* in interactions with persons of high status but not with those of lesser status, particularly in informal situations.

Research questions

This study will add to our knowledge of the acquisition of leave-taking in a second language in several important ways. The studies that have been published to date have not examined the acquisition of leave-taking from a language socialization theoretical perspective. Furthermore, they have not considered how the language used was connected to particular social values; that is, they did not examine how NSs socialized learners into the language and simultaneously into a set of cultural values, attitudes, and beliefs. To my knowledge, the present study is the first in second language acquisition pragmatics to address these issues. As such, it examines not only which linguistic features the learners acquired in certain contexts but also what values were acquired along with them.

This study is only the second to explore the acquisition of Indonesian leave-taking. It contrasts with Hassall's (2006) work in several important ways. Theoretically, Hassall's study focused on the pragmalinguistic aspects of leave-taking formulas from a cognitive perspective, whereas this study examines the learner's language socialization with regard to the relationship between asking permission during leave-taking (as expressed by the words *permisi* and *pamit*) and the values of *empan papan* ("proper place occupancy"), *andhap asor* ("humility") and *hormat* ("respect") toward those of higher status. Methodologically, while both my and Hassall's studies are based on diary data, they differ in the types of relationships that are examined. In Hassall's study, the encounters were typically between him and clerks, vendors, and people he met on the street; in this study, the interactions took place in government offices in a few cases but primarily within the host-family homes, where the learners were, to some extent, considered members of the families during their 4-month stays. Thus, I view these two studies as complementary to each other.

In this chapter, I explore the answers to the following questions:
1. What do study abroad learners learn about leave-taking routines in Indonesian?
2. How are learners socialized into leave-taking routines in home and office contexts in Indonesia?
3. What values are reinforced by the way that NSs realize leave-taking routines in these contexts?
4. What evidence is there to suggest that learners have acquired knowledge of these values?
5. To what extent do learners choose to conform to NS norms?

Method

Data

The data for this study were drawn from several sources: (a) diaries of my own acquisition of Indonesian when I was a student abroad in 1992 and 1993–1994; (b) journals of two other learners, Bruce and Charlene, who were part of a larger ethnographic study conducted in 1996 (DuFon, 2000) and whose journals were particularly rich in comments on leave-taking; and (c) field notes from the larger ethnographic study on which this chapter is based.

The situations examined for leave-taking for this analysis included leaving private homes (including the host families' homes) and government offices because these were the situations identified in which *pamit*-ing was often required.

These data were transcribed, imported into NVivo7 software, and coded for person, place, and reason for *pamit*-ing. The analysis was then narrowed to home and office settings and examined for the values connected with language use.

Learners

The learners included myself, Bruce, and Charlene.[2] All of us were students in Malang, although I was a student there 2 to 4 years before them and was in a different program. All of us lived with host families who spent time talking with us and teaching us about the culture, particularly during meal times. They were responsible in large part for socializing us into the language and culture on East Java, Indonesia.

Myself

At the time I began collecting data for this study in 1993, I was a white, 43-year-old, female PhD student, a sophisticated language learner and sojourner abroad, and an advanced learner of Indonesian. Prior to my arrival in Indonesia in 1993, I had completed 4 years of classroom instruction in Indonesian at the college level and had spent the previous summer in Indonesia in the Consortium for the Teaching of Indonesian Program for 10 weeks. Prior to studying Indonesian, I had acquired a minor in Spanish and had studied in Spain and worked in Uruguay. I had also studied Portuguese and American Sign Language and was fluent enough in these languages to converse at length albeit with reduced accuracy. Due to this degree of knowledge and experience, I differed in many ways from the more typical study abroad student. However, I did not always live and speak from the researcher perspective while abroad. Like other language learners, I at times suffered from language and culture shock as well as a certain degree of ethnocentrism. I accept this as part of the language-learning process abroad.

Bruce

Bruce was a 21-year-old, white male majoring in international business at a Midwestern university. He was born to an Australian mother and an American father in Australia and lived there until sometime in high school, when he moved to the United States. Bruce was a seasoned language learner and student abroad. His native language was English, but he had studied French both at home and in France and could speak French fluently. Prior to going to Indonesia to study, he had visited the country as a tourist, spending 2 weeks in Bali. He had also studied Indonesian for 6 months in the eighth grade and then for eight quarters in college. Upon arrival in Indonesia, he was placed in the intermediate class, where he was the most proficient learner both at the beginning and at the end of the 1996 program. He enjoyed living with the Djumandi family, which consisted of the parents, four boys, and a maid. They were a very experienced host family; Bruce was their 16th student.

Charlene

Charlene was a 20-year-old Japanese-American woman from Hawai'i, a junior majoring in anthropology at a West Coast university. Her native language was English. She had studied Japanese as a second language and could converse to some extent in Japanese. She was, however, a true beginner in Indonesian language at the time of her arrival, and this was her first experience living or studying abroad. Charlene chose Bu ("Mrs.") Hayati as her host mother. Along with Bu Hayati, the household in which Charlene lived consisted of Bu Hayati's mother, two other boarders, and a maid. Bu Hayati was a strong character, and Charlene had a great deal of respect for her and was happy with her choice of a host-family home. Bu Hayati was an influential socializing force in Charlene's life abroad. Furthermore, Charlene reported that her own father had taught her the value of respect and the importance of showing respect through language. Consequently, Charlene paid close attention to the way language was used to show respect and consciously attempted to imitate that in her own language use. Although only a beginner at the start of the program, she was pragmatically sophisticated in Indonesian by the end of the program, relative to even some of the intermediate learners.

Research site

The research for this study took place in Malang, an ethnically and linguistically diverse city located in the interior of the eastern section of the island of Java in Indonesia. Most residents are bilingual, speaking Indonesian, the national language, and a home language. Javanese is the dominant local language; however, there are a number of minority languages as well. Among the long-term residents, there are sizable communities of Madurese and Chinese, who speak various Chinese varieties as well as their own varieties of *ngoko* ("plain") Javanese and Indonesian (Kartomihardjo, 1981; Rafferty, 1984). The youth speak Bahasa Malang, a special code in which some words are said backwards. Because Malang is both an educational city with many universities and an industrial city with many factories, it attracts people from all over Indonesia, who speak their own local languages, as well as a small community of foreigners, including expatriates who live and work there, foreign students, and transient tourists. Thus, Malang is neither homogenous nor isolated but rather exposed to other cultures from both inside and outside Indonesia.

The Javanese are nevertheless the dominant group, and Bruce, Charlene, and I all lived with Javanese families. Javanese society is group oriented and views the individual as an interdependent member of the larger society. The needs of the society take first priority. What is best for the society as a whole is ultimately what is best for each of its members. Kartomihardjo (1981) noted that the highest ethical and aesthetic good in Javanese society is "an ordered universe in which everything is harmoniously placed in a location proper to it" (p. 18). There are many terms associated with this value; one is *empan papan* ("everything in its place" or "proper-place occupancy"). Knowing one's place includes the qualities of *andhap asor* ("to humble oneself politely") and granting proper respect (*hormat*) toward those of higher status (Geertz, 1960). These values are projected both in speech (e.g., in choice of terms of address) and in body language (e.g., the lower status person is more active and maintains a position that is physically lower, and the higher status person is more passive and maintains a physically higher position). Part of the task of the language learner in Indonesia is to learn to project these values in their own speech and accompanying behavior.

Socialization of leave-taking

The attention to proper-place occupancy, humility, and respect is evident in leave-taking routines in the use of two words that ask for permission to take leave: *permisi* and *pamit*. In this section, I first focus on the meanings of these words and our experiences as learners with them and then examine our acquisition of leave-taking routines with respect to socialization to use language and socialization through the use of language.

Words for leave-taking

My own experience in learning the words *permisi* and *pamit* differed from that of the other learners. In my acquisition of Indonesian, I learned *permisi* during the first weeks of instruction. It appeared in Chapter 1 of our Indonesian textbook, *Beginning Indonesian Through Self-Instruction* (Wolff et al., 1986, p. 11), a modified audiolingual text, whose first chapter began with a visit to the home of an Indonesian woman named Bu Tuti. The leave-taking portion of the dialog began with the following phrases.

Permisi dulu.
Ask permission first.
Excuse us.

Kami mau pulang.
We will go home.

Thus, from the very beginning, I was introduced to the concept of asking permission as part of the leave-taking routine. I was unaware, however, that asking permission was not always required when saying goodbye. Nor was I aware that permission could also be obtained by using the word *pamit* until after I had had 4 years of classroom instruction in Indonesian and was at the beginning of my 3rd month in my second study abroad there. At that time, I recorded the following incident in my diary:

Example 1
As Ritno left, she said something about Bu [Mrs.] Susila, which I correctly interpreted to mean something like say good-bye to Bu Susila for me. Then I realized I hadn't really paid attention to what she had said. I asked her to repeat it. It contained the word *pamit*, which I had never heard before. I asked her what it meant. She said "seperti permisi" [like permission]. I looked it up in the dictionary. It means to say *good-bye* or *farewell*. Amazing! I have been studying

Indonesian for such a long time and this is the first I have heard of this word, an important word for closings. (My diary, 10/31/93)

The second time I heard the word *pamit* was later the same day. This second occurrence reinforced the earlier incident. This time, I recognized its meaning instantly and began to wonder exactly how to use it:

Example 2
I went to Pak Prawiro's to study with him yesterday before the examination. When I first got there, there were some other people in the house. I'm not sure who they were or what they were doing there, but as they left, they said the word *pamit* in their parting sentence. I'm not sure if there is a formulaic sentence, but at least I know what the word for saying good-bye is. (My diary, 11/1/93)

When I returned to Indonesia for my dissertation research, the concept of *pamit*-ing was taught to the study abroad learners during their 3-day orientation upon arrival in Indonesia in August 1996. One of the concepts that was stressed both in the program booklet and orally during the orientation was the importance of *pamit*-ing or saying goodbye to your host mother before leaving the house. Consequently, this act was one that the learners were well aware of. Because I, too, had attended the orientation, it heightened my own awareness of the importance of *pamit*-ing. Still, my knowledge of its meaning was incomplete and was expanded only later in the semester as I recorded in the following incident:

Example 3
Pamit-ing is an issue that often arises. Bu Susila told me the other day *pamit* means *minta ijin* [ask permission], usually used in the context of leaving the house. But it need not be so. She *pamit*-ed (begged permission from) Bu B the other day saying that she could not help the Dharma Wanita [a faculty wives association] with Dies Natales [the college anniversary celebration] because of the man working on the house. (Field notes, 10/14/96)

Although used most often in the context of saying good-bye, *pamit*-ing is more than farewell. It also asks permission. Implicit in its use are the values placed on *empan papan* ("proper place occupancy") and its associated aspects of humility (*andhap asor*) and respect (*hormat*) for those of higher status in a given context.

Socialization to use language

We now turn to the data that shed light on how NSs socialized the learners to use language in a particular way during leave-taking. In some cases, socialization to use language can be a pleasant experience such as in the incident below, which occurred at a wedding reception held in the home of the host. All that was required was to follow the lead of my NS guide.

Example 4
Usually if I was unsure what to do, I just asked someone and they would help me out. For example, before I left the reception, I asked Bu E whom all I should *pamit*. She took me by the hand and led me to each person that I should say good-night too. I just followed her lead. (My diary, 1/5/94)

The next incident occurred 2 months later in a campus office. This socialization experience was one in which both parties suffered a loss of face and consequently was a more painful socialization experience:

Example 5
I went to A-3 to get my KHS [report card]. Pak [Mr.] Achmad sent me inside to Pak Sugeng's office [i.e., the administrator's office]. He [Pak Sugeng] gave me an official letter explaining that I had audited the four courses. Then a clerk started asking me questions about where I went to high school etc. So I immediately started answering him and moved over closer to him to make communication with him easier. I ended my business with Pak Sugeng in that way. When I finished with [the clerk] I...started to leave. Pak Achmad called me back and told me to *be polite and pamit* with *Pak Sugeng*. In America I feel it is rude to interrupt [an administrator] who would already be working on something else. (In fact in America, I would not have bothered a high status person at all, but a female secretary). So I often forget to go back, disturb people here just to say good-bye. But I really got called on the carpet for it. It was very embarrassing and I could not wait to get out of there. (My diary, 3/3/94)

From my point of view, I felt that if I went back to the Pak Sugeng, a higher status administrator, who had already returned to his work, I would be *disturbing* him and that I was being polite and respectful by leaving him alone. I learned instead that from the Indonesian point of view, it was important to show my respect by giving attention to the higher status person by asking his permission to leave. Not doing so was taken as a slight, and they let me know that by explicitly correcting my behavior. It was an embarrassing but powerful lesson.

The following incident, reported by Charlene, involved another case of explicit correction.

Example 6
The other day a strange thing happened. When Mbak Laksmi's friend *pamitted with Bu Hayati and not me, Bu corrected her and told her to pamit with me.* It was an awkward situation since I didn't even know her [Mbak Laksmi's friend] or how I should regard her. I was embarrassed for her. But *happy to realize Bu regarded me as a person who should also be pamitted to.* (Charlene's diary, 11/3/96)

In this incident, not only was it clear that Charlene and Mbak Laksmi were being socialized to use language in a particular way, but also that Charlene was being socialized through the use of language. Her comment that she was happy because her host mother regarded her as a person whom one should *pamit* to implies that she associated this with respect (*hormat*).

It is interesting that in this incident, it was a native speaker who was corrected. Perhaps she did not feel she needed to *pamit* to Charlene because Charlene was not the host mother. However, Charlene was present, and the host mother apparently felt that she should be acknowledged. Had Charlene not been present, the guest would not have needed to seek her out. As Examples 7 and 8 in the next section reveal, guests seek out the lady of the house to *pamit* to her when leaving. The action of seeking out the lady of the house to *pamit* or ask permission is one way of socializing respect (*hormat*) through the use of language. It also places the guest in a lower position from which they show their own humility (*andhap asor*).

Socialization through the use of language

I became aware of the practice of seeking out the host mother to say goodbye or ask permission to leave during my first few months of living in Indonesia on my second trip abroad. Example 7 illustrates an incident that occurred when a friend of mine wanted to say goodbye to my host mother before leaving my host home.

Example 7
When D left, she said she wanted to *pamit* Bu Susila so I went to get Bu Susila. She was watching TV and it seems like a *royal nuisance* to be disturbed to say good-bye to someone else's guest, but that is the way they do it here. I guess I am getting sort of used to it because *I like it when my guests pamit her.* I feel they look *more respectable* and in turn that reflects back on me in a very positive way. (My diary, 12/23/93)

This example indicates that at this point in time, I was ambivalent about the Indonesian practice of seeking the host mother out to ask permission to leave. On the one hand, I interpreted the interruption to my host mother as a nuisance, something that would disturb her. On the other hand, I realized that it was a gesture of respect and appreciated that. Bruce exhibited a similar pattern. After approximately 6 weeks in the study abroad program, Bruce reflected on what he had learned since his arrival. One area in which he felt he had improved was *pamit*-ing.

Example 8
I have also noticed that I can *pamit* with greater ease now. Yesterday I stopped by Charlene's house. Her Ibu [host mother] was a *little busy* and didn't talk to me all that much. Charlene and I were in the kitchen talking. When it came time to leave, *I went out to the living room/office where Ibu Hayati was.* I just said "*Permisi, Bu. Saya pulang*" [Excuse me, Ma'am, I am going home] She said "*Sudah?*" [Already?] I continued telling her that I should go before it starts to rain. I was surprised at how *'right' it felt to be pamit-ing* to her in somewhat formal language. Of course, this could be influenced by the fact that she is somewhat of a *strong character* and I may just feel more comfortable using a more polite language because of my fear of offending her.

I'm a lot more comfortable with *pamit*-ing at home also, but there is still one kind of situation that I'm not sure how to deal with. This is how to *pamit* if you're just going outside for about 5 minutes....By the time I went through *the hassle of pamit-ing* I could have already gone and been back! But in general *pamit*-ing seems *a lot more natural now*, and I often feel a void or even as if I'm being *rude if I don't pamit*. It's sort of *a sign of respect*, and *if I don't do it, I feel as if I'm not being respectful* to the other person. (Bruce's diary, 10/8/96)

Bruce referred to *pamit*-ing as a hassle, presumably because it involves interrupting the host mother, whom he described as "a little busy."

Nevertheless, he also saw it as respectful. His description of Charlene's host mother as a strong character implies that she was particularly deserving of respect because of her strength, and at the end, he explicitly stated that *pamit*-ing is a sign of respect, and the failure to *pamit* is disrespectful and rude.

Bruce also indicated that he had been socialized into Indonesian norms and that he had changed since his arrival. His admission that his response to his own *pamit*-ing behavior (it felt "right") surprised him and that *pamit*-ing seemed "more natural now" indicate that a shift had taken place.

Charlene's entry below also exhibits a degree of impatience with the *pamit*-ing routine, this time in a government-office setting. She implies that because of the status of the government officers, waiting for an extended period of time to simply ask permission to leave is necessary.

Example 9
We rode the bus to Pangala which took 2 hours on a totally bumpy road. Got there and went straight to the Kantor Kecematan and waited for the processing of my letter (1 hour). From there we went straight to the Kantor Lurah [village office] and spoke briefly to the Kepala Desa [the village chief], Pak R. He escorted us to his home; we had coffee and talked about family (of course). Pak Lurah [the village chief][3] left Mas Rampo, some official friend and I to talk about life. *We waited till he came back so we could pamit* and get to the PUSTU before it closed (*another 2 hours later*). By this time it was *siang* [late] and I was worried we wouldn't get to the PUSTU in time, *but we had to be patient and wait to pamit*. When we got to the PUSTU at 12:30, of course the doctor had already left, so we talked with the *pembantu* [assistant]. (Charlene's diary, 12/6/96)

From these examples, it is clear that the need to seek out and wait for the high status person, in a home (e.g., the host) or office (e.g., an administrator, a village chief) to ask their permission to leave is something that the learners were aware of and that they connected with the value of showing respect. It is possible in some cases to leave without following this protocol; instead, the guest can ask another person to *pamitkan*, or to *pamit* for them to the high status person (see Example 1).[4] The only other example of leave-taking that I recorded in my field notes where an Indonesian did not say goodbye to the high status person him- or herself concerned a time when Pak Suprapto visited me. In this case, he did not *pamit* or ask me to *pamit* for him, but instead made an excuse as to why he did not.

Example 10
When he left, Pak Suprapto did not make a lot of pretense about *pamit*-ing. He just said, "Rupanya Bu Susila sedang tidur" ["Apparently Mrs. Susila is napping"] and opened the door to leave. I said that I would *pamitkan*. He did not even ask me to, but after I said I would, he agreed to it. When he left, I walked to the kitchen. There she was working—not sleeping. I could have dragged her to the front for a *pamit* if Pak Suprapto had wanted to be bothered with it, but apparently he did not. (Field notes, 1/28/97)

By this time, I was so used to the routine that I felt a bit insulted that Pak Suprapto did not want to show respect to my host mother by *pamit*-ing her directly. Therefore, I offered to *pamitkan,* or *pamit* on his behalf.

When pamitting is not necessary

So far, the importance of asking permission in leave-taking as a sign of respect has been discussed. It is useful to contrast the contexts presented so far with those leave-taking scenarios in the home in which asking permission is not required. One such example is when leaving the table after a meal.

Leave-taking from the table

According to my field notes, in one of our group discussions on Indonesian politeness, Charlene raised the issue of *pamit*-ing at the table. She reported that she *pamit*-ed, but the other host children, who were Indonesian, did not. Thus, in her case, she was following her American family norms rather than what she was observing in Indonesia. The other five learners in the study reported that neither they nor anyone else asked permission to leave the table in their host homes. I also noted that in my own host home, we did not *pamit* from the dinner table.

Example 11
I remember that [excusing myself from the table] was something I struggled with the first time I was here. In my house, people don't really excuse themselves in any formulaic way. Usually it is done through body language, standing up and perhaps gradually moving away from the table. (Field notes, 10/7/96)

This is apparently not a situation in which one is required to ask permission to leave, and failure to ask permission is not perceived as a sign of disrespect.

Leave-taking from others

Pamit-ing is not required when saying goodbye to someone who is neither a host parent nor one of the heads of the household. In the following two examples, I noted how Mas Eko, another boarder, and Mas Setya, the son of my host parents, said goodbye to me when leaving the house.

Example 12
Today when Mas Eko left the house, he said *"Berangkat,* Peggy" [(I'm) leaving, Peggy]. Setya usually says "Peggy, *saya berangkat."* It's such an easy, straightforward way of saying good-bye. I like it. I've been saying *ayo,* but sometimes when I leave the house, I also say, *"Saya berangkat."* (My diary, 10/19/93)

Example 13
When leaving the house, Setya always says, *"Peggy, saya berangkat."* Mas Eko does not have a fixed expression, but today he said, *"berangkat dulu"* [(I'm) leaving now, literally "leave first"]. When I left the house, I also used that expression and it worked. (My diary, 10/28/96)

I observed that they both took leave simply by announcing their departure. No permission word was used. Nor was there any word that might be translated more literally as goodbye. I followed their example; thus, I was socialized through their examples to take leave in this way. This use of language also draws a distinction between the host parents, whom one asks permission to leave, and status equals, to whom one simply announces the departure, and in this way shows greater respect toward the host parents. Whether I was aware of this at that point is not clear; nevertheless, the social message is there. Furthermore, these individuals only took leave from me when they passed me on their way out. If I was not in their exit path, they did not seek me out to say goodbye as they would with the host mother. This difference also highlights the status difference and the importance of showing respect to those of higher status in a way that is not required toward those of equal or lower status.

When entering the home

Another situation in which asking permission was not necessary was upon entering the host-family home, as was noted by Charlene almost immediately upon her arrival in Indonesia.

Example 14
Sometimes I wonder if it is impolite not to announce one's arrival at home. In America when a person returns home, it is as polite to scream, "I'm home" as it is to *ask permission* for leave. However, I've found that *it really doesn't seem to matter whether you announce your arrival as long as you pamit before taking leave*. For example, when I inform Bu Hayati about my plans for school days, I just tell her what time she may expect me for dinner if I choose to eat lunch out. Although I may come home once or twice to retrieve something, I usually don't announce that I'm home. Just when I leave the house again do I more or less feel *obligated to pamit*, regardless if I just stop into retrieve a telephone number (which takes no more than two minutes). (Charlene's diary, Week 1)

Although Charlene had only recently arrived in Indonesia, she was already very much aware of the importance of *pamit*-ing to her host mother when leaving, perhaps because this point had been stressed during the orientation and because of the close attention she paid to the sociolinguistic and pragmatic norms. In contrast, greeting the host mother was not as important. Perhaps this is because it is the host mother's responsibility to know where her host children are. If they are out and someone calls, she needs to be able to say that immediately so as not to lose face.

The contrast between the situations in which *pamit*-ing or asking permission to leave was required and those in which it was not helped to socialize the learners concerning the importance of occupying their proper place (*empan papan*) and of showing proper humility (*andhap asor*) as the one in the low position and respect (*hormat*) toward the one in the high position within the household. The evidence presented here indicates that they were aware of the importance of *pamit*-ing and its links to these basic Javanese values.

Conclusions

The learners in this study learned that it is important to *pamit* or ask permission from higher status persons in homes and offices by using the words *pamit* or *permisi* when taking leave. The act of *pamit*-ing also requires seeking out or waiting for the higher status person to ask their permission to leave. *Pamit*-ing, then, performs a dual function semantically; it both informs the host that one wishes to leave and asks permission to do so. Such behavior is not required upon entering the host-family home or in leaving the dinner table; these are apparently not viewed as contexts in which permission is necessary even when interacting with higher status persons. Permission is also not necessary when taking leave of lower status persons; a simple announcement with a phrase such as *Saya berangkat* ("I'm leaving") or *Berangkat dulu* ("(I'm) leaving now"), which performs only a single function semantically, suffices, and even that is required only if the person is present. It is not necessary to seek him or her out. Thus, the linguistic formulas and the accompanying nonverbal behavior in each context socialized the learners to recognize the value placed on *empan papan* ("proper place occupancy") with regard to social status and its associated attitudes of *andhap asor* ("humility") and *hormat* ("respect"). The learners were socialized to use language through explicit instruction during their orientation program and in naturalistic interactions with their host families, tutors, and others both explicitly through instruction and correction and implicitly through modeling.

The diary data indicate that the learners in this study were aware of the connection between Indonesian leave-taking routines and showing respect to persons in authority, whether in the home or in government offices. They did experience some resistance to these norms, evident in the impatience and discomfort that they expressed in their diaries. This resistance stemmed from a conflict with the value they placed on time and expedience and from the belief that the leave-taking routine might disturb a higher status person who had to be sought out. Even then, their resistance was manifested mainly in their private grumblings in their diaries; in their actions, they attempted to follow the norms as they understood them to cooperate and show respect for their hosts. Eventually, they became more comfortable with *pamit*-ing and were usually able to let go of their need for leave-taking to take place rapidly and efficiently, at least to some extent. They learned to appreciate the act of *pamit*-ing and the respect associated with it both when *pamit*-ing and when being *pamit*-ed to.

Acknowledgements

The research for this study was supported by a Foreign Language and Area Studies Award, a Bilingual Education Fellowship, and a grant from the University of Hawai'i at Mānoa, College of Arts and Sciences during the data collection phases. The writing portion was funded by a California State University Summer Scholars Award.

Notes

1. In their analysis of leave-taking, Firth (1972) noted that leave-taking signals a transition to decreased access to the interlocutor and that many leave-taking behaviors seem to be attempts to communicate that although communicative access will be denied temporarily, it should not be perceived as "threatening the *end of our relationship*" (p. 184; emphasis in original).
2. All names of students and hosts in this chapter are pseudonyms.
3. *Kepala Desa* and *Pak Lurah* are synonyms, both meaning village head, and in this context, referring to the same person.
4. The morpheme *-kan* in *pamitkan* has a benefactive function; it means to do something for someone else, in this case, to "ask permission to leave on someone's behalf" or to "say goodbye for someone."

References

Cook, V. (1985). Language functions, social factors, and second language learning and teaching. *International Review of Applied Linguistics, 23*, 177–198.

Duff, P. A. (1996). Different languages, differing practices: Socialization of discourse competence in dual-language school classrooms in Hungary. In D. Nunan & K. M. Bailey (Eds.), *Voices from the language classroom* (pp. 407–433). Cambridge, England: Cambridge University Press.

Duff, P. A. (2003). New directions in second language socialization research. *Korean Journal of English Language and Linguistics, 3*, 309–339.

Duff, P. A. (2007). Second language socialization as sociocultural theory: Insights and issues. *Language Teaching, 40*, 309–319.

Duff, P. A. (2008a). Language socialization, higher education, and work. In P. A. Duff & N. Hornberger (Eds.), *Encyclopedia of language and education: Vol. 8. Language socialization* (pp. 257–270). Berlin: Springer.

Duff, P. A. (2008b). Language socialization, participation and identity: Ethnographic approaches. In M. Martin-Jones, A. M. Mejia, & N. Hornberger (Eds.), *Encyclopedia of language and education: Vol. 3. Discourse and education* (pp. 107–119). Berlin: Springer.

Duff, P. A., & Uchida, Y. (1997). The negotiation of teachers' sociocultural identities and practices in postsecondary EFL classrooms. *TESOL Quarterly, 31*, 451–486.

DuFon, M.A. (2000). *The acquisition of linguistic politeness in Indonesian by sojourners in naturalistic interactions*. PhD thesis, University of Hawai'i, 1999. Dissertation Abstracts International-A 60 (11), 3985.

DuFon, M. A. (2008). Language socialization theory and the acquisition of pragmatics in the foreign language classroom. In E. Alcón Soler & A. Martínez-Flor (Eds.),

Investigating pragmatics in foreign language learning, teaching and testing (pp. 25–44). Clevedon, England: Multilingual Matters.

Firth, R. (1972). Verbal and bodily rituals of greeting and parting. In J. S. La Fontaine (Ed.), *The interpretation of ritual* (pp. 11–38). London: Tavistock.

Fitch, K. (1990/1991). A ritual for attempting leave-taking in Colombia. *Research on Language and Social Interaction, 24*, 209–224.

Garrett, P. B., & Baquedano-López, P. (2002). Language socialization: Reproduction and continuity, transformation and change. *Annual Review of Anthropology, 31*, 339–361.

Geertz, C. (1960). *The religion of Java.* Chicago: University of Chicago Press.

Goffman, E. (1971). *Relations in public: Microstudies of the public order.* New York: Basic Books.

Hartford, B. S., & Bardovi-Harlig, K. (1992). Closing the conversation: Evidence from the academic advising session. *Discourse Processes, 15*, 93–116.

Hassall, T. (2006). Learning to take leave in social conversations: A diary study. In M. A. DuFon & E. Churchill (Eds.), *Language learners in study abroad contexts* (pp. 31–58). Clevedon, England: Multilingual Matters.

Hoffman-Hicks, S.D. (2000). *The longitudinal development of French foreign language pragmatic competence: Evidence from study abroad.* PhD thesis, Indiana University, 1999. Dissertation Abstracts International-A, 61:2, 591.

House, J. (2003). Teaching and learning pragmatic fluency in a foreign language: The case of English as a lingua franca. In A. Martínez Flor, E. Usó Juan, & A. Fernández Guerra (Eds.), *Pragmatic competence and foreign language teaching* (pp. 133–159). Castellón, Spain: Servei de Publicacions de la Universitat Jaume I.

Isabelli-García, C. (2003). Development of oral communication skills abroad. *Frontiers: The Interdisciplinary Journal of Study Abroad, 9*, 149–173.

Isabelli-García, C. (2006). Study abroad social networks, motivation and attitudes: Implications for second language acquisition. In M. A. DuFon & E. Churchill (Eds.), *Language learners in study abroad contexts* (pp. 231–258). Clevedon, England: Multilingual Matters.

Ide, R. (1998). 'Sorry for your kindness': Japanese interactional ritual in public discourse. *Journal of Pragmatics, 29*, 509–529.

Kartomihardjo, S. (1981). Ethnography of communicative codes in East Java. *Pacific Linguistics, Series D, No. 39.* Canberra: Australian National University.

Kinginger, C., & Farrell, K. (2004). Assessing development of meta-pragmatic awareness in study abroad. *Frontiers: The Interdisciplinary Journal of Study Abroad, 10*, 19–42.

Knapp, M. L., Hart, R. P., Friedrich, G. W., & Shulman, G. M. (1973). The rhetoric of goodbye: Verbal and nonverbal correlates of human leave-taking. *Communication Monographs, 40*, 182–198.

Kulick, D., & Schieffelin, B. (2004). Language socialization. In A. Duranti (Ed.), *A companion to linguistic anthropology* (pp. 349–368). Malden, MA: Blackwell.

Laver, J. (1981). Linguistic routines and politeness in greeting and parting. In F. Coulmas (Ed.), *Conversational routine: Explorations in standardized communication* (pp. 289–304). The Hague: Mouton.

Li, D. (2000). The pragmatics of making requests in the L2 workplace: A case study of language socialization. *The Canadian Modern Language Review, 57,* 58–87.

Omar, A. S. (1993). Closing Kiswahili conversations: The performance of native and non-native speakers. In L. F. Bouton & Y. Kachru (Eds.), *Pragmatics and language learning monograph series* (Vol. 4, pp. 104–125). Urbana-Champaign: University of Illinois, Division of English as an International Language.

Rafferty, E. (1984). Languages of the Chinese of Java: An historical review. *The Journal of Asian Studies, 43,* 247–272.

Scarcella, R. C. (1983). Developmental trends in the acquisition of conversational competence by adult second language learners. In N. Wolfson & E. Judd (Eds.), *Sociolinguistics and language acquisition* (pp. 175–83). Rowley, MA: Newbury House.

Schegloff, E., & Sacks, H. (1973). Opening up closings. *Semiotica, 8,* 289–327.

Schieffelin, B. B., & Ochs, E. (1986). Language socialization. *Annual Review of Anthropology, 15,* 163–191.

Schmidt, R. (1993). Consciousness, learning and interlanguage pragmatics. In G. Kasper & S. Blum-Kulka (Eds.), *Interlanguage pragmatics* (pp. 21–42). Oxford, England: Oxford University Press.

Siegal, M. (1995a). Individual differences and study abroad: Women learning Japanese in Japan. In B. F. Freed (Ed.), *Second language acquisition in a study abroad context* (pp. 225–244). Amsterdam: John Benjamins.

Siegal, M. (1995b). *Looking east: Learning Japanese as a second language in Japan and the interaction of race, gender and social context.* Unpublished doctoral dissertation, University of California, Berkeley.

Siegal, M. (1996). The role of subjectivity in second language sociolinguistic competency: Western women learning Japanese. *Applied Linguistics, 17,* 356–382.

Sukwiwat, M., & Fieg, J. (1987). Greeting and leave-taking. *PASAA, 17*(2), 1–12.

Takami, T. (2002). A study on closing sections of Japanese telephone conversations. *Working Papers in Educational Linguistics, 18*(1), 67–85.

Tchizmarova, I. K. (2005). Hedging functions of the Bulgarian discourse marker *xajde*. *Journal of Pragmatics, 37,* 1143–1163.

Wolff, J. U., Oetomo, D., & Fietkiewicz, D. (1986). *Beginning Indonesian through self-instruction.* Ithaca, NY: Cornell University Southeast Asia Program.

Zuengler, J., & Cole, K. (2005). Language socialization and second language learning. In E. Hinkel (Ed.), *Handbook of research in second language teaching and learning* (pp. 301–316). Mahwah, NJ: Lawrence Erlbaum.

Dinkas Down Under: Request Performance in Simulated Workplace Interaction

Lynda Yates

Macquarie University, Sydney, Australia

This study offers practical insights into the instruction needs of Dinka-background immigrants to Australia (and their teachers) and expands theoretical frameworks commonly used to investigate interlanguage requests. Data from 30 intermediate-level Dinka-background speakers of English and the same number of learners from other language backgrounds and native speakers of Australian English were collected as they negotiated complex requests in simulated workplace situations and analysed for evidence of stance as well as for the use of mitigation using a modified CCSARP (Cross Cultural Speech Act Research Project) framework. This analysis revealed that although both learner groups made fewer indirect requests and considerably fewer syntactic and lexical modifications than the native speakers, the Dinka used the least. Neither learner group made much use of preparators and disarmers to negotiate their requests, and the Dinka relied heavily on forceful reasons that were often repeated rather than reformulated. Overall, the Dinka were less successful in their use of empathetic and interpersonal markers and consultative devices, and although the native speakers tended to negotiate from a stance that established rapport and mutual responsibility, the Dinka more often took the role of supplicant. These differences appear to be motivated by both pragmalinguistic and sociocultural issues. Recommendations for instruction are given.

The Dinka have been arriving in Australia in increasing numbers as refugees from the civil war in Southern Sudan, and many have spent long periods in camps, where conditions were often very difficult. Although they constitute the largest ethnic group in southern Sudan, apart from some anthropological work on their traditional lifestyles (e.g., references available from the *Sudanese Online*

Research Association, n.d.), very little information is available on the linguistic and cultural influences that may impact their learning and use of English or on requestive practices in Dinka. For settlement agencies and providers of the national Adult Migrant English Program (AMEP)[1] who work with them in the early phases of their settlement, this is unfortunate because communication difficulties have been reported, resulting in the development of unhelpful stereotypes that learners from this background can be insistent and abrupt.

Many factors may underlie the reports of such stereotypes. As studies from cross-cultural perspectives have amply demonstrated, different cultural expectations and understandings of speakers from different backgrounds may contribute significantly to such communication difficulties (for a recent overview, see Boxer, 2004). Studies from an interlanguage-pragmatic perspective have also highlighted the role of not only sociocultural but also linguistic issues relating to transfer, resistance, awareness, and proficiency (e.g., Blum-Kulka, House, & Kasper, 1989; Hinkel, 1996; Houck & Gass, 1996; Siegal, 1996; Takahashi, 1996; Trosborg, 1995).

While the focus of this chapter is on the identification of such issues that may impact communication difficulties, it should be recognised that there are also larger social and political forces at play here. Dinka learners are highly visible in a country unused to migration from Africa, and as Piller (2007) warned, difficulties construed as cultural may conceal altogether more challenging problems of power relations and discrimination. Moreover, there are dangers in assuming the stability of categories of cultural membership because such categories can shift and mutate as we construct our identities through interaction. Ibrahim (2003), for example, illustrated the dynamics of shifting ethnic identity in response to the racism and other social pressures he experienced as a Sudanese refugee in North America. While in Africa, the fact that he was black was 'unmarked' so that different aspects of his identity were foregrounded, but this changed upon arrival in North America, where his blackness became more salient in his sense of self and in interaction. The constantly changing nature of identity highlighted in this example reinforces that care must be taken in extending generalisations about ethnic identity from one time to another or from individuals to groups.

A further difficulty with comparative studies of the kind reported in this chapter relates to the danger of constructing a deficit view of the learner group they are designed to assist. This danger is real but largely one of attitude and can scarcely be avoided where the aim is to discover what a group of learners may need in the way of instruction. Instruction that is targeted at areas of learner need is more likely to be useful in the learners' daily lives. From this perspective, comparative studies offer a kind of needs analysis that also provides practical insights to address communication difficulties, provided that the 'findings' they yield are used with caution. It is important, for example, that they do not perpetuate a 'deficit' view of speakers from other backgrounds, but rather that ensuing discussion should focus on providing insight into what native speakers do. Naturally, once this native-like behaviour is illuminated more clearly through empirical research, instruction, and reflection, the degree to which learners may adopt or adapt it for their own purposes is an entirely different matter. Learners must construct their own identities through their new language and chart their own communicative courses through the murky waters of hybrid existence.

The study[2] reported here was designed to investigate and compare how Dinka-background adult learners of English and native speakers of Australian English approached the same task involving the negotiation of a request and to do this in a way that could provide direct evidence on which to base teaching and learning materials to help raise awareness among both the learners themselves and the teachers and other professionals with whom they interact. On a practical level, then, its importance lies in its usefulness for teaching and its accessibility to teachers of the features that it investigates. On a theoretical level, it expands a commonly used analytical framework through the inclusion of attention to stance or subject position. In both spoken texts and written texts, the stance (Hyland, 2005; White, 2003), or position (Davies & Harré, 1990), taken by speakers or writers can be identified through of the linguistic choices that they make. An analysis of these selections can throw light on not only their attitudes to an issue, but also to how they regard themselves and their position in the world. Such dimensions can provide rich insight into the sociopragmatic underpinnings of complex requests negotiated over multiple turns and thus contribute to a more nuanced understanding of not only how but why speakers from different backgrounds may tackle these speech events in the ways that they do.

Teaching practice has not always kept up with research in interlanguage pragmatics. Although the pragmatic bases of cross-cultural miscommunication have been well documented (see Boxer, 2004), these insights have not always found their way to teachers in a useable form, and teaching materials still frequently lack precisely those features that speakers use to modulate what they say (McCarthy & O'Keefe, 2004). Even ESL teachers, who are used to interacting with speakers from other cultural and linguistic backgrounds, may lack a detailed awareness of exactly what may underlie misunderstandings in an interaction (Yates & Wigglesworth, 2005).

Moreover, issues of stance and the use of solidarity strategies have been largely overlooked in previous interlanguage-pragmatics studies. Through quantitative and qualitative analyses, this study contributes insights into how native speakers of Australian English make use of both solidarity and deference-oriented strategies in routine situations and the kinds of stances that they take, and therefore into some of the assumptions they may be bringing with them as they interact. By using data collection techniques that relate directly to appropriate curriculum tasks, it is hoped that the insights from this study can be easily incorporated into materials directly relevant to both language instruction and professional development.

Theoretical and practical considerations

Underpinning this study is the view that it is both possible and useful to identify regularities of interactive style shared by groups of speakers. Although speakers from a particular cultural background will show considerable individual variation (e.g., Yates, 2005) and, of course, variation across contexts, situations, and time, they will nevertheless also share interpretive assumptions based on repeated experiences within a sociocultural context and will use these to interpret and perform intentions within that context (Terkourafi, 2005). Regularities such as a preference for the use of particular devices or strategies can be detected through investigations of interactions in specific types of contexts, showing that recurring practices "are polite *because* they are regular" (Terkourafi, p. 248). While great caution should be taken not to generalize pragmatic regularities to the status of macrocultural 'norms' that reify a static view of culture, they can nevertheless form a useful starting point for instruction (see, e.g., numerous chapters in Rose & Kasper, 2001).

The ways in which we interact in relation to the expectations generated by pragmatic norms influence judgments that are made about us, and we may be viewed as competent or trustworthy or included in or excluded from certain groups on the basis of our displays of context-appropriate behaviour (Lakoff, 2005). The assumption here is that speakers who share a linguistic and cultural background also share understandings of the kinds of linguistic choices that are made in a certain situation according to the roles, rights, and obligations that they have in that situation and that the behaviour resulting from these choices is therefore intentional. Adult migrants[3] arriving in an English-speaking environment from other cultures and who are not yet fully proficient in English face a double challenge when communicating with members of the target community. Because they have grown up in a different culture, they are likely to have developed assumptions about interaction and how to do it that are different from those that are widely held in the wider community. However, because of the invisible nature of these assumptions, neither they nor the people they speak to will find this mismatch easy to recognise (Boxer, 2002). Further, because they do not have complete control over various aspects of English, for example, grammar and vocabulary, they are not always aware of the different ways of modulating what they say in English or the nuances of meaning involved in the choices of different words and so on. They may not know what devices are used by competent speakers to achieve a particular effect, or if they do, they may have trouble understanding or manipulating them (Cook & Liddicoat, 2002; Kasper & Roever, 2005).

Requests are likely to pose a particular communicative challenge: They are potentially face-threatening (Brown & Levinson, 1987), and both sociocultural and pragmalinguistic expectations and behaviour seem to vary enormously across different languages and cultures, making them a perilous undertaking in any cross-cultural situation. In addition, they pose particular challenges for learners, as the literature amply demonstrates (Blum-Kulka et al., 1989), even, or perhaps particularly, for those who are relatively proficient (e.g., see discussion in Dippold, 2006; Kasper & Roever, 2005). Learners of English not only have to understand the particular roles, rights, and obligations expected in any situation in which they find themselves, including the level of formality, jocularity, and so on expected, but also have to learn to understand the force of, and manipulate a wide range of, syntactic and lexical devices. This is a formidable task for any speaker and particularly demanding for refugees half a world away from anything familiar.

Although there has been considerable research on requests, there are still gaps in the literature. First, many studies from a speech-act perspective have looked at requests in terms of a single, initiating move, rather than as negotiated over several turns (but see Newton, 2004; Taleghani-Nikazm, 2006; Wigglesworth & Yates, 2007; Zhang, 1995 for some counterexamples). Although this has allowed detailed examination of the range of syntactic and lexical devices used to mitigate a principal request, it has left somewhat out of focus a range of other moves and factors that may contribute to the success of an interaction. In particular, the issues of the stance taken by the requester and how solidarity strategies are used to lubricate requests have received less focus than they deserve (but see Newton; Yates, 2005). The relative neglect of the role of rapport in the mitigation of requests has been encouraged by the hierarchy of politeness strategies suggested in Brown and Levinson's (1987) model of politeness. This may be a particularly important omission in relation to Australian culture, which has been argued to draw particularly heavily on values of egalitarianism, solidarity, and mateship (Goddard, 2006b; Wierzbicka, 1997). There seem to be real differences in both the communicative values and the way acts are performed in different varieties of English, and while American English has been much investigated, Australian English has been much less so (but see Achiba, 2003; Blum-Kulka et al., 1989; Yates; Yates & Wigglesworth, 2005).

Moreover, the workplace context is one that has particular importance in the lives of migrants and offers many opportunities for long-term misunderstandings that can seriously impact job prospects (Boxer, 2002), particularly if speakers are perceived as inappropriately assertive or abrupt. Because intuition is a notoriously unreliable source of information about what speakers in a culture actually do in a situation, there is a need for rigorous studies that provide evidence-based insights and models that can be used in the development of teaching and learning texts and activities. Although there has been increasing investigation of requests in professional and employment settings (e.g., Aronsson & Sätterlund-Larsson, 1987; Bilbow, 1997; Koester, 2002; Newton, 2004) and some work on workplace interactions in Australia (e.g., Clyne, 1994; Willing, 1992), these have focused on a range of acts, and we still lack the kind of detailed descriptions of how complex requests are negotiated in workplace-related contexts in Australia that are useful for instruction. Such descriptions need to come out of empirical evidence from situations that are routine in the workplace and illustrate not only how devices and strategies are used in combination over several moves, but also provide some insight into the larger sociocultural issues of how interlocutors approach situations and the stances they take with one another.

However, although many studies have been motivated by applied concerns in inter-cultural communication and language learning and teaching, the crossover between the worlds of research and the applications of the fruits of that research has not always been either happy or speedy. Despite the plethora of studies on requests, therefore, there is nevertheless very little good teaching material that can be used in classrooms to explicitly address the sociocultural underpinnings of communication in different cultures or pragmatic aspects of requestive situations in various contexts within those cultures. Many textbooks still offer dialogs that are fully scripted and acted and that lack features of spoken language that are routinely used by expert users to mitigate their speech, such as vague language and hedges (Burns, Joyce, & Gollin, 2001; McCarthy & O'Keefe, 2004; but see Good, 2006). An important aim of this study, therefore, was to provide descriptions and insights into the negotiation of complex workplace-related requests in a form that would be accessible to teachers and that could feed directly into the development of teaching and professional-development materials.

Study

The design of the study reported here draws on the comparative tradition used in cross-cultural and interlanguage-pragmatics studies that grew out of work done in the Cross-Cultural Speech Act Realization Project (Blum-Kulka et al., 1989). As Yuan (2001) noted, there are drawbacks to various kinds of data-gathering techniques, and indeed, they may not capture or measure exactly the same phenomenon (Sasaki, 1998), so it is important to match the techniques used with the research questions addressed. The study reported here was designed to provide qualitative as well as quantitative insights into both the negative politeness and solidarity strategies used, and into the stance taken in the interaction in ways that would be useful for instruction. Roleplays were used rather than discourse completion tasks (DCTs) because roleplays offer the opportunity for acts to be developed over time and to be co-constructed. However, they also have their drawbacks. People react differently to the roleplay situation, and the value of using elicited data at all has been questioned.

Although naturally occurring data collected from particular targeted contexts (e.g., Clyne, 1994; Newton, 2004; Yates, 2000, 2005) or from language corpora (e.g., Koester, 2002; Terkourafi, 2005) may give the clearest insight into what actually happens in a situation, they, too, have disadvantages, as McCarthy and O'Keefe (2004) noted. In addition to the difficulty of collecting exactly the kind of data that is required, that is, collecting enough examples of the target act or function to make any sort of comparison meaningful, the very naturalness and authenticity of such data impact their usefulness. Because naturally occurring language is dynamic and contingent, such data will also reflect factors relating very particularly to the contexts in which they were collected (e.g., whether the interlocutors like each other, the past history of interactions between them or the institutions they represent, how tired they are feeling) as well as factors such as contingency and urgency and their interactional manifestations (Curl & Drew, 2008; Thomas, 1995; Tsui, 1994).

In contrast, elicited roleplay data are more likely to reflect a more generalized sense of what is appropriate in a situation. They therefore offer models that are less affected by such considerations and thus more useful for instruction because they represent at least an attempt to capture what, all things being equal, someone is likely to say in a given situation. Golato (2003) reinforced this point in her comparison of different data-collection procedures, arguing that although conversation analyses of naturally occurring discourse illuminate the organization of talk, DCTs allow a kind of distillation of what the speaker knows about how to act in a situation. As McCarthy and O'Keefe (2004) argued, models based on a range of perspectives and methodologies can be important in providing insight into the nature of spoken language.

I would also like to briefly address questions that have been raised about the usefulness of the concept of 'native speaker' (e.g., Davies, 2003) and debates on whether (and which) native-speaker models might be appropriate for the teaching of spoken language (see McCarthy & O'Keefe, 2004). Although the concept is woefully over- and misused, I would argue that it can still be useful if appropriately operationalised, particularly in cross-cultural and interlanguage pragmatics research, where early sociocultural experiences are seen as influential in the development of pragmatic aspects of language use (see discussion in Kasper, 2001). Regarding the issue of which particular model is appropriate for use in instructional settings, in the context of migration to Australia it is perhaps less problematic to identify Australian models as being particularly useful for learners, at least in the short term. However, I would argue that the development of competence in English as a language of international communication and intercultural rather than only cross-cultural competence (Byram, 1997) should be an ultimate aim.

For this study, in order to compare speakers of different backgrounds performing the same complex negotiation task and to provide insights that would be directly relevant to the production of materials for learning and teaching in the AMEP, data were collected using two workplace-relevant tasks taken from the national curriculum, the Certificates of Spoken & Written English (CSWE), Level III.[4] This choice had the pedagogical advantage of providing direct insight into a situation that students are likely to encounter in their lives and for which instructive sequences could then be developed within the curriculum at the appropriate level. The two tasks involved the making of requests for which some negotiation was needed, a request for annual leave (Task 1) and for changing the appointment for a job interview (Task 2; see Appendix A for the role cards).

Three groups of individuals were recorded performing each of these tasks with a teacher from the AMEP, 30 learners from varied (non-Dinka) language and cultural backgrounds, 30 native speakers of Australian English (NS group), and 30 learners of English with Dinka backgrounds. The latter group all spoke Dinka, a language indigenous to Southern Sudan, and most also spoke Arabic and other languages common in the region. The data from the mixed background learners (MBL group) and the NSs had been collected in previous studies (Wigglesworth, 2001; Yates & Wigglesworth, 2005), and the Dinka-background (DBL group) data were collected specifically for the study reported here. The participants were from a range of sociocultural backgrounds, and all of the learners were at Level III in oracy in the CSWE (that is, intermediate). Although the participants in the MBL and NS groups were balanced for gender, it was not possible to do this in the DBL group because there were insufficient numbers of Dinka women with significant prior education and therefore intermediate levels of English. The Dinka ranged in age from 20 to 59 years old, and most had between 10 and 16 years of education (see Appendix B). Table 1 shows how the participants were distributed across the tasks.

Table 1. Distribution of participant categories and tasks (total of 180 dialogs)

	M		F	
	Task 1	Task 2	Task 1	Task 2
NNS	15	15	15	15
NS	15	15	16	15
DS	24	24	6	6

Each dialog was transcribed and analysed using the qualitative software program Atlas. Four principal types of mitigation were coded using an adapted and updated version of the framework developed by Blum-Kulka et al. (1989). The original framework was expanded to include an additional category of request form, *interlocutor formulation*. This was used to code those requests that were formulated by the interlocutor, usually because the requester was vague or unclear about what he or she wanted:

S14: But must be a...I'm coming I'm thinking good thinking I have good idea for this interview because I have problem before in some interview in first job, I don't come in like fresh I don't have good question and good answer about something in the job

Inter: Right, so you've got an interview tomorrow at two I think isn't it, your interview, um *but what are you saying you want to change the time to another day or something*?

(See Appendix C for the coding framework.)

Tokens of each category of the framework were coded, counted, and totalled for each group. In negotiated tasks of this kind, more than one request was frequently present in each event, and because all requests are likely to impact how the speaker is perceived, all were counted. Care was taken to code items that might have more than one function in context according to the function that they had in the event. A sample of the data was double-coded by two different researchers, and any disagreements were resolved.

The quantitative investigation was supplemented by a qualitative exploration of various types of mitigation used and the sequence of acts in each event. The use of greetings and address forms and the level of formality were taken as evidence of relational work and therefore as clues as to the tone of the interactions, the stances taken by the interlocutors, and the sociocultural values underpinning them. In addition, after they had completed the roleplays, the DBL group members were asked by the researcher why they had approached the tasks in the way that they had, and these data were used to provide additional insight into issues of stance and the approach taken to the request. Because this additional data collection task was included in response to feedback[6] from presentations based on a comparison of the two earlier datasets (MBL and NS), these insights are only available for the DBL group.

As there was the same number of participants in each group, the results for the use of different features is given in raw numbers for each group.[7] The differences between the groups were not tested for significance because there was frequently more than one token of any particular feature in the data from any one individual.[8] Because of the gender imbalance in the Dinka group, averages were also calculated for male and female groups to see if there were any differences. These calculations are given in Appendixes D through G. In most cases, the tendencies reported were not greatly different for the female and male groups, but exceptions are included in the discussion of the relevant findings.

Findings and discussion

The findings revealed a number of differences, not only between the learner and NS groups, but also between the DBL and MBL groups. First, as shown in Table 2, the DBL group used more direct, apparently assertive, that is, direct requests (e.g., "I want...") than either the MBL or NS groups (84, 39, and 47 requests for the DBL, MBL, and NS groups respectively) and fewer apparently negotiable requests (e.g., "Can you..."), although the differences here were less dramatic (51, 68, and 66). None of the NSs used any apparently advisory requests, although the learners used a few (3 and 4 for the DBL and MBL groups). An interesting finding was that the members of the DBL group left it to their interlocutor to clarify the request through a reformulation (coded as an interlocutor formulation) more often (17) than either the MBL (5) or NS (1) group. This pattern does not seem to be related to proficiency alone because the DBL group members were, if anything, at a slightly higher level of grammatical competence than the other learners in the study (see below). Rather, it may be part of a strategy that deliberately avoids spelling out completely a request that may be perceived as an imposition. Because only 1 of the 6 Dinka women used this strategy, but 14 of the 24 men opted out in this way (2 of them in each of the two tasks), there may be a difference here for gender (see Appendix B, averages for gender).

Table 2. Level of directness of request

	DBL	MBL	NS
interlocutor formulation	17	5	1
nonexplicit negotiable	0	2	0
apparently negotiable	51	68	66
apparently advisory	3	4	0
apparently assertive	84	39	47

Table 3. Use of syntactic mitigation

	DBL	MBL	NS
past	43	51	222
modal	35	39	169
continuous	4	8	51
embedding	51	8	84

Table 3 displays the results for the use of syntactic mitigation by the three groups. It shows, not surprisingly, that compared to the NS group, both the DBL and MBL groups used considerably used fewer *past* (43, 51, and 222 for the DBL, MBL, and NS groups), *modal* (35, 39, and 169), and *continuous* forms (51, 8, and 84) in their mitigating functions. That is, the NSs more often distanced themselves from the requested action syntactically as in the following examples:

I just *wanted* to ask you about my leave (past)

I *was hoping* we *could* make it the following the following even the following week (past and continuous)

ah *would* I be able to have 3 weeks annual leave next week (modal)

As shown in Appendix E, there was a gender difference for the DBL group's use of modals in that the females, on average, used twice as many as the males, but the numbers are too small to make any strong claims here. There was also a gender difference among the NSs: the females averaged 6.5 modals, whereas the males averaged only 4.8. The NS females also used more past modifications that the NS males (averages of 8.1 and 6.7, respectively). This is in line with claims of previous research that females may use more of such devices (e.g., Holmes, 1995; Yates, 2000).

The finding for the use of embedding (i.e., the use of frames such as "I was wondering if...") was a little different: Although both learner groups used fewer than the NS group (84), the DBL group used this device more frequently than the MBL group (51 vs. 8). This finding supports anecdotal impressions that those in the DBL group were more, rather than less, proficient in grammar and vocabulary than their counterparts in the MBL group.

Table 4. Use of lexical mitigation

	DBL	MBL	NS
"just"	11	19	68
understater	7	6	22
hedge	42	34	72
consultative device	23	8	26
empathetic marker	7	26	65
interpersonal marker	17	34	43

As far as the use of lexical mitigation is concerned, as can be seen from Table 4, the DBL group, like the MBL group, used fewer tokens of "just" and *understaters* than the NS group ("just": 11, 19, and 68, respectively; understaters: 7, 6, and 22) and used *hedging* slightly more than did the MBL group, but considerably less often than the NS group (42, 34, and 72). They also used *empathetic* (7, 26, and 65) and *interpersonal markers* (17, 34, and 41) less often than the MBL group and considerably less often than the NSs. Their usage was roughly balanced for gender (see Appendix F). Examples of these devices are given below:

so I'm *just* wondering if we can change it to 2 o'clock the day after? ("just")
is it possible to ah maybe *juggle* the time perhaps? (understaters)
I ahm I'm *kind of* hoping that we'll be able to ah (hedging)
I *realise* how hard it is (empathetic markers)
it's just like um *you know* like I said (interpersonal markers)

For example, NSs used "you know"[9] as an interpersonal marker relatively frequently to highlight a connectedness with their interlocutors (Trosborg, 1995). This had the effect of reinforcing a more egalitarian stance that established shared responsibility and from which requests appear to be more a matter of negotiation than supplication, as in the examples below:

> it's just like um *you know* like I said
>
> *you know* I don't mind working
>
> working extra extra time *you know* during Christmas and that

In these NS examples, "you know" is used to draw the interlocutor into what is being said in a kind of complicity (Schiffrin, 1987). In contrast, although some DBL group members seemed to be trying to use "you know" in this way, they were not always successful in making an appeal to alignment; that is, their use of "you know" did not increase the connection between the speaker and hearer, as in the following example (which was not, therefore, coded as an interpersonal marker):

> as *you know* you are my manager,

At times, even when their use was syntactically appropriate, their delivery tended to give too much prominence to the phrase, which had the effect of emphasizing its literal rather than pragmatic interpersonal function.

Similarly, the NS group more frequently used empathetic markers, that is, phrases such as "I realise," to introduce an expression of empathy with the interlocutor's position (65 and 7 uses for the NS and DBL groups respectively). In contrast, the few used by the DBL group more often introduced propositions that simply described the current state of affairs rather than expressing their concern about it. Such statements are liable to be interpreted as unsympathetic, especially if they are not delivered with an appropriate intonation. Compare the following examples from NSs

> I *realise* how hard it is
>
> I *know* that it's not a lot of ahm ahhh notice

with these examples in which members of the DBL group used "I know" to introduce apparent statements of fact:

> You know, I *know I know* we are so busy now, I know
>
> I *know* you are busy, all are busy

Thus, the NSs used "I realise" and "I know" to emphasise their empathetic understanding of the difficult general circumstances surrounding their requests and thus build a stance from which to negotiate, whereas the use of "I know" in the DBL examples almost has the opposite effect because it conveys acknowledgement of their boss's difficulty without managing to convey an appropriate degree of empathy.[10] In contrast to the use of interpersonal and empathetic markers discussed above, the DBL group used consultative devices (i.e., devices that appear to consult, such as "is there any chance that..."), more often than the MBL group and at frequencies similar to those of the NSs (23, 8, and 26, respectively). Qualitative analyses of these, however, showed that, again, there was often a difference in the functions of the markers used by the DBL group. The NSs used them to appear to consult about the matter in question or make an offer to alleviate the situation, as in the following examples:

okay *is there any way I could* make that later in the day

how about if I tried to organize something with one of the staff members

The DBL group, however, more often used them to 'pass the buck,' that is, to leave the responsibility with the boss or the system, as in the example below:

could you mind to arrange for me

Table 5. Use of propositional mitigation

	DBL	MBL	NS
greeting/title/name	54	44	49
reason	163	111	107
preparator	27	33	53
context	37	31	40
rapport	20	10	11
disarmer	20	29	76

Thus, although the NS group's use of consultative devices was oriented towards negotiation as a more egalitarian partner as part of a stance in which they shouldered some of the responsibility for a solution to the problems caused by their requests, the DBL group more often used them as a device to signal deference.

As can be seen from Table 5, the DBL group used *reasons* more than any other group (163, compared to 111 and 107 by the MBL and NS groups) and *context* (i.e., extra information to clarify the background to the request) as frequently as the NS group (37 vs. 40) and slightly more often than the MBL group (31). In this, both learner groups may well be illustrating the 'waffle phenomenon' (Edmondson & House, 1991), that is, the tendency of some L2 speakers to use reasons to justify their requests and ensure comprehension and compliance in compensation for other strategies and devices that they have less control over. Moreover, a qualitative analysis of the reasons used by the DBL group revealed that whereas the NSs used a range of reasons, including holidays, family, and personal reasons, the DBL group tended to use powerful family reasons, which exerted strong emotional pressure on their interlocutors. Thus, although the NSs often cited the need for a break or to get away with their partner, the DBL group often invoked the illness of a very close relative, childbirth, or study as reasons for their requests. These latter two reasons did not occur at all in the NS data. This may well reflect culture-specific assumptions related to the rights and obligations in a workplace situation and inexperience with the concept of paid leave and what it can be used for in an Australian setting. As discussed in the following section, the DBL group came to the task with a different perception of the relationship between the boss and employee and work and home life based on their cultural experiences in Africa. Also observable in the NS requests but not in those of the other groups was the tendency to develop the reasons behind the request slowly over several turns rather than repeating the same reason, which may lessen the pressure on the interlocutor, as in the following example:

A: ...as you know um my house went up for sale
B: yeah that's right yeah
A: ...and the settlements actually in a um weeks time...I have to move um and the thing is I'm moving out of the house cause I've sold my house and settlement day I've...

The DBL group's use of *preparators* was similar to that by the MBL group (27 vs. 33), but they used *disarmers* slightly less frequently (20 vs. 29). This usage was noticeably different from that of the NSs, who used twice as many preparators (53 vs. 27) and nearly four times the number of disarmers (76 vs. 20) as the DBL group. The NSs frequently used availability checks such as "are you busy?" to prepare the way for the principal request. Examples are given below:

Look just ahm sorry to disturb you (preparator)
look [name] I know this is a bit sudden but (disarmer)

However, the DBL group used twice as many *rapport* moves as the MBL group and almost twice as many as the NSs, although these were all simple greeting routines. An the exception was two moves that emphasized the hierarchical difference between the groups, for example:

and *with your personal consent* maybe you change this time for me to be today

The MBL group only used greeting routines (10). In contrast, the NSs used humour and self-deprecation in 4 of their 11 rapport moves (see the example below). No speakers from the other groups used these strategies.

I know this sounds really silly but I'm I'm an absolutely dopey Essendon supporter and I'm queuing up for tickets

Summary and interpretation of trends in Dinka-background and English NS negotiated requests

The list below summarises some of the trends emerging from the NS data that were less evident in DBL data. These features of NS requests could usefully be addressed in instruction.

- fewer apparently assertive request forms
- more frequent use of past, modal, and continuous forms to soften requests

- more embedding of requests in a polite frame using the continuous form.
- more frequent use of "just" as a softener
- more frequent vocabulary choices that understated the impact of the speaker's action
- more frequent use of empathetic markers to show understanding of the interlocutor's side
- more frequent use of interpersonal markers to emphasise connection
- use of consultative devices to check a course of action or suggest a solution rather than to pass responsibility for the solution to the interlocutor
- more frequent use of preparators such as availability checks
- more frequent use of disarmers to address potential problems, sometimes with offers of help
- tendency to develop the reasons behind the request slowly over several turns rather than repeating the same reason so that the interlocutor does not feel too pressured

As can be seen from the summary, the NSs mitigated the assertiveness of their requests through their choice of request forms and more frequent use of syntactic and lexical mitigation. They also prepared their requests carefully through the use of preparators and signaled empathy and mutual responsibility through disarmers, empathetic markers, interpersonal markers, and consultative devices. These devices were used less often and in some cases less successfully by learners from both groups, but particularly by the DBL group. Rather, the DBL group relied heavily on the provision of reasons, context, and greetings (rapport moves) to mitigate their requests. Alongside these strategies, however, like the MBL group, they made little use of syntactic mitigation and lexical devices like "just." Although they used hedges more frequently than the MBL group, they used them far less frequently than the NSs. They also made less use of preparators and disarmers than the MBL group and considerably less than the NSs and more often failed to articulate the requests clearly, but left it to their interlocutors to reformulate it.

These differences not only highlight those aspects of requesting behaviour in English in which Dinka-background learners may need awareness-raising activities but also suggest that they may be approaching the request in these workplace situations rather differently. Thus, although the NSs more often adopted a stance in which they signaled connectedness and mutual responsibility to their bosses, empathizing and offering solutions as they negotiated what they wanted, the DBL group sought to explain their requests as a supplicant.

As anticipated, the DBL group's responses to the post roleplay question about why they had approached the requestive tasks in the way that they had revealed that, like many other speakers, they were largely unaware of the strategies and devices that they were using. However, they did provide some insight into their experiences of workplace contexts and thus into why they may have adopted this rather different stance. A quarter of them had either never had paid employment at all or only casual employment, and those who had worked had often worked in very different environments in Egypt, Sudan, and Ethiopia (see Appendix B). This meant that the tasks and their underlying sociocultural conventions in Australia were unfamiliar to many of them. Many had little understanding, for example, of the notion of paid leave or a worker's rights and obligations at work and had to check that they understood the concept with the research assistant before they undertook Task 1.

Moreover, comments such as the example below from P63 suggest that the DBL group may have had a very different understanding of the relationship between the workplace and the community and between themselves, their families, and their boss:

> In Sudan if you give a reason such as you need to go and help your community, do something for your family, it is a very strong reason and the manager would be looked down upon if they refused. Work is not seen as being more important than doing something for your family or community.... If for example you said your mother is in hospital your manager likely to offer to go and visit with you. (P63)

Although it would be unwise to make any conclusive claims based on the available data, such comments do suggest a greater blurring of distinctions between work and home, between one's public, work self and one's more private, family self than is common in many workplaces in the current, postindustrial Anglo-Western world. Views of self in relation to community (e.g., Murphy-Berman & Berman, 2003) and the degree to which one's sense of self is different in different contexts are by no means universal across cultures. Although no studies, to my knowledge, have tackled such issues from the perspective of Dinka culture, nevertheless, anthropological work on traditional Dinka lifestyles suggests a very strong sense of community and communal responsibility. Deng (1998), for example, argued that respect for others (*atheek*) and dignity (*dheeng*) are very important values in Dinka culture, and they do not come automatically with power and wealth but must be earned. Reciprocity and mutual dependence are salient features of these attitudes. Deng described cooperation within the group as critical and the promotion of one's self interest above community interests as taboo in Dinka culture. It may well be, therefore, that such deeply held values influenced the Dinka participants' perceptions of mutual rights and obligations in workplace relations and that these would be rather different from those expected in an Australian workplace.

Implications and recommendations for learning and teaching

The findings of this study have provided some insight into features that Australian NSs might expect to see in workplace requests. Comparing these with the ways in which learners approached the same requests can throw light onto the question of what kinds of devices and strategies should be tackled in instruction. As noted above, an underlying assumption here is that because teachers themselves frequently lack a sophisticated awareness of contextually effective pragmatic actions, materials developed on the basis of these findings can be instructive for teachers and students alike. They could, therefore, be helpful as the basis for professional development and instructional materials from which not only the learners, but also the teachers, benefit (e.g., Yates & Wigglesworth, 2005).

As far as sociocultural issues are concerned, the findings suggest that it would be useful to tackle concepts relating to workplace conditions, rights, and responsibilities in Australia and the likely tenor of workplace interactions. 'Model' dialogs taken from the data and based on learners' past experiences would be a useful starting point for reflection and comparison with cultures with which learners (and teachers) are familiar (see Yates, 2004; Yates, 2008). Particular attention could be drawn to the way in which assumptions about rights and responsibilities and cultural values in communication can be reflected in the stance taken towards an interlocutor in a context. Professional development materials for employers and other professionals could also usefully focus on these issues as well as on understanding cultural differences in the role of family/community and the potentially blurred distinctions between responsibilities in each domain that different community members might have.

The summary of NS patterns above suggests the kinds of pragmalinguistic topics that might be usefully targeted in materials. Examples of how these might translate into items for instructional focus are given below. An idea of how some of these can be incorporated into a sample dialog can be found in the short extract from materials developed by teachers using the findings from this study in Appendix H.[11]

- indirect request forms and mitigation of direct request forms, for example:

    Have you got a few moments for me to pop in… (indirect request form, understated word choice)

    I'd really like to take 3 weeks annual leave now starting next week and I'm just wondering if we can arrange that? (direct request, mitigated using syntax)

- alternatives to repeated reasons for persuasion, for example:

    (developing rather than repeating a reason through providing more context)

- the use of additional lexis, including "just," and understated word choice to soften, for example:

    Could I just have a quick word?

- the use of disarmers, empathetic and interpersonal markers, and consultative devices to show connection and joint responsibility:

  I know we're really busy at the moment, and I know we are flat out at work, but... (disarmer)

  Yes I really understand that, but... (empathetic marker)

  How about if I... (consultative device used to make a suggestion/offer)

- the mitigating function of past, modal and continuous forms:

  I wanted to ask if I could... (past/modal)

  I was hoping to catch you... (past/continuous)

- the use of polite frames into which requests can be embedded:

  I was wondering if I could... (past/continuous/embedding)

It is unlikely that these features will be completely unfamiliar to learners at this level. However, they may be unaware of the mitigating functions of various forms or of how frequently they are used in everyday interaction. Although some of these may be quite complex (e.g., embedding frames such as "I was wondering if I could..."), they appear to be important in the negotiation of requests in Australian workplace contexts (as in some institutional contexts in British English, Curl & Drew, 2008), and they could be tackled as formulaic chunks. The importance of such sequences in the successful achievement of learners' communicative goals, providing as they do "islands of reliability" (Dechert, 1983) from which they can navigate the sometimes perilous open sea of unprestructured L2 production, has recently been reconsidered (Bardovi-Harlig, 2006, this volume; Bardovi-Harlig et al., this volume; House, 1996; Wray, 2000).

Such language features need to be related to the sociopragmatic values underpinning the informal interactive style suggested by the NS data. Thus, there should be a focus not only on individual devices such as consultative devices or empathetic markers, but also on why and how they are used to establish interpersonal connections during a negotiation and their role in the stance taken by a speaker in appearing to take an interlocutor's feelings into account. The way in which disarmers are used to show this kind of joint responsibility and how requests can be prepared with preparators to prefigure and soften the request can also be highlighted. There is no space here to provide extended samples of the kinds of materials that can be developed on the basis of this research, but, as noted above, the short sample dialog in Appendix H illustrates what can be developed by teachers for their own use in the classroom, and further examples can be found in the works of Yates and Springall (in press) and Springall (2007).

In this study, I have not been able to relate performance in English directly to the language and cultural practices of the Dinka. It is my hope that future research will address this gap in the literature so that we may more fully understand the motivations underlying the patterns seen here. In the absence of such studies of L1 performance, the immigrants arriving from many different backgrounds to settle in unfamiliar English-speaking environments and their teachers must rely on comparative studies such as the one reported here for insight into what areas might be useful for instruction.

In conclusion, this study has provided practical insights into the range of strategies and devices that native speakers and learners might use to negotiate a complex request in a workplace-related context and provided language samples that can be used in instruction and an evidence base that can be used in professional development and instructional settings. There is no place here for a detailed discussion of particular teaching activities that might be used with the models and materials arising out of the study, but there is mounting evidence that such features can be both taught and learned (Alcón & Martínez-Flor, 2007; Rose & Kasper, 2001; Slade, 1997), and many sources can provide ideas on how instruction in L2 pragmatics may be approached (e.g., Burns, Joyce, & Gollin, 2001; Hall, 1999; McCarthy & O'Keefe, 2004; Yates, 2004).

On a theoretical level, by complementing the CCSARP framework with a focus on stance, this study has contributed to the analytical tools that can be used to highlight sociocultural factors in the study of interlanguage pragmatics. These are frequently glossed over in comparative and interlanguage studies of pragmatics behaviours because the search for categories that are identifiable across cultures and learners can leave emic perspectives out of account (Goddard, 2006a). Yet, as I hope I have illustrated here, factors such as stance are important in understanding how, why, and when pragmalinguistic resources are deployed in context.

Notes

1. The AMEP delivers a national curriculum throughout Australia through a range of providers. Between 510 and 910 hours, depending on circumstances, are available free of charge to new arrivals who do not have functional English.
2. The study was conducted in 2006 through the AMEP Research Centre and funded by a Special Research Project grant from the Commonwealth Government of Australia, to whom thanks are due.
3. The word "migrant" is preferred over the term "immigrant" in Australia to refer to those who arrive with the intention of settling.
4. The AMEP is taught at three levels. Level III learners are at a low intermediate to intermediate level.
5. Learners placed at Certificate III level on arrival have usually had significant prior educational experiences in English. There is considerable gender disparity in educational level among the Dinka.
6. My thanks to Merrill Swain for this suggestion.

7   I did not calculate the frequencies of tokens in proportion to the number of words as in, for example, Dippold's (2006) study because my aim was to find out the number used by each speaker to achieve his or her aim, rather than in frequencies *per se*.
8   There were slight individual variations, but as these are not the particular focus of this chapter, they are not reported here.
9   Tokens of "you know" were counted as interpersonal markers where they had the function of a pragmatic marker inviting the addressee to align with the view expressed by the speaker (Schiffrin, 1987, p. 310).
10 My thanks to two anonymous readers for their insights on the use of interpersonal and empathetic markers.
11 Developed by Priti Mukherjee, Robyn Raleigh, Jacky Springall, and Clare Strack.

References

Achiba, M. (2003). *Learning to request in a second language*. Clevedon, England: Multilingual Matters.

Alcón, E. S., & Martínez-Flor, A. (Eds.). (2007). *Investigating pragmatics in foreign language learning, teaching and testing*. Clevedon, England: Multilingual Matters.

Aronsson, K., & Sätterlund-Larsson, U. (1987). Politeness strategies and doctor-patient communication. On the social choreography of collaborative thinking. *Journal of Language and Social Psychology, 6*, 1–27.

Bardovi-Harlig, K. (2006). On the role of formulas in the acquisition of L2 pragmatics. In K. Bardovi-Harlig, C. Félix-Brasdefer, & A. Omar (Eds.), *Pragmatics and Language Learning* (Vol. 11, pp. 1–28). Honolulu: University of Hawai'i, National Foreign Language Resource Center.

Bilbow, G.-T. (1997). Cross-cultural impression management in the multicultural workplace: The special case of Hong Kong. *Journal of Pragmatics, 28*, 461–487.

Blum-Kulka, S., House, J., & Kasper, G. (Eds.). (1989). *Cross-cultural pragmatics: Requests and apologies*. Norwood, NJ: Ablex.

Boxer, D. (2002). *Applying sociolinguistics: Domains and face-to-face interaction*. Amsterdam: John Benjamins.

Boxer, D. (2004). Discourse issues in cross-cultural pragmatics. *Annual Review of Applied Linguistics, 22*, 150–167.

Brown, P., & Levinson, S. (1987). *Politeness: Some universals in language usage*. Cambridge, England: Cambridge University Press.

Burns, A., Joyce, H., & Gollin, S. (2001). *"I see what you mean": Using spoken discourse in the classroom*. Sydney, Australia: National Centre for English Language Teaching Research.

Byram, M. (1997). *Teaching and assessing intercultural communicative competence*. Clevedon, England: Multilingual Matters.

Clyne, M. G. (1994). *Inter-cultural communication at work*. Cambridge, England: Cambridge University Press.

Cook, M., & Liddicoat, A. (2002). The development of comprehension in interlanguage pragmatics: The case of request strategies in English. *Australian Review of Applied Linguistics, 25(1),* 19–39.

Curl, T. S., & Drew, P. (2008). Contingency and action: A comparison of two forms of requesting. *Research on Language and Social Interaction, 41,* 129–153.

Davies, A. (2003). *The native speaker: Myth and reality* (Vol. 38). Clevedon, England: Multilingual Matters.

Davies, B., & Harré, R. (1990). Positioning: The discursive production of selves. *Journal for the Theory of Social Behaviour, 20,* 44–63.

Dechert, H. (1983). How a story is done in a second language. In C. Færch & G. Kasper (Eds.), *Strategies in interlanguage communication* (pp. 175–195). London: Longman.

Deng, F. M. (1998). The cow and the thing called 'what': Dinka cultural perspectives on wealth and poverty. *Journal of International Affairs, 52,* 101–129.

Dippold, D. (2006). Face in L2 argumentative discourse: Psycholinguistic constraints on the construction of identity. In R. Kiely, P. Rea-Dickens, H. Woodfield, & G. Clibbon (Eds.), *Language, culture and identity in applied linguistics* (pp. 163–179). London: Equinox.

Edmondson, W., & House, J. (1991). Do learners talk too much? The waffle phenomenon in interlanguage pragmatics. In R. Phillipson, E. Kellerman, L. Selinker, M. Sharwood Smith, & M. Swain (Eds.), *Foreign/second language pedagogy research* (pp. 273–286). Clevedon, England: Multilingual Matters.

Goddard, C. (2006a). Introduction. In C. Goddard (Ed.), *Ethnopragmatics* (pp. 65–97). Berlin: Mouton de Gruyter.

Goddard, C. (2006b). 'Lift your game Martina': Deadpan jocular irony and the ethnopragmatics of Australian English. In C. Goddard (Ed.), *Ethnopragmatics* (pp. 65–97). Berlin: Mouton de Gruyter.

Golato, A. (2003). Studying compliment responses: A comparison of DCTs and recordings of naturally-occurring talk. *Applied Linguistics, 23,* 90–121.

Good, S. (2006). *Getting on with the job. Book 2: Workplace communication skills.* Melbourne, Australia: AMES Victoria.

Hall, J. K. (1999). A prosaics of interaction: The development of interaction competence in another language. In E. Hinkel (Ed.), *Culture in second language teaching and learning* (pp. 137–151). Cambridge, England: Cambridge University Press.

Hinkel, E. (1996). When in Rome: Evaluations of L2 pragmalinguistic behaviors. *Journal of Pragmatics, 26,* 51–70.

Holmes, J. (1995). *Women, men and politeness.* Harlow, England: Longman.

Houck, N., & Gass, S. M. (1996). Non-native refusals: A methodological perspective. In S. M. Gass & J. Neu (Eds.), *Speech acts across cultures* (pp. 46–63). New York: Mouton de Gruyter.

House, J. (1996). Developing pragmatic fluency in English as a foreign language. *Studies in Second Language Acquisition, 18,* 225–252.

Hyland, K. (2005). Stance and engagement: A model of interaction in academic discourse. *Discourse Studies, 7*, 173–192.

Ibrahim, A. (2003). 'Whassup homeboy?' Joining the African diaspora: Black English as a symbolic site of identification and language learning. In S. Makoni, G. Smitherman, A. F. Ball, & A. K. Spears (Eds.), *Black linguistics: Language, society and politics in Africa and the Americas* (pp. 169–185). London: Routledge.

Kasper, G. (2001). Four perspectives on L2 pragmatic development. *Applied Linguistics, 22*, 502–530.

Kasper, G., & Roever, C. (2005). Pragmatics in second language learning. In E. Hinkel (Ed.), *Handbook of research in second language teaching and learning* (pp. 317–334). Mahwah, NJ: Erlbaum.

Koester, A. J. (2002). The performance of speech acts in workplace conversations and the teaching of communicative functions. *System, 30*, 167–184.

Lakoff, R. (2005). The politics of nice. *Journal of Politeness Research, 1*, 173–191.

McCarthy, M., & O'Keefe, A. (2004). Research in the teaching of speaking. *Annual Review of Applied Linguistics, 24*, 26–43.

Murphy-Berman, V., & Berman, J. J. (Eds.). (2003). *Cross-cultural differences in perspectives on the self*. Lincoln: University of Nebraska Press.

Newton, J. (2004). Face-threatening talk on the factory floor: Using authentic workplace interactions in language teaching. *Prospect, 19*, 3–21.

Piller, I. (2007). Linguistics and intercultural communication. *Language and Linguistics Compass, 1*, 208–226.

Rose, K. R., & Kasper, G. (Eds.). (2001). *Pragmatics in language teaching*. Cambridge, England: Cambridge University Press.

Sasaki, M. (1998). Investigating EFL students' production of speech acts: A comparison of production questionnaires and role plays. *Journal of Pragmatics, 30*, 457–484.

Schiffrin, D. (1987). *Discourse markers*. New York: CUP.

Siegal, M. (1996). The role of learner subjectivity in second language sociolinguistic competency: Western women learning Japanese. *Applied Linguistics, 17*, 356–382.

Slade, D. (1997). Stories and gossip in English. *Prospect, 12*, 72–86.

Springall, J. (2007). *Taking care—Trainer guide and DVD/CD pack. Melbourne*. Melbourne, Australia: AMES Vic.

Sudanese Online Research Association. (n.d.). Retrieved June 20, 2007, from http://sora.akm.net.au/

Takahashi, S. (1996). Pragmatic transferability. *Studies in Second Language Acquisition, 18*, 189–223.

Taleghani-Nikazm, C. (2006). *Request sequences: The intersection of grammar, interaction and social context*. Amsterdam: Benjamins.

Terkourafi, M. (2005). Beyond the micro-level in politeness research. *Journal of Politeness Research, 1*, 237–262.

Thomas, J. A. (1995). *Meaning in interaction: An introduction to pragmatics*. London: Longman.

Trosborg, A. (1995). *Interlanguage pragmatics.* Berlin: Mouton de Gruyter.

White, P. (2003). Beyond modality and hedging: A dialogic view of the language of intersubjective stance. *Text, 23,* 259–284.

Wierzbicka, A. (1997). *Understanding cultures through their key words: English, Russian, Polish, German and Japanese.* New York: Oxford University Press.

Wigglesworth, G. (2001). Influences on performance in task-based oral assessments. In M. Bygate, P. Skehan, & M. Swain (Eds.), *Task based learning* (pp. 186–209). London: Longman.

Wigglesworth, G., & Yates, L. (2007). Mitigating difficult requests in the workplace: What learners and teachers need to know. *TESOL Quarterly, 41,* 791–803.

Willing, K. (1992). *Talking it through. Clarification and problem-solving in professional work.* Sydney, Australia: Macquarie University.

Wray, A. (2000). Formulaic sequences in second language teaching: Principle and practice. *Applied Linguistics, 21,* 463–489.

Yates, L. (2000). *"Ciao, guys!": Mitigation addressing positive and negative face concerns in the directives of native-speaker and Chinese background speakers of Australian English.* Unpublished doctoral dissertation, La Trobe University, Melbourne, Australia.

Yates, L. (2004). The 'secret rules of language': Tackling pragmatics in the classroom. *Prospect, 19,* 3–21.

Yates, L. (2005). Negotiating an institutional identity: Individual differences in NS and NNS teacher directives. In K. Bardovi-Harlig & B. S. Hartford (Eds.), *Interlanguage pragmatics: Exploring institutional talk* (pp. 67–97). Mahwah, NJ: Lawrence Erlbaum.

Yates, L. (2008). *The not-so generic skills: Teaching employability communication skills to adult migrants.* Sydney, Australia: National Centre for English Language Teaching Research.

Yates, L., & Springall, J. (in press). Soften up! Successful requests in the workplace. In D. Tatsuki & N. Houck (Eds.), *Pragmatics from research to practice: Teaching speech acts.* Alexandria, VA: TESOL.

Yates, L., & Wigglesworth, G. (2005). Researching the effectiveness of professional development in pragmatics. In N. Bartels (Ed.), *Applied linguistics and language teacher education* (pp. 261–279). Amsterdam: Kluwer.

Yuan, Y. (2001). An inquiry into empirical pragmatics data-gathering methods: Written DCTs, oral DCTs, field notes, and natural conversations. *Journal of Pragmatics, 33,* 271–292.

Zhang, Y. (1995). Indirectness in Chinese requesting. In G. Kasper (Ed.), *Pragmatics of Chinese as native and target language* (pp. 69–118). Honolulu: University of Hawai'i, National Foreign Language Resource Center.

Appendix A: Role cards

Task 1: Requesting annual leave

Participant card

You have 4 weeks annual leave available this year. You would like to take 3 weeks leave now, even though it is a busy time at your workplace.
Talk to your manager about this situation, explain why you want to take the leave now and negotiate a solution.

Interlocutor card

You are the manager of a workplace. One of your employees has applied to take 3 weeks of their 4 weeks annual leave now.
It is a particularly busy time at your workplace. Find out why he/she wants to take leave now. Explain that employees normally take leave at Christmas when things are quieter. Ask the employee to suggest ways to resolve the situation.

Task 2: Changing job interview

Participant card

You have an appointment for a job interview with an employment agency tomorrow. The time that has been arranged is not convenient for you.
Go to the agency, introduce yourself and explain the situation.
Try and arrange another time for the interview.

Interlocutor card

You work at an employment agency. A job seeker calls in and wants to change the interview time you have arranged for him/her tomorrow, claiming that it is not convenient. Find out why the time is inconvenient. Point out that there are a number of applicants for the job and a limited time set aside for interviews. Ask the job seeker to suggest ways to resolve the situation.

Appendix B: Participant profile

ID	gender	age	no. months in Australia	years and place of education	occupation
1	m	50	6	24, Sudan & Egypt	teacher
2	m	34	14	12, Sudan	librarian
3	f	33	7	16, Sudan	teacher
4	f	33	7	20, Sudan	nurse
5	m	28	8	13, Sudan	casual
6	m	35	5	16, Sudan	teacher
7	m	44	9	16, Sudan	cleaner
8	m	43	6	12, Sudan	tax collector
9	f	32	5	8, Sudan & Uganda	none
10	m	20	5	12, Kenya	student teacher
11	m	34	3	12, Sudan	travel agent
12	f	25	7	12, Sudan	child care
13	m	46	11	9, Sudan	aged care
14	m	33	24	15, Sudan	sales
15	m	30	8	10, Ethiopia	never worked
16	m	43	7	12, Sudan	primary teacher/cleaner
17	m	22	1	5, Sudan; 5, Kenya	student
18	m	25	1	5, Sudan; 5, Kenya	student & NGO
19	m	40	24	12, Sudan	shop assistant
20	m	44	19	16, Sudan	assistant priest
21	m	25	2	3, Sudan; 6, Kenya	casual/labourer
22	m	41	13	12, Sudan	administration
23	m	59	1	13, Sudan	management (water)
24	m	30	8	6	customer service
25	f	27	13	15, Sudan	child care
26	m	30	4	12, Sudan	sales and Dinka teacher
27	m	22	3	3, Sudan; 2, Egypt	shop keeper
28	m	28	9	10, Sudan	sales/supermarket
29	f	25	24	10, Sudan	never worked
30	m	27	12	16, Sudan (in Arabic)	cleaner

Appendix C: Summary of coding framework

Five levels of directness/assertiveness of requests (semantic formulae)

Apparently assertive (direct)
Example: I *want* to change the time.

Apparently advisory (conventionally indirect)
Example: Maybe I *could* take the extra week I haven't had yet.

Apparently negotiable (conventionally indirect)
Example: So *could* we sort of do something about my leave now.

Nonexplicit negotiable (hints)
Example: *I really need to know what leave is available to me.*

Interlocutor formulation
Example: (Interlocutor) Right, so you've got an interview tomorrow at two I think isn't it, your interview, um *but what are you saying you want to change the time to another day or something*?

Syntactic modifications of requests

Past marking
Examples: I just *wanted* ...; I *was* just wondering if I could have a minute of your time.

Modals
Examples: I'*d* like to take some annual leave. I was wondering if we *might*...

Continuous
Example: I'm really *hoping* to...

Embedding
Example: I *was just wondering if* it would be possible

Lexical modifications of requests

Downtoner—"just"
Example: I *just* need these three weeks to finish that.

Understater
Example: I really would *appreciate* being able to...

Hedge
Example: *Maybe* I could take the days that I haven't had yet.

Consultative device
Example: *Would that be okay* with you?

Empathetic marker
Examples: *I think/know/realise/feel...*; *I [can] understand, appreciate...*

Interpersonal marker
Examples: *You know what I mean...; You see...; You know...*

Propositional support moves for requests

Context
Example: *I have some holiday left.*

Reason
Example: Ah well *my wife at the moment she's a bit ill.*

Preparator
Example: *I was wondering if I could have a minute of your time.*

Rapport
Example: *Ooh I've got to do a bit of grovelling.*

Disarmer
Example: *I know it's not a good time of the year.*

Appendix D: Average use of request formulae by gender

request formula	DBL			MBL			NS		
	m	f	tot	m	f	tot	m	f	tot
interlocutor formulation	0.7	0.2	**0.6**	0	0.3	**0.2**	0	0.1	**0**
apparently negotiable	1.7	1.7	**1.7**	2	2.5	**2.3**	2.3	2.1	**2.2**
apparently assertive		0.2		0.2	0.1	**0.1**			
assertive	2.8	2.7	**2.8**	1.1	1.5	**1.3**	1.8	1.3	**1.6**

Appendix E: Average use of syntactic mitigation devices by gender

syntactic device	DBL			MBL			NS		
	m	f	tot	m	f	tot	m	f	tot
past	1.4	1.7	**1.4**	2.7	0.7	**1.7**	6.7	8.1	**7.4**
modal	1	2	**1.2**	1.9	0.7	**1.3**	4.8	6.5	**5.63**
continuous	0.2	0	**0.1**	0.4	0.1	**0.3**	1.7	1.7	**1.7**
embedding	1.2	1.3	**1.7**	0.4	0.1	**0.3**	2.4	3.2	**2.8**

Appendix F: Average use of lexical mitigation devices by gender

lexical device	DBL			MBL			NS		
	m	f	tot	m	f	tot	m	f	tot
"just"	0.4	0.2	**0.4**	1	0.3	**0.6**	2.5	2	**2.27**
understater	0.2	0.3	**0.2**	0.3	0.1	**0.2**	0.6	0.9	**0.73**
hedge	1.5	1.2	**1.4**	1.4	0.9	**1.1**	2.1	2.7	**2.4**
consultative device	0.8	0.8	**0.8**	0.3	0.2	**0.3**	0.8	0.9	**0.87**
interpersonal marker	0.7	1	**0.7**	1.8	0.5	**1.1**	1.4	1.5	**1.43**
empathetic marker	0.2	0.5	**0.2**	0.9	0.8	**0.9**	2.3	2.1	**2.17**

Appendix G: Average use of propositional mitigation by gender

propositional mitigation	DBL			MBL			NS		
	m	f	tot	m	f	tot	m	f	tot
reason	6.2	6.2	**5.4**	3.4	4	**3.7**	3.3	3.9	**3.57**
preparators	0.9	0.8	**0.9**	1.1	1.1	**1.1**	1.5	2.1	**1.77**
context	1.3	0.8	**1.2**	1.2	0.9	**1**	1.3	1.4	**1.33**
rapport	0.8	0.2	**0.7**	0.3	0.4	**0.3**	0.4	0.3	**0.37**
disarmers	0.7	0.5	**0.7**	1.1	0.8	**1**	2.7	2.4	**2.53**

Appendix H: Dialog 2

Toni   Hello Simon, have you got a few moments for me to pop in and have a word with you please?

Simon   Yes sure come in.

Toni   Look Simon, I know we're really busy at the moment, and I know we are flat out at work, but I've got 4 weeks annual leave owing to me.

Simon   Yeah

Toni   I'd really like to take 3 weeks annual leave now starting next week and I'm just wondering if we can arrange that?

Simon   You know that it's not a good time at the moment?

Toni   Yes I really understand that, but my mother has taken sick in New Zealand and I have to go home and help Dad look after her.

Simon   I'm sorry to hear that Toni but it's a very awkward time…

Toni   Yes, I know it's not a good time of the year but I really need to be there for my family.

Simon   Well, I guess we'll have to work something out.

Toni   That would be great.
Thanks.

Recognition of Conventional Expressions in L2 Pragmatics[1]

Kathleen Bardovi-Harlig
Indiana University

It is widely noted that second language learners do not use conventional expressions where native speakers do. This pattern may be due in part to a lack of pragmalinguistic resources. This study investigates learners' recognition of conventional expressions and their ability to distinguish conventional-grammatical expressions from nonconventional-grammatical ones, an ability of native speakers that Pawley and Syder (1983) called nativelike selection. An aural recognition task of 60 items was administered using a 3-way scale in which learners indicated a level of recognition for each expression by circling the most descriptive rating: "I often/sometimes/never hear this." This cross-sectional study of 123 learners at 4 levels of proficiency and 49 native speakers found that the learners distinguished between the authentic, conventional expressions and the modified, nonconventional ones. Whereas the learners recognized some expressions early at lower proficiency levels, other conventional expressions were recognized later or at very low rates. In addition, the learners reported that they often or sometimes heard modified expressions that native speakers reported never hearing.

This chapter investigates second language learners' familiarity with conventional expressions used by native speakers. Conventional expressions consist of strings such as "No problem," "Nice to meet you," and "That'd be great," which native speakers use predictably in certain contexts. It has been widely observed that learners underuse such expressions both in research on L2 development in general (Nattinger & DeCarrico, 1992; Schmitt & Carter, 2004; Yorio, 1989) and L2 pragmatics in particular (Blum-Kulka & Olshtain, 1986; Edmondson & House, 1991; House, 1996; Kasper & Blum-Kulka, 1993; Kecskes, 2000; Roever, 2005; Scarcella, 1979). By investigating learners' recognition of conventional expressions, this study hopes to contribute to our understanding of why such expressions are underused in L2 pragmatics and to locate the source of difficulty in emerging interlanguage. This study begins with an investigation of conventional expressions as a pragmalinguistic resource. As Kasper and Blum-Kulka observed, "one area where insufficient control of pragmalinguistic knowledge is particularly obvious is that of pragmatic routines" (p. 9). Although production of conventional expressions has received substantial attention in L2 pragmatics, learners' abilities to recognize conventional expressions is relatively unexplored.

As is traditional in papers on conventional expressions, I take a short detour here to comment on terminology. Many readers will be familiar with the terms *formula* or *routine* (there are many others, but I restrict the discussion to L2 pragmatics; see Schmitt & McCarthy, 2004; Wray & Perkins, 2000). The terms *formula* and *routine* carry an implicit claim that the expressions under discussion are stored and retrieved whole. In the case of L2 learners especially, this claim is premature; it is, in fact, the object of investigation. Furthermore, the term *formula* has been used to describe at least two types of formulas discussed in ILP research (and in formula research more broadly): acquisitional formulas and social formulas (Bardovi-Harlig, 2006). The former arise spontaneously during the early stages of acquisition and are generally not analyzable by the interlanguage grammar (Krashen, Dulay, & Burt, 1982; Myles, Hooper, & Mitchell, 1998; Schmidt, 1983). These are thought to be stored and retrieved whole. In contrast, the latter are shared by a community and are used in specific social or discourse contexts. They may serve as input or targets for second language acquisition. It is these expressions that researchers describe as late learned and whose mastery may characterize highly advanced learners (De Cock, 2000; Foster, 2001; Granger, 1998; House, 1996; Howarth, 1998; Scarcella, 1979; Schmitt & Underwood, 2004; Spöttl & McCarthy, 2004; Yorio, 1989). In this chapter and other recent work, I refer to this second type as *conventional expressions* (instead of social formulas) to avoid implicit claims about storage or retrieval (see also Bardovi-Harlig et al., this volume; Yorio).

Learner familiarity with conventional expressions relates directly to what Pawley and Syder (1983) have called "the puzzle of nativelike selection," which describes the problem of how native speakers select conventional expressions from among a "range of grammatically correct paraphrases, many of which are nonnativelike or highly marked usages" (p. 90). According to Pawley and Syder, language learners need to learn a means of "knowing which of the well-formed sentences are nativelike—a way of distinguishing those usages that are normal or unmarked from those that are unnatural or highly marked" (p. 94).

Interlanguage pragmatics (ILP) research has long been concerned with developing measures by which to compare interlanguage development and native-speaker competence (Kasper & Schmidt, 1996). This study continues in that tradition with a contribution on conventional expressions. What Pawley and Syder (1983) called *nativelike* is defined in the pragmatics literature as community-wide use. Coulmas (1981) described conventional expressions as "tacit agreements, which the members of a community presume to be shared by every reasonable co-member. In embodying societal knowledge they are essential in the handling of day-to-day situations" (p. 4). Edmondson and House (1991) suggested that learners cannot necessarily handle social situations in the same way "because they do not have ready access to, and therefore do not make use of, standardized routines for meeting the social imposition... as native speakers do" (p. 284).

The goal of this study is to begin to explore what lies behind the reported underuse of conventional expressions in L2 pragmatics by examining recognition: If learners do not recognize conventional expressions, then the lack of use may stem from a lack of pragmalinguistic resources. If learners do recognize conventional expressions, the lack of use may stem from difficulty with retrieval or from a mismatch of L2 and target sociopragmatics, the pragmatic knowledge that governs use in context.

Previous ILP research on conventional expressions

Interest in conventional expressions in ILP parallels interest in formulas in SLA more generally, with early studies in the 1970s and a second push more recently in the first decade of 2000. The studies represent a range of approaches within ILP research. The earliest study to focus explicitly on conventional expressions in pragmatics was Scarcella (1979), which used a written dialog completion task to elicit 15 common conventional expressions including, among others, "Watch out," "Happy birthday," "Come in," and "I'm sorry." Two groups of learners were tested: 30 advanced English as a second language (ESL) students at the American Language Institute whose L1 was Spanish and 30 advanced ESL university students from mixed language backgrounds. Each response was coded as "correct," matching the control group responses, or "incorrect," not matching the control group responses. The first group showed 38% targetlike responses; the second, only 30%. Scarcella then conducted an error analysis that showed that 44% of the nonmatching responses were paraphrases (e.g., "Who's behind the door" for "Who's there?"), and 25% were partially acquired routines (e.g., "Watch up!" for "Watch out!"). The remaining 30% were divided equally among substitution, translations, and ambiguous cases. Scarcella concluded that adult second language learners have difficulty acquiring very common expressions.

Although not an empirical study, the often-cited book by Nattinger and DeCarrico (1992) brought conventional expressions, which they called *lexical phrases*, to the attention of teachers and pragmatics researchers by presenting an extensive inventory of expressions. A full chapter was devoted to the functions of lexical phrases, many of which were pragmatic in nature. An additional chapter on teaching spoken discourse included examples of conventional expressions used in the context of indirect speech acts.

The early 2000s saw a renewed interest in empirical investigations of conventional expressions in L2 pragmatics. Kecskes (2000) asked whether L2 learners of English know what conventional expressions mean. Eighty-eight learners from 10 countries responded to three written tasks: a dialog interpretation task, a dialog completion task (learners supplied missing turns in short dialogs), and a discourse completion task (learners supplied a response to a scenario). The dialog interpretation task included idioms that had both literal and figurative readings (e.g., "OK, shoot" [meaning "go ahead"], "get out of here" [meaning "don't fool me"], and "piece of cake" [meaning "easy"]). Kecskes reported that learners more readily recognized literal meanings than idiomatic ones; especially among the advanced Asian students, production was often grammatical and appropriate but not nativelike.

Roever (2005) investigated the identification of pragmatic formulas in specific situations. Roever used three tasks: an implicature task, a routines task, and a discourse completion task (DCT). The routines task is of particular interest here. The DCT presented 12 multiple-choice questions that included a brief description of a situation followed by a question such as, "What would Jack probably say?" The respondents then selected from four choices: the target expression and three distracters. The distracters were either relevant but nonidiomatic or idiomatic but irrelevant. Roever found that learners with exposure to the ESL environment scored higher than learners without such exposure: Even as little as 3 months (or less) in a target-language environment led to significantly better performance on selecting situational routines from a restricted set of options.

Bardovi-Harlig (2008) explored the relation between recognition and production of conventional expressions in a written recognition task paired with a written DCT. The recognition task presented a list of expressions from which learners were asked to identify the expressions that they knew (cf. Meara, 1989; Wesche & Paribakht, 1996 for similar procedures in vocabulary research). When the results from the recognition and production tasks were compared, the learners scored much higher on their self-reports of recognition than on production. However, because the learners from intermediate to advanced levels of proficiency reported knowing almost all of the expressions (including the distracters), one might conclude that the task was too easy or that the learner self-report of recognition was too generous. Vocabulary studies have observed that learners tend to be conservative in their judgments about whether they know words and that they underestimate rather than overestimate their knowledge (Meara), but it is possible that learners are not as conservative in their estimate of familiarity for expressions. In addition, the use of a written recognition task for what are essentially conversational expressions does not present the expressions in the same form in which they would be encountered in communication.

Developing an aural task

If testing the recognition of conventional expressions should respect the mode of expression in which the sequence normally occurs, expressions that generally belong to written discourse should be tested in writing (Granger, 1998; Nattinger & DeCarrico, 1992), and expressions that belong to conversation should be tested aurally. A written recognition task has a number of potential problems for the study of conversational expressions. Written presentations of oral expressions parse orthographically what may in speech be parsed differently. "That'd be great" looks like three words in print, but learners may not readily link its written form to the oral reduced form of [ðædbi greyt]. Results of Bardovi-Harlig (2008) suggest that tasks that ask learners to judge conversational expressions in written format may encourage them to overestimate their familiarity with an expression. In contrast, a listening-based recognition task could yield more modest self-reports and give a more accurate picture of the linguistic resources available to learners during conversation.

The methodological goal of this study is to refine the investigation of recognition of conventional conversational expressions reported by Bardovi-Harlig (2008) by using aural stimuli. Keeping in mind the learning task identified by Pawley and Syder (1983) as the puzzle of nativelike selection—that learners must develop a means of distinguishing the grammatical strings that are conventional from those that are not—this study addresses the following research question: Do adult second language learners recognize conventional expressions and distinguish between them and corresponding modified expressions that are grammatical but not conventional? The following two sections discuss how particular conventional expressions have been identified in previous studies and how they were identified in the present study.

Identifying conventional expressions in previous studies

At the heart of the task are the identification criteria and the resultant inventory of expressions, two elements that often differ considerably from study to study. The expressions have been selected for their literal and idiomatic interpretations (Kecskes, 2000), high rates of native speaker (NS) agreement (Roever, 2005), frequency and value in academic English (Schmitt, Dörnyei, Adolphs, & Durow, 2004), and use in previous studies (Bardovi-Harlig, 2008).

Roever (2005), following standard practice in ILP research, used high NS agreement to determine targetlike responses. In Roever's study, the multiple-choice items that tested the recognition of expressions in context were piloted three times. Each item was matched with one targeted expression and three distracters that took the form of plausible alternatives. The contexts were determined to be generally familiar to test-takers and included school, work, and everyday life. All targeted expressions showed high agreement among NSs of American English, but as Roever pointed out (p. 47), frequency or typicality was not empirically investigated.

Frequency was a central concern for Schmitt et al. (2004); although not a study of pragmatics, their approach is instructive. They used three main criteria for selection of instructionally relevant expressions: (a) frequency as determined by occurrence in three corpora (one each of a written, oral, and academic corpus); (b) connection to academic discourse, and (c) usefulness to students and worthiness of being taught. Candidate formulas identified by steps a and b were checked for their presence in program textbooks. From an original candidate list of about 150 expressions, 45 were presented to program ESL instructors, and a resultant list of 20 target expressions was chosen through instructor surveys and discussion.

Using published sources, Bardovi-Harlig (2008) constructed a list of 63 items, 59 of which were compiled from pragmatics production studies (Takahashi, 2005), recognition studies (Kecskes, 2000; Roever, 2005), formula lists (Nattinger & DeCarrico, 1992), and current usage suggested by ESL teachers (such as "my bad"). Although the majority of the items in the task had been supplied by NSs in previous studies, I had anticipated that the expressions that were unknown to individual learners would serve as controls for familiar ones, that is, that learners would rate unknown expressions as not recognized. This expectation was not met because the learners reported recognizing almost all of the expressions.

Method

Identifying conventional expressions in the present study

Taking previous studies into account, the objective of this study was to establish an inventory of conventional expressions that were used in the university community without restricting the context too narrowly to the university campus. The list of conventional expressions for the present study was developed through multiple stages: (a) observation of conversations, (b) scenario construction, (c) piloting, (d) further revision and culling of expressions, (e) repiloting, and (f) selection of final contexts and expressions. Steps a through e were carried out by students enrolled in the Seminar in Interlanguage Pragmatics, Spring 2006, at Indiana University. In the observation stage, the researchers collected spontaneous speech of graduate-student peers, undergraduates, friends, families, and community members. We used field notes and recordings to identify conventional expressions and the contexts in which they occurred. Following Myles et al. (1998, p. 325), we identified conventional expressions that were (a) at least two morphemes in length; (b) phonologically coherent—

that is, fluently articulated, nonhesitant; (c) used repeatedly and always in the same form; (d) situationally dependent; and (e) community-wide in use, the latter being interpreted as frequent in the sample collected. We next constructed 77 scenarios designed to elicit the same expressions in a controlled task.

The 77 scenarios were then piloted with NSs of English who were university students. Both oral and written responses were collected, and the results were reviewed by the seminar. Scenarios that did not elicit conventional expressions were eliminated. Scenarios that elicited conventional expressions and shared a word or phrase with the responses were rewritten to avoid the lexical overlap.

A subset of 44 retained and revised scenarios was retested in the second pilot study. The means of data collection was aural/oral. One of the researchers read the scenarios from a script. The participants' oral responses were digitally recorded on computers. Because an informal survey of the ESL teachers had indicated that undergraduates were the NS population with whom the learners had the most contact, 28 undergraduates who were not studying linguistics were recruited to complete the task.

Following the second pilot, the author and an assistant identified the most consistently used of the conventional expressions in 30 scenarios, yielding 35 expressions. Expressions that were selected either occurred in 50% or more of the responses or were one of up to three conventional expressions that exhaustively constituted the response set. In this way, the expressions that were selected for the recognition task were common to the university community in which the learners studied and lived.

Instrument

The recognition task consisted of 60 items that were based on the NS responses to the second pilot using the oral DCT as described above. Of the 60 items, 35 of the items were taken verbatim from NS production data in the pilot; these are the authentic expressions. These included complete expressions such as "I'm just looking," "Nice to meet you," and "Thank you for having me"; frames such as "Would you like to...?"; and phrases that recurred in NS production such as "my place" (in invitations) and "other plans" (in refusals to invitations). Of the 60 total items, most were complete expressions (56/60).

The other 25 items were modified either lexically or grammatically. No items were ungrammatical. For lexical modifications, a near synonym from the same word frequency band was substituted to make a grammatical expression that contained common words, and this resulted in a string that is neither a conventional expression nor often heard as a unit. The word frequency counts were those of Cobb (2006). The resulting pairs included conventional and modified expressions such as "Excuse the mess"/"Excuse the dirt," "I'm just looking"/"I'm just seeing," and "I'm late"/"I'm tardy." There were 18 pairs that differed by a lexical item. The other seven changes were more grammatical in nature. Three modified items provided a full form instead of the NS reduced form as in "You're welcome"/"You are welcome" or "Excuse me"/"You excuse me." One added a single morpheme, from the authentic "no problem" to "no problems"; another changed the particle in "watch out" to "watch up"; and two substituted the modal "could" for "would," resulting in the pairs "would you mind"/"could you mind" and "would you like to"/"could you like to." The authentic and modified items were separated, and their orders were randomized in the recorded presentation.

Procedure

The expressions were all digitally recorded by a single speaker in a sound booth and were played to participants through individual headsets. Each expression was heard twice. The items were separated by pauses of 7 s. The task was only presented aurally. The only thing the participants saw was their answer sheet. The full recognition task took about 12 minutes with instructions and examples. The list of expressions used in the task is given in the appendix.

Recognition was operationalized as the determination of how often the participants reported hearing a string of words together and in the same order.[2] The instructions were as follows:

If you hear these words together and always in the same order, and you hear them often, circle "I often hear this." If you hear a phrase less often, circle "I sometimes hear this." If you never hear these words together or in this order, circle "I never hear this."

Two training examples were given before the task began. The answer sheet was set up as shown in the examples. There was an item number and three choices for each expression.

Example A: Good morning
(I often hear this)   I sometimes hear this   I never hear this
Example B: Bad morning
I often hear this   I sometimes hear this   (I never hear this)

As in Bardovi-Harlig and Dörnyei's (1998) study, the learners were trained on a very obvious example. Obvious (and admittedly sometimes funny) examples are used so that learners immediately recognize the problem and what they are being asked to judge.

The recognition task was administered as the first of three tasks in a larger study: the audio recognition task discussed here, an audio-visual production task (Bardovi-Harlig et al., this volume), and a background questionnaire.

Participants

A total of 172 participants completed the task: 123 learners of ESL and 49 NSs of American English who attended or taught at the same university the learners attended. The learners ranged in age from 17 to 36 years with a mean of 23.8.[3] The NSs comprised two groups: undergraduates and ESL teachers. The 35 undergraduates ranged in age from 18 to 40 years with a mean age of

20.0. This group is called NS peers. The 14 teachers ranged from 23 to 62 years, with a mean of 43.1. Three of the ESL teachers were also graduate students. This group is called NS teachers.[4]

The learners were enrolled in four levels of classes in an intensive English program, from low-intermediate at level 3 to low-advanced at level 6. Each level of instruction is 7 weeks long, with 135 to 165 hours of instruction. The learners represented 11 language backgrounds: Arabic (n = 55), Chinese (n = 12), Korean (n = 28), Japanese (n = 13), Thai (n = 5), Spanish (n = 3), Turkish (n = 2), Portuguese (n = 2), and 1 each of Italian, Tibetan, and Kazakh. The L1s are fairly well distributed across the levels, with the exception of level 3, where 24 of the 35 learners reported Arabic as their L1. The learners reported a mean length of residence in the US of 5.0 months and among those who answered the question, a mean length of English study prior to their ESL experience of 4.7 years.

Analysis

Each response was converted into a number. "I never hear this" received 0 points; "I sometimes hear this," 1 point; and "I often hear this" received 2 points. A mixed model analysis was conducted to address the question of whether the participants recognized the authentic expressions more or less readily than the modified expressions and whether this difference depended on proficiency level. This analysis was chosen because it includes each of the individual item responses and appropriately accounts for the natural correlation of items within participants. In addition, it avoids loss of participants due to missing responses when participants failed to provide an answer or circled two options in their responses.

The model included fixed effects for group (four learner groups and two NS groups), authenticity (whether the conventional expression was authentic or modified), and the interaction between group and authenticity. A random effect was included for participant.

Results

The conventional expressions typically received higher scores than their modified counterparts. There was not a significant difference among the groups when all responses (modified and authentic) were taken as a whole (p = .067). However, there was a significant difference between responses given to modified and authentic conventional expressions (p < .001). Authentic expressions were accepted as being heard significantly more often than modified responses (Table 1). In addition, the interaction between group (learner levels 3–6, NS peers, and NS teachers) and authenticity (whether the conventional expression was authentic or modified) was also significant (p < .001). As the learner proficiency level increased, the acceptance of the modified expressions decreased, whereas their acceptance of authentic expressions increased (Figure 1).

Table 1. Mean recognition scores for authentic and modified expressions by level

	\multicolumn{10}{c}{level/group}
	3		4		5		6		NS peer		NS teachers	
	M	SE	M	SE	M	SE	M	SE	M	SE	M	SE
authentic	1.42	0.04	1.48	0.04	1.54	0.04	1.56	0.05	1.72	0.04	1.84	0.06
modified	0.86	0.04	0.85	0.04	0.80	0.04	0.69	0.05	0.31	0.04	0.32	0.06

note: Estimated marginal means from mixed model.

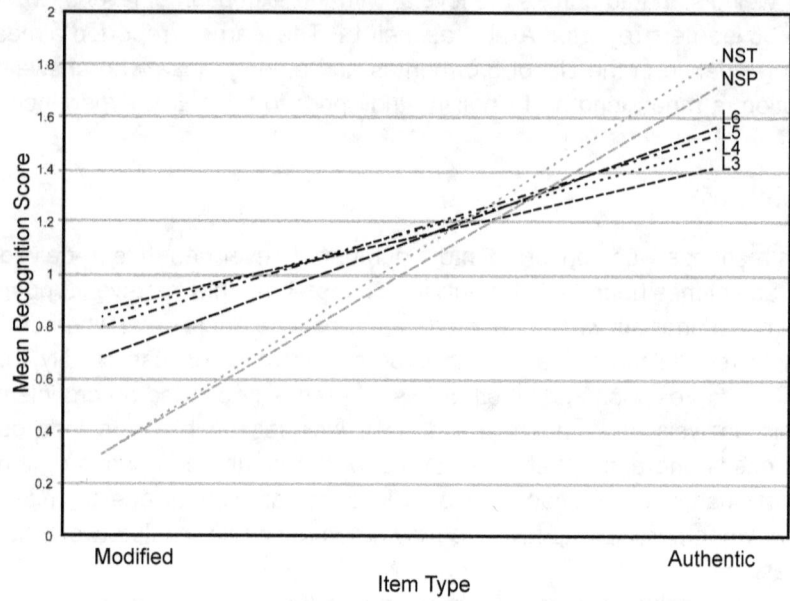

Figure 1. Mean recognition scores by item type by level.

Table 2 presents the level/group scores for each expression and is arranged in descending order of NS peer scores. The 25 modified expressions occupy the last 23 places in the table with two modified expressions, "I gotta leave" and "You are welcome," in places 26 and 27 from the bottom of the table.

Table 2. Self-reported recognition of expressions in descending order

	\multicolumn{6}{c}{level/group}
	3	4	5	6	NSP	NST
	n=35	n=31	n=32	n=25	n=35	n=14
No, thanks	1.83	1.84	1.91	1.83	2.00	2.00
Thank you	2.00	2.00	1.94	2.00	2.00	2.00
You're welcome	1.91	1.97	1.97	2.00	2.00	2.00
No problem	1.97	1.94	1.97	2.00	1.97	2.00
Excuse me	2.00	2.00	1.97	2.00	1.97	2.00

I'm sorry	2.00	1.97	2.00	2.00	1.94	2.00
That'd be great	1.46	1.77	1.70	1.48	1.91	1.93
Nice to meet you	2.00	2.00	2.00	2.00	1.91	1.93
Watch out!	0.80	1.19	1.24	1.44	1.91	1.93
I gotta go	1.60	1.77	1.55	1.64	1.89	1.93
Be careful!	1.83	1.81	1.97	1.88	1.89	1.86
You too	1.94	1.84	1.88	1.92	1.89	2.00
Shut up	1.31	1.42	1.58	1.42	1.86	1.54
I'm late	1.77	1.77	1.88	1.88	1.86	1.86
I'm just looking	1.89	1.84	1.76	1.92	1.80	2.00
I'd love to	1.20	1.26	1.48	1.76	1.80	2.00
I was wondering	0.80	1.35	1.27	1.52	1.80	1.71
Be quiet!	1.57	1.45	1.82	1.80	1.80	1.71
Want a ride?	0.86	0.71	0.94	0.96	1.77	1.93
Can I get a ride?	1.20	1.45	1.39	1.32	1.77	1.64
I'm looking for	1.91	1.84	1.88	2.00	1.74	1.57
Would you like to?	1.83	1.77	2.00	1.84	1.74	1.64
Thank you for having me	0.57	0.48	0.45	0.28	1.71	2.00
Do you have a minute?	0.91	1.35	1.55	1.52	1.71	2.00
Would you mind?	1.40	1.81	1.88	1.92	1.71	1.93
Can I leave a message?	1.65	1.63	1.71	1.73	1.66	2.00
Other plans	1.26	1.35	1.27	1.44	1.65	1.07
Thanks for your time	1.60	1.67	1.58	1.72	1.60	1.93
Nice to see you	1.71	1.61	1.70	1.92	1.54	2.00
That works for me	1.00	1.29	1.33	1.40	1.43	1.77
Sure thing	0.40	0.45	0.55	0.58	1.37	1.62
Keep it down	1.37	1.16	1.33	1.08	1.31	1.50
My place	1.03	0.81	0.73	0.96	1.29	1.64
I gotta leave	1.46	1.42	1.24	1.36	1.26	1.29
You are welcome	1.86	1.94	1.88	1.88	1.20	0.79
The place is messy	0.51	0.87	1.12	1.16	1.11	1.36
Excuse the mess	0.43	0.35	0.30	0.12	1.03	1.71
Other activities	1.09	1.03	1.12	1.20	1.00	1.07
I thank you for your time	0.94	1.16	0.85	1.00	0.91	0.86
I'm just seeing	1.14	1.03	1.13	1.04	0.63	0.36
Do you have an hour?	0.71	0.87	0.88	0.44	0.49	0.57
You also	1.14	1.23	1.03	0.76	0.40	0.43

continued...

Table 2. Self-reported recognition of expressions in descending order *(cont.)*

	level/group					
	3 *n*=35	4 *n*=31	5 *n*=32	6 *n*=25	NSP *n*=35	NST *n*=14
Be cautious!	0.20	0.35	0.44	0.32	0.37	0.36
No problems	1.83	1.55	1.06	1.24	0.26	0.00
Excuse the dirt	0.17	0.10	0.21	0.00	0.18	0.36
Be silent	1.03	0.81	0.79	0.60	0.21	0.21
No, please	1.31	1.23	1.12	0.92	0.14	0.57
I'm tardy	0.34	0.52	0.56	0.16	0.17	0.36
Could you mind?	1.31	1.19	1.06	1.21	0.14	0.07
My pad	0.60	0.39	0.36	0.28	0.14	0.21
The place is untidy	0.20	0.32	0.33	0.12	0.12	0.50
You excuse me	0.63	0.33	0.48	0.36	0.09	0.00
Certain thing	0.17	0.52	0.73	0.84	0.09	0.00
Quiet up	0.21	0.23	0.24	0.16	0.06	0.14
Make it down	0.83	0.77	0.73	0.36	0.03	0.00
Can I get a drive?	0.91	0.94	0.82	0.68	0.00	0.00
Nice to introduce you	0.66	0.71	0.36	0.32	0.00	0.00
Nice to look at you	0.77	0.48	0.53	0.32	0.00	0.00
Watch up!	0.94	1.06	1.21	1.16	0.00	0.00
Could you like to?	1.09	0.97	0.73	0.48	0.00	0.00

note: NSP = native-speaker peer; NST = native-speaker teacher.

Readers will notice that the NS teachers reported that they heard more expressions more often than the NS peers. Thirteen expressions received unanimous ratings of "I often hear this" (2.00) from NS teachers compared to three expressions from NS peers. Although it is possible that this relates to the difference in the sizes of the NS groups, NS teachers and peers also showed significant differences on a related oral-production task (Bardovi-Harlig et al., this volume). As a mother of two college students, I was amused to see that "Excuse the mess" showed the greatest difference between peers (1.03) and teachers (1.71).

Some modifications resulted in phrases that were more accepted by NSs than others. Table 3 presents the scores for each of the 25 pairs. The full form "You are welcome" was rated 1.20, "sometimes," by NS peers compared to 2.00 for the reduced form, "You're welcome." Similarly, "I thank you for your time" was rated .91, a weak "sometimes" by NS peers compared to "Thanks for your time" (1.60, peers; 1.93, teachers). In contrast, "You excuse me" was not recognized by even lower level learners. Of the lexical substitutions, "I gotta leave" was rated as 1.26 and 1.29, a strong "sometimes," by NS peers and teachers, respectively. This was a modification of "I gotta go," derived from a scenario in which the speaker is talking on a cell phone when his or her bus comes. "Other plans" was an expression that was widely used by NSs in an invitation-rejection scenario in the pilot study and ranked 1.65 and 1.07 by peers and teachers, respectively; the corresponding modification "other activities" was reported to be sometimes heard (1.00 and 1.07).

Table 3. Recognition of authentic and modified expressions

	level/group					
	3	4	5	6	NSP	NST
	n=35	n=31	n=32	n25	n=35	n=14
No, thanks	1.83	1.84	1.91	1.83	2.00	2.00
No, please	1.31	1.23	1.12	0.92	0.14	0.57
You're welcome	1.91	1.97	1.97	2.00	2.00	2.00
You are welcome	1.86	1.94	1.88	1.88	1.20	0.79
No problem	1.97	1.94	1.97	2.00	1.97	2.00
No problems	1.83	1.55	1.06	1.24	0.26	0.00
Excuse me	2.00	2.00	1.97	2.00	1.97	2.00
You excuse me	0.63	0.33	0.48	0.36	0.09	0.00
Nice to meet you	2.00	2.00	2.00	2.00	1.91	1.93
Nice to introduce you	0.66	0.71	0.36	0.32	0.00	0.00
Watch out!	0.80	1.19	1.24	1.44	1.91	1.93
Watch up!	0.94	1.06	1.21	1.16	0.00	0.00
I gotta go	1.60	1.77	1.55	1.64	1.89	1.93
I gotta leave	1.46	1.42	1.24	1.36	1.26	1.29
Be careful!	1.83	1.81	1.97	1.88	1.89	1.86
Be cautious!	0.20	0.35	0.44	0.32	0.37	0.36
You too	1.94	1.84	1.88	1.92	1.89	2.00
You also	1.14	1.23	1.03	0.76	0.40	0.43
I'm late	1.77	1.77	1.88	1.88	1.86	1.86
I'm tardy	0.34	0.52	0.56	0.16	0.17	0.36
Shut up	1.31	1.42	1.58	1.42	1.86	1.54
Quiet up	0.21	0.23	0.24	0.16	0.06	0.14
I'm just looking	1.89	1.84	1.76	1.92	1.80	2.00
I'm just seeing	1.14	1.03	1.13	1.04	0.63	0.36
Be quiet!	1.57	1.45	1.82	1.80	1.80	1.71
Be silent!	1.03	0.81	0.79	0.60	0.21	0.21
Can I get a ride?	1.20	1.45	1.39	1.32	1.77	1.64
Can I get a drive?	0.91	0.94	0.82	0.68	0.00	0.00
Would you like to?	1.83	1.77	2.00	1.84	1.74	1.64
Could you like to?	1.09	0.97	0.73	0.48	0.00	0.00
Do you have a minute?	0.91	1.35	1.55	1.52	1.71	2.00
Do you have an hour?	0.71	0.87	0.91	0.44	0.49	0.57

continued...

Table 3. Recognition of authentic and modified expressions *(cont.)*

	level/group					
	3 *n*=35	4 *n*=31	5 *n*=32	6 *n*25	NSP *n*=35	NST *n*=14
Would you mind?	1.40	1.81	1.88	1.92	1.71	1.93
Could you mind?	1.31	1.19	1.06	1.21	0.14	0.07
Other plans	1.26	1.35	1.27	1.44	1.65	1.07
Other activities	1.09	1.03	1.12	1.20	1.00	1.07
Thanks for your time	1.60	1.67	1.58	1.72	1.60	1.93
I thank you for your time	0.94	1.16	0.85	1.00	0.91	0.86
Nice to see you	1.71	1.61	1.70	1.92	1.54	2.00
Nice to look at you	0.77	0.48	0.55	0.32	0.00	0.00
Sure thing	0.40	0.45	0.55	0.58	1.37	1.62
Certain thing	0.17	0.52	0.73	0.84	0.09	0.00
Keep it down	1.37	1.16	1.33	1.08	1.31	1.50
Make it down	0.83	0.77	0.73	0.36	0.03	0.00
My place	1.03	0.81	0.73	0.96	1.29	1.64
My pad	0.60	0.39	0.36	0.28	0.14	0.21
The place is messy	0.51	0.87	1.12	1.16	1.11	1.36
The place is untidy	0.20	0.32	0.33	0.12	0.12	0.50
Excuse the mess	0.43	0.35	0.30	0.12	1.03	1.71
Excuse the dirt	0.17	0.10	0.21	0.00	0.18	0.36

note: NSP = native-speaker peer; NST = native-speaker teacher.

The learner data revealed that some expressions are recognized very early. Fourteen authentic expressions received a rating of 1.70 or better by learners in level 3. These include "No thanks," "Thank you," "You're welcome," "No problem," "Excuse me," "I'm sorry," "Nice to meet you," "Be careful," "You too," "I'm late," "I'm just looking," "I'm looking for," "Would you like to?", and "Nice to see you." An additional three conventional expressions received ratings of 1.57–1.60 by level 3 ("I gotta go," "Thanks for your time," and "Be quiet!"). In other cases, learners gradually came to recognize authentic expressions, and differences across levels show a developmental picture, as reported in Tables 2 and 3.

As Tables 1–3 show, the learner reports of recognition do not always match those of the NSs. Sometimes the learners rated the authentic expressions lower than the NSs did (e.g., "Want a ride?", "Thank you for having me," "Excuse the mess," and "Sure thing"), and other times, they rated the modified expressions higher than the NSs did (e.g., "I'm just seeing," "You also," and "No problems"). Each set of ratings is considered in turn below. Both "Thank you for having me" and "Excuse the mess" may violate some interlanguage grammars, which may explain their low rankings. "Thank you for having me" includes a stative predicate ("have") that is progressive, a highly nonprototypical form potentially ruled out by interlanguage grammars (Andersen & Shirai, 1996; Bardovi-Harlig, 2000). Although "Excuse me" was rated very high, with only one level reporting less than a perfect score of "I often hear this," the learners rejected both direct objects, "the mess" ("excuse the mess") and "the dirt" ("excuse the dirt"; Table 3). This response pattern suggests that "excuse" was not transitive in the learners' L2 grammar. In fact, "excuse" may allow no arguments other than "me" because "You excuse me" is also reported to be unfamiliar. If correct, this analysis would explain why the learners rejected these phrases; in past studies, learners have been reported to reject combinations in the input that are not consistent with their level of grammatical development (Bardovi-Harlig, 2001). Yorio (1989) also reported that conventional expressions are subject to interlanguage rules.

The reason for the low scores for "Want a ride?" is not obvious. On the one hand, the word "ride" might not have been recognized. However, the validity of this explanation is questionable considering that "Can I get a ride?" has scores of 1.20–1.45. On the other hand, the learners may have been offered rides less often than their NS peers and not often by NSs, who are more likely to offer a ride using this expression. The lower recognition of "Sure thing" is not surprising given the relatively weak rating by the peers (1.38). In the development phase of the task, "sure" alone was produced more frequently than "Sure thing," but "Sure thing" was selected for the recognition task because it was phrasal.

Equally important to the development of conventional expressions is recognizing what is possible but not generally said or heard. This is precisely the problem of nativelike selection (Pawley & Syder, 1983). In this dataset, this is an important source of difference between the NSs and the learners because the learners tended to overaccept unconventional strings. Modified expressions with relatively high ratings compared to the NS ratings include "I'm just seeing," "You also," "No problems," "No please," "Be silent," "Could you mind," "You excuse me," "Certain thing," "Could you like to?", and "Watch up!" (Table 3). Because all of the modified expressions are grammatical, increased grammatical competence should not influence recognition of expressions. Instead, additional input might help learners move from recognizing an undifferentiated set of grammatical strings to distinguishing a smaller subset of conventional strings.

In addition to NS-learner differences, changes across learner levels are instructive in the study of recognition. The learners allowed both "would" and "could" in "Would you mind" and "Would you like to" but slowly began to report that they did not recognize "Could you like to" by level 6, although "Could you mind" stays in the "I sometimes hear this" range. The pair of phrasal verbs also proved interesting: The learners rated "Watch up" higher than "Watch out" in level 3 and almost equal in level 4 before "Watch out" won out in level 6. It is interesting to note that although "Watch out" pulled ahead in recognition, the learners did not report not recognizing "Watch up" (Table 3).

Finally, it appears that some of the rankings are between truly pragmatic choices and are less likely to reflect L2 grammar. The choice of "Thanks for your time" and "I thank you for your time" may reflect distance between interlocutors or level of imposition of the thanked-for action, and the longer expression may also appeal to a learner's general preference for full forms because of their transparency.

The results in this section center on group scores for individual expressions. Another perspective on learner performance is to consider individual scores across expressions. Although treatment of this is beyond the scope of this chapter, individual variation is worth considering for what it reveals about a learner's receptivity to the input. On one end are the learners with low scores: The three lowest range from 0.63 to 0.72. Although considerably lower than NS rankings for authentic expressions, the lowest scores follow the NS pattern of distinguishing authentic from modified expressions, ranking authentic expressions 3 to 6 times higher than modified expressions. In contrast, the learners with the highest scores reported hearing the modified expressions as often as the conventional ones. The three highest scores are between 1.88 and 1.98. The ratings that these learners reported do not discriminate between authentic and modified expressions. Without discrimination, these learners seemed to respond to all of the items on the task by saying, "Yes, that's English." Differences in receptivity may lead to different acquisitional outcomes, a topic worth exploring in the future.

Discussion and conclusion

The learners' abilities to distinguish between conventional expressions and their modified counterparts suggest that they are on the path toward nativelike selection. In this task, nativelike selection, the discrimination of the conventional (and grammatical) from the merely grammatical, involves two judgments: recognizing what expressions are heard and recognizing what expressions are not heard. The cross-sectional results show that the learners in level 6 ruled out significantly more modified expressions than in levels 3 and 4, suggesting development. The identification of authentic expressions increased with level but not significantly. One possible interpretation is that proficiency (as represented by instructional level) is not as powerful a determinant as length of exposure (measured as length of stay), which Olshtain and Blum-Kulka (1985) and Roever (2005) found to be a good predictor. Length of stay information for most of the learners was provided on the background questionnaires and could be further investigated.

A second interpretation of the recognition scores for authentic expressions is that learners can reach only a modest level of recognition without instruction directed at conventional expressions, which these learners did not have. The summer that these data were collected, there was an elective course on slang in the intensive English program. Learners from this class were invited to participate in this project, although their numbers were too small to be included in the subsequent analyses. Given that the slang class focused on common expressions, presumably raising awareness, we were interested in comparing learners enrolled in this class with learners of comparable proficiency who did not have the benefit of this lexical instruction. This is certainly an interesting question to return to. Moreover, although recognizing conventional expressions may require greater exposure to the target language in use (including perhaps instruction), it may also require that learners overcome initial resistance to some expressions that are grammatically or semantically nonprototypical.

Looking at individual learner performance in the area of conventional expressions (Bardovi-Harlig, 2006; Kecskes, 2000) may prove to be important because the recognition results suggest that there may be a continuum of learners with respect to the ability or inclination to discriminate among expressions they hear in the target language. At one end of the continuum, there are learners who report low recognition of the conventional expressions. At the other end of the continuum, there are learners who report having heard every expression. In the middle are learners who discriminate among the expressions in a similar way to native speakers. Future work might profitably investigate whether these learner types behave differently on other recognition tasks, such as Roever's (2005) multiple-choice selection in context or Kecskes' interpretation task, or on production tasks (Bardovi-Harlig, 2009; Bardovi-Harlig et al., this volume).

The recognition task used here overcame problems of the binary recognition task used previously by Bardovi-Harlig (2008). Three important changes were made: the use of aural stimuli, presentation of three response choices ("I often/sometimes/never hear this"), and use of authentic expressions piloted in the local community with modified counterparts. As has long been the practice in ILP research, it would be interesting to compare this task with others, using the same learner populations across tasks. This task explores pragmalinguistic resources by testing the recognition of conventional expressions in isolation. Contextualized judgment tasks such as that used by Roever (2005) may yield different results. Respondents who rated authentic and modified expressions similarly may rate them differently if the expressions were presented in their original contexts. For example, whether learners would distinguish between "I gotta go" and "I gotta leave" in a telephone closing is an empirical question. Modifications would need to be made to the traditional written form of the multiple-choice questionnaires previously used, but one could envision web-based tests such as Roever used, including a–d choices that would play audio when clicked on rather than providing written selections. As an alternative, learners could be given a context and asked to rate a single aurally presented selection without competing distracters.

The list of 60 expressions tested here is small compared to the greater context of conventional expressions (see various estimates in Nattinger & DeCarrico, 1992, among others), and it is not a given that these results are generalizable because of the lexical nature of the expressions. However, there are likely to be classes of items to which participants would respond similarly. Revisions of the task might include substituting lower scoring authentic expressions for higher scoring ones (after additional piloting) and adding additional items with grammatical modifications to better balance the task between lexical and grammatical modification. Because tense-aspect morphology often functions in mitigation, pairs like "I was wondering" and "I am wondering" would be good candidates. Additional pairs of full and reduced forms would also explore the balance of target grammar, interlanguage grammar, and conventional expressions. One lesson to be learned from this task is to only select the first choice (i.e., most frequent) expression. In the original elicitation, for example, "The place is a mess" was the preferred expression and "The place is messy" was a runner-up in response to the same scenario. The latter was selected because it was easier to modify. However, the cost of doing that was an expression that was not highly rated by NSs.

Many studies of formulas conclude with suggestions for teaching them to second and foreign language learners (e.g., Foster, 2001; Granger, 1998; Nattinger & DeCarrico, 1992). It seems premature to make extensive recommendations based on this study; however, I venture one observation related directly to the aural stimuli used in this task. Based on a comparison of the results of the present and Bardovi-Harlig's (2008) studies, it would seem that needs assessment, presentation of input, and testing of conventional expressions should match the mode in which they are generally used. Conversational expressions should be identified aurally; expressions used in writing should be presented in writing.

The original goal of Bardovi-Harlig (2008) was to study the relationship of the recognition of conventional expressions to their production by learners in the context of L2 pragmatics. The motivation was to explore whether the lack of use of conventional expressions by learners reported in the literature was related to a lack of pragmalinguistic resources. As discussed above, elements of the design, including the binary choice, written presentation, means of selection of expressions, and the limited numbers of items that appeared on both the recognition and production tasks, hampered the interpretation of the pilot results. As a result of the new design, the present task yielded results that can now be compared to production results with some degree of confidence. The next stage of this ongoing project is to compare production on a related oral DCT (Bardovi-Harlig et al., this volume) to the recognition results presented here (Bardovi-Harlig, 2009). Possible matched outcomes include high recognition and high use of expressions and low recognition and low use. If nonuse relates to nonrecognition, interpretation—and pedagogical intervention—is fairly straightforward. However, if high recognition does not always lead to high and appropriate use, this will raise many interesting questions about access, retrieval, and contextualized use that remain to be investigated.

Notes

1 I would like to thank Edelmira Nickels and Amanda Edmonds for their extensive discussion of this chapter.
2 This is consistent with Schmidt's (1995) formulation of noticing, a low level of awareness, as the "conscious registration of the occurrence of some event" (p. 29).
3 A total of 131 background questionnaires were completed. Of those, 125 reported a numeric response to age; 90 reported length of English study.
4 The decision to keep the NS groups separate on the basis of age and status is justified by the fact that they were reliably significantly different from each other.

References

Andersen, R. W., & Shirai, Y. (1996). The primacy of aspect in first and second language acquisition: The pidgin-creole connection. In W. C. Ritchie & T. K. Bhatia (Eds.), *Handbook of second language acquisition* (pp. 527–570). San Diego, CA: Academic Press.

Bardovi-Harlig, K. (2000). *Tense and aspect in second language acquisition: Form, meaning, and use.* Oxford, England: Blackwell.

Bardovi-Harlig, K. (2001). Evaluating the empirical evidence: Grounds for instruction in pragmatics? In K. R. Rose & G. Kasper (Eds.), *Pragmatics in language teaching* (pp. 13–32). New York: Cambridge University Press.

Bardovi-Harlig, K. (2006). On the role of formulas in the acquisition of L2 pragmatics. In K. Bardovi-Harlig, C. Félix-Brasdefer, & A. S. Omar (Eds.), *Pragmatics and language learning* (Vol. 11, pp. 1–28). Honolulu: University of Hawai'i, National Foreign Language Resource Center.

Bardovi-Harlig, K. (2008). Recognition and production of formulas in L2 pragmatics. In Z.-H. Han (Ed.), *Understanding second language process* (pp. 205–222). Clevedon, England: Multilingual Matters.

Bardovi-Harlig, K. (2009). Conventional expressions as a pragmalinguistic resource: Recognition and production of conventional expressions in L2 pragmatics. *Language Learning, 49*, 755–795.

Bardovi-Harlig, K., & Dörnyei, Z. (1998). Do language learners recognize pragmatic violations? Pragmatic vs. grammatical awareness in instructed L2 learning. *TESOL Quarterly, 32*, 233–259.

Blum-Kulka, S., & Olshtain, E. (1986). Too many words: Length of utterance and pragmatic failure. *Studies in Second Language Acquisition, 8*, 165–180.

Cobb, T. (2006). *Compleat lexical tutor.* Retrieved July 6, 2006, 2006, from http://132.208.224.131/

Coulmas, F. (1981). *Conversational routine: Explorations in standardized communication situations and prepatterned speech.* The Hague: Mouton.

De Cock, S. (2000). Repetitive phrasal chunkiness and advanced EFL speech and writing. In C. Mair & M. Hundt (Eds.), *Corpus linguistics and linguistic theory* (pp. 51–68). Amsterdam: Rodopi.

Edmondson, W., & House, J. (1991). Do learners talk too much? The waffle phenomenon in interlanguage pragmatics. In R. Phillipson, E. Kellerman, L. Selinker, M. Sharwood Smith, & M. Swain (Eds.), *Foreign/second language pedagogy research: A commemorative volume for Claus Færch* (pp. 273–287). Clevedon, England: Multilingual Matters.

Foster, P. (2001). Rules and routines: A consideration of their role in the task-based language production of native and non-native speakers. In M. Bygate, P. Skehan, & M. Swain (Eds.), *Researching pedagogical tasks: Second language learning, teaching and testing* (pp. 75–93). Harlow, England: Longman.

Granger, S. (1998). Prefabricated patterns in advanced EFL writing: Collocations and formulae. In A. P. Cowie (Ed.), *Phraseology: Theory, analysis, and applications* (pp. 145–160). Oxford, England: Clarendon.

House, J. (1996). Developing pragmatic fluency in English as a foreign language: Routines and metapragmatic awareness. *Studies in Second Language Acquisition, 17*, 225–252.

Howarth, P. (1998). The phraseology of learners' academic writing. In A. P. Cowie (Ed.), *Phraseology: Theory, analysis, and applications* (pp. 161–186). Oxford, England: Clarendon.

Kasper, G., & Blum-Kulka, S. (1993). Interlanguage pragmatics: An introduction. In G. Kasper & S. Blum-Kulka (Eds.), *Interlanguage pragmatics* (pp. 1–17). New York: Oxford University Press.

Kasper, G., & Schmidt, R. (1996). Developmental issues in interlanguage pragmatics. *Studies in Second Language Acquisition, 18*, 149–169.

Kecskes, I. (2000). Conceptual fluency and the use of situation-bound utterances. *Links & Letters, 7*, 145–161.

Krashen, S., Dulay, H., & Burt, M. (1982). *Language two.* New York: Oxford University Press.

Meara, P. (1909). Matrix models of vocabulary acquisition. *AILA Review, 6*, 66–85.

Myles, F., Hooper, J., & Mitchell, R. (1998). Rote or rule? Exploring the role of formulaic language in classroom foreign language learning. *Language Learning, 48*, 323–363.

Nattinger, J. R., & DeCarrico, J. S. (1992). *Lexical phrases and language teaching.* Oxford, England: Oxford University Press.

Olshtain, E., & Blum-Kulka, S. (1985). Degree of approximation: Nonnative reactions to native speech act behavior. In S. M. Gass & C. Madden (Eds.), *Input in second language acquisition* (pp. 303–325). Rowley, MA: Newbury House.

Pawley, A., & Syder, F. H. (1983). Two puzzles for linguistic theory: Nativelike selection and nativelike fluency. In J. C. Richards & R. W. Schmidt (Eds.), *Language and communication* (pp. 191–226). London: Longman.

Roever, C. (2005). *Testing ESL pragmatics: Development and validation of a web-based assessment battery.* Berlin: Peter Lang.

Scarcella, R. C. (1979). Watch up! *Working Papers in Bilingualism, 19,* 79–88.

Schmidt, R. (1983). Interaction, acculturation, and the acquisition of communicative competence: A case study of an adult. In E. Judd & N. Wolfson (Eds.), *Sociolinguistics and language acquisition* (pp.137–174). Rowley, MA: Newbury House.

Schmidt, R. (1995). Consciousness and foreign language learning: A tutorial on the role of attention and awareness in learning. In R. Schmidt (Ed.), *Attention and awareness in foreign language learning* (pp. 1–63). Honolulu: University of Hawai'i, Second Language Teaching and Curriculum Center.

Schmitt, N., & Carter, R. (2004). Formulaic sequences in action: An introduction. In N. Schmitt (Ed.), *Formulaic sequences: Acquisition, processing and use* (pp. 1–22). Amsterdam: Benjamins.

Schmitt, N., Dörnyei, Z., Adolphs, S., & Durow, V. (2004). Knowledge and acquisition of formulaic sequences. In N. Schmitt (Ed.), *Formulaic sequences: Acquisition, processing and use* (pp. 55–86). Amsterdam: Benjamins.

Schmitt, N., & Underwood, G. (2004). Exploring the processing of formulaic sequences through a self-paced reading task. In N. Schmitt (Ed.), *Formulaic sequences: Acquisition, processing and use* (pp. 173–190). Amsterdam: Benjamins.

Spöttl, C., & McCarthy, M. (2004). Comparing knowledge of formulaic sequences across L1, L2, L3, and L4. In N. Schmitt (Ed.), *Formulaic sequences: Acquisition, processing and use* (pp. 191–224). Amsterdam: Benjamins.

Takahashi, S. (2005). Pragmalinguistic awareness: Is it related to motivation and proficiency? *Applied Linguistics, 26,* 90–120.

Wesche, M., & Paribakht, T. S. (1996). Assessing second language vocabulary knowledge: Depth vs. breadth. *Canadian Modern Language Review, 53,* 13–40.

Wray, A., & Perkins, M. R. (2000). The functions of formulaic language: An integrated model. *Language and Communication, 20,* 1–28.

Yorio, C. (1989). Idiomaticity as an indicator of second language proficiency. In K. Hyltenstam & L. K. Obler (Eds.), *Bilingualism across the lifespan* (pp. 55–72). Cambridge, England: Cambridge University Press.

Appendix: List of expressions used in the task

The students only heard this part; there was no written input; portions of expressions that were modified to yield less common strings are italicized

#	expression	#	expression
1	Can I leave a *note*?	31	Watch *up*!
2	Shut up	32	I'm looking for
3	That works for me	33	Nice to see you
4	Sure thing	34	*Could* you like to?
5	*Could* you mind?	35	No problem
6	*I* thank you for your time	36	Would you mind?
7	I'd love to	37	I'm just looking
8	Excuse the mess	38	Excuse me
9	I gotta go	39	Can I get a *drive*?
10	Can I get a ride?	40	Thank you
11	My *pad*	41	Would you like to?
12	Keep it down	42	Be careful!
13	That'd be great	43	Other *activities*
14	Nice to meet you	44	Be quiet!
15	You *also*	45	I'm late
16	Want a ride?	46	Do you have a minute?
17	You *are* welcome	47	Be *cautious*!
18	Want a *drive*?	48	I'm *tardy*
19	I'm just *seeing*	49	The place is messy
20	Nice to *look at* you	50	You too
21	I was wondering	51	Thank you for having me
22	*Make* it down	52	The place is *untidy*
23	Thanks for your time	53	Other plans
24	I gotta *leave*	54	Nice to *introduce* you
25	My place	55	No problem-*s*
26	Quiet *up*	56	*Certain* thing
27	Can I leave a message?	57	*You* excuse me
28	You're welcome	58	Be silent
29	Do you have *an hour*?	59	Excuse the *dirt*
30	I'm sorry	60	Watch out!

The Use of Conventional Expressions and Utterance Length in L2 Pragmatics

Kathleen Bardovi-Harlig
Maria-Thereza Bastos
Beatrix Burghardt
Eric Chappetto
Edelmira L. Nickels
Marda Rose
Indiana University Bloomington

Previous research based on written discourse completion tasks has claimed that learners talk more than native speakers when producing the same speech acts and that this results in pragmatic failure (Blum-Kulka & Olshtain, 1986; Edmondson & House, 1991). This cross-sectional study used a computer-delivered oral production task to determine if learners use the same expressions as native speakers and if learner responses are longer. The task was completed by 123 adult learners of English as a second language and 49 native speakers of American English. This study analyzes the results of 22 scenarios, representing a variety of speech acts that fostered high use of conventional expressions among the native speakers. Results show that the learner use of conventional expressions varied by scenario. Results also suggest that the acquisition of a conventional expression may begin with a lexical core, with learners building toward the target form through grammaticalization and elaboration. This study finds that the learners did not use significantly more words or semantic formulas than the native speakers, and there are no significant differences in responses that contain conventional expressions.

Studies in pragmatics and language learning have compared the production of second language learners to that of native speakers (NSs) along a variety of parameters. These include the speech acts produced in given contexts, the semantic formulas used to realize those speech acts, the content encoded in the semantic formulas, and the forms with which they are realized (Bardovi-Harlig, 2001). This study investigates one particular aspect of form: the construction and use of conventional expressions. Conventional expressions such as "Nice to meet you" or "Good to see you" are used predictably in certain contexts. They are often called *conversational routines* (Coulmas, 1981), *formulas* (Wray, 2002), or *formulaic sequences* (Schmitt & Carter, 2004). Although conventional expressions go by many names (Bardovi-Harlig, 2006; Wray), terms such as *formula* or *formulaic sequence* make a psycholinguistic claim that the word strings are stored and retrieved as one lexical item. In this study, we make no assumption about how expressions are stored or retrieved, which is a psycholinguistic issue. Instead, we focus on the word strings themselves and their syntax, morphology, and lexis. We address two basic questions: Do learners use the same expressions as NSs? What happens to the length of their contributions when they do?

Knowledge of conventional expressions forms part of a speaker's pragmalinguistic competence, and knowledge of their use and the contexts in which they occur is part of sociopragmatic competence. Coulmas (1981) described conventional expressions as "tacit agreements, which the members of a community presume to be shared by every reasonable co-member. In embodying societal knowledge they are essential in the handling of day-to-day situations" (p. 4). As second language learners become co-members of the target-language community, the use of conventional language may be expected of them. From a pedagogical and sociolinguistic perspective, House (1996) wrote that "it is important to learn routines at any learning stage because they embody the societal knowledge that members of a given community share.... Routine formulae are thus essential in the verbal handling of everyday life" (pp. 226–227).

The literature identifies at least four benefits to learners (and others) who use conventional expressions (Bardovi-Harlig, 2006): making a language learner appear nativelike (Yorio, 1989), allowing for fluency in production and faster processing (Weinert, 1995), saving the speaker planning time that can be used where it is needed more (Peters, 1983), and increasing a speaker's confidence that speech acts will be understood by interlocutors in the intended way (Wildner-Bassett, 1994). The middle two have been attributed to the psycholinguistic aspects of storage and retrieval of routines.

Conventional expressions are a type of "I know it when I hear it" category. Viewers of police shows will recognize the use of "I'm sorry for your loss" as a police officer's conventional means for opening a conversation with the family of a victim. To operationalize the identification of conventional expressions, we adopted four of the characteristics used by Myles, Hooper, and Mitchell (1998, p. 325): They are at least two morphemes in length, used repeatedly and always in the same form, situationally dependent, and community-wide in use.[1] Because we are investigating the use of the conventional expressions rather than claims about their storage, fluency criteria were not used for identification.[2]

The use and nonuse of conventional expressions by learners and nonnative speakers has been related to length of contribution. Previous research has claimed that learners talk more than NSs when completing the same speech acts, and this concept of "too much talk" has been equated with pragmatic failure (Blum-Kulka & Olshtain, 1986; Edmondson & House, 1991). Studying requests and apologies through written discourse completion tasks (DCTs), Blum-Kulka and Olshtain and Edmondson and House concluded that intermediate and advanced learners produce longer responses than NSs. Blum-Kulka and Olshtain attributed this to "the learners' general lack of confidence in their communicative competence" (p. 176).[3] Likewise, Edmondson and House attributed learners' verbosity at least in part to insecurity, although they acknowledged that it may also be due to the nature of the written DCT.[4] According to Edmondson and House, learners do not use standardized routines in their responses as NSs do (p. 284); therefore, the length of a learner's response is seen as a compensatory strategy that reflects the learner's "perception of the communicative 'problem'" (p. 283) and, at the same time, indicates that learners do not use formulas (p. 284). Scarcella (1979) reported that 44% (97/220) of the nontargetlike responses to a written DCT were paraphrases of the targeted conventional expressions; although she did not discuss length directly, the example paraphrases are longer than the targets (e.g., "please reduce your speed" for "slow down," p. 83).

Length has been calculated in both number of words and number of semantic formulas. On a written DCT that elicited five requests, Blum-Kulka and Olshtain (1986) found that nonnative speakers used significantly more words per contribution than NSs. They also reported that nonnative speakers used significantly more external modification than NSs in four of the five request scenarios. (External modification may be understood as the number of supportive moves or the total number of semantic formulas less the head act.) Blum-Kulka and Olshtain linked the greater number of words to the greater number of supportive moves used by nonnative speakers, a relationship that we test in this study. A second study by Edmondson and House (1991) investigated the number of supportive moves in seven apologies and five requests, using the same DCT as Blum-Kulka and Olshtain. Results on the five request scenarios showed that learners used significantly more supportive moves than NSs, corroborating Blum-Kulka and Olshtain's finding. The learners also used more supportive moves than the NSs in apologies; however, the difference was not significant and was less important than in requests.

Measuring length in number of words should be sensitive to a respondent's paraphrase and circumlocution occasioned by the lack of a word or expression that would lengthen a response (Jourdain & Scullen, 2001; Scarcella, 1979). On the other hand, it may also be sensitive to grammatical development if learners use fewer words than NSs through the use of null articles or predicates without copulas. In contrast, measuring length in the number of semantic formulas tallies the number of components speakers use to realize the speech act set. This attends to the number of moves a person makes, rather than the number of words it takes to say them.

In light of the claims of previous studies, this chapter focuses exclusively on the use of conventional expressions and addresses two research questions:
1. Do learners use the same expressions that NSs do when performing the same speech act in the same context?
2. Are learners' contributions longer than those of NSs?

Method

Participants

A total of 172 participants completed the task: 123 learners of English as a second language and 49 NSs of American English who attended or taught at the same university that the learners attended. The learners ranged in age from 17 to 36 years with a mean of 23.8.[5] The NSs comprised two groups: undergraduates and English as a second language (ESL) teachers. The undergraduates were included to provide an appropriate age group for comparison, and the teachers were included because they provide input to the learners. The 35 undergraduates ranged in age from 18 to 40 years with a mean age of 20.0. This group is called *NS peers*. The 14 teachers ranged from 23 to 62 years, with a mean of 43.1. Three of the ESL teachers were also graduate students. This group is called *NS teachers*.[6]

The learners were enrolled in four levels of classes at the Intensive English Program, from low-intermediate at level 3 to low-advanced at level 6. Each level of instruction is 7 weeks long, with 135 to 165 hours of instruction. The learners represent 11 language backgrounds: Arabic (*n* = 55), Korean (*n* = 28), Japanese (*n* = 13), Chinese (*n* = 12), Thai (*n* = 5), Spanish (*n* = 3), Portuguese (*n* = 2), Turkish (*n* = 2), and 1 each of Italian, Kazakh, and Tibetan. The first languages are fairly well distributed across the levels with the exception of level 3, where 24 of the 35 learners reported Arabic as their first language. The learners reported a mean length of residence in the US of 5.0 months, and among those who answered the question, a mean length of English study prior to their ESL experience of 4.7 years.

Tasks

This study is part of a larger investigation of conventional expressions. On the day of data collection, two elicitation tasks plus a questionnaire were completed during a 50-minute session in the language lab in the following order: an audio recognition task of 60 conventional and modified expressions (12 minutes; Bardovi-Harlig, this volume), an audio-visual production task (20 minutes, including instructions and examples), and a background questionnaire (approximately 5–10 minutes).[7]

The production task was based on two pilot studies that identified contexts that fostered the high use of conventional expressions by NSs of American English in the same university community as the ESL population to be tested. The 32 scenarios used in this task were selected from an original set of 77 scenarios derived from observation, 44 of which were retested in a second pilot (Bardovi-Harlig, this volume). The piloting resulted in an empirically identified conventional expression for each of the scenarios included.

The production task consisted of 32 scenarios; 13 required the respondents to initiate an interaction, and 19 scenarios required them to respond to an interlocutor's turn. The production task had two versions that reversed the order of the responses and the initiators. The task was computer delivered; respondents listened to the scenarios over individual headsets while they read their computer screens and recorded their responses through headset microphones onto digital files. They were trained with two examples of each type. The task with instructions is in the appendix. An example of each type is provided here.

Example A.		The phone rings. You pick it up. [oral and written] *You say:* [screen only] *NNS respondent:* "*Hello*" [audio only]
(Initiating-1)		You see your friend standing on a chair trying to reach a book at the top of the bookshelf. You know that the chair she is standing on has a broken leg. *You say:* [screen only]
(Responding-12)		You go to a clothing store and you need to find a new shirt. A salesperson approaches you. You don't want the salesperson's assistance. "*Can I help you?*" [audio only] *You say:* [screen only]

Analysis

In the first stage of the analysis, we transcribed the 5504 responses (172 respondents by 32 scenarios). Each author transcribed approximately 1/6 of the corpus and verified the transcription of another 1/6. In this manner, all transcription was verified by two people. Consistent implementation of transcription conventions was assured through comparison and discussion. The transcriptions included all repairs, pauses, and noteworthy prosodic features like rate, intonation, stress, and volume. Pauses of 0.5 s and greater were timed to 0.1 s.

To determine that there were clear preferences among the NSs and to establish an identifiable target expression for the university community in the study, the NS responses were analyzed first for means of expression. If the NS responses showed at least 50% use of a string, the responses to the scenario were included for further analysis.[8] Scenarios that did not show clear use of a single expression were eliminated from the analysis. This led to 22 scenarios divided among a variety of speech acts: expressions of gratitude (4), warnings (3), leave-takings (3), apologies (2), condolences (2), declining offers (2), accepting offers (2), and one each of a request, accepting a request, deflecting thanks, and an introduction.

The responses to the scenarios were then coded. A lack of response was coded as "no answer." Responses that indicated that the learners did not understand the scenario were coded accordingly in an individual category. Reponses that addressed the scenarios were further coded for means of expression. Coding was completed separately by two researchers with any discrepancies resolved by a third.

The target expression for each scenario was identified as the longest string that captures the greatest percentage of the NS responses. For example, "just look" or "just looking" are too short to capture the NS use or to reflect learner development toward the target. "No thanks, I'm just looking" was too long a string because it excluded other thanking expressions and other positions (cf. "I'm just looking, thanks"). However, "I'm just looking" is common to both strings and was therefore identified as the target expression.

A careful analysis of the elicited data led to three additional refinements of the analysis. First, thanking scenarios are distinguished by the use of intensifiers: Where one scenario elicits responses of "thanks" or "thank you," another elicits "thanks so much." Second, we allowed for variation in some target expressions. Consistent with what is reported in the formula literature (Nattinger & DeCarrico, 1992; Schmitt & Carter, 2004), some expressions exhibited variability. At the end of a conversation with a friend whom the speaker has not seen for a long time, 71% of the undergraduates said either "{Good/nice/great/glad} to see you" or "{Good/nice/great} seeing you," the dominant choice being "Good to see you" (40%), followed by "Good seeing you" (11%). Such variation was taken into account by describing the expression as "Adj {to see/seeing} you."

Third, we adopted an analysis that allows for minor grammatical differences between the NSs and learners. The use of the noncontracted copula is the most common allowance. For example, although the NSs said "I'm just looking," and the learners used both "I'm just looking" and "I am just looking," their use of both forms was counted as using the targeted expression. In other cases, such as "I'm sorry" and "I am sorry," the NSs used both the full and contracted copulas. Variations in tense, however, were not included because these were not part of the NS variation. We return to a discussion of the role of the learners' grammar in the development of conventional expressions later. In addition to the analysis that compares the learner production to the NS production, we also include an interlanguage analysis that shows the lexical and grammatical development of expressions across levels.

Length was calculated in both number of words and number of semantic formulas. Semantic formulas are the components that make up a speech-act set. For example, in declining an offer, someone might include an explanation and an expression of gratitude. In the following example, the learner is declining a salesperson's offer to help him. The learner first offers a refusal ("No"), followed by an explanation ("I'm just looking"), and an expression of gratitude ("thank you").

3. No::. I'm just looking, thank you! (level 3, learner 8)

This response was coded as having six words and three semantic formulas.

Because repetition is one way that participants upgrade the illocutionary force of their utterances, most repetitions were included in our analysis. For example, the following response to a condolence scenario was coded as having nine words and three semantic formulas. Even though all three semantic formulas are apologies, it is through the use of all three that the learner is able to express the gravity of the situation.

4. I'm sorry about that. (2.1) I'm sorry. (0.6) I'm so sorry. (level 3, learner 3)

However, when participants offered an exact repetition of their entire response after a pause, only the first response was included in the analysis. Therefore, the following response was coded as having five words and two semantic formulas (decline and explanation).

5. No thank you I'm fine. (1.9) No thank you I'm fine. (level 3, learner 7)

In addition, if repetition occurred as part of a repair sequence, we included the total number of words in the response, but we did not count the repaired portion as an additional semantic formula. So, in the following example, the response was coded as having 18 words and three strategies. The correction of tense in "I have some problem" was not counted as a separate strategy because here it is clear that the learner is correcting himself. However, the second "I'm so sorry" was counted as a second strategy because it strengthens his apology.

6. I am sorry from late. I am::, so sorry but uh, I have some problem- I had some problem. (level 3, learner 4)

A mixed model analysis was conducted for each of the following outcomes: number of words for all responses, number of words when the target expressions were used, number of semantic formulas for all responses, and number of semantic formulas when the target expressions were used. This analysis was chosen because it includes each of the individual item responses and appropriately accounted for the natural correlation of items within participant. In addition, it avoids the loss of participants due to missing responses when participants fail to respond or their responses demonstrate that they did not understand the scenario. The fixed effects were group (four learner groups and two NS groups), scenario, and the interaction between group and scenario. The random effect was for participant. Bonferroni post-hoc tests were performed on the differences between the proficiency levels.

Results

This section reports on the expressions that the learners used in comparison to the target and developmentally, across proficiency levels. We then investigate the effect that using conventional expressions has on length.

Use of conventional expressions by NSs and learners

The learner responses fell along a continuum from very high use of the conventional expression favored by the NSs to very low use (Table 1). Moving from the left-most column to the right, Table 1 gives the item number and a descriptive title for each scenario. The conventional expressions are given in italics using standard linguistic notation. Curly brackets {} show alternation, and parentheses indicate optional elements: "{I'm/I am} (intensifier) sorry" may be realized as "I'm sorry," "I am sorry," or both, with the addition of "so" or "very." The next columns give the percentage and raw scores of response by level and NS group. The rightmost column gives the total number of responses for the learners and NSs combined.

At the high end, invariant and frequent expressions such as "Nice to meet you" in response to an introduction (R15) and "You too" to reciprocate to "Have a nice day" (R6) were used early and frequently. There are 156 and 154 responses (out of 172), respectively. The next most widely used expression by the NSs and learners combined is the offer of condolences "{I am/I'm} (intensifier) sorry" for a dog hit by a car (R1).

At the opposite end are responses to scenarios with little or no use of the conventional expressions by the learners. Seven scenarios showed no use of the target expression in one or more levels. These include "Watch out!" (I3, I12), "Gotta go" (I11), "That {'d/would} be great" (R2, R18b), "Thanks for {having/inviting} me" (R3), and "Sure no problem" (R5). Some of these target expressions seem to be dependent on grammatical development as in "That{'d/would} be + adj" (R2), or on input and grammar as in the case of "Thanks for having me" (R3). The NSs used "I'm stuffed" as a strong alternative to "I'm full" (R19), whereas no learner attempted this. Of the lowest scoring expressions, four reach only 12% or lower use by level 6 ("Gotta go," "That {'d/ would} be + adj," "Thanks for {having/inviting} me," and "Sure no problem"). The closing response "Adj {to see/ seeing} you" is among the least used formulas; its highest use is still only 16% by level 6.

Two of the scenarios elicited somewhat lower use of the conventional expressions by the NSs. The ride in the rain scenario has two target expressions for the NSs that occur in complementary distribution: a thanking expression and "That{'d/ would} be + adj." Together, these expressions account for 71% of the NS peer responses (3 speakers used both). Likewise, "Sure no problem" in Save Place (R5) was the other expression that the NSs used less frequently. This was included as a pair with "No problem," which deflected an expression of gratitude in Gave Ride (R9). Whereas Gave Ride turned out to be a genuine "No problem" scenario, Save Place elicited "Sure" as the most common recurring word among both NSs and learners. Including "Sure no problem" and "Sure" alone or with another minimizing statement accounts for 86% of the NS teacher responses, 81% of the peer responses, and as much as 50% of the responses in level 5.

The remaining expressions showed increased use by the learners or at least attempts at construction. In response to More Food (R19), the learners' use of the alternative "I'm full" increased steadily from level 3 through levels 5 and 6, with a high of 81% use, although they did not use the more colloquial "I'm stuffed," as noted above.[9] Among these expressions are "Sorry I'm late," "Be quiet," "I'm looking for," "I'm just looking," "No problem," and "Thanks/Thank you +intensifier + much." Even slow starters like "Watch out!" show a steady climb up to 44% by level 6 in Bus (I12) and 36% in Puddle (I3).

As with any L2 analysis, the comparison of learner to NS production is only a partial story. The acquisition story rests on what learners do en route to being targetlike. Although the developmental paths of all the expressions are interesting, we illustrate the development of expressions with a few examples. Because we are working with cross-sectional data, these observations will need to be corroborated by longitudinal data; nevertheless, the rather large number of learners ($N = 143$) and 22 scenarios provides a reasonable starting point.

The use of conventional expressions may begin with a lexical core. Consider the expression "I'm just looking" used by NSs in No Help (R12). The learners show a steady increase in the use of the expression from 14% in level 3 to 52% in level 6. As Table 2 shows, however, the expression builds earlier, and the presence of the core lexical items "just look" at earlier levels shows that learners associate them with the scenario. One learner in level 5 produced "just look," and one learner in level 4 produced "just looking." Although the latter is idiomatic (and used by 3 NSs), we see that both expressions occur with a subject and no auxiliary in "I just look" and "I just looking." One case each of "I'll just looking" and "Just I'm looking" further suggests that mastery of expressions is at least partially dependent on the learner's emergent grammar. The learners also show increasing grammatical development with each level as shown in Table 1. However, Table 2 shows that even as learners use the target expression, use of the full auxiliary "am" is present through level 6 and is a form not used by the NSs who consistently used the contraction "I'm."

Table 1. Use of NS-dominant expressions by level

			level/group											
			3 n=35		4 n=31		5 n=32		6 n=25		NSP n=35		NST n=14		total
ID	context	expression	%	(n)	%	(n)	%	(n)	%	(n)	%	(n)	%	(n)	(N)
I1	Broken chair	Be careful	34	(12)	35	(11)	28	(9)	44	(11)	60	(21)	64	(9)	(73)
I3	Puddle	Watch out	0	(0)	13	(4)	19	(6)	36	(9)	86	(30)	50	(7)	(56)
I4	Closing	Adj {to see/seeing} you	11	(4)	6	(2)	13	(4)	16	(4)	71	(25)	64	(9)	(48)
I8	Late (25 min)	Sorry {I am/I'm} late	14	(5)	23	(7)	19	(6)	36	(9)	60	(21)	64	(9)	(57)
I9	Movies	Be quiet	26	(9)	48	(15)	38	(12)	40	(10)	60	(21)	21	(3)	(70)
I10	Busy teacher	{Thanks/Thank you} for	17	(6)	35	(11)	44	(14)	56	(14)	94	(33)	71	(10)	(88)
I11	Cell phone	Gotta go	3	(1)	0	(0)	6	(2)	12	(3)	57	(20)	50	(7)	(33)
I12	Bus	Watch out	20	(7)	10	(3)	16	(5)	44	(11)	71	(25)	71	(10)	(61)
R1	Dog hit by car	{I am/I'm} (intensifier) sorry	63	(22)	48	(15)	41	(13)	76	(19)	71	(25)	64	(9)	(103)
R2	Offer of help	That {'d/would} be + adj	0	(0)	0	(0)	8	(2)	4	(1)	66	(23)	57	(8)	(34)
R3	Closing, party	{Thanks/thank you} for {having/inviting} me	0	(0)	3	(1)	6	(2)	12	(3)	74	(26)	50	(7)	(39)
R4	Shopping help	I'm looking for	14	(5)	26	(8)	22	(7)	56	(14)	54	(19)	43	(6)	(59)
R5	Save place	Sure no problem	3	(1)	0	(0)	6	(2)	12	(3)	34	(12)	43	(6)	(24)
R6	Have a nice day!	You too	83	(29)	94	(29)	94	(30)	84	(21)	94	(33)	100	(14)	(156)
R7	Late (5 min)	Sorry {I'm/ am} late	17	(6)	32	(10)	31	(10)	48	(12)	69	(24)	71	(10)	(72)
R9	Gave ride	No problem	14	(5)	26	(8)	16	(5)	32	(8)	80	(28)	64	(9)	(63)
R12	Shopping no help	{I'm/am} just looking	14	(5)	35	(11)	38	(12)	52	(13)	71	(25)	64	(9)	(75)
R15	Introduction	Nice to meet you	100	(35)	84	(26)	94	(30)	80	(20)	89	(31)	86	(12)	(154)
R16	Father died	{I am/I'm} + intensifier + sorry	40	(14)	19	(6)	31	(10)	44	(11)	77	(27)	93	(13)	(81)
R17	Make-up test	Thank you + intensifier + much	40	(14)	29	(9)	34	(11)	60	(15)	86	(30)	71	(10)	(89)
R18	Ride in rain	{Thanks/thank you} {so/very} much	26	(9)	16	(5)	16	(5)	28	(7)	37	(13)	43	(6)	(45)
R18b	Ride in rain	That {'d/would} be + adj	0	(0)	0	(0)	0	(0)	0	(0)	37	(13)	29	(4)	(17)
R19	More food	I'm (adv) full	31	(11)	55	(17)	81	(26)	76	(19)	40	(14)	29	(4)	(91)
R19b	More food	I'm stuffed	0	(0)	0	(0)	0	(0)	0	(0)	37	(13)	50	(7)	(20)

note: I = initiating utterance; R = responding utterance; NSP = native-speaker peer group; NST = native-speaker teacher group; Total = total number of responses that used the target expression; {} show alternation; () indicates an optional element.

Table 2. Building an expression from a lexical core (number of responses)

emergent expressions	3 n=35	4 n=31	5 n=32	6 n=25	NSP n=35	NST n=14
Just look			1			
I just look	1	2		1		
Just looking		1			2	1
I just looking	3		2			
I'll just looking	1					
Just I'm looking			1			
I am just looking	2	2	1	6		
I'm just looking	3	9	11	7	25	9
total	10	14	16	14	27	10

note: NSP = native-speaker peer group; NST = native-speaker teacher group.

Even expressions that show very low rates of use suggest that learners build toward the use of the target form. In affirmative replies to offers of help (R2) or a ride (R18), the NSs most often realized "That {'d/would} be adj" as "That'd be great." Three learners used the expression in R2, 2 in level 5, and 1 in level 6.

7a. Oh, that'd be great. Thanks a lot.   (L5B7)
 b. That would be great! Sank-, thanks so much! (L5C9)
 c. O:h thank you! That would be nice from you! (L6C19)

Five more learners attempted the expression in R2 and R18 combined (not reflected in Table 1). These learners seemed to recognize these scenarios as contexts for a positive adjective: 4 learners used "great" and 1 used "wonderful":

8a. That will be great. Thank you >very much.< (R2; L6C19)
 b. Oh, thank you! (1.6) It's great! (R2; L6C22)
 c. Thanks a lot. That wo- that will be wonderful. (R18; L5B2)
 d. Ye:s, thank you:, that's (0.5) great! (R18; L3BS8)
 e. If you hel-, if you help me I will: be great. (R18; L3A8)

Perhaps more revealing is the emergence of the frame. Two learners in levels 5 and 6 used "That will be great/wonderful." The level 5 learner appears to have started to say "that would" but repaired to "that will." Another 2 used present-tense contractions "that's" and "it's," and the final learner used "I will be great." The use of "will" and the present is understandable given the late acquisition of "would" (Salsbury & Bardovi-Harlig, 2000). The contracted alternative "That'd be great" may be additionally difficult for learners to parse. Both of these interpretations presuppose that learners construct the expressions on the basis of their interlanguage grammar (Bardovi-Harlig, 2006).

If grammatical development is one way learners build up conventional expressions, as shown in the case of "I'm just looking," elaboration is another way. The many scenarios eliciting "thank you" and "I'm sorry" illustrate elaboration. Reponses to the thanking scenarios show variation in the use of "thank you" and "thanks" as well as in the use of intensification: "so much" and "very much." The apologies and condolences show that learners, like NSs, may elaborate the lexical core "I'm sorry" with complements as well as intensifiers (e.g., "I'm *so* sorry *to hear about your father*").

Table 3. Distribution of thanking expressions in make-up test scenario

	level/group										total
	3 n=35		4 n=31		5 n=32		6 n=25		NSP n=35		NST n=14	
target expression	%	(n)	%	(n)	%	(n)	%	(n)	%	(n)	%	(n)	(N)
Thank you (all expressions)	66	(23)	65	(20)	84	(27)	92	(23)	91	(32)	71	(10)	(135)
Thank you+intensifier+much	40	(14)	29	(9)	34	(11)	60	(15)	86	(30)	71	(10)	(88)
Thank you very much	26	(9)	13	(4)	22	(7)	36	(9)	6	(2)	7	(1)	(32)
Thank you so much	14	(5)	16	(5)	12	(4)	24	(6)	80	(28)	64	(9)	(56)

note: NSP = native-speaker peer group; NST = native-speaker teacher group.

In response to Make-Up Test (R17), 86% of the NS peers and 71% of the teachers used an intensifier with "thank you" (Table 3). As row 1 shows, 66% of the learners as early as level 3 replied to the scenario with "thank you," increasing to 92% by level 6. However, the use of intensifiers, which are typical in the NS responses, builds more slowly, from a low of 29% in level 4 to 60% in level 6. Although the learners preferred "very much" to the NSs' use of "so much" (rows 3 and 4), the increase nevertheless shows that the learners increasingly recognized and responded to this scenario as a context that requires intensification of the "thank you" expression. Note, too, that this scenario favors the full form of "thank you" and does not alternate as in other scenarios.

A second example of expansion by elaboration comes from the condolence scenarios (R1 and R16). In addition to the use of intensifier "so" in "I'm so sorry," speakers may elaborate the basic expression through complementation, "I'm sorry to *hear that*." The NS responses show relatively little elaboration in the Dog Hit by Car scenario, but much greater use when offering condolences at the death of the speaker's father. Learners, however, respond to both scenarios more similarly than NSs do, although Table 4 shows that learners use more elaboration in Father Died (R16), with the exception of level 6. The responses to this scenario suggest that both the grammar underlying the pragmalinguistic resources and the sociopragmatic knowledge of when to use these resources are developing at the same time.

The intensifier with "hear that" occurred more when the NSs extended condolences for the father than for the dog. Based on the NS features, one would expect an increased word count in the learners' responses in R16. However, some of the learners did not use full frames, for example, "I'm so sorry," but rather used single-word utterances such as "Sorry." This may lead to decreased word counts in the learner responses. For example, the shortest target-like response, "I'm sorry" without a complement, was given by 12 learners in level 4. Other levels not only used the pronoun but also included a complement, either "about that" or "to hear about it." This may help explain the observed difference in response length between level 4 and the other three levels (as discussed in the following section).

Table 4. The use of complements with expressions of condolence

target expression	level/group												total
	3 n=35		4 n=31		5 n=32		6 n=25		NSP n=35		NST n=14		
	%	(n)	%	(n)	%	(n)	%	(n)	%	(n)	%	(n)	(N)
dog hit by car (R1)													
about	17	(6)	19	(6)	9	(3)	12	(3)	0	(0)	0	(0)	(18)
for/with	6	(2)	0	(0)	3	(1)	4	(1)	0	(0)	0	(0)	(4)
to hear	3	(1)	6	(2)	6	(2)	28	(7)	9	(3)	29	(4)	(19)
total elaborated		(9)		(8)		(6)		(11)		(3)		(4)	(31)
father died (R16)													
about	29	(10)	16	(5)	16	(5)	8	(2)	6	(2)	7	(1)	(25)
for/with	3	(1)	0	(0)	16	(5)	12	(3)	3	(1)	0	(0)	(10)
to hear	3	(1)	16	(5)	6	(2)	24	(6)	51	(18)	50	(7)	(39)
total elaborated		(12)		(10)		(12)		(11)		(21)		(7)	(74)

note: R = responding utterance; NSP = native-speaker peer group; NST = native-speaker teacher group. The learner in level 3 used "Ø hear." One learner in each of levels 3 and 5 used "with."

Length

In this section, we address the claims that learners' contributions are longer than NSs'. We break this down into four subquestions: Are learner responses longer than NS responses when measured in words? Are learner responses longer than NS responses when measured in semantic formulas? Are learner responses with conventional expressions longer when measured in words? Are learner responses with conventional expressions longer when measured in semantic formulas? Each section compares the learners by level to the NSs.

Length in number of words

The findings did not corroborate earlier reports that learner responses are longer than NS responses when measured in number of words. The mixed-model analysis with Bonferroni post-hoc comparisons revealed no significant differences between the learners and NS peers across all scenarios.[10] The learners in levels 3 and 5 used more words than the NS peers, but these differences are not statistically significant (Table 5, second and third columns). The NS teachers consistently produced longer responses, by all measures, than either the learners or NS peers. The performance of the NS teachers is discussed separately at the end of this section.

Table 5. Length in number of words

level/group	all responses		with conventional expressions	
	M	SE	M	SE
3 (n=35)	6.725	.338	6.410	.409
4 (n=31)	5.674	.354	6.177	.394
5 (n=32)	6.656	.346	6.830	.380
6 (n=25)	6.030	.389	6.318	.388
NS peers (n=35)	6.379	.327	6.494	.283
NS teachers (n=14)	8.272	.517	8.272	.456

note: Estimated marginal means from mixed model.

Length in number of semantic formulas

A comparison of the cross-sectional sample of the learners when length is measured in number of semantic formulas shows that the learners used more semantic formulas than the NS peers at all levels; however, these differences are not statistically significant (Table 6, second and third columns). The learners in levels 3 and 5 used more semantic formulas than the other participants; this is the same direction as the number of words.

Table 6. Length in number of semantic formulas

level/group	all responses		with conventional expressions	
	M	SE	M	SE
3 (n=35)	2.161	.078	2.176	.106
4 (n=31)	1.904	.082	1.939	.102
5 (n=32)	2.145	.080	2.164	.099
6 (n=25)	1.919	.090	1.930	.102
NS peers (n=35)	1.903	.076	1.972	.076
NS teachers (n=14)	2.283	.120	2.395	.121

note: Estimated marginal means from mixed model.

Length in number of words in responses with dominant NS expressions

The analysis revealed no significant differences between the four learner groups and NS peers when contributions exhibiting the dominant NS expressions are compared in number of words. Only level 5 used more words than the NS peers, but this difference was not statistically significant (Table 5).

Does the use of the dominant NS expression reduce learner response length? The learners in level 3 show shorter responses and in levels 4–6 show longer responses in number of words when they used the favored conventional expression compared to all of the relevant responses combined (Table 5). It is not possible to compare conventional to nonconventional expressions because the distinction is not so much a dichotomy as a scale (Nattinger & DeCarrico, 1992; Wray & Perkins, 2000). In addition, the combined responses (for NSs and learners) may also contain conventional expressions that were not the dominant ones used by the NSs.

Length in number of semantic formulas of responses with dominant NS expressions

There are no significant differences between any of the learner levels and the NS peers in number of semantic formulas when the preferred conventional expression is used.

Does the use of the dominant NS expression reduce learner response lengths when measured in number of semantic formulas? The learners in levels 3–6 show slightly longer responses in the number of semantic formulas that they used when they included the favored conventional expression than they did in all of the relevant responses combined (Table 6).

NS Teachers

The NS teachers consistently produced longer responses by all measures than either the learners or NS peers. All of the learner groups used fewer words than the NS teachers. This difference is significant for level 4 ($p = .001$) and level 6 ($p = .010$). All of the learner groups also used fewer semantic formulas than the NS teachers, but these differences were not significant. Moreover, when contributions with the target expressions are compared, all of the learners used fewer words than the NS teachers, and this difference is significant for level 3 ($p = .039$), level 4 ($p = .009$), and level 6 ($p = .020$). All of the learner groups use fewer semantic formulas with targeted expressions than the NS teachers, but these differences were not significant at the .05 level.

The NS teachers also produced longer responses than the NS peers on all measures. These differences are significant for the number of words ($p = .035$) and the number of words when contributions with the target expressions are compared ($p = .017$). When the number of semantic formulas with targeted expressions are compared, the differences between the NS peers and NS teachers approached significance ($p = .054$).

Variation in length by scenario

Examining the number of semantic formulas used by the learners and NSs by scenario shows that in some cases, the learners used more semantic formulas than the NSs and in others, they used fewer. In this section, we explore the two scenarios with the highest NS and learner use of expressions: Introduction (R15) with "Nice to meet you" and Have a Nice Day! (R6) with "You too." In response to Introduction, the learners used more semantic formulas than the NSs, whereas in response to Have a Nice Day!, the learners used fewer semantic formulas than the NSs. These differences indicate that even though the learners used the targeted expressions in scenarios where their use is felicitous, the learners seemed to have a different sociopragmatic sense of what else should be included in their contribution.

The learners used more semantic formulas than the NSs in response to Introduction at all four levels, but especially in level 3. Whereas 63% of all of the NS responses included only the target or the target with a greeting, only 42% of all of the learner responses included just these semantic formulas. In level 3, for example, 54% of the responses also included a self-introduction, thereby making their responses considerably longer when an introduction of the self is added to the greeting and target formula, as can be seen in Example 9.

9a. Hi Bill, this i:s NAME, nice to meet you. (L3A6)
b. Hi Bill nice to meet you my name is NAME. (L3A13)

The inclusion of a reciprocal self-introduction occurred at all levels, but not to the same extent. Levels 4–6 used reciprocal self-introduction in 30% of the responses, which is still higher than the NSs, who included a reciprocal introduction in 22% of their responses, but noticeably lower than level 3. Another semantic formula that was used by learners was a question such as, "How are you?" (Example 10). This occurred at all four levels of learners, but was not as common. Learners included this type of question in 9% of their responses, whereas NSs included it only twice (4%).

10a. O::::h, >Nice to meet you.< My name NAME. How are you today? (L4C11)
b. Hi:: (.7) >how are you?<(.7) Nice to meet you. (L5A2)

In this scenario, differences between the learners and the NSs were also observed within the semantic formulas, which in turn led to differences in the number of words. First, the NSs included the name of the person to whom they were introduced in 67% of their responses. The learners, on the other hand, only included the addressee's name in 32% of their responses. The inclusion of the name increased slightly as the learners increased in proficiency. Second, 100% of the learner responses that included the target produced it exclusively in its simplest form, "nice to meet you," without expansion. However, 31% of the NS responses used the target expression in the phrase "It's nice to meet you." This, along with the use of the name, contributed to the length of the NS contributions. The use of this phrase was more common among the NS peers (40%) than teachers and may be a reflection of the importance of roommates to students. For students, meeting roommates may be comparable to meeting family members; it may be for this reason that they emphasized the importance of meeting this person by using the complete sentence.

In response to Have a Nice Day! (R–6), the learners used fewer semantic formulas than the NSs, with 50% of all of the learners using only the target, "you too," in their response. In contrast, only 18% of all of the NS participants used only the reciprocating expression. It was far more frequent for the NSs to include an expression of gratitude in their response, as in Example 11.

11. Thanks. You too. (NSP11)

This occurred in 74% of the NS responses. The learners, on the other hand, used this combination noticeably less, in only 29% of their responses.

A similar case occurs in the Shopping No Help scenario, in which the speakers declined help. In addition to "I'm just looking," 71% of the NS peers and 64% of the teachers used an additional formula that included a thanking expression ("No thanks, I'm just looking" or "<Thanks> I'm just looking<thanks>").[11] The learners gradually added the thanking formula to the declining expression, starting with 9% of the responses in level 3, going to a high of 31% in level 5 and 28% in level 6, showing increased sociopragmatic sensitivity to the context.

Discussion

Results from this study suggest that when learners are given an oral-production task that simulates turns, the learners do not use significantly more words than NSs. This is the case both for all responses taken together and responses with conventional expressions. In contrast, the learners may use more semantic formulas than NS peers (but not significantly so); and there is no significant difference in responses with conventional expressions.

This suggests that when interlanguage development is taken into account, the number of words is not a suitable measure of learner facility with conventional expressions or otherwise knowing what to say. As we have demonstrated, learners may identify a lexical core that is appropriate to a context and build up to it. As the interlanguage grammar develops, utterances become longer. The development from short to long utterances is offset by a number of features characteristic of oral production, including word searches, repetitions, and self-repair (see Examples 4–6 and the accompanying discussion).

In contrast, the number of semantic formulas is independent of grammatical development and the pressures of word retrieval and production. Semantic formulas may more readily capture a speaker's sense of saying enough in a given situation. Although using more semantic formulas may increase word the number of words, it need not. Two short semantic formulas can have fewer words than one elaborated formula, and a learner's stage of grammatical development may also contribute to the length.

Although the results of this study do not corroborate the finding that nonnatives used significantly more words per scenario than NSs did on written DCTs (Blum-Kulka & Olshtain, 1986), they are consistent with the finding that there was no evidence of increased length in roleplays (Edmondson, House, Kasper, & Stemmer, 1984). The use of written tasks to investigate oral features may influence the outcome. On the other hand, mode seems to have less effect on the number of semantic formulas. Both the present study and Blum-Kulka and Olshtain found greater use of semantic formulas by nonnative speakers.

However, the contrast between findings that nonnative speakers used significantly more semantic formulas in requests (Blum-Kulka & Olshtain, 1986;

Edmondson & House, 1991) and the finding that this did not hold to the same extent for apologies (Edmondson & House) suggests that the speech act may be an additional factor. This study confirms earlier reports that participants respond differently to individual scenarios even when the same speech acts are used, as is the case when we compare the subsets of thanking, apology, or condolence scenarios (Cohen, 2004; Nickels, 2006). This study combined all speech acts for the quantitative analysis, but an alternative would be to study multiple instantiations of the same speech act together and separately from others. It is interesting to note that the request scenarios—which would form the most direct comparison to Blum-Kulka and Olshtain's study—did not yield clearly dominant conventional expressions and were excluded either at the piloting stages during instrument construction or at the analysis phase of the present study.

Implicit in our discussion has also been the developmental nature of this study. We used a cross-sectional design and tested low-intermediate learners to low-advanced learners. This contrasts with participants in the Cross-Cultural Speech Act Realization Project studies, who were described only as nonnative speakers in university courses (Blum-Kulka, House, & Kasper, 1989). Level clearly influences production, but a more detailed comparison by level is not possible with the earlier studies.

The greatest difference between this study and those that guided it is the identification of conventional expressions. Previous studies either did not specify what expressions were targeted or investigated a predetermined set of expressions (Bardovi-Harlig, 2008; Kecskes, 2003; Roever, 2005; Scarcella, 1979). In contrast, we operationalized the notions of *targetlike use* and *social routines* as specific conventional expressions identified by pilot studies with NSs and reconfirmed by NS participation on the final task. The difference between the NS peers and teachers highlighted the importance of NS participants. This analysis clearly shows that although learners and NSs may use the same semantic formulas, a number of factors determine whether they use the same expressions. This approach introduces analytic issues of where to draw the line between use and nonuse of a targeted conventional expression for quantitative analysis. But as we showed, the approach also provides a rich framework in which to investigate the development of conventional expressions.

When the scenarios are pooled, we find, consistent with Blum-Kulka and Olshtain's (1986) findings, that the learners used more semantic formulas than the NS peers. We also find that when conventional expressions are used, the learners showed no difference from the NS peers. This may reflect what Blum-Kulka and Olshtain and Wildner-Bassett (1994) referred to as a speakers' confidence in communication. As we have shown, the picture is somewhat more complex in that the number of semantic formulas may differ by scenarios, speech acts, the expressions attempted, and the level of the learner, all of which bear continued investigation in the future.

Notes

1. The requirement that formulas be at least two morphemes long comes from psycholinguistic—not sociolinguistic—investigations. Formulas are thought to be stored and retrieved whole, like individual words. For this claim not to be vacuous, formulas must be at least two morphemes long. In this chapter, we use the term *conventional expressions* because we believe that, in the case of learners, the storage and retrieval of social expressions remains to be investigated. There are, of course, one-word conventional expressions such as "sorry" and "pardon." However, because they are mono-morphemic, they are not investigated here.
2. Fluency criteria for the identification of formulas include phonologically coherent, fluently articulated, and nonhesitant delivery of the sequence in question.
3. Recall that other scholars have cited confidence in communication as one of the benefits of using conventional expressions (Wildner-Bassett, 1994).
4. Roleplay data that allowed for face-to-face interaction did not produce the effect (see Edmondson, House, Kasper, & Stemmer, 1984).
5. A total of 131 background questionnaires were completed. Of those, 125 reported a numeric response to age; 90 reported length of English study.
6. The decision to keep the NS groups separate on the basis of age and status is justified by the fact that they were significantly different from each other.
7. This chapter reports the results of the production task. For a detailed discussion of the recognition task, see Bardovi-Harlig's study (this volume).
8. The 50% criterion led to 21 items. "Sure, no problem" (Save Place, R5) was also included because with a pair formed "no problem" (Gave Ride, R9).
9. One learner responded "I'm pure." Whereas we could make a plausible argument for phonological processes leading from "full" to "pure," the fact that a listener would be unlikely to recognize the target persuaded us not to include this response. Other accented pronunciations in this and other learner responses that were recognizable and did not result in extant words were included as using the conventional expressions. "Full" occasioned the largest number of pronunciation difficulties.
10. For all reports of significant differences, $p < .05$, unless otherwise noted.
11. The angled brackets indicate that "thanks" may occur either at the beginning or the end of the utterance.

References

Bardovi-Harlig, K. (2001). Evaluating the empirical evidence: Grounds for instruction in pragmatics? In K. R. Rose & G. Kasper (Eds.), *Pragmatics in language teaching* (pp. 13–32). New York: Cambridge University Press.

Bardovi-Harlig, K. (2006). On the role of formulas in the acquisition of L2 pragmatics. In K. Bardovi-Harlig, J. C. Félix-Brasdefer, & A. Omar (Eds.), *Pragmatics and language learning* (Vol. 11, pp. 1–28). Honolulu: University of Hawai'i, National Foreign Language Resource Center.

Bardovi-Harlig, K. (2008). Recognition and production of formulas in L2 pragmatics. In Z.-H. Han (Ed.), *Understanding second language process* (pp. 205–222). Clevedon, England: Multilingual Matters.

Blum-Kulka, J. House, & G. Kasper (Eds.). (1989). *Cross-cultural pragmatics: Requests and apologies.* Norwood, NJ: Ablex.

Blum-Kulka, S., & Olshtain, E. (1986). Too many words: Length of utterance and pragmatic failure. *Studies in Second Language Acquisition, 8,* 165–180.

Cohen, A. D. (2004). Assessing speech acts in a second language. In D. Boxer & A. D. Cohen (Eds.), *Studying speaking to inform second language learning* (pp. 302–327). Clevedon, England: Multilingual Matters.

Coulmas, F. (1981). *Conversational routine: Explorations in standardized communication situations and prepatterned speech.* The Hague: Mouton.

Edmondson, W., & House, J. (1991). Do learners talk too much? The waffle phenomenon in interlanguage pragmatics. In R. Phillipson, E. Kellerman, L. Selinker, M. Sharwood Smith, & M. Swain (Eds.), *Foreign/second language pedagogy research: A commemorative volume for Claus Færch* (pp. 273–287). Clevedon, England: Multilingual Matters.

Edmondson, W., House, J., Kasper, G., & Stemmer, B. (1984). Learning the pragmatics of discourse: A project report. *Applied Linguistics, 5,* 113–127.

House, J. (1996). Developing pragmatic fluency in English as a foreign language: Routines and metapragmatic awareness. *Studies in Second Language Acquisition, 18,* 225–252.

Jourdain, S., & Scullen, M. E. (2001). A pedagogical norm for circumlocution in French. In S. Gass, K. Bardovi-Harlig, S. S. Magnan, & J. Walz (Eds.), *A pedagogical norm for second and foreign language learning and teaching* (pp. 221–239). Amsterdam: John Benjamins.

Kecskes, I. (2003). *Situation-bound utterances in L1 and L2.* Berlin: Mouton.

Myles, F., Hooper, J., & Mitchell, R. (1998). Rote or rule? Exploring the role of formulaic language in classroom foreign language learning. *Language Learning, 48, 323–363.*

Nattinger, J. R., & DeCarrico, J. S. (1992). *Lexical phrases and language teaching.* Oxford: Oxford University Press.

Nickels, E. L. (2006). Interlanguage pragmatics and the effects of setting. In K. Bardovi-Harlig, J. C. Félix-Brasdefer, & A. Omar (Eds.), *Pragmatics and Language Learning* (Vol. 11, pp. 253–280). Honolulu: University of Hawai'i, National Foreign Language Resource Center.

Peters, A. M. (1983). *The units of language acquisition.* Cambridge, England: Cambridge University Press.

Roever, C. (2005). *Testing ESL pragmatics: Development and validation of a web-based assessment battery.* Berlin: Peter Lang.

Salsbury, T., & Bardovi-Harlig, K. (2000). Oppositional talk and the acquisition of modality in L2 English. In B. Swierzbin, F. Morris, M. E. Anderson, C. A. Klee, & E. Tarone (Eds.), *Social and cognitive factors in second language acquisition:*

Selected proceedings of the 1999 Second Language Research Forum (pp. 57–76). Somerville, MA: Cascadilla Press.

Scarcella, R. (1979). Watch up! *Working Papers in Bilingualism, 19,* 79–88.

Schmitt, N., & Carter, R. (2004). Formulaic sequences in action. In N. Schmitt (Ed.), *Formulaic sequences: Acquisition, processing and use* (pp. 1–22). Amsterdam: Benjamins.

Weinert, R. (1995). The role of formulaic language in second language acquisition: A review. *Applied Linguistics, 16,* 180–205.

Wildner-Bassett, M. E. (1994). Intercultural pragmatics and proficiency: 'Polite' noises for cultural appropriateness. *International Review of Applied Linguistics, 32,* 3–17.

Wray, A. (2002). *Formulaic language and the lexicon.* Cambridge, England: Cambridge University Press.

Wray, A., & Perkins, M. R. (2000). The functions of formulaic language: An integrated model. *Language and Communication, 20,* 1–28.

Yorio, C. (1989). Idiomaticity as an indicator of second language proficiency. In K. Hyltenstam & L. K. Obler (Eds.), *Bilingualism across the lifespan* (pp. 55–72). Cambridge, England: Cambridge University Press.

Appendix: Task with instructions

Part A
Instructions: Initiating utterances
In this part of the task, you will see a description on the screen. Read along with the speaker. Imagine that you are speaking to a friend. When you see "you say" on the screen, speak to your friend. Say the first thing you think of. You have seven seconds to respond. Speak clearly.

Here are two examples.

> Example A. The phone rings. You pick it up. [oral and written]
> *You say:* [screen only]
> NNS respondent: "Hello" [audio only]

> Example B. You are talking to your friend from a cell phone on a noisy city street. You couldn't hear something she said.
> *You say:* [screen only]
> NNS respondent: "Could you say that again?" [audio only]

Now, let's begin. This part will take about 10 minutes.

Initiators (eight, included in the analysis of the present chapter). All scenarios are followed by a visual prompt on the screen that says *"You say:"*.

I-1 You see your friend standing on a chair trying to reach a book at the top of a bookshelf. You know that the chair she is standing on has a broken leg.

I-3 After class you're walking to the library with a friend. It's been raining all morning, and you notice that your friend is about to step into a big puddle.

I-4 You are in the library and you see an old friend who you have not seen for a long time. You talk for a little while and as you are leaving you say,

I-8 You made an appointment with your teacher. Unfortunately you arrive 25 minutes late for the meeting, and the teacher is already leaving.

I-9 You are in the theater. There is a group of young teenagers sitting behind you. They are talking so loudly that you cannot hear a word.

I-10 You stop by your teacher's office to ask a question about the assignment. She takes time to answer your question. You know she is very busy, so before you say good-bye, you say,

I-11 You are at the bus stop. While waiting, you are talking with your friend on your cell phone. The bus arrives and you need to hang up.

I-12 You and a friend are about to cross the street when you see the campus bus coming. Your friend does not see the bus and is about to step in front of it.

Part B
Instructions: Responding utterances
In this part of the task, you are talking to your friend, and your friend speaks first. When your friend finishes, you answer. You have 7 seconds to respond. Remember to speak clearly.

Here are two examples.

Example A. You see your old friend at a party. [oral and written]

Friend: How are you? [audio only]

You say: [screen only]

NNS response: *Good, how are you?* [audio only]

Example B. Your friend needs some help moving a heavy old desk out of her dorm room.

Friend: Could you help me move my desk? [audio only]

You say: [screen only]

NNS response: *I'd be happy to.* [audio only]

Now let's begin. This part will take about 18 minutes.

Replies (14, included in the analysis of the present chapter): All scenarios are followed by an oral turn and visual prompt on the screen that says "You say:".

R–1   You're talking outside with your longtime neighbor and she tells you about her dog's accident. Audio only (AO): "Last Sunday my dog got hit by a truck."

R–2   You need to pick up a book at the bookstore, but you don't have any free time today. (AO): "I can pick it up for you."

R–3   There is a reception on campus. The organizer invited you and a few other students as well. It is getting late, and you decide to leave. You go over to the organizer. (AO): "Thanks for coming"

R–4   You go to a clothing store and you need to find a new shirt. A salesperson approaches you. You want the salesperson's assistance. (AO): "Can I help you?"

R–5   You are waiting in line at the movie theatre and the person in front of you says, (AO): "Could you hold my place in line? I'll be right back."

R–6   You are in the supermarket. After you pay, you are ready to pick up your bags. The cashier says, (AO): "Have a nice day!"

R–7   You made an appointment with your teacher. Unfortunately you arrive five minutes late for the meeting. Your teacher says, (AO): "Hello. Come on in."

R–9   You give your classmate a ride home. He lives in the building next to yours. He gets out of the car and says, (AO): "Thanks for the ride."

R–12 You go to a clothing store and you need to find a new shirt. A salesperson approaches you. You don't want the salesperson's assistance. (AO): "Can I help you?"

R–15 Your friend introduces you to his new roommate. (AO): "This is my new roommate, Bill."

R–16 You go to ask your teacher if he will be having office hours tomorrow, and he tells you about his father. (AO): "I won't be having office hours tomorrow. My father died, and I have to go to the funeral."

R–17 You have been studying very hard for your test. But on the morning of the test, your alarm does not go off and you oversleep. You ask your teacher for a make-up test. (AO): "Okay. I'll give you a make-up test this time, but don't let it happen again."

R–18 It's raining really hard and you are walking to the bank. A friend pulls his car over to offer you a ride. (AO): "Hey, want a ride?"

R–19 You are having dinner at a friend's house. Your friend offers you more food, but you couldn't possibly eat another bite. (AO): "Would you like some more?"

Effects of Cultural Background in a Test of ESL Pragmalinguistics: A DIF Approach

Carsten Roever
University of Melbourne, Australia

Very little is known about possible effects of test takers' linguistic and cultural background in tests of interlanguage pragmatics. Where tests are not designed for test takers from a specific first language (L1) background, this becomes an important issue because certain test takers may be unfairly advantaged by their native languages and cultures over others. In test analysis, such an advantage can be detected as differential item functioning (DIF). This study analyzes a dataset of 254 test takers with European and Asian first languages from Roever's (2005) test of ESL pragmalinguistics for evidence of DIF. Two well-established DIF techniques were used, the Mantel-Haenszel Odds Ratio and logistic regression. Analyses identified 9 items (25% of the total test) for which at least one of the DIF techniques found a large DIF. Closer inspection of the items and the test-taker response patterns indicates that the DIF was construct-irrelevant in some cases and therefore, evidence of bias. In other cases, the DIF was due to a confounding of test-taker background variables, most commonly exposure and group membership. In these cases, it constituted a legitimate difference between test takers and not bias. Implications for the design of pragmatics tests are discussed.

Testing of second language (L2) pragmatics is still a young area of research. Although we now have sufficient knowledge about learners' pragmatic development to build assessment instruments, only a few formal tests have actually been trialed and validated. Some of these instruments are designed for specific L1-L2 pairs, but for the ones that claim usability for learners from any native language and cultural background, the specific issue of bias arises: Are test takers of certain L1s or language groups disadvantaged on the test?

And is this disadvantage truly unfair or simply a reflection of factors that would also be impeding in real-world interaction? This study investigates bias effects in Roever's test of ESL pragmalinguistics (Roever, 2005, 2006) using two supplementary bias detection techniques: the Mantel-Haenszel odds ratio and logistic regression.

Assessment of L2 pragmatics

Although pragmatics is a recognized component of general communicative competence (Bachman, 1990; Canale, 1983; Canale & Swain, 1980), there are still very few assessment instruments available. This is probably due to a challenge that is in principle present in all areas of language testing, but it is especially foregrounded in the assessment of pragmatics (McNamara & Roever, 2006): the tension between designing instruments that are at same time practical, that is, not overly resource-intensive, but also cover a broad construct like "pragmatic ability," which by its very nature would require context-rich, performance-based types of assessment. There are in principle two ways to handle this dilemma: testers can expend the necessary resources to establish context in a way that resembles real-world context and design tasks that elicit online performance or they can limit the construct to aspects of pragmatics that can be assessed without establishing rich context and limit tasks to the elicitation of offline knowledge.

A second construct-related challenge that runs parallel to the context issue is the design of pragmatics tests as either contrastive for a specific L1-L2 pairing or generally applicable to test takers of any L1. Although a contrastively designed test is more limited in its usability, it avoids concerns over possible bias introduced through test takers' L1. On the other hand, the validity of any test that claims to be universally applicable would be attenuated if test takers' L1 backgrounds were to influence the measurement of the construct and give some test takers an illegitimate advantage.

The issues of practicality and L1-specific design are apparent in all research on L2-pragmatics test development along the sociopragmatics-pragmalinguistics divide (Leech, 1983). Tests that focus on the social side of pragmatics and investigate sociopragmatics and appropriateness tend to be more context rich and performance oriented and investigate a broader construct but are less practical and focus on a specific L1-L2 combination. For example, Hudson, Detmer, and Brown's (1995) test battery was designed as a prototypical measure to assess cross-cultural pragmatic ability in performing selected speech acts with different types of discourse completion tasks (DCTs) as well as roleplays and self-assessments. Yamashita's (1996) adaptation of Hudson et al.'s instrument was designed for native-English-speaking learners of Japanese, and Liu's (2006) set of multiple written measures targets the pragmatic knowledge of Mandarin Chinese speakers of English.

On the other hand, tests that focus on the linguistic side of pragmatics and investigate pragmalinguistics and pragmatic comprehension and encoding tend to be more context limited and knowledge oriented and investigate a narrower construct, but are more practical and applicable to test takers from any L1 background. Such instruments are discussed in more detail in the following section.

Tests of L2 pragmalinguistics: Limited construct but broader use

Two tests of ESL pragmalinguistics have been developed: Bouton's (1988, 1994, 1999) test of implicature and Roever's (2005, 2006) test battery assessing knowledge of implicature, routines, and speech acts. The present study is based on data from Roever's test, which integrates Bouton's work.

Roever (2005, 2006) developed a test battery for offline pragmalinguistic knowledge of implicatures, situational routines, and the speech acts of apology, request, and refusal. All sections consisted of 12 items, which were in multiple-choice format for the routines and implicature sections and discourse completion task (DCT) format with rejoinder for the speech act section.

The implicature section was based on Bouton's (1988, 1994) work and contained eight items assessing comprehension of idiosyncratic implicature and four items assessing comprehension of formulaic implicature (the "Pope question" and indirect criticism). Following Bouton, idiosyncratic implicature is equivalent to conventional implicature ("Has the mail come?" "It's not even noon yet!"), whereas formulaic implicature includes indirect criticism ("Did you like your food?" "Let's just say it was colorful.") and the Pope question ("Is the Pope Catholic?"). Similar to Bouton's (1999) findings, formulaic implicature was significantly more difficult than idiosyncratic implicature, but the effect size was small (Roever, 2005). Unlike Bouton, Roever found that development of implicature comprehension was not related to learners' L2 exposure but rather to their proficiency. The following is an example of an idiosyncratic implicature item:

> Jack is talking to his housemate Sarah about another housemate, Frank.
> Jack: "Do you know where Frank is, Sarah?"
> Sarah: "Well, I heard music from his room earlier."
> *What does Sarah probably mean?*
> 1. Frank forgot to turn the music off.
> 2. Frank's loud music bothers Sarah.
> 3. Frank is probably in his room.
> 4. Sarah doesn't know where Frank is.

The routines section assessed recognition of situational routines ("For here or to go?", "No thanks, I'm full."), functional routines ("Here you go," "Do you have the time?"), and second pair parts ("You're welcome," "That's okay."). Unlike for the other sections, exposure had a significant effect on the learners' knowledge of routines, and even short-term exposure of up to 3 months had a large effect. Routines items looked like the following example:

> Jack was just introduced to Jamal by a friend. They're shaking hands.
> *What would Jack probably say?*
> 1. "Nice to meet you."
> 2. "Good to run into you."
> 3. "Happy to find you."
> 4. "Glad to see you."

The speech act section consisted of 12 discourse-completion items, equally split between apologies, requests, and refusals. Within the three speech acts, 2 items used high-imposition situations, and 2 items used low imposition ones. All items contained rejoinders to aid contextualization and limit the range of acceptable responses. Although interlocutor reactions are not conclusively predictable in real-world interaction, the focus of the assessment was on eliciting knowledge of pragmalinguistic strategies for implementing speech acts. The rejoinders were constructed to aid such elicitation. Also, the role of context factors was acknowledged but kept to a minimum by instructing raters not to judge appropriateness unless a response was grossly offensive or far over-polite.

In the following example, the situation requires an apology, and the rejoinder elicits a supportive move, namely, an offer of repair:

> Ella borrowed a recent copy of *TIME Magazine* from her friend Sean but she accidentally spilled a cup of coffee all over it. She is returning the magazine to Sean.
> Ella: "_____."
> Sean: "No, don't worry about replacing it, I read it already."

The test takers were instructed to fill the gap in a way that completes the conversation so that it "makes sense." Unsurprisingly, knowledge of speech acts was mostly related to L2 proficiency, and high imposition speech acts were more difficult than low-imposition ones.

Roever's (2005) instrument assesses a broader construct of pragmalinguistic knowledge than Bouton's (1999) test, which was limited to knowledge of implicature. Like Bouton, Roever did not design the instrument for a particular L1 group, although some distractors were built in that were likely to appeal to a specific L1 population, namely, native German speakers. The Pope question implicature in particular was suspected of being easier for test takers coming from cultures with strong Judeo-Christian influences than for others. Investigating the possible effects of test-taker language and culture background on Roever's test is the purpose of this study. Such an investigation is best framed in terms of differential item functioning (DIF).

Differential item functioning

Investigations of DIF are common in large-scale assessments such as the GRE, SAT, and TOEFL (see O'Neill & McPeek, 1993, for a summary), but not a great deal of DIF work has been undertaken in language testing, and only one study exists on the testing of pragmatics (Roever, 2007).

DIF describes a situation where a test item is easier for a certain group of test takers than for another, matched group that has the same ability. For example, a population of ESL test takers could be broken down into those of European linguistic and cultural background and those of Asian linguistic and cultural background. When both populations are matched by ESL proficiency, they should have an equal likelihood of getting a certain test item correct. However, if the European group is much more likely to answer the item correctly than the Asian group, the groups' linguistic and cultural background may be interacting with a feature of the item and make it easier for the European test takers than the Asian ones. This would, of course, violate the construct of the test, which is language proficiency, not L1 background. A situation where test takers from one group have a consistently higher likelihood of a correct response than test takers from the other group across all (or most) ability levels is known as "uniform DIF."

There could also be a somewhat more complex situation where proficiency interacts with L1 background so that, for example, European low-proficiency learners are more likely than Asian low-proficiency learners to get the item correct, but the tendency is reversed for high proficiency learners, where the Asian group has a higher likelihood to respond correctly. This situation is known as "nonuniform DIF."

The major purpose of DIF investigations is to detect whether a certain test item unfairly advantages one group of test takers over the other. But sometimes differences between groups can be legitimate in terms of the construct. For example, the European test takers may be advantaged on an item because they can use positive transfer due to the typological similarity of their native languages with English, whereas the Asian test takers may not have this option. One could then argue that the European group would have a similar advantage in real-world language use, so the test is not actually unfair to the Asian test takers but simply reflects reality. In this case, a finding of DIF would be considered "statistical DIF," whereas in cases where DIF is actually determined to indicate an unfair advantage, it is known as "substantive DIF." Substantive DIF is akin to bias, which not only is unfair to test takers but also lowers the general validity of the test because inferences and decisions based on scores can lead to negative social consequences (McNamara & Roever, 2006; Messick, 1989).

It is important to emphasize that the differentiation between the two types of DIF is based on judgment rather than a statistical outcome. In fact, understanding what causes the differential functioning of an item is a difficult task at best. Expert judgments are used to hypothesize possible reasons for DIF, and researchers may use verbal protocols as well (Uiterwijk & Vallen, 2005). However, although hypotheses about causes may be generated this way, it is often difficult to test them.

Various approaches exist for the detection of DIF, but not all are equally useful in second language testing situations, where the numbers of participants are often not very large. All DIF detection approaches have in common that they split a larger test-taker population into two groups: a focal group and a reference group. The focal group is the group of interest, usually where a disadvantage is suspected. The reference group is the comparison group, for which an advantage is usually suspected. However, this nomenclature is purely conventional and has no inherent statistical relevance.

DIF detection techniques can be roughly grouped as contingency-table approaches, model-comparison approaches, and a range of other techniques (for an overview, see Camilli & Shepard, 1994). By far the most common contingency-table approach is the Mantel-Haenszel odds ratio (Dorans & Holland, 1993).

The Mantel-Haenszel odds ratio

To use the Mantel-Haenszel approach, researchers first group test takers into ability levels based on their total test scores or the scores on a criterion measure. For every item, they then compare the reference and the focal group's likelihood of success at each score level and compute the overall relative odds of getting the item right. An odds ratio of 1 indicates equal likelihood of a correct response (no DIF), and the odds ratio can be tested with a chi-square-based test as to whether it is significantly different from 1. If one group has a significantly higher likelihood of getting the item correct, DIF in favor of that group can be suspected.

To classify the size of DIF, the Mantel-Haenszel odds ratio is first converted to a statistic known as MH D-DIF by multiplying the logarithmic transformation of the odds by −2.35 (Holland & Thayer, 1985). A value of 0 indicates the absence of DIF, whereas negative values show an advantage for the reference group, and positive values show an advantage for the focal group. Following Zwick and Ercikan (1989), items with nonsignificant chi-square values or an MH D-DIF of less than 1 are considered to have negligible DIF. For an item to be classified as showing large DIF, MH D-DIF must have an absolute value larger than 1.5, which is not only significantly different from 0 but also significantly different from 1. All other items are considered to have moderate DIF.

Mantel-Haenszel has two potential shortcomings. One problem is the difficulty of determining ability levels if samples are small. Ability levels are usually based on the score for the test, a relevant subsection, or the score on a criterion measure if this measure can be assumed to measure the same construct as the test under investigation. Breslow (1981) showed that the more score levels can be identified, the better Mantel-Haenszel will work. However, if samples are small or skewed, there may be few or no test takers at a given score level. This can lead to a reduction in score levels, known as "fat matching" (Dorans & Holland, 1993), which reduces the usefulness of Mantel-Haenszel. Donoghue and Allen (1992) suggested various approaches to avoid empty cells in score-level tables, including combining score levels at the top and bottom extremes and having unequal intervals (i.e., some score levels may cover a broader range of scores than others). However, most analysts prefer equal score intervals and attempt to strike a balance between the number of score levels and having sufficient numbers of participants at each level.

A second problem of the Mantel-Haenszel technique is its inability to detect nonuniform DIF. In fact, if the reference group is advantaged at lower score levels, and the focal group is advantaged at higher score levels, the outcome of Mantel-Haenszel will look like there is no DIF at all in the item.

Mantel-Haenszel has been used in some large-scale studies in second language DIF research, though none of them was concerned with pragmatics. As part of their study comparing ETS's TOEFL and Cambridge's First Certificate in English test, Ryan and Bachman (1992) investigated DIF based on gender and test-taker L1, splitting their population of 1,426 test takers into speakers of Indo-European and non-Indo-European languages for the latter analysis. They found no appreciable gender-based DIF, but when comparing L1s, they detected a large DIF for nearly one third of their items, mostly in the vocabulary sections of the two tests. In a later study, Elder (1996) investigated DIF in the Australian Language Certificate with 6,863 teenage learners of Chinese, Italian, and Greek. She compared native speakers (NSs) and heritage learners on the one hand with true L2 learners (NNSs) on the other. Her study showed very large DIF for the sample with Chinese as a target language, identifying nearly two thirds of items as having DIF. Nearly a third of the items in the Italian exam and just over 10% in the Greek exam showed appreciable DIF. After a closer analysis of the items and consultation with experts, Elder concluded that much of the DIF was statistical and simply an indication that NSs process language differently from NNSs. In a recent study, Uiterwijk and Vallen (2005) applied Mantel-Haenszel to 180 items from three test papers of the Final Test of Primary Education in the Netherlands, taken at the end of elementary school by students about 12 years old. Uiterwijk and Vallen investigated DIF for a sample of nearly 8,000 native speakers of Dutch and second-generation immigrant students, finding DIF for about 17% of items, in most cases to the disadvantage of the immigrant students. Pae (2004) applied the Mantel-Haenszel technique to data from 14,000 test takers who took the English section of the Korean National Entrance Exam. He found DIF in about one third of the items, with the majority of DIF items advantaging science over humanities students. Finally, Pae and

Park (2006) investigated gender-based DIF on the English language section of the Korean College Scholastic Aptitude Test with a sample of 15,000 test takers. They found gender-based differences in two thirds of items, with the majority advantaging male over female test takers.

Although Mantel-Haenszel is by far the most popular DIF detection approach, logistic regression has gained in popularity recently.

Logistic regression

Logistic regression functions differently from Mantel-Haenszel and is essentially a model-comparison approach (for more details, see Zumbo, 1999). Like any regression, it tries to predict a dependent outcome variable from an independent predictor variable. Although other regression approaches use continuous outcome variables, logistic regression uses dichotomous outcome variables so that it can handle items scored as incorrect or correct (0/1). Logistic regression analyses for DIF proceed in three steps. In the first step, ability level alone serves as the predictor variable. This builds a regression model without DIF because ability level is supposed to be the only factor influencing the likelihood of getting an item correct: high ability test takers should have much higher likelihoods than low ability test takers. In the second step, a new regression model is built again using ability but adding group membership (reference or focal group). If the prediction from the new model with group membership is significantly better than from the previous model without group membership, uniform DIF is present because membership in the reference or focal group has an effect on test takers' scores, and scores are not determined by ability alone. In a third step, the interaction between ability and group membership is integrated to detect nonuniform DIF. At each step, an effect-size statistic (usually Nagelkerke's R2) is computed, which shows the contribution that the addition of the variable makes towards explaining the variance in the data. The effect size is accompanied by a significance level based on chi-square, which shows whether the increase in variance explained is significant.

What level of effect size indicates serious DIF is a matter of some debate. Following Cohen (1992), Zumbo (1999) suggested that nonsignificant effect sizes or those of less than .13 should be considered negligible in terms of indicating DIF, significant effect sizes from .13 to .26 should be considered medium, and more than .26 should be considered large. However, Jodoin and Gierl (2001) used a radically different classification scheme after showing that by applying Zumbo's approach, only a minuscule number of DIF items in their simulation study would be identified. They considered negligible DIF to be an effect size of less than .035; medium DIF, from .035 to .07 with a significant chi-square; and large DIF, greater than .07 with a significant chi-square.

Overall, logistic regression is superior to Mantel-Haenszel in its ability to detect nonuniform DIF, but at the same time, it is much more mathematically complex than Mantel-Haenszel, and the integration of interaction terms can make its results difficult to interpret. It has not been used as extensively as Mantel-Haenszel in language-testing DIF research, but recent studies exist, though again with very large sample sizes.

Kim (2001) used logistic regression on data from the SPEAK test. She divided a sample of 1,038 test takers into speakers of Indo-European and non-Indo-European languages and found a significant effect of group membership and the interaction between group membership and ability. However, neither factor had a particularly large effect. In a series of even larger-scale studies, a team of researchers at ETS investigated the effects of native language (Lee, Breland, & Muraki, 2004), gender (Breland, Lee, Najarian, & Muraki, 2004), and response mode (Breland, Lee, & Muraki, 2004) on scores for TOEFL CBT writing prompts. Because writing prompts only render a single score, an aggregated score from the other TOEFL sections was used as the ability variable. Investigating over 80 essay prompts with samples of over 200,000 essays in the native-language study and over 600,000 in the gender and response-mode studies, the researchers identified instances of uniform and nonuniform DIF caused by the background variables, but the effect sizes were overwhelmingly negligible.

Evaluation of logistic regression and Mantel-Haenszel

Both techniques have the advantages that they can be computed using standard statistical software and do not require specialized programs. They are also, in principle, capable of finding DIF in smaller datasets, although most previous research has used very large samples. One conceptual issue for both is the effect-size criterion. Classifying DIF as "large," "moderate," or "small" is essentially a value judgment, and the MH D-DIF approach or Zumbo's (1999) classification schemes make it quite difficult for items to be classified as having "large" DIF, though Jodoin and Gierl's (2001) approach is more liberal.

Despite their shortcomings, these two procedures were chosen for this study because they are practical and should supplement each other well.

Study

Tests of interlanguage pragmatics that are designed for test takers of any L1 (rather than a specific L1-L2 pair) are more versatile than tests designed for specific L1s. However, they may be affected by construct-irrelevant factors introduced by test takers' native languages or cultures. In this exploratory DIF study, the first question to be answered is whether L1-induced DIF exists in Roever's test of ESL pragmalinguistics; the second is whether the DIF is statistical and construct-relevant (no bias) or substantive and construct-irrelevant (bias). The dividing factor for the reference and focal groups is native-language background, and like in Ryan and Bachman's (1992) study and Lee, Breland, and Muraki's (2004) comparison by native language, the test-taker population was split into Indo-European (German and Polish) and non-Indo-European

(Chinese, Japanese, Korean, Thai, and Vietnamese) first languages. This is not to imply that speakers of these language groups are in some way culturally "the same" but that they differ in at least two respects. Indo-European languages are typologically closer to American English, thus allowing more linguistic transfer. Speakers of Indo-European languages also share a multitude of historical, religious, and cultural ties with Anglo speakers of American English, thereby also possibly facilitating transfer.

As a secondary goal, this study examines the suitability of Mantel-Haenszel and logistic regression for small sample sizes, which are more common in language-testing research than the large samples used in many past studies.

Research questions

Which items show DIF in either or both methods?

If the methods are indeed supplementary, it would be expected that they both identify the same cases of uniform DIF and that logistic regression might also find nonuniform DIF.

Which items can be classified as showing large DIF, and what are their characteristics?

The classification criterion for DIF sizes is a matter of judgment, and the supplementary use of two techniques should help judge the size of DIF. DIF needs to be further understood in terms of which group is advantaged and whether the DIF is uniform or nonuniform. For reasons of space, only items with large DIF are considered in detail.

Is the DIF in these items substantive or statistical, and what might its cause be?

It is a matter of value judgment and argumentation whether any DIF detected simply shows a construct-relevant difference between groups or constitutes construct-irrelevant variance. This necessarily entails thinking about the possible causes of DIF in these items.

Method

Participants

The participants were 254 test takers, of which 164 spoke European languages and 90 non-European languages. Specifically, in the European-languages group, 159 test takers gave German as their L1 or German and another European language, most commonly Russian. Five test takers had Polish as their first language, but because all of these participants were located in Germany and recruited at a German high school or university, it is likely that even the L1 Polish test takers had high proficiency in German. The non-European-languages group was more linguistically and culturally diverse and comprised 57 Japanese speakers, 15 Chinese speakers, 12 Korean speakers, 5 Thai speakers, and 1 Vietnamese speaker. The vast majority of these participants were located in the US, with a smaller group located in Japan.

Table 1 shows the test takers' average age1, length of residence in English-speaking countries, and gender distribution.

Table 1. Population characteristics

	reference	focal
age (years)	16.5	25.6
length of residence (years)	0.4	2.6
male/female/undisclosed	61/93/10	25/47/8

Instruments

The data for this study came from Roever's (2005) test of ESL pragmalinguistics. The test was delivered through a web browser (usually Internet Explorer) and consisted of three sections: implicature, routines, and speech acts. The test takers chose the correct answer for the multiple-choice items in the implicature and routines sections and typed in their responses for the speech-acts section. Each section was preceded by an interactive example, and the entire test was preceded by a bio questionnaire. The sequence of the sections as well as the sequence of the items within a section was randomized to avoid sequencing effects. The sections were time-limited and automatically terminated when the maximum time was reached (12 minutes for implicatures and routines, 18 minutes for speech acts). All of the responses were sent to the researcher via a form e-mail. The multiple-choice sections were self-scoring, and the test takers could elect to see their section scores at the end. The speech-act section was hand-scored by the researcher, and three raters scored a subset of the speech-act responses.

Table 2 shows the reliabilities of the sections and the whole test.

Table 2. Section and whole-test reliabilities (Cronbach's Alpha)

section	Alpha
implicature	.815
routines	.728
speech acts (total)	.894
interrater reliability for subset	.96
total test	.913

All section reliabilities are in the acceptable range, with the speech-acts section being particularly reliable.

Tables 3, 4, and 5 show the individual item mean scores for the reference and focal groups.

Table 3. Implicature difficulty for focal and reference group; difficulty and discrimination for whole sample

item	focal group		reference group		total sample		
	n	M	n	M	N	M	discrim.
Imp 1	67	.8955	144	.7431	211	.7915	.532
Imp 2	64	.7031	143	.5874	207	.6232	.701
Imp 3	64	.7188	143	.5315	207	.5894	.592
Imp 4	65	.6769	143	.5804	208	.6106	.598
Imp 5	64	.3906	143	.2937	207	.3237	.356
Imp 6	65	.7231	144	.5486	209	.6029	.544
Imp 7	65	.5538	142	.6127	207	.5942	.513
Imp 8	66	.5303	144	.3819	210	.4286	.531
Imp 9	62	.7419	143	.6993	205	.7122	.625
Imp 10	64	.6406	142	.5282	206	.5631	.540
Imp 11	66	.7879	143	.6014	209	.6603	.714
Imp 12	65	.6154	142	.7113	207	.6812	.606
mean	67	.6592	144	.5667	211	.5961	

Table 4. Routines difficulty for focal and reference group; difficulty and discrimination for whole sample

item	focal group		reference group		total sample		
	n	M	n	M	N	M	discrim.
Rout 1	73	.9041	151	.8028	210	.8381	.322
Rout 2	70	.7143	144	.2535	210	.4095	.655
Rout 3	69	.6377	147	.6197	210	.6286	.463
Rout 4	71	.5915	145	.3028	210	.4048	.529
Rout 5	71	.8873	146	.5775	210	.6810	.467
Rout 6	69	.2754	145	.1972	210	.2238	.365
Rout 7	69	.9855	147	.4366	210	.6143	.618
Rout 8	71	.9718	144	.8521	210	.8952	.408
Rout 9	70	.9714	145	.6197	210	.7333	.472
Rout 10	69	.7971	146	.3028	210	.4667	.578
Rout 11	71	.9155	145	.5493	210	.6667	.526
Rout 12	69	.8406	144	.4225	210	.5571	.541
mean	68	.7990	142	.4947	210	.5933	

Table 5. Speech act difficulty for focal and reference group; difficulty and discrimination for whole sample

item	focal group n	M	reference group n	M	total sample N	M	discrim.
Prg 1	65	.6615	132	.4848	197	.5431	.550
Prg 2	40	.7250	109	.4862	149	.5503	.697
Prg 3	51	.7647	125	.6160	176	.6591	.703
Prg 4	48	.8333	120	.6333	168	.6905	.765
Prg 5	59	.4746	117	.4103	176	.4318	.583
Prg 6	55	.7636	117	.5983	172	.6512	.695
Prg 7	56	.5179	116	.3362	172	.3953	.577
Prg 8	59	.6102	119	.2857	178	.3933	.654
Prg 9	54	.7222	120	.8750	174	.8276	.492
Prg 10	57	.2632	119	.1597	176	.1932	.472
Prg 11	61	.7541	120	.6833	181	.7072	.697
Prg 12	41	.8049	102	.6863	143	.7203	.671
mean	65	.6434	132	.5170	197	.5587	

It is noticeable that the focal group scores were higher than the reference group scores on all sections and most items, with the difference being particularly pronounced on the routines section. This difference is probably due to the focal group being generally higher proficiency and having had more exposure. It is somewhat unusual in DIF research to have a focal group with a higher score than the reference group, but this does not affect the statistical calculations.

Procedures

The test takers' scores on all items and their background information were entered into an SPSS 14.0 spreadsheet. The test takers were divided into a focal group and a reference group, based on their self-reported L1s, and section totals for the three test sections were computed. These section totals then served as ability proxies for the two DIF analyses that were undertaken: Mantel-Haenszel and logistic regression.

In preparation for the Mantel-Haenszel statistic, the section scores were first subdivided into score levels with the help of the SPSS FREQUENCIES function[2]. The small number of test takers and the importance of not having empty cells for either group at a given score level necessitated "thick matching" (Donoghue & Allen, 1992). For the implicature and speech-act sections, 10 score levels were used, each 10 percentage points wide, that is, 0–10%, 10.1–20%, 20.1–30%, and so on, up to 90.1–100%. For the routines section, only six score levels could be identified, each 16.67% wide, that is, 0–16.67%, 16.68–33.33%, and so on, up to 83.34%–100%.

The Mantel-Haenszel statistic was obtained separately for every item through the SPSS crosstabs function, with the item as a column, group membership in the focal or reference group as a row, and the score level of the relevant section as a layer. This produced the Mantel-Haenszel odds ratio for each item, together with its significance level and the logarithmic transformation of the odds. The logarithmic transformation of the odds was multiplied by −2.35 to obtain MH D-DIF, and items with significant results and whose MH D-DIF was larger than 1.5 were further analyzed to find whether the D-DIF value was significantly larger than 1, which would indicate a large DIF according to Zwick and Ercikan (1989).

Logistic regression was computed through the binary logistic function in SPSS. The item score was the dependent variable, and the section score, group membership, and interaction between score and group membership were entered sequentially into the regression equation. In other words, in the first step, section score was considered by itself. In the second step, group membership was added as a predictor, and in the third step, the interaction term between section score and group membership was added. The output included the omnibus test of model coefficients for each step, indicating through a chi-square test whether the additional variable improved the model prediction over the previous model. So, for example, does the model predict significantly better if group membership is added to section score than if section score is the only predictor? The output also included Nagelkerke's R^2 for each step, which shows how much of the total variance is accounted for by the model.

The significance levels for all of the analyses were set at $\alpha = .05$, and to confirm the credibility of the results, the analyses were rerun with group membership randomly assigned to participants. Given that 36 Mantel-Haenszel odds ratios, 36 logistic regressions for uniform DIF, and 36 logistic regressions for nonuniform DIF were computed, two significant results that are in fact Type I errors can be expected for each of these computations in the simulated condition.

Results and discussion

Which items show DIF in either or both methods?

Table 6 lists the items that exhibited significant DIF in Mantel-Haenszel and/or logistic regression. Only items obtaining a significant result in at least one of the procedures are shown.

Table 6. Items with DIF

item	total DIF	uniform	non-uniform	MH odds	D-DIF	advantaged group or interaction	DIF size (Zumbo, 1999)	DIF size (Jodoin & Gierl, 2001)	DIF size (Zwick & Ercikan, 1989)
Imp 5	.125	.001	.124**	0.60	1.20	interaction	negl.	large	negl.
Imp 7	.034	.033**	.001	3.02	(2.60*)	reference	negl.	negl.	mod.
Imp 12	.080	.079**	.001	6.82	4.51**	reference	negl.	large	large

Rout 3	.153	.148**	.005	12.82	5.99**	reference	mod.	large	large
Rout 4	.026	.005	.021*	1.89	1.49	interaction	negl.	negl.	negl.
Rout 5	.037	.008	.029*	0.49	1.68	interaction	negl.	mod.	negl.
Rout 6	.199	.065**	.134**	34.42	8.32*	reference/ interaction	mod.	large	large
Rout 7	.089	.089**	.000	0.02	9.52**	focal	negl.	large	large
Rout 9	.045	.044**	.001	0.10	5.49*	focal	negl.	mod.	large
Rout 10	.086	.022*	.064**	0.40	(2.15*)	focal/ interaction	negl.	large	mod.
Rout 12	.039	.009	.030*	0.71	.80	interaction	negl.	mod.	negl.
Prg 8	.044	.041**	.003	0.20	3.76**	focal	negl.	mod.	large
Prg 9	.233	.198**	.035*	9.89	5.38**	reference	mod.	large	large

note: *significant at p < .05, **significant at p < .01; D-DIF values in parentheses mean significant at Δ = 0 but not significant at Δ = 1, that is, the item has mod. DIF according to Zwick and Ercikan (1989).

Altogether, three implicature items, eight routines items, and two speech-act items were identified as showing DIF, accounting for just over one third of the total number of items on the test. However, two thirds of the routines section has some degree of DIF.

It is noticeable that in all cases where logistic regression finds significant uniform DIF, Mantel-Haenszel also detects the item as showing DIF. This is comforting because it strengthens the case that DIF actually exists in the item. However, in cases where only the nonuniform DIF portion is significant, Mantel-Haenszel does not detect the item as showing DIF, which is unsurprising because Mantel-Haenszel cannot detect nonuniform DIF. It was never the case that Mantel-Haenszel identified an item that logistic regression did not also identify.

In the simulation study with random group membership, two items were identified by Mantel-Haenszel and logistic regression as showing uniform DIF, and two further items as showing nonuniform DIF. It is therefore likely that two to four of the items shown above do in fact not have DIF.

Which items can be classified as showing large DIF, and what are their characteristics?

Using Zumbo's (1999) criteria for effect size in logistic regression, out of 13 possible DIF items, 10 have negligible DIF, only 3 items have moderate DIF, and none have large DIF. However, when Jodoin and Gierl's (2001) more relaxed criteria are used, only 2 items have negligible DIF, 4 have medium DIF, and 7 items have large DIF.

The outcome of the MH D-DIF statistic is quite similar to Jodoin and Gierl's (2001) analysis. Following Zwick and Ercikan's (1989) classification, seven items have large DIF, two items have medium DIF, and the rest have negligible DIF. It must be noted, however, that the items shown in Table 6 that were classified as having negligible DIF by MH D-DIF were always items where only the nonuniform DIF portion was significant, so Mantel-Haenszel could not detect these items.

Of the items that show large DIF, most have overwhelmingly uniform DIF, except Imp 5, Rout 6, and Rout 10, which had more nonuniform DIF. The item with the largest DIF size in the logistic regression analysis was Prg 9, a high-imposition refusal item (see appendix), which uniformly and strongly advantaged the reference group. The other items that advantaged the reference group were Imp 12 (Pope question) and Rout 3 (a restaurant routine). The items that uniformly advantaged the focal group include Rout 7, a second pair part response to "Thank you," which had the largest MH D-DIF statistic, and Prg 8, a high-imposition apology in a university setting.

Imp 5 (indirect criticism) had nonuniform DIF and generated the graph in Figure 1.

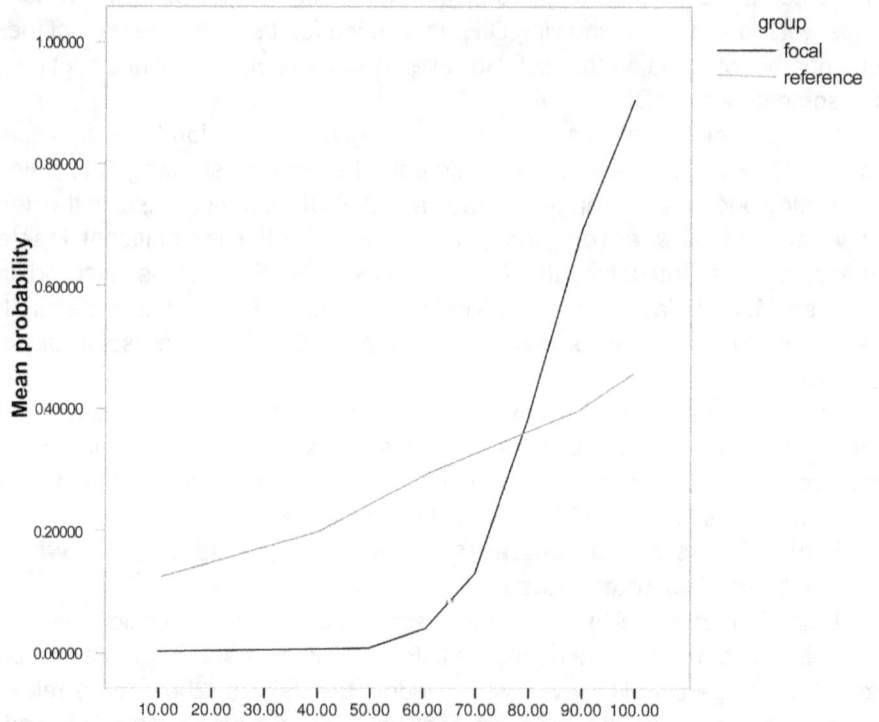

Figure 1. Mean probability of a correct response on Imp 5 for focal and reference groups by score level.

It is noticeable that the reference group has a higher likelihood of answering the item correctly for all but the highest ability levels.

As Figure 2 shows, Rout 10 (take-out restaurant) followed a similar pattern, although the reference group was only advantaged at the lower ability levels, whereas at the higher levels, the likelihood of a correct response was much larger for the focal group.

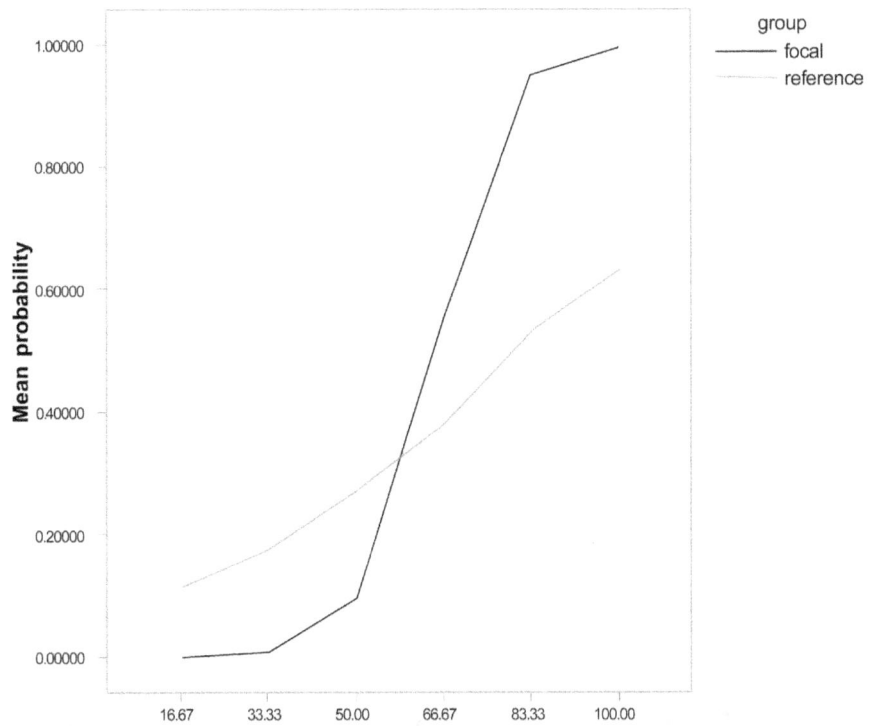

Figure 2. Mean probability of a correct response on Rout 10 for focal and reference groups by score level.

The third item with more nonuniform than uniform DIF was Rout 6 (invitation), which showed a strange curve (Figure 3).

This item was possibly not appropriate for the focal group because it discriminated overly sharply. Virtually only focal-group members with perfect ability even had a chance of answering the item correctly—all other focal-group members invariably got it wrong. Also, statistical indices associated with logistic regression showed possible data problems, which caution against drawing conclusions from the item: The b-value in the regression equation exceeded 300 trillion and had unacceptably large confidence intervals, whereas b-values are commonly in the one- to two-digit range.

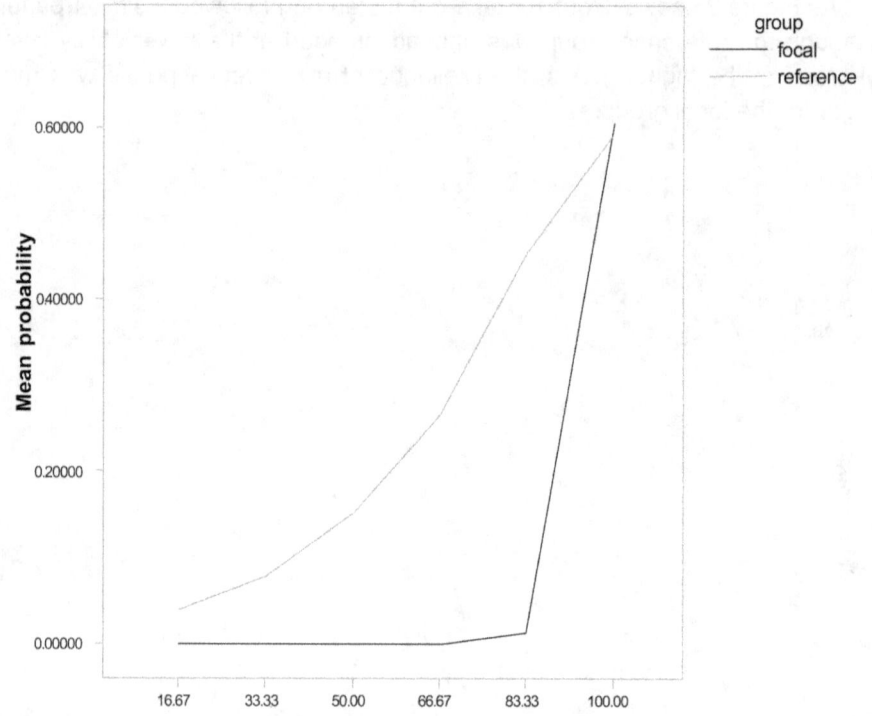

Figure 3. Mean probability of a correct response on Rout 6 for focal and reference groups by score level.

Is the DIF in these items substantive or statistical, and what might its cause be?

Understanding the sources of DIF can be challenging and is necessarily a somewhat speculative undertaking. For the implicature items with DIF, an explanation is easiest to find for Imp 12, the Pope question. The test takers of European background had nearly seven times greater likelihood of answering this item correctly than the test takers of Asian L1 background. However, a comparable item (Imp 6, "Do fish swim?") showed only negligible DIF. It is likely that sociocultural background knowledge is the cause for this outcome. Test takers of German or Polish background come from cultures with strong Judeo-Christian influences, and, independent of their own beliefs, would be exposed to knowledge about what a Pope is and that he is Catholic. Test takers of Asian cultural backgrounds are much less likely to have such exposure because their cultures are less influenced by Christianity. However, test takers of both L1 groups are equally likely to know that fish do in fact swim.

Whether the DIF introduced by test takers' background knowledge about the Pope is deemed statistical or substantive depends on whether one considers background knowledge an essential part of the construct of implicature. If the focus of the construct is on the interpretation of nonliteral utterances, then cultural background knowledge may be considered construct-irrelevant variance. However, if the construct is broadened to include some degree of background knowledge, as was the case in this test, then the Pope question is a legitimate component of an implicature measure. In any case, this finding raises awareness of the effect of specific cultural background knowledge, and test designers would be well advised to consider to what extent they are intending to test it alongside implicature interpretation ability.

Imp 5 (indirect criticism) showed an interaction effect, with the focal group having a very low likelihood of a correct answer at lower ability levels but equaling and then surpassing the reference group at high levels. It is noticeable that for the reference group, the likelihood of a correct response only rose relatively slowly with ability, as the shallow slope of the graph shows, and it never reached 50% likelihood. This indicates that the item is difficult, and it may take an additional "boost" above and beyond proficiency to have a substantial chance of getting it correct. It is possible that exposure provided such a boost. The test takers in the Asian group who answered the item correctly had longer average residence in English-speaking countries (3 years, 7 months) than test takers who did not (2 years, 1 month), although the difference was not statistically significant (t = 1.085, df = 57, ns). Although implicature knowledge is mostly related to proficiency, exposure to formulaic patterns of implicature certainly aids interpretation and may help explain the interaction effect in this item. Such an explanation points to statistical rather than substantive DIF because exposure would confer a legitimate advantage in real-world settings as well.

Among the routines items, Rout 7 ("You're welcome") strongly advantages the focal group to the point that membership in the focal group almost guarantees that test takers will answer it correctly. This is not surprising because this extremely high-frequency routine would certainly be easily learned by anyone with even a short residence in an English-speaking speech community. Rout 9 ("Can I leave a message?") behaves in a similar fashion, though not quite as deterministically. Even low-ability focal-group members have a better than even chance of getting the item correct, and most likely an exposure effect is at work here as well. This advantage due to residence on these two items indicates statistical DIF; however, another feature of Rout 7 might also introduce some substantive DIF to the reference group's disadvantage. One distractor ("please") was attractive to many reference-group members (chosen by nearly one third of the reference group) due to transfer from German, where this is an appropriate response to "thank you." So, the attractiveness of the distractor may have contributed to lowering the reference group's likelihood of getting the item correct and may have misled reference-group members who might otherwise have chosen the correct response. However, it could just as well be argued that the reference-group members might resort to negative transfer in real-world interaction as well, so their choice of a transfer-based distractor indicates lower competence in terms of the construct and not DIF.

The uniform advantage for reference-group members on Rout 3 ("Can I get you anything else?") is much more difficult to explain. The choice of the correct response is not facilitated by positive transfer from German, nor did the focal group fall prey to transfer effects. Except for the lowest score level, the focal group had longer residences than the reference group and should therefore have had more opportunities to encounter this routine. So, why this item greatly advantages the reference group is unclear, and this may actually be a case of Type I error.

For the items with large interaction terms, the outcome for Rout 10 ("For here or to go?") might be interpreted in a similar way as Imp 5 above. The high-ability focal-group members surpassed the reference group in their likelihood of a correct response, and those focal-group members who got the item right had nearly 2 years longer residence in English-speaking countries than focal-group members who did not. So, once again, residence may have given a boost to knowledge of this routine, but its lower frequency than that of "you're welcome" in Rout 7 required a longer residence to be assured of a correct response.

The outcome for Rout 6 ("Do you think you could make it?") is uninterpretable due to the statistical behavior of the item.

Of the speech act items, Prg 8, a high-imposition apology, advantages the focal group. This might be due to the item being set in a university context, which would be unfamiliar to many of the reference-group members, who were high school students. Although the apology situation could just as well have been situated in a high school or other setting, their lack of familiarity with sociopragmatic rules of discourse in a university setting may have led to reference-group members underperforming their actual competence in producing apologies. It is noticeable that the other high-imposition apology item on the test (Prg 11) did not show any noticeable DIF. Prg 8 would therefore be another likely candidate for substantive DIF because the setting of the speech act should not influence the test taker's likelihood of producing it correctly if they have the ability.

Finally, Prg 9, a high-imposition refusal item, advantages the reference group and was identified by logistic regression as having the single largest amount of DIF on the whole test, including the single largest amount of uniform DIF. Even reference-group members who only achieved a total score of 10–20% on the section had a nearly 80% chance of getting this item correct, and ones whose total scores were between 30–40% or above were virtually certain to produce a correct response. By comparison, to have an 80% likelihood of a correct response, focal-group members had to have total scores in the 50–60% range, and even among the highest scorers in the focal group, some test takers still did not answer this item successfully. In the item, an interlocutor is asked by a friend for a $500 loan, but the friend refuses and only offers to lend $200. A possible explanation for the vastly lower scores of the focal group might be the cultural inappropriateness of a refusal in this situation. It may be more difficult for Asian test takers to refuse a friend's request for help due to sociopragmatic norms of reciprocity and mutuality (Young, 1994). The item may therefore have required test takers to produce a response that they would not give in real-world interaction, which may have greatly increased its difficulty for the focal group. It is again difficult to decide whether the DIF here is substantive or statistical: It could be argued that the ability to produce refusals is "fair game" in a test of pragmatics, and test takers can be expected to produce them regardless of whether they would choose to do so in actual interactions. This is analogous to a grammar test assessing test takers' knowledge of the present perfect progressive, regardless of whether they ever wish to use it in reality. However, such an argument ignores the shortcomings of a testing instrument such as the DCT, which only allows a one-shot response and is in this case further constrained by a rejoinder. In real-world communication, test takers might be able to convey their refusal differently, for example, by expressing their reluctance to lend their friend money and hoping that the friend will then drop the request. This element of interactive negotiation is necessarily missing in a DCT, and it could be the case that the test instrument itself was unable to tap the test takers' competence in this instance. This highlights the problematicity of using DCTs for assessing speech acts that might in real-world communication unfold over several turns. In any case, if the test format makes it easier for one group of test takers to answer correctly than for the other group, an argument can certainly be made for substantive DIF.

Conclusion

This study identified cases of L1-based DIF in a test of second language pragmalinguistics. Most DIF was statistical and justifiable in terms of the construct, but the cases of substantive DIF that did occur highlight the necessity of carefully delineating the construct, for example, with regard to how much background knowledge should be tested. They also show that it is important to design situation descriptions carefully so that they do not advantage or disadvantage certain groups of test takers and to be aware of the shortcomings of the test instrument.

The test takers' L1 backgrounds were in some instances confounded with other background factors, most commonly residence, and the absence of matching of the focal and reference groups according to background variables remains a limitation of this study: It would have been preferable to have equal distributions of residence, age, and educational background in both groups, which might have prevented some findings of statistical DIF.

At the same time, this "messy" situation is often encountered in language testing and applied linguistics research, where sample sizes are small and samples are often "found" because they happen to be available to the researcher rather than carefully assembled from a large random population. The great deal of overlap between procedures as mathematically distinct as Mantel-Haenszel and logistic regression shows that it is possible to use such DIF detection procedures with reference and focal groups of 100–200 participants, although, of course, larger samples are always preferable.

Future research into designing pragmatics assessments should continue to consider DIF as an issue for non-L1-specific instruments and might use DIF analyses to aid the adaptation of L1-specific tests for larger groups of native languages. Understanding differential item functioning in pragmatics assessments and its causes can help testers gain insight into the ways that test tasks tap learners' L2 pragmatic knowledge and contribute to a detailed picture of learners' L2 pragmatic competence.

Notes

1   Although the groups differed strongly in average age, Rose (2000) indicated that age in itself has very little effect on L2 pragmatic competence. Exposure can, of course, affect it much more strongly, but this is expected and relevant to the construct.
2   Although total scores are often used for classification, a factor analysis indicated that the sections had fairly large amounts of unique variance, and their reliabilities were considered sufficiently high to serve as the ability proxy in this study.

References

Bachman, L. F. (1990). *Fundamental considerations in language testing.* Oxford, England: Oxford University Press.
Bouton, L. (1988). A cross-cultural study of ability to interpret implicatures in English. *World Englishes, 17,* 183–196.
Bouton, L. F. (1994). Conversational implicature in the second language: Learned slowly when not deliberately taught. *Journal of Pragmatics, 22,* 157–167.
Bouton, L. F. (1999). Developing nonnative speaker skills in interpreting conversational implicatures in English: Explicit teaching can ease the process. In E. Hinkel (Ed.), *Culture in second language teaching and learning* (pp. 47–70). Cambridge, England: Cambridge University Press.
Breland, H., Lee, Y. W., & Muraki, E. (2004). *Comparability of TOEFL CBT writing prompts: Response mode analyses* (TOEFL Research Report No. 75). Princeton, NJ: Educational Testing Service.

Breland, H., Lee, Y. W., Najarian, M., & Muraki, E. (2004). *An analysis of TOEFL CBT writing prompt difficulty and comparability for different gender groups* (TOEFL Research Report No. 76). Princeton, NJ: Educational Testing Service.

Breslow, N. (1981). Odds ratio estimates when the data are sparse. *Psychometrika, 46*, 443–460.

Camilli, G., & Shepard, L. A. (1994). *Methods for identifying biased test items*. Thousand Oaks, CA: Sage.

Canale, M. (1983). From communicative competence to communicative language pedagogy. In J. Richards & R. Schmidt (Eds.), *Language and communication* (pp. 2–27). London: Longman.

Canale, M., & Swain, M. (1980). Theoretical bases of communicative approaches to second language teaching and testing. *Applied Linguistics, 1,* 1–47.

Cohen, J. (1992). A power primer. *Psychological Bulletin, 112*, 155–159.

Donoghue, J. R., & Allen, N. L. (1992). *"Thin" versus "thick" matching in the Mantel-Haenszel procedure for detecting DIF* (ETS Research Report No. 92–76). Princeton, NJ: ETS.

Dorans, N. J., & Holland, P. W. (1993). DIF detection and description: Mantel-Haenszel and standardization. In P. W. Holland & H. Wainer (Eds.), *Differential item functioning* (pp. 35–66). Hillsdale, NJ: Lawrence Erlbaum.

Elder, C. (1996). The effect of language background on "foreign" language test performance: The case of Chinese, Italian, and Modern Greek. *Language Learning, 46*, 233–282.

Holland, P. W., & Thayer, D. T. (1985). *An alternative definition of the ETS delta scale of item difficulty* (ETS Research Report No. 85–43). Princeton, NJ: Educational Testing Service.

Hudson, T., Detmer, E., & Brown, J. D. (1995). *Developing prototypic measures of cross-cultural pragmatics* (Technical Report No. 7). Honolulu: University of Hawai'i, Second Language Teaching and Curriculum Center.

Jodoin, M.G., & Gierl, M.J. (2001). Evaluating type I error and power rates using an effect size measure with the logistic regression procedure for DIF detection. *Applied Measurement in Education, 14*, 4, 329–349.

Kim, M. (2001). Detecting DIF across the different language groups in a speaking test. *Language Testing, 18*, 89–114.

Lee, Y. W., Breland, H., & Muraki, E. (2004). *Comparability of TOEFL CBT writing prompts for different native language groups* (TOEFL Research Report No. 77). Princeton, NJ: Educational Testing Service.

Leech, G. (1983). *Principles of pragmatics*. London: Longman.

Liu, J. (2006). *Measuring interlanguage pragmatic knowledge of EFL learners*. Frankfurt, Germany: Peter Lang.

McNamara, T. F., & Roever, C. (2006). *Language testing: The social dimension*. Oxford, England: Basil Blackwell.

Messick, S. (1989). Validity. In R. L. Linn (Ed.), *Educational measurement* (3rd ed., pp. 13–103). New York: American Council on Education & Macmillan.

O'Neill, K. A., & McPeek, W. M. (1993). Item and test characteristics that are associated with differential item functioning. In P. W. Holland & H. Wainer (Eds.), *Differential item functioning* (pp. 255–276). Hillsdale, NJ: Lawrence Erlbaum.

Pae, T. (2004). DIF for students with different academic backgrounds. *Language Testing, 21*, 53–73.

Pae, T. I., & Park, G. P. (2006). Examining the relationship between differential item functioning and differential test functioning. *Language Testing, 23*, 475–496.

Roever, C. (2005). *Testing ESL pragmatics*. Frankfurt, Germany: Peter Lang.

Roever, C. (2006). Validation of a web-based test of ESL pragmalinguistics. *Language Testing, 23*(2), 229–256.

Roever, C. (2007). DIF in the assessment of second language pragmatics. *Language Assessment Quarterly, 4*, 2, 165–189.

Ryan, K., & Bachman, L. F. (1992). Differential item functioning on two tests of EFL proficiency. *Language Testing, 9*, 12–29.

Uiterwijk, H., & Vallen, T. (2005). Linguistic sources of item bias for second generation immigrants in Dutch tests. *Language Testing, 22*, 211–234.

Yamashita, S. O. (1996). *Six measures of JSL pragmatics* (Technical Report No. 14). Honolulu: University of Hawai'i, Second Language Teaching and Curriculum Center.

Young, W. L. (1994). *Crosstalk and culture in Sino-American communication*. Cambridge, England: Cambridge University Press.

Zumbo, B. D. (1999). *A handbook on the theory and methods of differential item functioning (DIF): Logistic regression modeling as a unitary framework for binary and Likert-type (ordinal) item scores*. Ottawa, Ontario, Canada: Directorate of Human Resources Research and Evaluation, Department of National Defense.

Zwick, R., & Ercikan, K. (1989). Analysis of differential item functioning in the NAEP history assessment. *Journal of Educational Measurement, 26*, 1, 55–66.

Appendix: Items with DIF

Note that the correct answers are underlined below for the reader's convenience. Of course, nothing was underlined in the operational test version.

Imp 5: Jose and Tanya are professors at a college. They are talking about a student, Derek.
Jose: "How did you like Derek's essay?"
Tanya: "I thought it was well-typed."
What does Tanya probably mean?
1. She did not like Derek's essay.
2. She likes it if students hand in their work type-written.
3. She thought the topic Derek had chosen was interesting.
4. She doesn't really remember Derek's essay.

Imp 7: Jenny and her housemate Darren go to college in Southern California. They are talking one morning before going to class.
Jenny: "Darren, is it cold out this morning?"
Darren: "Jenny, it's August!"
What does Darren probably mean?
1. It's surprisingly cold for August.
2. It's so warm that it feels like August.
3. It's warm like usual in August.
4. It's hard to predict the temperature in August.

Imp 12: Mike is trying to find an apartment in New York City. He just looked at a place and is telling his friend Jane about it.
Jane: "Is the rent high?"
Mike: "Is the Pope Catholic?"
What does Mike probably mean?
1. He doesn't want to talk about the rent.
2. The rent is high.
3. The apartment is owned by the church.
4. The rent isn't very high.

Rout 3: Tom ordered a meal in a restaurant and the waitress just brought it. She asks him if he wants to order additional items.
What would the waitress probably say?
1. "Would you like anything extra?"
2. "Is there more for you?"
3. "What can I do for you?"
4. "Can I get you anything else?"

Rout 6: Ted is inviting his friend to a little party he's having at his house tomorrow night.
Ted: "I'm having a little party tomorrow night at my place.

How would Ted probably go on?
1. "How would you like to come in?"
2. <u>Do you think you could make it?"</u>
3. How about you're there?"
4. Why aren't you showing up?"

Rout 7: The person ahead of Kate in line at the cafeteria drops his pen. Kate picks it up and gives it back to him. He says "Thank you."
What would Kate probably reply?
1. "Thank you."
2. "Please."
3. <u>"You're welcome."</u>
4. "Don't bother."

Rout 9: Claudia calls her college classmate Dennis but his roommate answers the phone and tells her that Dennis isn't home. Claudia would like the roommate to tell Dennis something.
What would Claudia probably say?
1. "Can you write something?"
2. "Can I give you information?"
3. <u>"Can I leave a message?"</u>
4. "Can you take a note?"

Rout 10: Tim is ordering food at a restaurant where you can sit down or take the food home with you.
What would the woman behind the counter probably ask Tim?
1. "For home or here?"
2. "For going or staying?"
3. "For taking it with you?"
4. <u>"For here or to go?"</u>

Prg 8: Henry is working on a class project with his classmate Lydia. He was supposed to meet with her yesterday but he had to stay late at work and he couldn't make it. He's running into Lydia now.
Lydia: "Hey, where were you yesterday? We have to finish our project by Monday or Professor Johnson is going to lower our grade!"
Henry:
Lydia: "You better. And be real convincing when you talk to her, I don't want to ruin my grade because of you!"

Prg 9: Kevin's paycheck is late but he has to pay rent today. He decides to ask his friend Carol to help him.
Kevin: "Carol, I really need $500 for rent. I'll pay you back tomorrow."
Carol:
Kevin: "$200 is great. Thanks so much, Carol."

Part II

**Second Language Interaction
in Pedagogical Settings**

Achieving Distinction Through Mock ESL: A Critical Pragmatics Analysis of Classroom Talk in a High School[1]

Steven Talmy
University of British Columbia, Canada

This chapter investigates the widely noted yet little investigated stigma that is associated with English as a second language (ESL) as an institutional and social-identity category in North American public schools. Drawn from a critical ethnography conducted in an ESL program at a large urban high school in Hawai'i (Tradewinds High), the chapter examines how linguistic prejudice, linguistic nationalism, xenophobia, and assimilationism are constituted, instantiated, and circulated through use of a linguistic style referred to as "Mock ESL." Four occasionings of Mock ESL are analyzed, which were voiced by oldtimer, generation 1.5 ESL—or "Local ESL"—students in public displays of distinction from low English-proficient newcomer classmates, or "FOBs" (i.e., students "fresh off the boat").

For the analysis of these data, an ethnographically informed, socially constituted critical pragmatics conceptual framework is outlined, which situates the microanalysis of classroom talk within broader critical and ethnographic perspectives and views them as mutually informing. This not only works to ground, warrant, and elaborate particular critical ethnographic claims about the stigma of ESL in data-near, participant-relevant terms, but to demonstrate how the "micropolitics" of Mock ESL is linked to the "macropolitics" of language and education in Hawai'i and in the US more generally. Specifically, by considering Mock ESL in terms of the language-ideological processes of iconization, erasure, and fractal recursivity, the chapter illustrates how the recursive projection of social processes at several different levels of the "macro"/"micro" relationship ultimately undermines this binarism, demonstrating instead how the "macro" is constituted in the "micro," and vice versa.

The chapter concludes with a brief consideration of certain pedagogical interventions informed by the critical pragmatics analysis, which are aimed at interrupting the (re) production of linguistic chauvinism.

At: Thank god there's no ESL in college.
Mr. Talmy: There's ESL in college, At.
At: No way. No way!
China: If I have to take ESL in college, I'm gonna kill myself.²
Brahdah: Wat? Get ESL in calij? Ho, jas falo yu araun!...So iz ESL calij diploma les dan reglr calij diploma?
            What? There's ESL in college? Damn, it just follows you around!... So is an ESL college diploma less than a regular college diploma?
            (Talmy, 2005, p. 586)³

In 2.5 years of critical ethnographic fieldwork in the English as a Second Language (ESL) program at Tradewinds High,⁴ a public high school in Hawai'i, one of the most pervasive perspectives I heard voiced, from ESL students and teachers alike, was how utterly, how totally uncool it was to be a student in the school's ESL program. This view is implied in the data excerpts above, in which three oldtimer (Lave & Wenger, 1991) "Local ESL"⁵ students referenced the stigmatized status of ESL: At, who had lived in Hawai'i for 3 years, assuredly, but mistakenly, applauds the absence of ESL programs in college; China, who had lived in Hawai'i for 5 years, vows suicide if assigned to college-level ESL; and Brahdah, a 9th grader who had spent his entire school career in ESL, wonders whether the deficiencies accorded to ESL translate into an "ESL college diploma" that is somehow less than a "regular" one.

Similarly negative views about the status of ESL in the social orders of North American public schools have been noted repeatedly in the literature on Kindergarten–12th grade (K–12) ESL (see, e.g., Derwing, DeCorby, & Jamieson, 1999; Duff, 2002; Faltis, 1999; Gunderson, 2006; Harklau, 1994; Johnson, 1996; McKay & Wong, 1996; Talmy, 2009c; Toohey, 2000; Valdés, 2001; Watt & Roessingh, 2001; Willett, 1995). Despite this, few studies have directly addressed why ESL might be so "uncool," and fewer still have examined how this "uncoolness" might actually happen. In fact, despite the rapid increase in the number of ESL students in North America in recent years, there remains comparatively little applied linguistics research that concerns K–12 ESL at all, particularly for the high school years (Duff, 2005). This is of some concern because ESL students in North America are far more likely than non-ESL students to come from families living in poverty (by some estimates, as high as 75%; August & Hakuta, 1997), and secondary ESL students, in particular, are among the most likely school-age populations to drop out, be "pushed out," and to "disappear" (Gunderson) from school, with rates ranging from twice the national average in the US (Ruiz de Velasco, Fix, & Clewell, 2000) to three quarters of ESL students at one large urban Canadian high school (Watt & Roessingh). As Faltis has argued, the empirical silence concerning secondary ESL can only work to perpetuate a status quo in which these students' access to equal educational opportunity remains seriously compromised.

This chapter thus takes up Faltis' (1999, p. 1) call for increased attention to what he referred to as "one of the most unexamined and overlooked areas of education": secondary ESL. It concerns the widely noted yet little investigated stigma associated with ESL, focusing in particular on the linguicism (Skutnabb-Kangas, 2000) or linguistic prejudice that informs it. It does so by privileging in microanalytic detail the actions of students such as At, China, and Brahdah, whose experiences are similarly underrepresented in the research literature, by examining Local ESL students' use of a parodic language variety that I call Mock ESL. As I argue below, use of Mock ESL worked to project within the Tradewinds ESL classes assimilationist language ideologies concerning ESL, second-language (L2) English, and ESL speakers that were also evident in the wider school and societal contexts.

In addition, I outline in this chapter the theoretical framework that I use to make this argument. Considering that the larger study (Talmy, 2005) from which the data below are drawn is a critical ethnography (see, e.g., Anderson, 1989; Levinson, Foley, & Holland, 1996; Quantz, 1992; Simon & Dippo, 1986) and one that incorporates the analysis of classroom talk-in-interaction, the term that I have appropriated for this framework is "critical pragmatics" (cf. Mey, 2001). However, I should note that my aim in elucidating what I mean by critical pragmatics is not intended to be definitional; it is primarily illustrative, meant to demonstrate the benefits that accrue when critical ethnography and an analysis of talk-in-interaction are used complementarily (Miller & Fox, 2004). That notwithstanding, elucidation of a critical pragmatics theoretical framework necessitates discussion of analytic traditions that investigate talk-in-interaction, such as (applied) conversation analysis (CA) and membership categorization analysis (MCA), and those that undertake the analysis of discourse from critical perspectives, including Fairclough's (e.g., 1989, 1992, 2001) version of critical discourse analysis (CDA) and certain iterations of (critical) discourse analytic work in discursive and rhetorical psychology (e.g., Billig, 1996; Edley, 2001; Wetherell, 1998; Wetherell & Edley, 1999) and feminist psychology (e.g., Kitzinger, 2000, 2007, 2008; Kitzinger & Rickford, 2007; Speer, 1999; Stokoe, 2000, 2003, 2006, 2010; Stokoe & Edwards, 2007; Stokoe & Smithson, 2001; Wilkinson & Kitzinger, 2003, 2008; cf. Wowk, 2007).

In the next section, I discuss in more detail this critical pragmatics framework. I then sketch a brief historical context of linguicism in language and education policy in Hawai'i before introducing the Tradewinds study and some of its primary findings. Next, I consider research done on mock language varieties as a means to contextualize Mock ESL, the focus of my analysis. Following this, I analyze four excerpts of Mock ESL use by oldtimer Local ESL students in classroom interaction. Afterward, I discuss the implications of instances of Mock ESL use, particularly in terms of three language-ideological processes formulated by Irvine and Gal (2000) and Irvine (2001): iconization, erasure, and fractal recursivity. I conclude with consideration of how this all relates to the perspectives voiced by At, China, and Brahdah at the start of this chapter concerning the stigmatized status of ESL.

Toward a critically oriented, socially constituted, ethnographically situated pragmatics

> If critical approaches to language use in the context of social practices fail to be convincing as a result of a lack of theoretical and methodological rigour... they destroy their own *raison d'être* and make the task all the more difficult for anyone who does observe the basic rules of documentation, argumentation and explicit presentation (Verschueren, 2001, p. 60)
>
> As is often the case for more marginal research traditions, [critical discourse] research has to be 'better' than other research in order to be accepted.
> (van Dijk, 2001, p. 353)

In this section, I discuss the theoretical framework that I have adopted for the critical pragmatics analysis below. I first discuss my conceptualization of pragmatics and then outline some general principles of critical research. Afterward, I engage some of the problematics that can arise in a critical analysis of classroom talk, namely, tensions between two streams of empirical work in pragmatics: research in critical discourse analysis and in the analysis of talk-in-interaction. It is in this discussion that I argue for a respecification of the term "critical pragmatics" so that it represents a greater diversity of approaches in pragmatics that can attend to the critical analysis of discourse.

Pragmatics

It is important to state at the outset that I do not consider myself a pragmaticist. Nor, for that matter, do I consider myself a conversation analyst, a membership categorization analyst, or—speaking of membership categories—a discourse analyst. Rather, I consider myself a critical ethnographer. This has implications for how I conceptualize pragmatics as well as how I believe pragmatics could be recruited for critical pragmatics research in (language) education.

To begin with, this means that I take a necessarily broad view of pragmatics, consistent with what Verschueren (e.g., 1998) called a "pragmatic perspective." This is a "more sociological conception of pragmatics" (Horn & Ward, 2004, p. xi), which draws on and shares objects of study with neighbor disciplines such as sociolinguistics and linguistic anthropology, to name two traditions that I draw upon in this chapter. It is a perspective that contrasts with a "component perspective" of pragmatics (Verschueren), and the "narrowly circumscribed, mainly Anglo-American conception of linguistic and philosophical pragmatics" advanced by Horn and Ward (p. xi), among others.

Additionally, I approach pragmatics from a broadly social interactionist perspective, consistent with what Kasper (2006) termed a "discursive pragmatics," whereby action, meaning, and context are "constituted not only *in* but *through* social interaction" (p. 284). I also embrace a theoretically principled analytic opportunism; that is, I do not claim allegiance to any one analytic framework but appropriate them as necessary.[6] As well, I take an unabashedly ethnographic approach (Blommaert, 2005), one that is situated theoretically in cultural studies (e.g., Hall, 1996; Williams, 1977; Willis, 1977), critical education studies (e.g., Giroux, 1997), and poststructural critical applied linguistics (Pennycook, 2001).

Locating "critical"

The task of elaborating what I mean by "critical" is challenging in that there is a plurality of critical theories, based on the diverse work of a range of scholars, from Marx to Freire, Vološinov to Foucault. Just as critical theories are not monolithic, neither are they static as they change and shift due to ongoing, "synergistic" relationships among themselves and with cultural studies, poststructuralism, postmodernism, and postcolonialism (Kincheloe & McLaren, 2000).

However, although there is no single agreed-upon definition of "critical," there are certain principles and objectives shared in the critical "project" (cf. Simon & Dippo, 1986). At the risk of reducing an extremely complex cluster of theoretical alignments and fissures, these include variants of some of the following principles:

- that society is stratified and marked by inequality, with differential structural access to material and symbolic resources;
- that power arrangements are asymmetrical;
- that there is a reciprocal, mutually constitutive relationship between social structures and human agency;
- that social structures mediate social practices but do not determine them;
- that society, power, agency, and culture do not exist atemporally, but are sociohistorically situated;
- that there is no such thing as "value-free" research: all knowledge is "interested" (Foucault, 1972);
- that it is not enough to simply describe inequality; it must be transformed through sustained critique and direct action, or praxis (this "emancipatory impulse" has garnered considerable criticism, e.g., Ellsworth, 1989, resulting in recent conceptions of praxis as more circumspect, situated, collaborative, and reflexive).

When the two subsections above are considered together, the theoretical framework that I adopt for this study can be glossed as a critically oriented, socially constituted, ethnographically situated pragmatics (also see Blommaert, 2005).

Respecifying "critical pragmatics"?

Consideration of the two subsections above also logically results in the collocation "critical pragmatics." Interestingly, however, there are comparatively few references to work that is in some way identified by this label (but see, e.g.,

Koyama, 2004; McHoul, 1988), prompting Jacob Mey, in the second edition of *Pragmatics: An introduction* (2001), to comment thus:

> Since nobody, to my knowledge, has appropriated the term yet, I suggest letting the...work done...mainly [by] the so-called 'Lancaster School' of critical language awareness, centered on Norman Fairclough and his co-workers...be suitably captured by the common denominator of 'critical pragmatics.' (p. 316; also see p. xi)

Faircloughian CDA is, in many respects, a plausible candidate for the mantle of critical pragmatics. Over the years, there has been a considerable amount of important research on language-in-use that has adopted Fairclough's increasingly elaborated, quasi systemic-functional analytic framework. At the same time, however, it should be noted that there is no compelling reason to delimit "critical pragmatics" to Faircloughian CDA, especially in light of the many substantive critiques that have been made of it (see, e.g., Blommaert, 2005; McHoul, 1988; Slembrouck, 2001; Verschueren, 2001; also see Pennycook, 2001, 2003). It is in this respect that I would argue for a critical pragmatics that is respecified to include a wider, more inclusive, and more representative range of analytic frameworks that can (and do) attend to the critical analysis of discourse (cf. Blommaert, 2005) and the critical analysis of talk-in-interaction.[7]

Much has been written in recent years of paradigmatic tensions between traditions in CDA and the analysis of talk-in-interaction (see, e.g., Billig, 1999a, 1999b; Blommaert, 2005; Fairclough, 1989, 1992; Kitzinger, 2000, 2008; Schegloff, 1997, 1998, 1999a, 1999b; ten Have, 2007; Verschueren, 2001; Wetherell, 1998; Wilkinson & Kitzinger, 2008; Wooffitt, 2005; Wowk, 2007). This includes, of course, CA and Faircloughian CDA, two methods closely associated with pragmatics, as well as divergent lines of CDA that are not, including from discursive and rhetorical psychology (e.g., Billig, 1996; Edley, 2001; Wetherell & Edley, 1999) and feminist psychology (e.g., Kitzinger, 2000, 2007, 2008; Kitzinger & Rickford, 2007; Speer, 1999; Stokoe, 2000, 2003, 2006, 2010; Stokoe & Edwards, 2007; Stokoe & Smithson, 2001; Wilkinson & Kitzinger, 2003, 2008). I am not going to rehearse these debates in any detail (for a summary, see Wooffitt, pp. 137–157), but they essentially go as follows: CA, with its "naïve epistemology," its insistence on "unmotivated looking," its overriding commitment to endogenous orientations, and its restricted conceptualization of context, is overly formalistic, scientistic, technicist, and "micro." Because CA does not necessarily attend to matters of social justice, discrimination, and inequality, it is argued, it is complicit in their perpetuation. Conversely, CDA has been criticized for "theoretical imperialism," inadequate methodological rigor, and a corresponding failure to provide sufficient warrant for critical claims,[8] telling more about the analyst's politics than how racism, sexism, or homophobia, for example, might actually be accomplished in everyday life.[9]

From my perspective, there is substance to both sets of critiques. For example, the notion of ideological neutrality in CA is, in my view, disingenuous, because obviously, such a position is itself ideological. Relatedly, to suggest that data can be approached with a "clean gaze" (Stokoe & Smithson, 2001, p. 6) implies what amounts to an omniscient analytic position: that research can be conducted and data analyzed "from nowhere in particular" (Pavlenko, 2007, p. 167). As well, I find the restricted view of context in "basic" (Heritage, 2005), "pure" (ten Have, 2007), or Schegloffian (e.g., 2007) CA unduly limiting (though this is not the case for "applied" CA; see note 9 and below; also see Kitzinger, 2008; Stokoe & Smithson; Talmy, 2009c).

At the same time, however, I find myself too often wanting critical empirical work, especially in applied linguistics, to push beyond a nominal functional analysis of a document, a thematic analysis of an account generated in an interview, or an ungrounded abstraction like "dominant discourse," which is frequently posited as if it simply exists or is so self-evident that it requires no further elaboration. As many scholars, including those with critical interests, have shown, more than a few critical studies play fast and loose with warrants for claims, with inadequate evidence of the analytic legwork undertaken to substantiate what otherwise amounts to a collection of predictable "theory-induced judgement[s]" (Verschueren, 2001, p. 69; also see Schegloff, 1997). As a result, returning to Verschueren's hyperbolic warning, these studies may ultimately wind up "destroy[ing] their own *raison d'être*" (p. 60) or perhaps more plausibly, "undermin[ing] the practical and political utility of [their] analyses" (Widdicombe, 1995, p. 111).

With these points in mind, and in line with the stance of analytic opportunism mentioned above, I adopt more of an agnostic position than has characterized the frequently partisan debates between critical discourse analysts and analysts of talk-in-interaction, and argue not for the superiority of one or another tradition, but for a stronger commitment in critical discourse research to empirically grounded and demonstrable "documentation, argumentation and explicit presentation" (Verschueren, 2001, p. 60). One analytic means that critical pragmaticists might adopt for this endeavor is CA or at least, "applied" CA, which, in contrast to the scientific interests of "pure" CA (i.e., to "discover the basic and general aspects of sociality," ten Have, 2007, p. 174), "'uses' CA concepts and methods for accomplishing its own particular [i.e., critical] agenda" (p. 56; cf. Kitzinger, 2008). Other analytic approaches that can be used include, but are not limited to, MCA (e.g., Sacks, 1972, 1992; also see Antaki & Widdicombe, 1998), interactional sociolinguistics (Gumperz, 1982), the ethnography of communication (e.g., Saville-Troike, 2003), language socialization (e.g., Ochs, 1990, 1993, 1996), discursive psychology (e.g., Edwards & Potter, 1992), and linguistic anthropology (e.g., Duranti, 1997). However, it is important to underscore that the call for demonstrability and defensibility in this respecification of critical pragmatics in no way aspires to any form of analytic objectivity nor aims to deny the "creative act of researcher interpretation" (Anderson, 1989, p. 252). It is my hope, rather, that by more substantively warranting claims in critical discourse research, more work can go toward mobilizing efforts to change social injustice, rather than debating whether this point or that is indeed supported by the data that a particular analysis encompasses. More to the point, high standards of rigor and care in critical pragmatics research will help to ensure that whatever means ultimately *are* chosen to promote transformation are empirically grounded, locally relevant, judiciously circumspect, collaboratively produced, and thus, one might hope, more effective (cf. Gore, 1992).

Language and national identity in Hawai'i: Linguicism in historical context

> As fellow citizens, we need a common language. In the United States, that language is English. Our common history is written in English. Our common forefathers speak to us, through the ages, in English.
> U.S. Secretary of Education William Bennett (1985, in Crawford, 2008, p. 5)

> Speak American! To speak American is to *think* American!...Here in Hawai'i the language is AMERICAN. The majority of us *speak* American...but there are still some of us who...still speak other languages...[However, e]very citizen has been given the advantage of American school education...and *knows* the language!
> "Speak American" advertisement, *Hawai'i Magazine*, 1943 (in Roberts, 2003)

> If you can read this, thank a teacher. If you can read this in English, thank a soldier.
> bumper sticker

In this section, I provide a brief historical discussion of language and education in Hawai'i, framed in terms of linguistic anthropological work on language ideologies. I do this to sketch what some might call a "macro" context for the analysis of Mock ESL below, but that I term instead a framework for interpretation.[10] Specifically, I consider a one nation/one language, or nationalist language ideology (Woolard, 1998) in the US and in colonial and postcolonial Hawai'i, in which nation, language, culture, and social identity are mapped onto one another in one-to-one correspondence. Crudely put, this is a monolingual ideology, whereby a mythic, homogeneous variety of (American) English, erased (Irvine & Gal, 2000) of any variation, is cast as a central criterion for US-American national identity. In contrast, languages other than English, different varieties of English, and "marked" accents of English are exactly that: other, different, marked—indexes of non-US-American or "foreign" identity (cf. Bucholtz & Hall, 2004; Irvine & Gal; Woolard).

The history of language education and politics in Hawai'i is typified by linguistic nationalism, as well as by linguicism, the "[i]deologies, structures, and practices which are used to legitimate, effectuate, regulate, and reproduce [social inequality]...on the basis of language" (Skutnabb-Kangas, 2000, p. 30).[11] Both linguistic nationalism and linguicism were evident from the very institutionalization of Hawai'i's formal education system. Established in 1820 by *haole*[12] missionaries, the public school system was organized into two tiers, based on language. The language of the "select schools," created for the children of missionaries and Hawaiian royalty, was English; in the "common schools," which enrolled the children of Hawaiian non-elites, the medium of instruction was Hawaiian (Benham & Heck, 1998; Buck, 1986; Kawamoto, 1993).

In 1896, 3 years following the US-backed overthrow of the Hawaiian monarchy, Hawaiian was banned as a language of instruction, replaced by English throughout the Islands' schools (Buck; Kawamoto; Reinecke, 1969; Sato, 1985). This policy led to a perilous decline in the use of the Hawaiian language, a decline that, until recent revitalization efforts, threatened the existence of the language (Buck; Reinecke). It also marked the start of a period in which race as a factor in educational segregation would be complemented, and later superseded, by language.

By the turn of the 20th century, thousands of immigrant laborers from China, Portugal, Japan, the Philippines, Korea, and Puerto Rico had come to Hawai'i to work the Territory's sugar and pineapple plantations. A contact language, or pidgin, developed as a result of these workers' need to communicate. Eventually, this pidgin developed into a creole, a fully elaborated code spoken as a first language by immigrant children and used throughout the wider community.[13] By the 1930s, Pidgin, as Hawai'i Creole came to be widely called, was spoken by approximately 40% of the Islands' population and had become a critical, if often stigmatized, symbol of Local culture and identity. Due to its origins, the sociopolitical context of its development, and the racial, ethnic, and socioeconomic backgrounds of many of its speakers, Pidgin was (and for many still is) seen as "broken English," a sloppy way of speaking, negative views perpetuated by decades of efforts aimed at "correcting" Pidgin out of existence (Buck, 1986; Kawamoto, 1993; Sato, 1985, 1991; Tamura, 1993).[14]

Any implicit ideological association of English with US-American identity prior to the turn of the 20th century in Hawai'i became overt when campaigns to Americanize immigrants swept the US, an effort that Tamura (1993) characterizes as a "crusade" (also see Buck, 1986). As Crawford (2004) notes, during World War I, Americanization efforts "took a coercive turn," as "proficiency in English was increasingly equated with political loyalty; for the first time, an ideological link was forged between speaking good English and being a 'good American'" (p. 88; also see Crawford, 2008). In the Territory of Hawai'i, (English) linguistic nationalism was manifested in Americanization efforts that led to the suppression of a multilingual press, the eventual closure of heritage language schools, ongoing attempts to eradicate Pidgin, and the creation of yet another mechanism to segregate middle-class *haole* children from immigrants, children of color, and the working class: the formation of the English Standard Schools (Agbayani & Takeuchi, 1986; Benham & Heck, 1998; Buck; Kawamoto, 1993; Sato, 1985).

Whereas many of the "select" schools went on to form the basis of Hawai'i's extensive system of private schools, the English Standard Schools (ESS), established in 1924, were part of the public education system. According to Sato

(1985), because *haole* middle-class parents "could not afford private school tuition, their only alternative was to call for segregation in the public school system" (pp. 263–264); in other words, the ESS were "an attempt at having private schools at government expense" (Agbayani & Takeuchi, 1986, p. 33). As with the "select" schools, several institutions were set aside; this time, however, admission was based not on race or class, but on proficiency in English. Yet, as Skutnabb-Kangas (2000) points out, linguicism frequently produces the same results as racism and classism (and is increasingly used as their proxy). Such was the case with the ESS: In the year following its designation as the first English Standard School, for example, Honolulu's Lincoln Elementary had a student body that comprised 19 Japanese, 27 Chinese, and 572 *haole* children (Benham & Heck, 1998, p. 149).

After 25 years, the ESS system began to be phased out, with the 1960 class of Honolulu's Roosevelt High School eventually becoming the last of the ESS graduates. However, segregation remained, both in the form of Standard English classes within schools and in the continuing expansion of private schools. In fact, at nearly 17% (Office of the Superintendent, 2008), the state of Hawai'i today has the one of the highest percentages of children in North America who attend private school, as the public education system continues to rank among the worst in the US, based on indices that include standardized test scores, per-pupil spending, graduation rates, out-of-field teaching, and teacher salaries (see Talmy, 2005, pp. 145–149, 215–236).

There have also been significant problems in contemporary Hawai'i with the public schooling of students who speak languages other than English. As Haas (1992) has chronicled, until the early 1990s, the Hawai'i Department of Education consistently flirted with the minimum standards set by federal law for bilingual and ESL students, and was repeatedly cited by federal oversight agencies for not adequately serving them.[15] The pattern of misconduct receiving federal sanction included under-identification of students needing bilingual or ESL services, under-servicing of those who were identified, inappropriate staffing of bilingual/ESL programs, disproportionate placement of bilingual/ESL students in special education programs, segregation, and improper mainstreaming procedures.[16]

This is not to suggest that Hawai'i is the only state that has inadequately supported students for whom English is a second language. At the federal level, successive reauthorizations of the 1968 *Bilingual Education Act* increasingly promoted "special alternative" ESL programs over bilingual education (Crawford, 2004). This particular manifestation of linguicism culminated in the elimination of the *Bilingual Education Act* altogether in 2002 as part of the Bush administration's *No Child Left Behind* legislation. Federal policy under *The English Language Acquisition, Language Enhancement, and Academic Achievement Act* now reinforces an assimilationist ideology of English monolingualism by making no reference to bilingualism at all. At the same time, around the US, efforts to cap the time students can remain enrolled in ESL classes are ongoing, reductions in ESL staffing continue, and cuts in funds for ESL teacher training, professional development, and support services are being made. According to a recent survey (Zehler et al., 2003), ESL students increasingly receive instruction delivered completely in English, more than half receive instruction not specifically designed for L2 learners, and ESL curricula are far less aligned with content standards than "regular" subject areas are. Finally, only 30% of public school teachers with ESL students have received the training necessary to teach them; of these teachers, fewer than 3% have degrees in ESL or bilingual education.

Taken together, the material and symbolic privileges accorded to English in pre- and post-statehood Hawai'i dovetails in many ways with the nationalist language ideology discussed above, an orientation that views multilingualism as a nuisance at best, and at worst, evidence of disloyalty or a lack of patriotism. In Figure 1, I have represented certain ideological linkages that are implied from the association of English with US-American identity (also see Crawford, 2004, 2008; Lippi-Green, 1997; Zentella, 2003), with "native" speaker and "standard" English serving as indexes (if not basic constituents) of this in-group identity, and languages other than English, "nonnative" speakers, and "nonstandard" varieties of English as indexes of a relational out-group or "foreign" identity. I return to the implications of this discussion further below. Next, however, I introduce the Tradewinds High study.

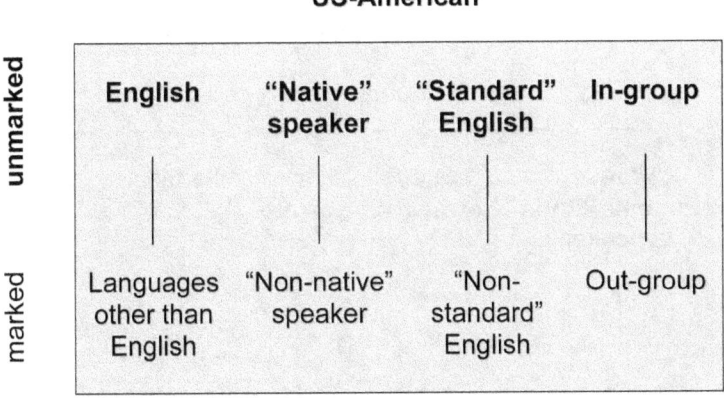

Figure 1. Representing hierarchical oppositions deriving from U.S. linguistic nationalism.

Study

> One of the greatest errors in education is to assume that the larger social context of the school is irrelevant or even secondary to learning....The social structure

of the school is not simply the context of learning; it is part of what is learned.
(Eckert, 1989, p. 179)

They say [ESL] is meant to help mainstream the kids. But I think a lot of it is to keep them out of the regular classes and out of the other teachers' hair....[I]t's become sort of a...dumping ground for kids that they don't want to deal with.
Ms. Ariel, ESL teacher (in Talmy, 2005, p. 287)

The Tradewinds study consisted of 625 hours of observation in 15 high school classrooms, including 8 dedicated-ESL classes, over 2.5 years. Observational data were generated in field notes and supplemented by 158 hours of audio-recorded classroom interaction. A total of 58 formal interviews were recorded with 10 teachers and 37 students, and classroom materials, schoolwork, and other site artifacts were collected for analysis.

The larger study concerned the production of ESL as a negatively marked (Bucholtz & Hall, 2004) or stigmatized identity category, with a focus on the role that linguicism played in this. As its appellation connotes, "mainstream student" at Tradewinds was indicative of the category's unmarked status; conversely, "ESL student" was marked, relationally defined by how it diverged from the "mainstream" norm (cf. Barth, 1969). What I call a "mainstream || ESL" hierarchy that was prevalent at Tradewinds was constituted by and constitutive of language ideologies concerning these divergences, whereby "native speakers," "the mainstream," and "regular students" were valorized as ideals, normalized by the explicit aim of the ESL program to "mainstream" its students. In Figure 2, I have represented

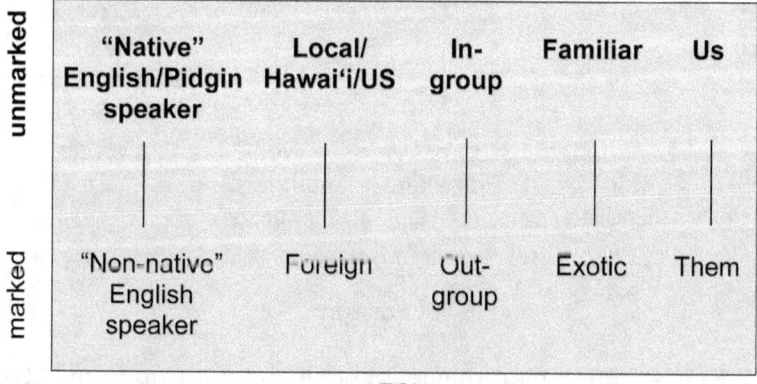

Figure 2. Representing the mainstream || ESL relational hierarchy at Tradewinds.

the mainstream || ESL hierarchy in diagram form and included an array of hierarchically associated dualities implied by it: native || nonnative speaker,

US-American || foreign, in-group || out-group, familiar || exotic, and us || them (see Talmy, 2009a, for more details).

The larger study examined the production of the "stigma" of ESL in two ways: first, in the "official" or school-sanctioned "cultural productions of the ESL student" (cf. Levinson et al., 1996), and second, in the oppositional "cultural productions of the ESL student" generated by a community of practice (CoP; Lave & Wenger, 1991) of oldtimer Local ESL students that spanned all eight of the dedicated-ESL classes I observed over 2.5 years.

The official or school-sanctioned productions of the ESL student were manifested in Tradewinds ESL policy, curriculum, and instruction (see Talmy, 2005, pp. 237–286). Although the ESL population was large and diverse, the category "ESL student" was institutionally articulated in undifferentiated terms. The homogeneity of the category was connoted variously, from the Tradewinds ESL placement policy, in which the length of enrollment at the school rather than L2 expertise (Rampton, 1990) or educational needs determined which ESL classes students were to take, to the ESL program's uniform literature-based curriculum, whereby students, regardless of L2 expertise, received the same materials, assignments, and activities. The centerpiece of this curriculum was popular juvenile fiction such as *James and the Giant Peach* (Dahl, 1961) and *Are You There God? It's Me, Margaret* (Blume, 1970), which was below grade-level and often had peripheral relevance to academic content or L2 English learning. In addition to such books were assignments that presumed that students "automatically affiliated" with the cultures, customs, and languages of "their" countries (Talmy, 2008, 2009a). As well, assignments introducing newcomers to customs and holidays of the US were common, as were other ESL mainstays, such as family-tree activities, which many Local ESL students stated they had been assigned repeatedly in prior grades.

Local ESL students' responses to the school-sanctioned productions of the ESL student, were, as might be expected, largely negative. I have detailed a number of these students' (resistant) social practices elsewhere (Talmy, 2008, 2009a, 2009b, 2009c, in press), but they included leaving assigned materials "at home," not doing homework, and completing assignments that required minimal effort (e.g., worksheets) but not others (e.g., writing activities). The more overt, interactionally mediated practices included bargaining for reduced requirements on classwork, refusal to participate in instructional activities, and the often delicate negotiations with teachers that resulted. There was also a cluster of practices in which Local ESL students engaged in public displays of "distinction" (Irvine, 2001; Irvine & Gal, 2000; also see Bucholtz & Hall, 2004) from their lower-L2-expert and newcomer ESL classmates, whom many Local ESL students dismissively referred to as FOBs (i.e., "fresh off the boat"). These displays, in which sociopolitical relations of difference, hierarchy, and stratification were produced and underscored (Bucholtz & Hall, p. 384), took form in many ways, including the targeted use of Mock ESL.

Mock ESL

> Negative attitudes toward other [language varieties] are rarely developed on the basis of [language] differences themselves; rather they are formed because of attitudes toward the *speakers* of those [varieties]. A suspicion of difference arises mostly from viewing other ethnic or social groups as less deserving, less educated, less intelligent, less acceptable—and these attitudes get transferred to the languages these groups of people speak. Language becomes the scapegoat for racist and classist stereotypes and biases. (Wilson, 2001, p. 34)

In recent years, there has been a considerable increase in research on mock language. Mock language is a form of linguistic style, that is, "an organization of distinctiveness that operates on a linguistic plane yet is constitutive of social distinctiveness as it does so" (Irvine, 2001, p. 42). Research on mock styles has included Mock Ebonics (Ronkin & Karn, 1999), Injun English (Meek, 2006), Mock Filipino (Labrador, 2009), Mock Asian (Chun, 2009), Mock Standard Dutch (Jaspers, 2006), FOB accent (Reyes, 2007), Stylized Asian English (e.g., Rampton, 1995, *inter alia*), and, perhaps best known, Jane Hill's influential work on Junk or Mock Spanish (1993, 1995, 1998; also see Zentella, 2003). Features of this latter variety include the insertion of morphosyntax, words, or phrases, particularly in Anglo English-speakers' talk, that are stereotypically associated with Spanish, for example, "no problemo," "no way, José," "hasta la vista, baby," "el cheapo," and "correctomundo." Semiotically, Mock Spanish, like other mock languages, functions in terms of direct and indirect, or "dual," indexicality (Ochs, 1990), signifying "directly," in this case, the Mock Spanish speaker's "desirable qualities: a sense of humor, a playful skill with a foreign language, authentic regional roots, an easy-going attitude toward life" (Hill, 1995, para. 3) while at the same time "indirectly" or "covertly" "reproduc[ing] highly negative racializing stereotypes of Chicanos and Latinos" (Hill, 1998, p. 680).

Mock ESL shares similar semiotics to other mock language styles but has a greater relational range, indexing an archetypal, pan-ethnic Foreigner rather than a specific racial or ethnolinguistic group (cf. Rampton, 2001, p. 271; Reyes, 2007, pp. 32–37). In terms of *indirect indexicality*, Mock ESL represents a form of "derisive crossing" (Rampton, 1995, p. 45), as the absurd syntactic error, hyperbolic phonology, lexical parody, and oral disfluencies that characterize the style connote negative attributes including pragmatic incompetence, cognitive impairment, and a general, all-encompassing lack of social desirability. These language-ideological associations also attach to the "figure" (Goffman, 1974) that is animated by the Mock ESL style shift, which can be glossed, in Local ESL students' terminology, as a FOB. At the same time, derisive crossing into Mock ESL *directly indexes* the speaker's distinction (Irvine, 2001; Irvine & Gal, 2000) from the real or imagined target of the style shift (i.e., the FOB figure), in terms of the ironic, metapragmatic comment the style shift achieves (if successful; see Excerpt 1). Additionally, Mock ESL directly indexes the L2 English expertise and interactional competence of the Mock ESL crosser, who in performing the style displays an often expert ability to manipulate L2 resources, as well as a discerning understanding of *which* linguistic resources can be recruited for these performances (see Excerpts 2, 3, and 4 below). It is in this respect that Mock ESL style shifts featured as an important social practice in Local ESL students' performative displays of distinction from their lower-L2-expert and newcomer classmates. I turn now to the data to elaborate.

Achieving distinction through Mock ESL

All four of the excerpts that I analyze come from two first-year ESL-A classes that I observed in my second year of fieldwork at Tradewinds: ESL-A (2W), taught by Ms. Ariel, an experienced ESL instructor in her first year of high school teaching, and ESL-A (2X), taught by Mr. Day, an industrial-arts instructor with no background in teaching ESL, who was also in his first year at Tradewinds. I observed Ms. Ariel's ESL-A (2W) for 68 hours and Mr. Day's ESL-A (2X) for 64 hours, and supplemented fieldnotes with 26 hours of audio recording in ESL-A (2W), and 29 hours in ESL-A (2X). These included whole-class recordings, whereby a digital recorder was placed at the front (or rear) of a class, as well as student-carried recordings, in which individual students were outfitted with microphones and recorders to record localized, especially student-student, interaction.

The ESL-A classes were the largest, most heterogeneous, and instructionally challenging in the Tradewinds ESL program. Both the ESL-A (2W and 2X) classes averaged over 30 students during the course of the school year, with students aged 14–18, about one third of whom were at early levels of L2 development and/or had interrupted formal educations; another third of whom had lived in the US for between 3–10 years, many of whom I identified as Local ESL (see Talmy, 2008, Table 1, p. 624); with the remainder at levels of English expertise in between.

The first excerpt I consider involves China and Raven, two 9th-grade oldtimers of the Local ESL CoP in Ms. Ariel's class. Ms. Ariel was absent on this day, and Ms. Jackson, a frequent substitute in the ESL program, was teaching. The interaction commences as Ms. Jackson is at the front of the classroom, pointing out instructions for a "freewriting" activity that Ms. Ariel has assigned. Ms. Jackson aims to allot 15 minutes for the activity—that is, until "ten-thirty"—but China attempts to bargain for twice that (see appendix for transcript conventions).

Excerpt 1 How do you spell 'A'? [ELA42WmdS10: 104–122]

```
01   Ms J:        [so today we are going to be doing] our jour↑nals.
02   Raven:       [((shuffling cards)) (            )]
03                (2.6) ((backpack zippering))
04   Ms J:        you need to write a journal entry about,
05                (1.1)((T pointing at board))
06   CKY:         >freewriti[ng
07   ?FS:                   [free[(writing)
08   China:                      [>freewriti[ng<
09   Ms J:                                   [<freewriti[ng.>
10   Eddie*:                                             [((Miss)=
11   ?FS:         =(freewriting)=
12   ?FS:         =(>I don't [know.<)]
13   Ms J?:                  [(sh!) ]=
14   Raven:       =(   common in here.)
15   Ms J:        students! (0.4) pay <attenti[on.>
16   China:                                   [ba::::h!
17                (0.5)
18   Ms J:        okay. (0.7) <you pick something that you want to write about.>
19                (1.0)
20   Ms J:        ((pointing at board; reading voice)) [do you have something in
21                your mi:nd, (0.3) ↓write about it. (0.4) (write it down.)]
22   ?Ss:                                              [(
23                                                                             )]
24   Dannica:     you stole my book?
25   Ms J:        for ↑this, (0.5) I will give you: until:=
26   China:       =like half hour we need.
27   Ms J:        no tehn-[<thirty> ((i.e., 15 minutes))
28   ?FS:                 [(                )
29   China:       no half hour.
30                (0.4)
31   Ms J:        fifteen minutes should be suff[(icient.)
32   China:                                     [>twenty-five! twenty-five.<
33   ?FS:         fif[teen
34   Ms J:           [ten-]thirty.
35   ?FS:         (okay)
36   ?FS:         (          )
37   Ms J:        >you know why=because< [this (0.4) this class (0.4)]=
38   ?Ss:                                [(                          )]
39   China:       ((Pidgin)) so [ha(d)!]
                               is so hard!
40   Ms J:                      =[today ] is (0.5) early release right?
41   China:       yeah [bu-
42   Ms J:             [we (mu[st)
43   China:                   [bu- [bu-
44   Ms J:                         [>we have to hurry<
45   ?FS:         (          )
46   China:       ((higher pitch, light nasal quality)) but we E-S-L student!
                                                       (([bʰʌ wi iɛsɛl studɛn]))
47   Raven:       ((Pidgin)) wi= wi ↑so ↓dam!
                             we're- we're so dumb!
48   Ms J:                                       [that's o↑ka:y!
49   China:       ((higher pitch, light nasal quality)) ↑we no English!
                                                       (([wi no ɪŋgəlɪʃ:]))
50   ?FS:         (     [                                                    )]
51   Raven:             [(((Pidgin)) haw du yu spel ↓'A':: .]=
                                    how do you spell 'A'?
52   Ms J:        =((to the class)) ten-[thirty!  ]
53   Benz:                               [( got ]her. (.)       her.)
54                (0.5)
55   ?FSs:        (okay let's be[gin.)
56   Ms J:                      [begin! ready begin.
```

Bargaining for fewer assignments, reduced requirements on them, and the extension of deadlines was a central social practice of the Local ESL CoP (see Talmy, 2005, pp. 442–453). It was as successful as it was widespread, too, and was one of the primary reasons that the official ESL curriculum slowed down and became increasingly restricted over the course of an academic year. It is worth noting that such practices as bargaining in part helped to create an ESL program that was easy, unchallenging, and academically inconsequential: precisely what Local ESL students claimed to dislike about it (cf. Willis, 1977).

The bargaining in this interaction begins just as Ms. Jackson is determining the amount of time for the freewriting activity (line 25). China latches her turn with "like half hour we need.", which leads to a series of preemptive counter-accounts in which both Ms. Jackson and China provide rationales concerning the duration of the assignment: Ms. Jackson maintains that 15 minutes (i.e., until 10:30) should be enough and that the class is shorter than usual ("early release") and thus needs "to hurry," with China countering, in Pidgin, that the class is "so hard" (line 39). It is when Ms. Jackson is in the midst of her final two accounts (lines 40, 44) that China crosses into the style that I call Mock ESL, uttering in line 46, with a higher pitched, nasal quality, "but we E-S-L student!" The prosodic styling extends to coda /t/ deletion in "but" and is accompanied by equally marked syntactic "error," namely, copula deletion and plural neutralization in "student." The shift in line 49, "we no English!", is styled in similar prosodic terms and also features absurdly marked "error."

Mock ESL is recruited by China as a resource in his dispute with Ms. Jackson, similar to the participants in Rampton (1995), who crossed into Stylized Asian English while negotiating participation in an "interactional enclosure" where an authority figure had "control or influence over them" (p. 80). In this respect, it appears that China return to exploits his incumbency as a member of the category "ESL student" and the omnirelevance of having difficulty with English, and thus, an English assignment, that is normatively bound to the category. Indeed, the linguistic resources that China marshals in the Mock ESL performance enact precisely this indexical linkage, providing an additional and hearable warrant, beyond the utterance that the class is "so hard," for his claim that he requires more time for freewriting.

China's style shift represents a semiotic process that Irvine and Gal (2000) have called iconization, that is, "the [association] of certain linguistic features or varieties as formally congruent with [a particular] group" (Bucholtz & Hall, 2004, p. 380) that "binds them together in a linkage that appears to be natural" (Irvine & Gal, p. 38). The group iconized by China's shift into Mock ESL is, as he states in line 46, a general, essentialized group of ESL speakers, the figure of an archetypal ESL student, or FOB.

The phonological, morphological, and syntactic features constituting this mock language variety are in essence the embodied performance of the activity that China binds to the category of "ESL student" in line 49, "we no English!", and the attribute that Raven assigns it, in Pidgin: "so dumb" (line 47). The condition of cognitive deficit is expanded dramatically in line 51 to needing help to spell the letter 'A.'

Although China and Raven have packaged this performance with several metapragmatic cues indicating that they have keyed an ironic frame, Ms. Jackson does not at first orient to it; indeed, it is apparent from her sympathetic "that's oka:y!" (line 48) that she treats China and Raven's line 46 and 47 utterances as genuine. This creates a context for the boys to continue their display, which they do: China, with his intensified line 49 Mock ESL utterance, followed by Raven's absurd "how do you spell 'A'?" It is at this point (line 52) that Ms. Jackson finally orients to the boys' mockery: She abandons the negotiation with China, discontinues her sympathetic tone from line 48, and shifts footing (Goffman, 1981) to address the class now, repeating with an exclamatory intonation her original deadline of 10:30. Following this, Benz, another Local ESL student, appears to congratulate China and Raven for their display, with "got her" (line 53).

In abandoning her negotiation with China and abruptly shifting her footing (and tone), Ms. Jackson displays her orientation not only to the boys' mockery of *her*, but to their ridicule of the category of "ESL student," accomplished as it has been through the Mock ESL style shifts and the farcical attributes of ineptitude and cognitive deficit assigned to it.[17] In this respect, then, Ms. Jackson also orients to the *distinction* that China and Raven have performed through their ludic display: that is, as students who *do* "know" English, who are not "dumb," in contrast to the archetypal ESL student/FOB figure they have iconized through their parodic performance.

In addition to iconization and distinction, two related semiotic processes are evident in the display above: what Bucholtz and Hall (2004) calls authentication and adequation. Authentication refers to the agentive "construction of a credible or genuine identity" (p. 385), for example, through the use of a code that is ideologically linked to a particular identity. Adequation, whereby "potentially salient differences are set aside in favor of perceived or asserted similarities" (Bucholtz & Hall, p. 384), is the converse of distinction. In the interaction above, then, China and Raven not only iconize the figure of an archetypal ESL student/ FOB and produce their distinction from it, their expert use of Pidgin and English produces identities of similarity, alignment, and authenticity with "Local" and "mainstream," the social types that are ideologically linked to those codes. In this respect, the Mock ESL style shifts and the negative attributes associated with the ESL student/FOB figure, both "indirectly" (Ochs, 1990; also see Hill, 1998) (re)produce the stigma associated with ESL and serve as resources for China and Raven to differentiate themselves "directly" from the category "ESL student"; simultaneously, their use of Pidgin and English aligns and authenticates them as members of its relational counterpart: Local/mainstream.

The next excerpt provides an indication of how style shifts to Mock ESL could be used to target lower L2-English-expert students in very public ways. This interaction occurred during a whole-class vocabulary correction activity in Mr. Day's ESL-A (2X). As both this excerpt and Excerpt 3 suggest, such activities provided rich opportunities for practices such as Mock ESL crossing because they made available a range of candidate resources that were necessary for its occasioning: that is, putative L2 English "mistakes" that could be singled out for ridicule.

Here, Bush, a lower L2-English-proficient student from Hong Kong, volunteers a sentence he has written for the word "moment." The sentence that he wrote was "a cruel murderer have used a few moment to kill four little girl and buried her." As becomes evident, Mr. Day has difficulty comprehending Bush's answer, a difficulty that is subsequently recruited as a resource by Mack Daddy, a Local ESL student from Chuuk, Federated States of Micronesia.

Excerpt 2 Moment [ELA32Xmd7: 2007–2017]

```
01  ?FSs:         [((overlapping talk))
02  Mr. Day:      [ moment! who's doing moment?
03  Bush:         ((raises hand))
04  Mr. Day:      alright good Bush, go. ((to talking students)) hey!=sh!
05  Mochenia:     (                )
06  Bush:         ((reading from paper)) a cru:el murderer have used (a few
07                moment to kill four little girl and buried her).
08  Mr. Day:      huh? used a what type of moment?
09                (0.5)
10  Tony:         a few.=
                  (([ə fju:]))
11  Bush:         =a few moment.
                  (([ə fɛu mowmɛn]))
12                (2.3) ((Mr. Day goes to Bush's desk, looks at his paper))
13  Ioane:        ((singing)) (                          ) mo:me:nts.
14  Jonelle:      shut up.
15                (0.2)
16  Mack Daddy:   ((low pitch, nasal monotone)) I don't speak no English.
                                          (([aɪ don spik no i:ŋglɪʧ]))
17                (0.5)
18  Mr. Day:      uh excuse me Mack?
19                (1.7)
20  Mr. Day:      ((to Bush)) a few moment. so that would be s=
21  Ioane:        [((singing)) (come o:n)
22  Mr. Day:      =[a few moments.
```

Bush's line 6–7 utterance evidently proves to be a trouble source for Mr. Day as he utters a next-turn repair initiator ("huh?"; Schegloff, Jefferson, & Sacks, 1977) and indicates that whatever has modified "moment"—"a what type of moment?"—is a repairable. However, there is a considerable delay following Mr. Day's repair initiation. By providing the candidate repair "a few," [ə fju:], Bush's friend Tony treats the silence in line 9 as Bush's and as evidence that Bush has not understood the source of Mr. Day's difficulty. Bush latches Tony's turn to finally provide a self-repair, but with identical pronunciation as his initial reading of the sentence (in line 7), that is, [ə fɛu]. Unlike Tony, it appears that Bush is either unaware of the source of Mr. Day's difficulty, or is unable to correct it; as a result, Bush's self-repair in line 11 becomes a repairable itself. It is at this point that the teacher abandons oral negotiation with Bush and initiates what amounts to an embodied other-initiated repair, as he moves to Bush's desk, looks over his shoulder, and reads Bush's sentence himself. If there had been any question that Bush's L2 expertise and interactional competence were at issue here, there is no longer. Bush's initial mispronunciation of "few" in his sentence reading, his initial lack of sequentially projected uptake to Mr. Day's repair initiation (line 9), his lack of uptake to Tony's other-initiated repair (line 10), his failure to adequately self-repair the trouble source (line 11), Mr. Day's subsequent embodied other-initiated repair (line 12), the extended time this latter action requires, and the sing-song correction of another "mistake" by a Local ESL student, Ioane (who supplies in line 13 the plural morpheme in "moments"; cf. lines 20, 22): All of these actions form the context in which Mack Daddy's style shift occurs in line 16.

Mack Daddy's Mock ESL voicing is uttered in a lower pitch monotone with a nasal quality. Similar to China's style shift in the previous excerpt, this utterance features exaggerated syntactic "error" and hyperbolic phonological styling indexical of "foreign" English. Also similar is the convergence of propositional content with embodied performance as Bush is iconized as an archetypal incumbent of the category "ESL student": a FOB. In contrast, Mack Daddy's style shift points to his awareness that such actions as Bush's are resources for a Mock ESL performance—that is, are candidate "mockables"—as well as Mack Daddy's L2 expertise and interactional competence to actually accomplish the parody. Mack Daddy has, in other words, indexed his distinction from Bush and the "ESL student" category.

In fact, Mr. Day appears to orient to Mack Daddy's display of distinction, and by extension, the hierarchical dualities that constitute it: low L2-English-expert ESL student in the subordinate position and Mack Daddy's unmarked counterpart in the superior. Mr. Day's line 18 utterance, "uh ex<u>cu</u>se me Mack?", is a repair initiation, but as the emphasis and use of the vocative, and the preceding delay suggest, it is contextualized as a condemnation. This, and the fact that Mack Daddy does not provide a sequentially projected second-pair part indicate both his and Mr. Day's orientations to the sanctionability of the Mock ESL performance, and to the stigmatized status of ESL that it connotes.

Mock ESL style shifts in participation frameworks involving teachers tended to be much more subtle than they were in Excerpt 2, likely because of the potential for punishment for such bald, on-the-record (Brown & Levinson, 1987) conduct. Such subtlety is evident in the next excerpt. Here, students are peer-correcting a vocabulary quiz with their teacher, Ms. Ariel. Nat*, a Local ESL student from the Marshall Islands, singles out an apparent mistake on the quiz he is correcting, which belongs to 618. 618 was also a Local ESL student but one whose L2-English proficiency was such that she was a more peripheral member of the Local ESL CoP; it also made her an occasional target of performances such as this one. The entire class is aware that Nat is correcting 618's paper because he made this public a few minutes earlier. The vocabulary word in question is "falter," and the "correct" definition is "to hesitate" or "move unsteadily."

Excerpt 3 Stradily [ELA32Wmd6: 2144-2160]

```
01  Ms. Ariel:   does anyone have an answer for number fourteen (("falter"))?=
02  Raven:       =yes,=hesitate.
03  ?MS:         (hesitate.)
04  Nat:         (              [    )       ]
05  Ms. Ariel                   [hesitated.]
06  Eddie:       hesitate.
07  ?MS:         (oh                                    wrong.)
08  Ms. Ariel:   or to move unsteadily?
09               (0.8)
10  Ms. Ariel:   either of [those (0.5)           ]
11  ?MS:                   [(                    )]
12  Ms. Ariel:   will work.=
13  Nat:         =what about stradily.
                 (([strædɪli]))
14               (0.6)
15  Nat:         stradily.=
16  Ms. Ariel:   =hh
17               (0.6)
18  Nat:         (they put) stradily:!
19  Ms. Ariel:   I think hhh
20  ?Ss:         hhhhh[hhhh
21  618:              [hu:[:h!
22  Ms. Ariel:        [what they mean:t wa:s (0.3) unsteadily=you know
23               what?=this is [what I-  ]=
24  618:                       [(shut up)]
25  Ms. Ariel:   =everyday this is what I correct. and I try to figure out
26               okay what did that person mea[:n?
27  ?Ss:                                      [he hh
28  ?MS:         (nice      )
29  Ms. Ariel:   so I try not to grade them on spelling=on the defin[itions=
30  Raven:                                                          [mistake!
31  Ms. Ariel:   =because [I want to know they know the meaning.]
32  618:                  [(             [           )          ]
33  Raven:                               [(                    )]
34  CKY:         mistake!
35  China:       Miss.
36  Ms. Ariel:   so I try to decipher what they meant.
37  China:       so wait you correct 618's paper every day?=
38  Nat:         =unstradily?
                 (([ənstrædɪli]))
39               (0.8)
40  ?S:          hhhh
41  Nat:         unstra[dily (is a                     ).]
42  Ms.Ariel:          [okay number fifteen, over ]there, G-Koput.
```

There is much to comment on in this excerpt, but I concern myself with the way the Local ESL students find in the structure of a peer-review activity the affordances for a display of distinction, specifically in terms of the Mock ESL voicings of "stradily" (lines 13, 15, 18) and "unstradily" (lines 38, 41). In contrast to Excerpt 2, only one apparent "mistake" has been singled out and made public here: 618's evidently incorrect definition for the word "falter."

The first point to note is the occasioning of the style shift. Nat has voiced this in a strategic way, as an ostensible check about a classmate's quiz answer, which throws into question the frame of the "stradily" voicing: ironic or just checking an answer? This has important implications for the trajectory of the interaction as Ms. Ariel in fact orients to Nat "just checking an answer"; indeed, she aligns herself with him and his amazement at such a mistake, as her extended explanation, spanning lines 22–23, 25–26, 29, 31, and 36, indicates. This clears the way for Nat to repeatedly revoice "stradily" without sanction and for Nat's classmates, including Raven, CKY, and China (all Local ESL students), to laugh and comment upon 618's "mistake" (lines 30, 34, 35, 37; also see lines 20, 27, 28, 33, 40) in a similarly unsanctionable manner. They are, all could conceivably claim, simply reacting to an amusing error, not Nat's display of distinction,[18] which they have, it seems clear, oriented to themselves (see, e.g., lines 30, 34, 37).

The second point to note is the mode of the putative "mistake" that Nat has recruited for his performance: It is written. That is, no one has voiced "stradily" until Nat does in line 13, as he animates the quiz "answer" that 618 is publicly known to be author and principal of (Goffman, 1981). But has she in fact authored it? The apparent mistake involves a minimal misspelling, not of the vocabulary word "falter," but of a word in the definition. In fact, the ostensible "mistake" may not be 618's but *Nat's*, who may just as well have *misread* 618's handwritten answer, "mistaking" with his stylized "unstradily" an "e" for an "r." There is, in fact, some warrant for this assertion, in terms of how 618 contextualizes her line 21 "hu::h!," with the intonation, emphasis, and sound stretch indexing an unequivocal stance of astonishment.

As this interaction underscores, then, even the seemingly most insignificant L2 "mistake" could serve as a resource in the occasioning of Mock ESL style shifts, a mistake so evidently minor that it may have involved the misspelling of a single letter in one word of a definition, or was, perhaps, a result of illegible handwriting, or perhaps even involved a misreading by the Mock ESL language crosser himself. Regardless, the indexical effects of such a display are identical to those that attended "mistakes" of a far greater magnitude (as, e.g., in Excerpt 2).

In fact, the hierarchical ordering of categories made relevant in Excerpt 3 is evident in a brief analysis of the pronouns in these data, with Nat and Ms. Ariel's "theys" and "thems" (lines 18, 22, 29, 31, 36) signifying an out-group of students who "everyday" (line 25) make mistakes such that Ms. Ariel has to "figure out okay what did that person <u>mea</u>:n?" As a consequence, she states, she cannot grade them on spelling or definitions—an utterance that in its very mention, displays her orientation to such an accommodation as marked—but on whether she can determine if "they know the meaning." As China explicitly notes in line 37, 618 has been iconized as an incumbent of this "they/them" out-group. This out-group simultaneously invokes a relational "we/us" in-group of advanced, perhaps even "native" English speakers, the incumbents of which are Ms. Ariel, Nat, China, and the students who have aligned themselves with them through their laughter and sarcastic commentary (also see Talmy, 2009a).

The final interaction that I analyze took place among several Local ESL classmates during a classroom "study hall" session, when students were essentially given free time to "catch up" on overdue work. China had been walking around the classroom, talking to classmates and to Ms. Ariel, before stopping at Eddie's desk. After a few moments, China asked Eddie how long he had lived in Hawai'i. Eddie orients to an apparent peculiarity in China's utterance, and Mock ESL is used to interesting effect as a consequence.

Excerpt 4 Me no English [ELA42WmdS11: 658–667]

```
01  China:     how long you come to Hawai'i.
02             (6.2)
03  China:     I come here [two days only.
04  Eddie:                 [how long you come Hawai(h)'i. China, you don't
05             know how to speak En(hh)glish. how long you come to Hawai'i.
06             ((laugh))
07  Raven:     ((laugh))
08  Ash:       ((laugh))
09  China:     ((higher pitch; light nasal quality)) I- I- I come over here
10             only two day.
                                     (([aɪ- aɪ- aɪ kʰʌm obə hiə
               onli tʰu de]))
11  Eddie:     ((laugh))
12  China:     ((higher pitch; light nasal quality)) me no English. me come
13             here two day [only.
                                     (([mi no ɪŋɡəlɪʃ] [mi kʰʌm hiə
               tʰu de onli]))
14  Eddie:                  [((laugh))
15             (1.0)
16  China:     ((higher pitch; light nasal quality)) me kick your ass after
17             school.
                                     (([mi kʰɪk jɔ æs æftə
               skuʷ]
18             (1.1)
19  China:     and P-E.
               (([æn pi i.]))
```

China's question to Eddie in line 1, "how long you come to Hawai'i.", is followed by a substantial silence. Unfortunately, because I was working with other students at this time, I do not have a record of what transpired during this pause. However, it appears that either the marked duration of the silence in line 2 and/or a combination of nonverbal actions from Eddie and/or his copresent Local ESL peers Ash and Raven, provided China with some indication that they had treated his line 1 utterance as improprietous. In line 3, China appears to anticipate some form of sanction because he shifts footing to utter what seems a precursor of the Mock ESL performance to come: Although the style shift here lacks elements of a full-on shift to Mock ESL, such as those that come in lines 9–10, 12–13, 16–17, and 19 (note the plural morpheme on "days"; cf. lines 10, 13, and the lack of prosodic styling), Eddie, Raven, and Ash know that China has not "come here two days only." This latter utterance is overlapped by Eddie in line 4, who provides metapragmatic comments about China's initial question, first indexically, by revoicing it and contextualizing the revoicing with laughter, and then denotatively, with "China, you don't know how to speak En(hh)glish." Raven and Ash then join Eddie in laughter.

It is at this point that China crosses into a fully stylized Mock ESL. The variety includes similar features as those enumerated in the analysis of Excerpt 1, but over the course of the interaction, becomes progressively more exaggerated. In fact, it is the absurdity of China's performance, from the increasingly hyper-incorrect syntax and styled prosody to the physical threats in his last two turns, that becomes what is hearably humorous— *instead of* China's initial utterance. In a clear testament to China's L2 expertise and interactional competence, the metapragmatic cues achieved by the style shift have worked to align the original L2 impropriety with a social other, a FOB, the same social other that Eddie makes relevant with his line 5–6 assessment, "you don't know how to speak En(hh)glish." With the line 1 mistake now "authored" by a "FOB," rather than its (mere) animator, China, the style shift at once mitigates China's incumbency as a member of that category, and remarkably, aligns him with the very Local ESL classmates who had singled out his impropriety in the first place. In an extraordinary display, China has transformed being "targeted" by Eddie and the others for his own L2 "mistake" into an ostensibly ludic, aligning *display of distinction*. It is unlikely that students with lower L2 expertise or interactional competence could have achieved such an adept reversal.

Iconization, erasure, and fractal recursivity

In line with the critical pragmatics analytic framework sketched earlier, I aim in the next two sections to situate the analysis in a broader ethnographic context, to consider the instances of Mock ESL style shifts just discussed in terms of their sociohistorical, sociopolitical, and language-ideological significance: specifically, in this section, through the lens of the three semiotic processes formulated by Irvine and Gal (2000), iconization, erasure, and fractal recursivity.

Iconization

The analysis has already made reference to the process of iconization, whereby "[l]inguistic features that index social groups or activities appear to be iconic representations of them, as if a linguistic feature somehow depicted or displayed a social group's inherent nature or essence" (Irvine & Gal, 2000, p. 37). Through this process, the Mock ESL style shifts analysed earlier iconized the identity category

"ESL student," binding the following "inherent" attributes to it: rudimentary L2 English expertise, interactional incompetence, and pragmatic ineptitude ("Me no English," "I don't speak no English"); incomprehensibility and awkwardness ("stradily," "a what type of moment?"); low mental capacity, infantilism, and befuddlement ("how do you spell A?", "but we ESL student"); and naïveté and novicehood ("I come here two day only").[19] Through practices such as Mock ESL crossing, the category of "ESL student" came to signify an archetypal social other, a FOB, that was relationally distinct from the perpetrators of these displays, and whose abnormality stemmed in myriad ways from a lack of familiarity with, experience of, and socialization into a wide range of L2 English, school, Hawai'i, and U.S. social practices.

Erasure

Erasure is the process by which difference is downplayed in an effort to underscore social and/or linguistic uniformity. As Irvine and Gal (2000) argued, "in simplifying the sociolinguistic field," the process of erasure "renders some persons or activities (or sociolinguistic phenomena) invisible. Facts that are inconsistent with the ideological scheme either go unnoticed or get explained away" (p. 38). In terms of the analysis above, what was "erased" through displays of distinction such as Mock ESL crossing included the many *similarities* shared by Local ESL students and their lower L2-English-expert and newcomer classmates. By the same token, a great deal of variation in terms of L2 expertise and interactional competence among Local ESL students was suppressed, particularly in displays that involved several of these students (e.g., in Excerpt 3). However, the fluidity and fragility of these processes of erasure, the inherently contingent character of producing "difference" from FOBs and "similarity" with other Local ESL students, made their vulnerability to being "unerased" omnirelevant because *anyone* in the ESL classes could (and did) make L2 "mistakes": The common targets of practices such as Mock ESL—lower L2-expert and newcomer ESL students—made them, to be sure, but then, so did Local ESL students. Thus, irrespective of who authored them, *any* L2 mistakes could be recruited as candidate mockables for displays of distinction (ludic or otherwise) by Local ESL students at any time, and, as was the case with 618 (in Excerpt 2) and China (in Excerpt 4), Local ESL students could find themselves the targets of these practices as well.

Fractal recursivity

Social practices such as Mock ESL styling worked to create a system of hierarchical oppositions between the targets of Mock ESL—the FOBs—and the Mock ESL crossers—the Local ESL students. The iconic attributes of the "ESL student" category enumerated earlier (lack of English expertise, interactional incompetence, low mental capacity, novicehood, etc.) were ascribed to the Mock ESL targets, while the Mock ESL crossers signaled through this practice their distinction from them. Schematically, this system of oppositions can be represented as a Local ESL || FOB hierarchy as in Figure 3.

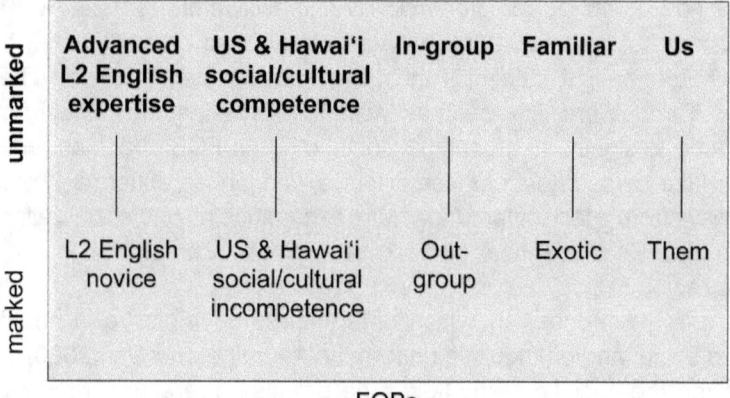

Figure 3. Representing of the Local ESL || FOB relational hierarchy in the Tradewinds ESL program.

The relations represented in Figure 3 should recall those depicting the mainstream || ESL hierarchy from Figure 2 (p.226) and the US-American || Foreign hierarchy from Figure 1 (p. 225). The relationship between these systems of oppositions is adequately described by the third-language ideological process posited by Irvine and Gal (2000), *fractal recursivity*. Fractal recursivity "involves the projection of an opposition, salient at some level of relationship, onto some other level" (p. 38). This is a process "by which meaningful distinctions (between groups, linguistic varieties, etc.) are reproduced *within each side of a dichotomy*, creating subcategories and subvarieties" (Irvine, 2001, p. 33, my emphasis). That is, the Local ESL || FOB hierarchy can be seen as the local projection *within* the Tradewinds ESL program of the relational dualities constituting the mainstream || ESL hierarchy in the wider school context. In view of the brief discussion of linguicism in Hawai'i and the US—the Speak American campaigns, for example, the ongoing challenges associated with state and federal policy concerning the education of students for whom English is a second language—the mainstream || ESL hierarchy, and its recursive system of subcategories, the Local ESL || FOB hierarchy, can *themselves* be seen as the recursive projection of systems of oppositions from a supralocal context, that is, of an iconic "U.S. citizen," defined in contrast to a "foreigner" (see Figure 4). In each of these recursive self-other iterations, it is English, or some "marked" or (mock) variety thereof, that figures centrally in the iconization process and the recursive projection of these systems of distinctiveness.

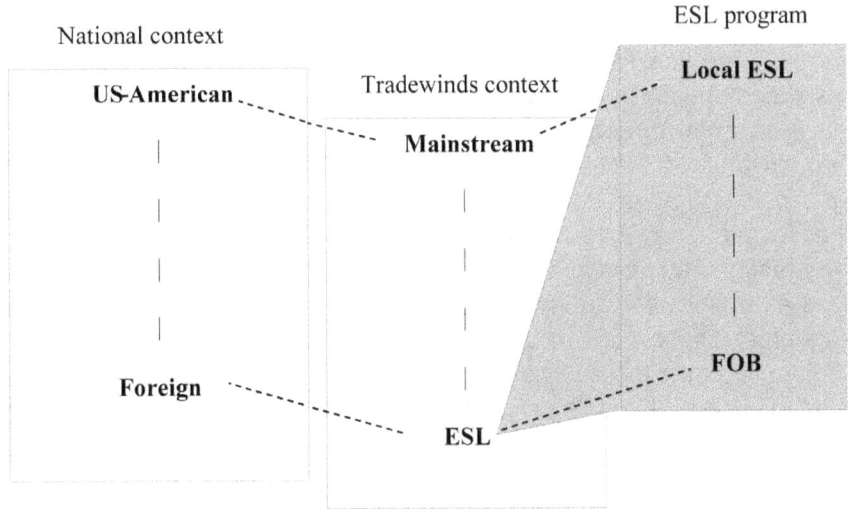

Figure 4. Representing of fractally recursive language-ideological oppositions at the supralocal, school, and ESL program levels.

Distinction and stigma

To return to the perspectives voiced by At, China, and Brahdah at the beginning of this chapter (and referenced by other Local ESL students throughout), I have discussed one way that the stigma of ESL was achieved at Tradewinds High: through these students' Mock ESL style shifts.[20] The low prestige associated with ESL was not, in other words, merely a matter of discriminatory language and educational policies, assimilationist discourses concerning immigrants, negative language ideologies about multilingualism, or historical linguicism, nor did it simply stem from the actions of administrators, educators, or "regular" students in the mainstream. Rather, ESL students themselves were central players in the production of the stigma of ESL at the high school as well, especially the oldtimers featured in the analysis above, in the micropolitics of mundane, everyday classroom conduct. In fact, it was apparent to me in my time at Tradewinds that an important index of (language) learning for many students in the ESL classes was a developing desire, and a corresponding development in ability, to publicly display a stance toward ESL that ranged from subtly negative to explicitly contemptuous. These abilities included embodied social actions such as leaving materials "at home" or not completing coursework, as well as those that were interactionally mediated, including, par excellence, engagement in practices such as Mock ESL crossing. Though the practices varied, all in some way worked to index the practitioner's distinction from "FOBs."

Having considered how the low prestige of ESL was achieved through indexical displays of distinction such as Mock ESL crossing, the question remains: *Why* was ESL stigmatized at Tradewinds? This question is, of course, far more challenging to answer than how it was stigmatized, but I hope to have provided through the analysis above a defensible and adequately warranted answer. I'd like to suggest that in part, a pervasive nationalist language ideology, in which language, nation, and identity were iconized and associated in one-to-one terms, accounts for the production of ESL as a low prestige category at Tradewinds, as it converged with (and frequently served as a proxy for) racism, nativism, exclusionism, assimilationism, and xenophobia. These convergences operated in such a way that to "Speak American" became the equivalent of a shibboleth; to not speak it, or to speak it with "an accent" (Lippi-Green, 1997), was to index one's status as an iconic outsider, an alien, a foreigner, someone who could be safely mocked and ridiculed, even in front of (and at times in concert with) teachers, because "they" did not belong.

Pedagogical implications

> It's unfair to ask educators, overstressed and underpaid as they are in the USA, to moonlight as political activists. The last thing they need is distraction from their important work in the classroom. Yet, like it or not, for educators determined to do their best for English language learners...advocacy is part of the job description.   (Crawford, 2008, p. 1)

Although I agree with Crawford (2008) that ESL teachers must work as advocates for their students, their jobs, and their programs (see Crookes & Talmy, 2004), I also believe that part of their "job description" is to ensure that students become advocates for themselves. One way to go about this is not to consider advocacy a "distraction" (Crawford, p. 1), but to integrate advocacy into the ESL curriculum itself. For this endeavor, I would argue that close attention to interactional data can provide a remarkable resource, both in terms of informing curricular and instructional decisions and as a basis for materials development, that is, for principled, grounded, and empirically based pedagogical interventions, critical and otherwise.

For example, in an effort to raise awareness (among students, teachers, administrators, and parents) about linguicism as a frequently unexamined form of socially accepted discrimination, activities could be formulated based on instances of Mock ESL crossing such as those discussed in this chapter, on other research that concerns mock language (e.g., Mock Spanish, Mock Ebonics, Mock Asian), or other forms or instances of linguicism (see Lippi-Green, 1997, for ideas). Such activities might involve debates, poetry or story writing, playwriting and performance, critical analyses of pop cultural artifacts, and research reports. Students could be asked to pose problems (Freire,

1993) about linguicism, to discuss and write about incidents of linguistic prejudice that they themselves have experienced (and/or perpetrated), or to research examples of it in the cultural forms and social practices of everyday life, for example, on the web, in mass media such as magazines, television, or movies, in history, and in literature. These activities could also ask students to consider linguicism in relation to assimilationism, (English) monolingualism, linguistic nationalism, xenophobia, racism, and nativism; they would also, ideally, relate these matters to the status of ESL speakers in North America and especially of ESL students in schools. In the broader goal of promoting L2 and subject-area learning and self-advocacy, such activities would allow teachers and students to usefully and creatively address issues related to linguicism, to work toward change, and to help to make coursework more relevant to students' lives.

Conclusion

In this chapter, I have outlined an ethnographically informed, socially constituted critical pragmatics analytic framework "respecified" beyond the Faircloughian "school" (Blommaert, 2005, p. 24) of CDA to include a wider range of analytic resources that can attend to the critical analysis of language-in-use. As an example, the critical pragmatics framework I used drew on applied CA, MCA, interactional sociolinguistics, and linguistic anthropology to complement, in data-near, participant-relevant microanalytic terms, an analysis that was first and foremost a critical ethnography. With this framework, I examined four occasionings of a linguistic style that I call Mock ESL as it was used by oldtimer Local ESL students in displays of distinction from lower L2-English-expert and newcomer ESL classmates at Tradewinds High. I interpreted these style shifts in terms of the language ideological processes of iconization, erasure, and fractal recursivity. I did so as a means to demonstrate how the politics of Mock ESL use could be sociohistorically linked to the politics of language and education in Hawai'i and to illustrate the recursive projection of social processes at several different levels of relationship, ranging from "macro" to "micro," or to put it more precisely, how the "macro" was *constituted* in the "micro" and vice versa. Finally, having endeavored to illustrate one way that the stigma of ESL was produced at Tradewinds High, I sought to address the matter of why it was stigmatized. I located one important source in the consequences and repercussions of a pervasive nationalist language ideology that circulated in the ESL program and, I argued, in the wider school and societal contexts. I followed this discussion with a brief consideration of certain pedagogical interventions that might be pursued using discourse data such as those involving Mock ESL style shifts, so that the Ats, the Chinas, and the Brahdahs of the future might have less reason to malign and much more to gain from ESL.

Notes

1. I am indebted to the students and teachers at Tradewinds High for granting me access to their classroom worlds and for allowing me to represent those worlds. I am also grateful to the Pragmatics and Language Learning (PLL) conference organizers, Gabriele Kasper, Hanh Nguyen, Dina Yoshimi, and Jim K. Yoshioka for extending me the opportunity to present an early draft of this chapter at PLL 17 in Honolulu. My thanks also to Sarah J. Roberts, who supplied me with resources drawn from her exceptional archival research on Pidgin. Finally, my gratitude to The Spencer Foundation and The International Research Foundation for English Language Education, two organizations that helped fund this study. The views expressed and any errors are my own. This article is dedicated to the memory of Terri Menacker, a kind mentor, outstanding scholar, and tireless advocate for Pidgin and speakers of Pidgin.
2. The data in the epigraph are from fieldnotes, in contrast to the audio-recorded excerpts I analyze below, and so are formatted differently and not subjected to analysis.
3. All utterances in Pidgin (Hawai'i Creole) in this chapter, such as Brahdah's here, are transcribed in the phonemic Odo orthography (see Sakoda & Siegel, 2003), accompanied by an English gloss in italics.
4. The names of the students, the teachers, and the school in this chapter have been changed. The students chose their own pseudonyms, unless denoted at first mention by an asterisk (*).
5. "Local," an identity category in wide circulation in Hawai'i, refers to someone born and raised in the islands (see Okamura, 1994; cf. Trask, 2000); "Local ESL," an etic category, thus aims to signify ESL students whose actions indexed "Local" affiliations and oldtimer status in Hawai'i, the US, and in U.S. ESL programs, as well as advanced L2 (English and Pidgin) expertise (see Talmy, 2008, pp. 623–625).
6. By a "theoretically principled" analytic opportunism, I mean that the analytic frameworks must be theoretically compatible, as they indeed can be for critical analyses of talk-in-interaction (see Kitzinger, 2000, 2008; Miller & Fox, 2004; Speer, 1999; Stokoe, 2000; ten Have, 2007, pp. 42–64, 73–78; Wilkinson & Kitzinger, 2008).
7. For those, including Fairclough (e.g., 1992, pp. 85–86), who might argue that there is no need for such a respecification because CDA has utilized methods from CA, I suggest comparing how CA is used in Faircloughian CDA to how it is used, for example, in feminist psychology (e.g., Kitzinger, 2000, 2007, 2008; Stokoe, 2003, 2010; Stokoe & Edwards, 2007; Stokoe & Smithson, 2001; Wilkinson & Kitzinger, 2003, 2008), where there is greater demonstrable adherence to analysis that takes seriously the commitment to endogenous orientations.
8. There are other critiques of (Faircloughian) CDA that are not necessarily linked to CA, including those of McHoul (1988), Pennycook (2001, 2003), and Verschueren (2001).
9. G. Kasper (personal communication, June 2009) offers an important insight concerning the CA/CDA polemic, arguing that it does not take into account the

distinction between "pure"/"basic" and "applied" CA (see below for more on this distinction): "the entire Billig/Wetherell/Schegloff debate suffers from a confusion of the explanandum. The explanandum of basic CA is the procedural infrastructure of interaction, no more, no less. Unless one argues that this explanandum is illegitimate (which would make as little sense to me as proscribing the study of grammar as an object in its own right), I think it needs to be accepted for what it is. Critical [discursive psychology], CDA, pragmatics, ethnography; institutional, feminist, critical CA, or CA-SLA for that matter, have different explananda. CA can be necessary as part of the explanans but it often cannot go the entire way."

10 The term "macro context" would suggest that the historical discussion that follows is relevant, a priori, to my analysis of Mock ESL (Schegloff, 1997; ten Have, 2007, pp. 73–78). However, following points made in the previous section, it is my task to demonstrate in a defensible manner its relevance. See below.

11 Tove Skutnabb-Kangas and Robert Phillipson have been charged (see Blommaert, 2001a, 2001b) with condoning a nationalist language ideology because their arguments concerning linguistic human rights appear predicated on a conflation of language with ethnic group and ethnolinguistic group with nation. For the record, Skutnabb-Kangas (2002) has denied working within "the outdated (Herderian) nation-state ideology" (p. 540), maintaining that critics have mistaken her use of arguments from international human rights law as evidence for it. Although this point is arguable, it should be obvious that I use "linguicism" as a gloss for discrimination based on language, not to connote linguistic nationalism.

12 *Haole*, from the Hawaiian word for "foreigner," has over time come to denote "white" or "Caucasian."

13 More thorough discussions on the genesis and development of Pidgin can be found, for example, in works by Roberts (2000), Sakoda & Siegel (2003), Sato (1985, 1991), and Siegel (2000).

14 At the same time, although Pidgin currently is still stigmatized in many circles, in others it is celebrated (e.g., among Local authors, poets, educators, and activists). Regardless, in many communities and contexts in Hawai'i, Pidgin remains the usual, unmarked code for communication. This was, indeed, the case in the Tradewinds mainstream, where Pidgin was commonly spoken, as was standardized English. In the Tradewinds ESL program, those students who spoke Pidgin most frequently were the long-term, oldtimer, Local ESL students. Unfortunately, the different statuses, functions, and domains of use of Pidgin and standardized English at Tradewinds were not a focus of the original study.

15 Violations dwindled as funds were cut (and mandates reduced) to oversight agencies such as the Office of Civil Rights (Crawford, 2004).

16 Although there is a long history of linguicism in Hawai'i in which indigenous, Local, and immigrant populations have been denied the right to their L1s, Hawai'i is noteworthy for having two official state languages (English and Hawaiian) and is currently a leader in developing school programs aimed at indigenous language

revitalization, with over 1,500 children, at the time of this writing, in K–12 Hawaiian immersion schools across the state (see http://www.k12.hi.us/~kaiapuni).
17 Indeed, China and Raven's mockery of Ms. Jackson is achieved in substantial part *because* she treats their performance as members of the category "ESL student" as genuine.
18 This would be an example of a "defensible fall-back" account, an interactional practice that featured prominently in the Local ESL CoP communicative repertoire (see Talmy, 2009b).
19 Other attributes, including "disrespect" and "immorality" were also bound to the category (see Talmy, 2009c).
20 In fact, the negative representations of ESL in formal interviews with students such as At, Brahdah, and China can be considered another social practice that produced identities of distinction (see Talmy, in press).

References

Agbayani, A., & Takeuchi, D. (1986). English Standard Schools: A policy analysis. In N. Tsuchida (Ed.), *Issues in Asian and Pacific American education* (pp. 30–47). Minneapolis, MN: National Association for Asia and Pacific American Education & Asian/Pacific American Learning Resource Center.

Anderson, G. (1989). Critical ethnography in education: Origins, current status, and new directions. *Review of Educational Research, 59*, 249–270.

Antaki, C., & Widdicombe, S. (Eds.). (1998). *Identities in talk*. London: Sage.

August, D., & Hakuta, K. (1997). *Improving schooling for language-minority children: A research agenda*. Washington, DC: National Academy Press.

Barth, F. (1969). Introduction. In F. Barth (Ed.), *Ethnic groups and boundaries: The social organization of cultural difference* (pp. 9–39). Bergen-Oslo, Norway: Universitets Forlaget.

Benham, M. K. P., & Heck, R. H. (1998). *Culture and educational policy in Hawai'i: The silencing of native voices*. Mahwah, NJ: Lawrence Erlbaum.

Billig, M. (1996). *Arguing and thinking: A rhetorical approach to social psychology* (2nd ed.). Cambridge, England: Cambridge University Press.

Billig, M. (1999a). Conversation analysis and the claims of naivety. *Discourse & Society, 10*, 572–576.

Billig, M. (1999b). Whose terms? Whose ordinariness? Rhetoric and ideology in conversation analysis. *Discourse & Society, 10*, 543–558.

Blommaert, J. (2001a). The Asmara Declaration as a sociolinguistic problem: Reflections on scholarship and linguistic rights. *Journal of Sociolinguistics, 5*, 131–142.

Blommaert, J. (2001b). [Review of the book *Linguistic genocide in education—or worldwide diversity and human rights?*]. *Applied Linguistics, 22*, 539–542.

Blommaert, J. (2005). *Discourse: A critical introduction*. Cambridge, England: Cambridge University Press.

Blume, J. (1970). *Are you there God? It's me, Margaret*. New York: Yearling.

Brown, P., & Levinson, S. C. (1987). *Politeness: Some universals in language usage.* New York: Cambridge University Press.

Bucholtz, M., & Hall, K. (2004). Language and identity. In A. Duranti (Ed.), *Companion to linguistic anthropology* (pp. 369–394). Malden, MA: Blackwell.

Buck, E. (1986). English in the linguistic transformation of Hawai'i: Literacy, languages, and discourse. *World Englishes, 5*(2/3), 141–152.

Chun, E. W. (2009). Ideologies of legitimate mockery: Margaret Cho's revoicings of Mock Asian. In A. Reyes & A. Lo (Eds.), *Beyond Yellow English: Toward a linguistic anthropology of Asian Pacific America* (pp. 261–287). New York: Oxford University Press.

Crawford, J. (2004). *Educating English learners: Language diversity in the classroom* (5th ed.). Los Angeles: Bilingual Educational Services.

Crawford, J. (2008). *Advocating for English language learners: Selected essays.* Clevedon, England: Multilingual Matters.

Crookes, G., & Talmy, S. (2004). S/FL program preservation and advancement: Literatures and lessons for teachers and teacher education. *Critical Inquiry in Language Studies, 1*, 219–236.

Dahl, R. (1961). *James and the giant peach.* New York: Knopf.

Derwing, T. M., DeCorby, J. I., & Jamieson, K. (1999). Some factors that affect the success of ESL high school students. *Canadian Modern Language Review, 55*, 532–547.

Duff, P. A. (2002). The discursive co-construction of knowledge, identity, and difference: An ethnography of communication in the high school mainstream. *Applied Linguistics, 23*, 289–322.

Duff, P. A. (2005). ESL in secondary schools: Programs, problematics, possibilities. In E. Hinkel (Ed.), *Handbook of research in second language teaching and learning* (pp. 45–63). Mahwah, NJ: Lawrence Erlbaum.

Duranti, A. (1997). *Linguistic anthropology.* Cambridge, England: Cambridge University Press.

Eckert, P. (1989). *Jocks and burnouts: Social categories and identity in the high school.* New York: Teachers College Press.

Edley, N. (2001). Analysing masculinity: Interpretative repertoires, ideological dilemmas and subject positions. In M. Wetherell, S. Taylor, & S. J. Yates (Eds.), *Discourse as data: A guide for analysis* (pp. 189–228). London: The Open University/Sage.

Edwards, D., & Potter, J. (1992). *Discursive psychology.* Thousand Oaks, CA: Sage.

Ellsworth, E. (1989). Why doesn't this feel empowering? Working through the repressive myths of critical pedagogy. *Harvard Educational Review, 59*, 297–324.

Fairclough, N. (1989). *Language and power.* London: Longman.

Fairclough, N. (1992). *Discourse and social change.* Cambridge, England: Polity Press.

Fairclough, N. (2001). The discourse of New Labour: Critical discourse analysis. In M. Wetherell, S. Taylor, & S. J. Yates (Eds.), *Discourse as data: A guide for analysis* (pp. 229–266). London: The Open University/Sage.

Faltis, C. J. (1999). Creating a new history. In C. J. Faltis & P. M. Wolfe (Eds.), *So much to say: Adolescents, bilingualism, and ESL in the secondary school* (pp. 1–9). New York: Teachers College Press.

Foucault, M. (1972). *The archeology of knowledge*. New York: Pantheon.

Freire, P. (1993). *Pedagogy of the oppressed* (M. B. Ramos, Trans.). New York: Continuum. (Original work published 1970)

Giroux, H. A. (1997). *Pedagogy and the politics of hope: Theory, culture, and schooling*. Boulder, CO: Westview.

Goffman, E. (1974). *Frame analysis: An essay on the organization of experience*. New York: Harper & Row.

Goffman, E. (1981). *Forms of talk*. Philadelphia: University of Pennsylvania Press.

Gore, J. (1992). What we can do for you! What *can* "we" do for "you"? Struggling over empowerment in critical and feminist pedagogy. In C. Luke & J. Gore (Eds.), *Feminisms and critical pedagogy* (pp. 54–73). New York: Routledge.

Gumperz, J. J. (1982). *Discourse strategies*. New York: Cambridge University Press.

Gunderson, L. (2006). *English-only instruction and immigrant students in secondary schools: A critical examination*. Mahwah, NJ: Lawrence Erlbaum.

Haas, M. (1992). *Institutional racism: The case of Hawai'i*. Westport, CT: Prager.

Hall, S. (1996). New ethnicities. In D. Morley & K. Chen (Eds.), *The Stuart Hall reader: Critical dialogues in cultural studies* (pp. 441–449). London: Routledge.

Harklau, L. (1994). ESL versus mainstream classes: Contrasting L2 learning environments. *TESOL Quarterly, 28*, 241–272.

Heritage, J. (2005). Conversation analysis and institutional talk. In K. L. Fitch & R. E. Sanders (Eds.), *Handbook of language and social interaction* (pp. 103–147). Mahwah, NJ: Lawrence Erlbaum.

Hill, J. H. (1993). Hasta la vista, baby: Anglo Spanish in the American Southwest. *Critique of Anthropology, 13*, 145–176.

Hill, J. H. (1995). *Mock Spanish: The indexical reproduction of racism in American English*. No longer available online. Retrieved May 13, 2010, from http://language-culture.binghamton.edu/symposia/2/part1/index.html.

Hill, J. H. (1998). Language, race, and white public space. *American Anthropologist, 100*, 680–689.

Horn, L. R., & Ward, G. (Eds.). (2004). *The handbook of pragmatics*. Malden, MA: Blackwell.

Irvine, J. T. (2001). "Style" as distinctiveness: The culture and ideology of linguistic differentiation. In P. Eckert & J. R. Rickford (Eds.), *Style and sociolinguistic variation* (pp. 21–43). Cambridge, England: Cambridge University Press.

Irvine, J. T., & Gal, S. (2000). Language ideology and linguistic differentiation. In P. V. Kroskrity (Ed.), *Regimes of language: Ideologies, polities, and identities* (pp. 35–83). Santa Fe, NM: School of American Research Press.

Jaspers, J. (2006). Stylizing Standard Dutch by Moroccan boys in Antwerp. *Linguistics and Education, 16*, 131–156.

Johnson, K. E. (1996). The vision versus the reality: The tensions of the TESOL practicum. In D. Freeman & J. C. Richards (Eds.), *Teacher learning in language teaching* (pp. 30–49). Cambridge, England: Cambridge University Press.

Kasper, G. (2006). Speech acts in interaction: Toward discursive pragmatics. In K. Bardovi-Harlig, C. Felix-Brasdefer, & A. S. Omar (Eds.), *Pragmatics and Language Learning* (Vol. 11, pp. 283–316). Honolulu: National Foreign Language Resource Center/University of Hawai'i.

Kawamoto, K. Y. (1993). Hegemony and language politics in Hawai'i. *World Englishes, 12*, 193–207.

Kincheloe, J. L., & McLaren, P. (2000). Rethinking critical theory and qualitative research. In N. K. Denzin & Y. S. Lincoln (Eds.), *Handbook of qualitative research* (2nd ed., pp. 279–313). Thousand Oaks, CA: Sage.

Kitzinger, C. (2000). Doing feminist conversation analysis. *Feminism & Psychology, 10*, 163–193.

Kitzinger, C. (2007). Is 'woman' always relevantly gendered? *Gender and Language, 1*, 39–49.

Kitzinger, C. (2008). Developing feminist conversation analysis: A response to Wowk. *Human Studies, 31*, 179–208.

Kitzinger, C., & Rickford, R. (2007). Becoming a 'bloke': The construction of gender in interaction. *Feminism & Psychology, 17*, 214–223.

Koyama, W. (2004). Honorifics in critical-historic pragmatics: The linguistic ideologies of modernity, the national standard, and modern Japanese honorifics. *Journal of Pragmatics, 36*, 2023–2054.

Labrador, R. N. (2009). 'We can laugh at ourselves': Hawai'i ethnic humor, Local identity, and the myth of multiculturalism. In A. Reyes & A. Lo (Eds.), *Beyond Yellow English: Toward a linguistic anthropology of Asian Pacific America* (pp. 288–308). New York: Oxford University Press.

Lave, J., & Wenger, E. (1991). *Situated learning: Legitimate peripheral participation.* Cambridge, England: Cambridge University Press.

Levinson, B. A., Foley, D. E., & Holland, D. C. (Eds.). (1996). *The cultural production of the educated person: Critical ethnographies of schooling and local practice.* Albany: State University of New York Press.

Lippi-Green, R. (1997). *English with an accent: Language, ideology, and discrimination in the United States.* London: Routledge.

McHoul, A. (1988). Language and the sociology of mind: A critical introduction to the work of Jeff Coulter. *Journal of Pragmatics, 12*, 339–386.

McKay, S. L., & Wong, S.-L. C. (1996). Multiple discourses, multiple identities: Investment and agency in second-language learning among Chinese adolescent immigrant students. *Harvard Educational Review, 66*, 577–608.

Meek, B. A. (2006). And the Injun goes "How!": Representations of American Indian English in white public space. *Language in Society, 35*, 93–128.

Mey, J. L. (2001). *Pragmatics: An introduction* (2nd ed.). Malden, MA: Blackwell.

Miller, G., & Fox, K. J. (2004). Building bridges: The possibility of analytic dialogue between ethnography, conversation analysis, and Foucault. In D. Silverman (Ed.), *Qualitative research: Theory, method, and practice* (2nd ed., pp. 35–55). London: Sage.

Ochs, E. (1990). Indexicality and socialization. In J. W. Stigler, R. A. Schweder, & G. Herdt (Eds.), *Cultural psychology* (pp. 287–308). Cambridge, England: Cambridge University Press.

Ochs, E. (1993). Constructing social identity: A language socialization perspective. *Research on Language and Social Interaction, 26*, 287–306.

Ochs, E. (1996). Linguistic resources for socializing humanity. In J. J. Gumperz & S. C. Levinson (Eds.), *Rethinking linguistic relativity* (pp. 407–437). Cambridge, England: Cambridge University Press.

Office of the Superintendent. (2008). *The Superintendent's 18th annual report: 2007.* Honolulu: Hawai'i State Department of Education.

Okamura, J. Y. (1994). Why there are no Asian Americans in Hawai'i: The continuing significance of local identity. *Social Process in Hawai'i, 35*, 161–178.

Pavlenko, A. (2007). Autobiographic narratives as data in applied linguistics. *Applied Linguistics, 28*, 163–188.

Pennycook, A. (2001). *Critical applied linguistics: A critical introduction.* Mahwah, NJ: Lawrence Erlbaum.

Pennycook, A. (2003). Nostalgia for the real or refashioning futures: A response. *Discourse & Society, 14*(6), 808–811.

Quantz, R. A. (1992). On critical ethnography (with some postmodern considerations). In M. D. LeCompte, W. L. Millroy, & J. Preissle (Eds.), *The handbook of qualitative research in education* (pp. 447–505). San Diego, CA: Academic Press.

Rampton, B. (1990). Displacing the 'native speaker': Expertise, affiliation, and inheritance. *ELT Journal, 44*, 97–101.

Rampton, B. (1995). *Crossing: Language and ethnicity among adolescents.* London: Longman.

Rampton, B. (2001). Language crossing, cross-talk, and cross-disciplinarity in sociolinguistics. In N. Coupland, S. Sarangi, & C. Candlin (Eds.), *Sociolinguistics and social theory.* Upper Saddle River, NJ: Pearson.

Reinecke, J. E. (1969). *Language and dialect in Hawai'i: A sociolinguistic history to 1935.* Honolulu: University of Hawai'i Press.

Reyes, A. (2007). *Language, identity, and stereotype among Southeast Asian American youth: The other Asian.* Mahwah, NJ: Lawrence Erlbaum.

Roberts, S. J. (2000). Nativization and the genesis of Hawaiian Creole. In J. McWhorter (Ed.), *Language change and language contact in pidgins and creoles* (pp. 257–300). Philadelphia: John Benjamins.

Roberts, S. J. (2003, August). *Viper Pidgin, good English, and the language of the enemy: Language ideology in Territorial Hawai'i.* Paper presented at the Society for Pidgin and Creole Linguistics, Honolulu, HI.

Ronkin, M., & Karn, H. E. (1999). Mock Ebonics: Linguistic racism in parodies of Ebonics on the Internet. *Journal of Sociolinguistics, 3*, 360–380.

Ruiz de Velasco, J., Fix, M., & Clewell, B. C. (2000). *Overlooked and underserved: Immigrant students in US secondary schools*. Washington, DC: The Urban Institute.

Sacks, H. (1972). On the analyzability of stories by children. In J. J. Gumperz & D. Hymes (Eds.), *Directions in sociolinguistics: The ethnography of communication* (pp. 325–345). New York: Holt, Rinehart, and Winston.

Sacks, H. (1992). *Lectures on conversation* (Vols. 1 & 2). Oxford, England: Blackwell.

Sakoda, K., & Siegel, J. (2003). *Pidgin grammar: An introduction to the creole language of Hawai'i*. Honolulu, HI: Bess Press.

Sato, C. J. (1985). Linguistic inequality in Hawai'i: The post-creole dilemma. In N. Wolfson & J. Manes (Eds.), *Language of inequality* (pp. 255–272). Berlin: Mouton de Gruyter.

Sato, C. J. (1991). Sociolinguistic variation and language attitudes in Hawai'i. In J. Cheshire (Ed.), *English around the world* (pp. 647–663). Cambridge, England: Cambridge University Press.

Saville-Troike, M. (2003). *The ethnography of communication: An introduction* (3rd ed.). Malden, MA: Blackwell Publishing.

Schegloff, E. A. (1997). Whose text? Whose context? *Discourse & Society, 8*, 165–187.

Schegloff, E. A. (1998). Reply to Wetherell. *Discourse & Society, 9*, 413–416.

Schegloff, E. A. (1999a). Naivete versus sophistication or discipline versus self-indulgence: A rejoinder to Billig. *Discourse & Society, 10*, 577–582.

Schegloff, E. A. (1999b). Schegloff's texts as "Billig's data": A critical reply. *Discourse & Society, 10*, 558–572.

Schegloff, E. A. (2007). *Sequence organization in interaction: Vol. 1. A primer in Conversation Analysis*. Cambridge, England: Cambridge University Press.

Schegloff, E. A., Jefferson, G., & Sacks, H. (1977). The preference for self-correction in the organization of repair in conversation. *Language, 53*, 361–382.

Siegel, J. (2000). Substrate influence in Hawai'i Creole English. *Language in Society, 29*, 197–236.

Simon, R., & Dippo, D. (1986). On critical ethnographic work. *Anthropology and Education Quarterly, 17*, 195–202.

Skutnabb-Kangas, T. (2000). *Linguistic genocide in education—or worldwide diversity and human rights?* Mahwah, NJ: Lawrence Erlbaum.

Skutnabb-Kangas, T. (2002). Review or emotional reaction? A rejoinder. *Applied Linguistics, 23*, 536–541.

Slembrouck, S. (2001). Explanation, interpretation and critique in the analysis of discourse. *Critique of Anthropology, 21*, 33–57.

Speer, S. A. (1999). Feminism and conversation analysis: An oxymoron? *Feminism & Psychology, 9*, 471–478.

Stokoe, E. H. (2000). Toward a conversation analytic approach to gender and discourse. *Feminism & Psychology, 10*, 552–563.

Stokoe, E. H. (2003). Mothers, single women and sluts: Gender, morality and membership categorization in neighbour disputes. *Feminism & Psychology, 13*, 317–344.

Stokoe, E. H. (2006). On ethnomethodology, feminism, and the analysis of categorical reference to gender in talk-in-interaction. *The Sociological Review, 54*, 467–494.

Stokoe, E. H. (2010). 'I'm not gonna hit a lady': Conversation analysis, membership categorization and men's denials of violence towards women. *Discourse & Society, 21*, 1–24.

Stokoe, E. H., & Edwards, D. (2007). 'Black this, black that': Racial insults and reported speech in neighbour complaints and police interrogations. *Discourse & Society, 18*, 337–372.

Stokoe, E. H., & Smithson, J. (2001). Making gender relevant: Conversation analysis and gender categories in interaction. *Discourse & Society, 12*, 217–244.

Talmy, S. (2005). *Lifers and FOBs, rocks and resistance: Generation 1.5, identity, and the cultural productions of ESL in a high school.* Unpublished doctoral dissertation, University of Hawai'i at Mānoa, Honolulu.

Talmy, S. (2008). The cultural productions of the ESL student at Tradewinds High: Contingency, multidirectionality, and identity in L2 socialization. *Applied Linguistics, 29*, 619–644.

Talmy, S. (2009a). Forever FOB?: Resisting and reproducing the Other in high school ESL. In A. Reyes & A. Lo (Eds.), *Beyond Yellow English: Toward a linguistic anthropology of Asian Pacific America* (pp. 347–365). New York: Oxford University Press.

Talmy, S. (2009b). Resisting ESL: Categories and sequence in a critically "motivated" analysis of classroom interaction. In H. t. Nguyen & G. Kasper (Eds.), *Talk-in-interaction: Multilingual perspectives* (pp. 181–213). Honolulu: University of Hawai'i, National Foreign Language Resource Center.

Talmy, S. (2009c). "A very important lesson": Respect and the socialization of order(s) in high school ESL. *Linguistics and Education, 20*, 235–253.

Talmy, S. (in press). The interview as collaborative achievement: Ideology, identity, and interaction in a speech event. *Applied Linguistics.*

Tamura, E. (1993). The English-only effort, the anti-Japanese campaign, and language acquisition in the education of Japanese Americans in Hawai'i, 1915–1940. *History of Education Quarterly, 33*, 37–58.

ten Have, P. (2007). *Doing conversation analysis: A practical guide* (2nd ed.). London: Sage.

Toohey, K. (2000). *Learning English at school: Identity, social relations, and classroom practice.* Clevedon, England: Multilingual Matters.

Trask, H.-K. (2000). Settlers of color and "immigrant" hegemony: "Locals" in Hawai'i. *Amerasia Journal, 26*, 1–24.

Valdés, G. (2001). *Learning and not learning English: Latino students in American schools.* New York: Teachers College Press.

Van Dijk, T. (2001). Critical discourse analysis. In D. Schiffrin, D. Tannen, & H. E. Hamilton (Eds.), *The handbook of discourse analysis* (pp. 352–371). Oxford, England: Blackwell.

Verschueren, J. (1998). *Understanding pragmatics*. London: Arnold Publications.

Verschueren, J. (2001). Predicaments of criticism. *Critique of Anthropology, 21*, 59–80.

Watt, D., & Roessingh, H. (2001). The dynamics of ESL drop-out: Plus ça change... *Canadian Modern Language Review, 58*, 203–222.

Wetherell, M. (1998). Positioning and interpretative repertoires: Conversation analysis and post-structuralism in dialogue. *Discourse & Society, 9*, 387–412.

Wetherell, M., & Edley, N. (1999). Negotiating hegemonic masculinity: Imaginary positions and psycho-discursive practices. *Feminism & Psychology, 9*, 335–356.

Widdicombe, S. (1995). Identity, politics and talk: A case for the mundane and the everyday. In S. Wilkinson & C. Kitzinger (Eds.), *Feminism and discourse: Psychological perspectives* (pp. 106–127). London: Sage.

Wilkinson, S., & Kitzinger, C. (2003). Constructing identities: A feminist conversation analytic approach to positioning in action. In R. Harré & F. Moghaddam (Eds.), *The self and others: Positioning individuals and groups in personal, political and cultural contexts* (pp. 157–180). Westport, CT: Praeger.

Wilkinson, S., & Kitzinger, C. (2008). Using conversation analysis in feminist and critical research. *Social and Personality Psychology Compass, 2*, 555–573.

Willett, J. (1995). Becoming first graders in an L2: An ethnographic study of L2 socialization. *TESOL Quarterly, 29*, 473–503.

Williams, R. (1977). *Marxism and literature*. Oxford, England: Oxford University Press.

Willis, P. (1977). *Learning to labour: How working class kids get working class jobs*. New York: Columbia University Press.

Wilson, M. (2001). The changing discourse of language study. *The English Journal, 90*, 31–36.

Wooffitt, R. (2005). *Conversation analysis and discourse analysis: A comparative and critical introduction*. London: Sage.

Woolard, K. A. (1998). Introduction: Language ideology as a field of inquiry. In B. B. Schieffelin, K. A. Woolard, & P. V. Kroskrity (Eds.), *Language ideologies: Practice and theory* (pp. 3–47). New York: Oxford University Press.

Wowk, M. T. (2007). Kitzinger's feminist conversation analysis: Critical observations. *Human Studies, 30*, 131–155.

Zehler, A. M., Fleischman, H. L., Hopstock, P. J., Stephenson, T. G., Pendzick, M. L., & Sapru, S. (2003). *Descriptive study of services to LEP students and LEP students with disabilities* (Vol. 1). Arlington, VA: Development Associates/U.S. Department of Education.

Zentella, A. C. (2003). José, can you see? Latin@ reactions to racist discourse. In D. Sommer (Ed.), *Bilingual games: Some literary investigations* (pp. 51–66). New York: Palgrave.

Appendix A: Transcript conventions

.	falling intonation
,	continuing intonation
?	rising intonation
!	exclamatory intonation
underline	emphasis
—	abrupt sound stop
LOUD	louder than surrounding talk
°quiet°	quieter than surrounding talk
(.)	micropause
(n.n)	pause of more than 0.2 second
[ ]	overlapping speech
=	latched speech
:	sound stretch
( )	questionable transcription
(( ))	transcriber comments
gloss	English gloss of Pidgin (Hawai'i Creole English)
> <	faster than surrounding talk
> <	slower than surrounding talk
↑↓	rising/falling shift in intonation
hhh	laugh tokens
.hh	audible in-breath
?M/FS	unknown male/female student

Teacher Deployment of Applause in Interactional Assessments of L2 Learners

Yuri Hosoda
David Aline
Kanagawa University, Yokohama, Japan

Previous studies in second language learning have revealed a systematic mismatch between teachers' expected patterns of interaction and actual classroom interaction. The present conversation analytic study explores how the forms of assessments may reveal teachers' orientations to their own expectations of student behaviors. The analysis of 15 video-recorded English as a foreign language classes in a Japanese elementary school revealed various ways teachers have of providing positive assessments. Particular to this context was the frequently observed combination of verbal assessment with applause. When this combination was used, the sequence of interaction invariably moved to a next activity or next sequence. Furthermore, the examination of nonoccurrence (i.e., verbal assessment only) and delayed cases of applause revealed that the teacher withheld applause until the learner carried out the teacher's own lesson plan in the form of the precise interactional patterns that the teacher had envisaged. Thus, the teachers' orientation to their communicated expectations constrained the occurrence of applause. Moreover, the learners oriented to the teachers' communicated expectations as they adjusted their performance to conform to the format introduced by the teacher for that class.

In this chapter, we examine teachers' utilization of applause in their feedback turns and how the use of this interactional resource might index the teachers' expectations of students' behaviors. These expectations can be considered to be part of the teachers' "workplans," which, following Breen (1989), includes both planning prior to instruction in the classroom and teacher expectations of what students should do with the task at hand in the classroom. Our chapter looks specifically at the teachers' communicated expectations in the classroom interaction as it is publicly revealed in and through the interaction on a moment-by-moment basis. We can observe the teacher's expectations because the teachers themselves demonstrably orient to some patterns within the interaction. One indicator of their orientation to expectations is, as we discuss throughout the chapter, the deployment of applause.

Before we describe applause as an interactional resource in teachers' feedback turns, it is important to note that teachers' expectations of what students should do in a given teaching activity and students' actual behaviors may not match. Breen (1989), for example, argued that task-as-workplan differs from task-in-process and task outcomes because a teacher's predesigned task (i.e., task-as-workplan) "may not be followed according to the 'frame' which it offers to its users" (p. 188). Recent studies using a conversation analytic approach reported differences between the teachers' "workplan" and the actual interaction. Mori (2002) analyzed a *zadankai,* discussion meeting event, between students of Japanese as a foreign language and native Japanese speaker guests. Although the speech event was intended to generate natural interaction between the students and guests, the actual interaction involved a series of question-answer adjacency pairs with minimal third-turn acknowledgements, making the organization of the interaction look similar to that of structured interviews. Seedhouse (2001, 2004) examined a large database of second language (L2) classrooms with a variety of language backgrounds. Focusing especially on form-and-accuracy contexts, Seedhouse demonstrated how the teachers pursued their task-as-workplan through turn-taking and repair when the trajectory of classroom interaction deviated from the teachers' original workplan. On the other hand, when the learners' production fit the teachers' workplan, the teachers provided positive assessments and moved on to a new interactional sequence.

In many previous studies on the gap between teachers' plans and the actual activities, after the tasks were completed by the learners, the researchers judged whether the tasks had been carried out according to the task planners' intent. In these studies, there was no focus on the disparity between the plan and the actual activity that was oriented to by the participants in interaction, either in teacher-student interaction (e.g., Coughlan & Duff, 1994) or in student-student interaction (Mori, 2002; Ohta, 2001). In contrast, in our study, as in studies by Seedhouse (2001, 2004), we examine how the teachers, during teacher-fronted interaction, displayed in their talk and other conduct that students' behaviors do not match the teachers' communicated expectations, expectations that may have been based on previously established patterns of sequential organization and instructions. We do not apply a priori knowledge of what the teachers' tasks are designed to accomplish. Similarly to Seedhouse's studies, we investigate teachers' displayed orientation to their expectations in their feedback turns.

Unlike Seedhouse, however, we focus specifically on the use of one particular interactional resource: applause.

Teachers' positive feedback in third position[1]

Positive assessment tokens by teachers may include "okay," "yes," "good," "that's right," and the like (Seedhouse, 2001, 2004). However, the same tokens can be used even when the teacher does not completely accept a student's answer. For example, in the following excerpt, although the teacher initially responds with "That's right," he does not subsequently move to a next sequence. After producing, "That's right," the teacher supplies the correct form and asks the student to repeat the correct answer.

Excerpt 1 ("L" stands for "learner" and "T" stands for "teacher.")

```
L: When did Fred joined army?
T: That's right. Only when did Fred join the army?
   When did Fred join the army? Say it again.
           (Willis, 1987, p. 154, cited in Seedhouse, 2001, p. 358)
```

As evidenced in this excerpt, the verbal form of the assessment token alone does not indicate the action of the token. The positive token in the teacher's response only partially accepts the answer (in this case, for its content but not its accuracy), and this is evidenced by the fact that the teacher does not transition into a new sequence.[2] When the teacher uses positive assessment tokens and moves to a next activity or sequence, one may infer that the learner's response fits the teacher's expectation of what is acceptable in the student response slot.

Another way that teachers provide positive assessments to students is through repetition of students' responses in third positions. However, as is the case with tokens such as "okay," "good," or "yes," repetitions are not always used as positive assessments; the functional variability of repetitions may depend on prosody and intonation. Hellermann (2003), for example, found a difference in prosody between when repetition in the third turn is used as a positive assessment and when it is used as a negative assessment. He analyzed interaction in physics and history classes in the United States and focused his analysis on the teachers' repetition of the students' responses in the third turn in three-part classroom discourse sequences, that is, evaluation turns in initiation-response-evaluation (IRE) patterns (Mehan, 1979), feedback turns in initiation-response-feedback patterns (Sinclair & Coulthard, 1975), and comment turns in question-answer-comment patterns (McHoul, 1978). Hellermann discovered that although the teachers' repetitions were used as both positive and negative assessments, there were systematic differences in prosody between when the repeats were used as positive assessments and when they were used as negative assessments.

Contributing to this line of research, our study examines applause as another feature in addition to prosody and verbal expressions that can determine the actions of teachers' turns in third positions. Specifically, we explore what kind of teachers' third-position feedback allows the interaction to move forward and how the teachers' orientations to their communicated expectations is reflected in their third-position turns.

Study

Method

The data analyzed for this study come from 15 audio- and video-recorded English as a foreign language (EFL) classes in a Japanese elementary school. The observed classes were at 12 different schools randomly selected from throughout Japan as part of a research project to evaluate the new Japanese curriculum, which recently introduced English language classes to elementary schools (MEXT Grant No. 16520359). At the time of this project, English classes were not held by all schools on a regular basis, and English language instruction per se was not yet required but was taught under the umbrella term of "international understanding." The curriculum specified that the primary purpose of the classes was to foster an interest in and desire to understand foreign cultures and languages through experiential learning rather than learning language through formal instruction (Ministry of Education, Culture, Sports, Science and Technology, 2004).

Eleven of the observed English classes were taught by eight different visiting teachers (VT) who were non-Japanese expert speakers of English. In those classes, the Japanese homeroom teacher (JT) remained in the classroom and participated in the activities under various conditions of team teaching (Aline & Hosoda, 2006), from coteaching to covert assistance, but with the VT as the main teacher, who always initiated the main sequences of the classroom interaction.[3] The other four classes were taught only by Japanese teachers.

Our unmotivated examination of the transcripts and videos (Sacks, 1984) drew our attention to the unique occurrence of applause by the teachers in response to the students' performances. We found applause throughout the VTs' classes and in two combined classes taught by groups of JTs. (There were no instances of applause found in the two classes individually taught by the two Japanese homeroom teachers.) The two combined classes were special in that individual classes were combined (all school or all sixth-grade classes together) for public performance, and the applause was audience-initiated applause rather than teacher-initiated applause. Because we focus on teacher-initiated applause in this chapter, we excluded these two combined classes and included only the classes with the VTs. In these classes, we found over 100 instances of applause. All of the recordings were transcribed using the transcription system commonly used in conversation analysis (Jefferson, 1984), and the data were repeatedly examined in data sessions. In our analysis, we paid attention to the applause in the teachers' third-position turns as well as the functions of verbal tokens accompanying these applauses.

What constitutes applause in this chapter differs from applause as understood in previous CA studies. Atkinson (1984b), in a study on applause in political speeches, defined applause as an audience's affiliative response to a public speaker's speech and noted that clapping only becomes applause when several people do so simultaneously. In this chapter, however, we examine a quite different institutional context in that the teacher holds rights to evaluate students in a way that is similar to the rights held by the audience to affiliate with the speaker in public speaking contexts. In other words, the teacher, by affiliating with the student's performance, is doing an assessment.

In the teacher-fronted classroom setting, it is almost always the teacher who has exclusive rights to evaluation of student performance (McHoul, 1978; Mehan, 1979). Therefore, we use the terms *applause* and *clapping*[4] interchangeably because when it is done by the teacher, even when the clapping is not joined by the others (i.e., students), it has an affiliative function. This point is discussed further in the section on applause as teacher-initiated action.

Forms of positive assessment

Unlike conversational interaction in which allocations and designs of turns are not specified in advance but locally managed (Sacks, Schegloff, & Jefferson, 1974), in traditional, Western-style language classrooms, teachers tend to control the content and direction of classroom talk by initiating questions to students (Markee, 2000). The majority of the elementary school English classes examined for this study maintained this interactional pattern. The classes were conducted in teacher-fronted style, and the interaction was predominantly initiated by teachers through asking questions, giving commands, and evaluating student responses. This is different from what Cook (1999) found in non-EFL classes in Japanese elementary schools. The classes she examined had an initiation-presentation-reaction-evaluation pattern in which the students were expected to react to peer presentations prior to teacher evaluations. Cook concluded that through this pattern, Japanese pupils are socialized into a culture in which listening is valued. In the same fashion, through teacher-initiated exchange patterns in English classes, the students in the present data were learning not only the language but also the social norms of formal education in Western countries.

In the present data, in the feedback turns, the teachers produced various verbal tokens such as "good," "very good," "okay," and repetition of the students' responses, and in many cases, the sequences or activities that were in progress were terminated after these verbal tokens.[5] Nevertheless, as seen in Seedhouse's (2001, 2004) data, these verbal tokens alone do not always guarantee the closing of the sequences, and in many cases, further repair work follows. Consider Excerpt 2 below from our data. In this excerpt, the teacher shows the students an oval-shaped ball and asks S11 what it is.

Excerpt 2 [Shizuoka: 12:20–13:03] The visiting English teacher, VT, takes out an oval-shaped ball and shows it to the students. VT then selects S11 to answer his question.

```
01  VT:        what's this. you know?
02             (0.4) ((some Ss whisper "rugubii ball"))
03  (S11):     ragubii ball
04  VT:        >↑oh↓[h<
05  S11:            [ragubii ball
06  VT:        rugby ba:ll. oka:y. (1.0) in Canada, we say
07             (.) football. >football but rugby ball.< (.)
08             okay yeah.
```

In line 5, S11 answers, "ragubii ball" (rugby ball). Then in the following line, the teacher repeats "rugby ball" and says, "oka:y." The use of repetition and "oka:y," however, does not close the sequence. The "oka:y" in line 6 accepts the action that the student provided an appropriate second pair part, appropriate in that it is an answer to the question, but this positive assessment does not close the sequence, as evidenced in the subsequent repair work by the teacher in lines 6 and 7. After saying "oka:y," he repairs S11's response and says, "in Canada, we say (.) football," which shows that not "rugby ball" but "football" was the answer he was attempting to elicit.

In the interaction in the classes observed, however, when verbal tokens, such as "okay," "good," "very good," and repetition of a student's response were accompanied by applause, the sequence of interaction invariably moved forward to a next activity or next sequence. This does not mean that the combination [verbal tokens + applause] is essential to close a sequence but that when the combination occurred, it definitely closed the sequence. As seen in the data excerpts presented below, the [verbal tokens + applause] sequences in the dataset were found to close a sequence in three participation structures: teacher-whole class interaction, teacher-student interaction in front of the whole class, and student-student interaction in front of the whole class.

In Excerpt 3, the two teachers' verbal token "goo::::d" is accompanied by applause. The words, the clapping sound, and the clapping action function as a multimodal assessment that closes the sequence between the VT and a student. Prior to the interaction shown in this excerpt, one student, S1, volunteered to answer a question in front of the class. The expert English-speaking VT then placed a stuffed toy dog on a chair as a referent for this language learning activity.

Excerpt 3 [Tokyo: 04:06–13] VT: visiting English teacher; JT: Japanese homeroom teacher

```
01 VT:         Where is the dog?
02 JT:         [°it's on°
03 VT:         [(  )?
04 JT:         °i[t's on°
05 VT:           [°it's on°
06 S1:         [it's o::n the dog ah chair.
07 (VT/JT):    goo:[:::|::d. oka::y.
08 (VT/JT):        |((clapping))
09                 --(3.0)---------
10 (JT/VT):    [goo:|::|:d
11 (JT/VT):         |((clapping))
12                 --(2.5)----
13 Ss:              |((clapping))
14                 ---(3.0)------
15 VT:         [anybody else?
16 S2:         [((raises a hand))
```

In the first line, the VT asks S1 where the dog is. With assistance from the VT and the JT, S1 answers the question in line 6. Then in line 7, the VT or the JT (because their voices are similar, it is difficult even with the video to determine which) produces "goo::::d" and starts clapping her hands. The two teachers produce "goo::::d" in overlap, one starting immediately before the other, and then the students start applauding for 3 s. Immediately after the clapping ends, the VT asks the class if there is anyone else who wants to volunteer to answer a question, and S2 simultaneously raises her hand. The simultaneity of the action shows that S2 orients to the fact that applause implicates closing and that the teacher is going to select the next student. In other words, both the teacher and the student orient to the fact that the multimodal assessment, namely, the combination of verbal tokens such as "good" plus applause, can close the current sequence and open up a new sequence.

The combination [verbal tokens + applause] functioned in the data as a sequence-closing device even when the learner's performance was obviously not self-constructed but received overt or covert assistance from a teacher or teachers (see Excerpt 3, lines 2–5), fellow student or students, or from both teachers and students. In Excerpt 4, the VT and one student are performing a dialog in front of the whole class. After the greetings with this student, the teacher asks a question concerning the day of the week.

Excerpt 4 [Fukushima: 01:35–02:07] Before the extract, the teacher selected S1 to perform a dialog with the teacher in front of the class.

```
01  VT:        hello.
02  S1:        °hello°
03  VT:        h(h):i. h::i.
04  S1:        °hi°
05  VT:        okay. what day is it today. what day is it
06             today.
07             (0.5)
08  VT:        day day day.
09  S2:        °°it's [monday°° ((to S1))
10  S1:               [it's (.) monday.
11  VT:        it's MONday. oh|h|kay that's good. yey.
12  VT:                      |((clapping))
13  Ss:                      |((clapping))
14                           ------(3.0)-----------
15  VT:        okay. h:i, ((The teacher greets the next
               student.))
```

Upon completion of the greeting sequence, which marks the opening of a teacher-single student interaction in front of the whole class, the teacher asks S1 for the name of the day of the week. After the teacher repeats the question twice without a pause in between (thus indicating that the question was not repeated due to a lack of a response; line 5), there is a short pause (line 7), followed by the teacher's repetition of "day" three times (line 8). The short pause evidences S1's delay in responding to the teacher's question, and the repetition of "day" appears to be an attempt by the teacher to assist the learner by focusing on the key word of the question. However, there is still no immediate response from S1. Instead, S2, who is sitting near S1, turns around and whispers to S1 the likely answer; likely because it is in the form previously taught by the teacher. After hearing the start of S2's utterance, S1 begins to answer in slight overlap with the whispered prompt. Although the end of S2's utterance is overlapped with the beginning of S1's answer, it is likely that S1 hears what S2 says because even in overlap, speakers are able to comprehend and orient to what other speakers say (Schegloff, 2000). Upon the completion of S1's turn, the teacher accepts S1's answer with a repetition of the phrase, with extra stress on the first syllable, carrying the pertinent information, "MONday." The teacher then adds other verbal tokens, "ohhkay that's good. yey.", and applauds in overlap with the verbal tokens. The other students join the teacher's applause in overlap with his verbal tokens. Even though S1's answer was initially delayed, and S1 may have utilized S2's whispered phrase in production of the answer, S1's on-record answer was accepted as appropriate, and it received the sequence-closing positive assessment, consisting of repetition, positive verbal tokens, and applause.

Applause as a teacher-initiated action

Because the applause in the data occurred in overlap with the verbal tokens "good," "okay," and so on and was used as a part of the teachers' positive assessment in the third position, it was almost always teacher initiated, as shown in Excerpts 3 and 4 above. In Excerpt 3, the two teachers' applause is followed by the students' applause, and similarly, in Excerpt 4, the VT's applause is followed by the students' applause.

Applause in public speaking events has been seen as a collaborative activity that is accomplished in unison with others (Atkinson, 1984a, 1984b, 1985, 1986; Heritage & Greatbatch, 1986). Consequently, starting to applaud by oneself without affiliative applause from the other participants is considered to be embarrassing, and the person applauding will stop clapping after a few claps (Heritage & Greatbatch). However, in the English classes in this dataset, this convention does not always apply: The teachers can and frequently do applaud by themselves without the response applause from the students. Consider the interaction in Excerpt 5, in which the whole class is practicing how to ask and answer questions about the weather as the VT points to picture cards representing various weather conditions and playfully changes the speed of her speech.

Excerpt 5 [Nagano3: 7:01–11] Students' laughter turns in lines 2, 4, and 6 overlap somewhat with teacher's turns

```
01  VT:       how's the: wea:ther::::
02  Ss:       ((laugh)) i(h)t's ra(h)iny::.
03  VT:       how::
04  Ss:       ((laugh))
05  VT:       s the::::
06  Ss:       ((laugh))
07  VT:       w:::::::ea:::::::::::ther::::::::::
08  Ss:       i:::::::::::t's (.) clo::::::udy::::::::::::::.
09  VT:       how's the weather.
10  Ss:       it's sunny.
11  VT:       very |goo::::::d.
12  VT:            |((clapping))
13                 ---(2.1)----
14  VT:       oh do you remember the so:ng?
```

At line 11, the teacher closes the activity by saying "very goo:::::::d" and clapping her hands in overlap with the prolonged "goo:::::::d." After clapping her hands for 2.1 s, she introduces a next activity in line 12. Notice that the teacher's applause in line 11 is not joined by the others. Nevertheless, she continues applauding for more than 2 s. In the present data, the duration for applause was normally from 2 to 3 s, and thus, the 2.1-s applause in this excerpt is not noticeable as being short. (In contrast, in some political speeches, applause can last for around 8 s; Atkinson, 1985, p. 165).

In the rare cases in our data when individual students in the observed classes applauded by themselves without initiation from the teacher, they stopped after about 1 s, as shown in Excerpt 6.

Excerpt 6   [Shizuoka: 10:01–09]

```
01 VT:       hello:.
02 S5:       HELLO:
03 VT:       >uhh< my name is Donald. what's your name.
04 S5:       my name is Yu°taro°.
05 VT:       uh nice to meet |you.
06 S:                        |((a S claps))
07                           ---(1.2)-----
08           (.)
09 VT:       nice to meet you.
10 S5:       nice to meet you.
11 VT:       wohw:|:|:::::::::::: yey.
12 VT:            |((turns around to face class, starts
13                 clapping with exaggerated gestures))
14                ----------------(3.5)------------
15 Ss:            |((clapping))
16                -------------(3.5)-------------
17 VT:       yey. Good. hai next
18           yes
```

In this excerpt, the teacher and S5 are practicing a dialog in front of the whole class. When the teacher is about to finish saying, "nice to meet you" in line 5, one student starts clapping. However, the student's clapping is not joined by others, and the student stops clapping after 1.2 s. Then, in line 9, the teacher redoes the first pair part of an adjacency pair that can close the introduction sequence by saying "nice to meet you." By redoing the first pair part, the teacher sequentially deletes the student's clapping and treats the clapping as an interruption. This time, S5 produces the second pair part of the adjacency pair, "nice to meet you" (line 10). Then, in line 11, the teacher starts clapping while saying, "wohw::::::::::: yey." Interestingly, when the teacher starts clapping, he turns around to everybody and invites everyone to join in the applause. This clapping is joined by all students except S5, and it continues for 3.5 s.

As illustrated in these excerpts, applause was found to be a teacher-initiated action. Teachers decided when the students' responses were worthy of being applauded and used applause as part of a positive assessment of students' performances and to close the current sequence. Moreover, the teachers occasionally invited the other students to join in providing positive feedback in the form of applause.

Applause as a positive assessment of teachers' communicated expectations

As demonstrated above, the [verbal token + applause] pattern occurred in the teacher's turns in the third position as a positive assessment, and it could close the current sequence. This multimodal assessment format can move the interaction forward to a next sequence without further expansion. Moreover, applause itself implicates affiliation and carries a positive connotation (Atkinson, 1984a, 1984b).

However, the students' responses that could be considered "appropriate" or "acceptable" from an outside observer's point of view did not always result in the teacher's use of the apparent approbation combination [verbal token + applause], but sometimes resulted in only verbal assessments such as "good," "okay," and repetition of the student's response without applause. Consider Excerpt 7 below. In Excerpt 7, the students' contribution could be considered to be "correct" in other contexts, but it did not seem to fit in the teacher's communicated expectations of students' next actions, and it was not followed by applause. Prior to this excerpt, the teacher explained to the whole class that the student who is holding the card with the name that the class calls should say, "Yes, I am."

Excerpt 7 [Fukushima: 14:14–20] S12 has the card that says "Ian Thorpe."

```
01 VT:      Ian Thorpe? Ian Thorpe? oka:y. ohkay.
02          ARE YOU IAN THORPE?
03 Ss:      are you Ian Thorpe?
04 (        3.5) ((other Ss chatting))
05 S12:     °no I'm not°
06 VT:      n(h)o I'm n(h)ot. ohhh. uh:. yes? n(h)o?
07 S12:     no.
08 VT:      no. ((covers his face with hands)) okay.
```

Initially, the teacher confirms that the students want to find out who has the Ian Thorpe card. The teacher asks the question "ARE YOU IAN THORPE?" in line 2, and the students repeat the question in chorus in line 3. According to the teacher's directions for the activity, the student who is holding the "Ian Thorpe" card should stand up and say "Yes, I am." However, following a long pause, in line 4, S12, who has the "Ian Thorpe" card says, "°no I'm not°." Outside of the context of the classroom, this would be a perfectly acceptable answer because the student's name is not Ian Thorpe. However, S12's answer in line 5 does not follow the teacher's (previously provided) instructions, and in response to S12's answer, the teacher repeats the student's answer, "*n*(h)o I'm *n*(h)ot.", without applauding and utters "ohhh. uh:." The teacher then checks the student's answer with "yes?

n(h)o?" The student confirms his previous answer with the response "no." This time the teacher repeats "no," covering his face with his hands, which possibly indicates feigned shock or embarrassment at the student's answer, and finally says, "okay." In this excerpt, none of the teacher's utterances is accompanied by applause.

As shown in Excerpt 7, even if the students' contributions could be construed as perfectly acceptable outside of the language learning classroom context, when they deviated from the teacher's communicated expectations, the teacher did not applaud.

Also observed were instances in which the teacher delayed applauding until the precise pattern of interaction that the teacher introduced previously in the class was completed. In Excerpt 8 below, the class is practicing how to ask and answer the question, "How are you?" Prior to this excerpt, the VT selected S1 and S2 to practice a dialog in front of the whole class.

Excerpt 8 [Nagano3: 19:22–20:05]

```
01  VT:       please. ask her. how are you.
02            (0.5)
03  VT:       °ask her. how are you. say how are you°
04  S1:       how are you.
05  VT:       °>kay<°=
06  S2:       =I:'m hot.
07  VT:       oh|ka:::y.
08  VT:          |((clapping))
09  VT:           ---(0.7)---
10  VT:       hai sit down.
11            yes
12  VT:       ((signals the next two students to stand up))
```

In line 1, the teacher prompts S1 to ask S2 the question, "How are you?" However, because S1 does not immediately follow the teacher's direction, as indicated by the 0.5-s pause (line 2), in line 3, the teacher repeats the direction, this time using a quieter voice, and uses an additional repetition with the directive to speak, "say how are you." Subsequently, in line 4, S1 looks at S2 and says, "how are you." The teacher accepts this with a quickly and quietly spoken "°>kay<°." This "°>kay<°" functions to move the sequence forward, as indicated in S2's production of the second pair part to S1's question, "how are you." However, this "°>kay<°" is not followed by applause. Only after S2 produces the second pair part, "I'm hot," does the teacher applaud while producing, "ohka:::y" (line 7). This combination of ["okay" + applause] is followed by a transition to the next students: After applauding for 0.7 s, the teacher asks S1 and S2 to sit down and signals the next two students to stand up. Perhaps the teacher's expectation of what the students should say, an expectation that was made public through verbal instructions prior to the excerpt, included both "How are you?" and a response, so until the second pair part to "How are you?" was produced, the teacher withheld applause.

Excerpt 9 below is also an instance of the teacher withholding applause until the sequence of actions that the teacher previously communicated to the students is completed. At this point in the lesson, the VT is asking the students questions about the story that she has just read to them. For this question and answer activity, the teacher explained to the students that they were to answer how many pieces of fruit the caterpillar in the story ate on each day and then to go to the front of the classroom and put the corresponding number of fruit cards on the blackboard. Prior to this excerpt, the whole class went over this pattern of actions from Monday to Thursday.

Excerpt 9 [Kagoshima: 27:21–18:08] After reading the story "Very hungry caterpillar," the visiting native speaking teacher(VT) is asking the students questions about the story.

```
01 VT:        'kay, how many oranges (.) [did he eat.
02            how many.
03 JT:                                   [how many
04 S1:        HAI ((raises a hand))
05 S2:        HAI ((raises a hand))
06 S3:        HAAAh ((raising a hand))
07 VT:        ((gestures to S4))
08 S4:        five
09 VT:        fi::ve, very goo:d, very good.
10 S?:        °a::lright°
11 JT:        alright.
12 S4:        ((walks to the front, grabs strawberry cards,
              and starts putting them on the board.))
13 VT:        kay, o::ne=
14 JT:        =one
15 VT:        two::=
16 JT:        =two:
17 JT:        (hairi kiru) kasira::
              I wonder if they fit {on the board}
18 VT:        three::=
19 JT:        =three:::
20 S2:        ((whispering to the other student))
21 VT:        fou:[:r
22 JT:            [fou:::r, four
23 VT:        fi:ve
24 S4         ((finishes putting five strawberry cards on the board))
25 VT:        oka::y, (2.0) very good, very g|oo|d.
26 VT:                                       |((clapping))
27 Ss &JT:                                   |((clapping))
```

The teacher asks the students, in line 1, how many strawberries the caterpillar ate on Friday. In response to the question, S4 answers "five" in line 8. Although this answer is correct and the teacher accepts the answer saying, "fi::ve, very goo:d, very good," the teacher does not applaud at this point. From line 12 to line 23, S4 walks to the front and puts five strawberry cards on the blackboard. After S4 finishes putting the cards on the blackboard, the VT produces "oka::y" and "very good," and the second "very good" (line 25) is accompanied by applause (line 26). Thus, in this excerpt, the teacher refrains from providing the multimodal positive assessment, [verbal token + applause], until the complete set of activities that includes not only answering the question verbally but also putting the cards on the board is accomplished.

Similarly, in Excerpt 10, the teacher withholds applause until the student completes the exact phrase of a dialog that the teacher had previously introduced in the class. This excerpt also demonstrates that the students' deviation from the teacher's (previously communicated) expectation is a bit of a surprise to the teacher.

In this activity, the VT has two students performing an introduction in front of the whole class.

Excerpt 10 [Shizuoka: 20:20–21:20] The teacher asks S18 and S19 to come to the front of the class to demonstrate the modeled dialog. Anpanman and Mario are names of animated characters.

```
01  T:       OKAY. ready:? shh. Hello.
02  S18:     hello?
03  S19:     hello.
04  T:       my name is,
05  S18:     °°m(h)y n(h)ame i(h)sh°°
06  T:       my name is,
07  S18:     °my name is,°
08  T:       sorede?
             Go on
09  S18:     °my name is °°Anpanman°°
10  Ss:      ((laugh))
11  S1:      ima nante itta?
             what did he say now?
12  Ss:      Anpanma:n.
13  T:       ( ), Anpanman.
14  Ss:      UWA::::
15  T:       Anpanman. oh. what's your name.=
16  S18:     =°what's your name.°
17  S19:     my name is (.) my name is Mario.
18  T:       MA:RIO:. Oh::::
19  Ss:      UWA::::((a few Ss clap their hands for 1 second))
20           ((S18 & S19 start to return to their seats))
21  T:       >Oh oh oh oh.< >oh oh.< ((gestures S18 & S19 to
22           come back to front of class))
23  T:       nice to meet you.
24  S18:     °nice to meet you.°
25  S19:     nice to meet you.
26  T:       hai. °akushu°
             Yes. Shake hands.
27           ((S18 & S19 shake hands))
28  Ss:      ((a few Ss clap hands for 0.6 seconds))
29  T:       |OH|HKA::::Y.
30  T:       |((starts to rise from crouching position))
31  T:       |((clap hands.))
32  Ss:          |((clap hands))
33              -----(3.0)---------
```

After S18 and S19 introduce themselves and a few students start clapping their hands for three or four claps (line 19), S18 and S19 start to return to their seats (line 20). However, the students' closing of the introduction routine seems to be an unexpected event for the teacher. With utterances displaying surprise, ">Oh oh oh oh.<>oh oh<," the teacher gestures for the two students to come back to the front of the class. "Oh" as a "change of state token" (Heritage, 1984) is often observed in mundane conversation outside classroom contexts as a marker showing a change in the speaker's knowledge by virtue of something that happened in the prior turn. In classroom contexts, teachers do not usually acknowledge students' answers to display questions with "oh" because the teachers' knowledge state is not normally transformed by the students' answers (Heritage, 2005). The variation of "oh" in line 21 shows that for the teacher, the students' behavior in the prior turn was unexpected.[7] In addition, as demonstrated by Stivers (2004), multiple sayings in which the same word or phrase is repeated under a single intonation contour signifies that the speaker is proposing that the entire course of action should be stopped because there is a flawed understanding of the activity. In this example, the students displayed their understanding of the activity as asking for each other's names, but the teacher's expectation, as displayed by the multiple productions of "oh" in line 21, was to have the students perform a whole first-encounter dialog with a "Nice to meet you" exchange and shaking each others' hands. Given that the teacher's expectation of what the students should say here (giving their names, saying "nice to meet you," and shaking hands) has been communicated to the students in previous instructions, the teacher's prompt for the two students to go past their closing in lines 21 and 22, the students' immediate compliance with the teacher's request, and the class' applause when the two students have finished their roleplayed introduction (line 32) seem to exhibit everybody's co-constructed orientation to the teacher's previous instructions. In short, the teacher and students were displaying their socially shared cognition (Schegloff, 1991). It is noteworthy that the teacher provides a multimodal positive assessment (emphatic "okay," plus applause) only after the previously taught pattern was completely carried out by the students.

So far, we have shown how the teachers oriented to their (communicated) expectations through multimodal assessments. Interestingly, this orientation to the teachers' expectations was also manifested in the students' behavior. In Excerpt 11, one of the students displays his orientation to the teacher's communicated expectations by correcting another student even after the teacher has accepted the other student's answer.

Excerpt 11 [Fukushima: 11:18–28] The same activity as in Extract (8). The visiting teacher explained to the class that the student who is holding the card the class calls should say "Yes, I am."

```
01  VT:         oka:y. First one.
02  JT:         hai.
03  VT:         are you Jackie Chan? ((hearing gesture))
04  All:        are you Jackie Chan?
05  VT:         oka:y
06  JT:         yes ((signals S1 to stand up))
07  S1:         ((stands up))
08  Ss:         ((some Ss)) $Jackie Cha:n$
09  JT:         °(>kotae<) yes:° I am
                   answer
10  S1:         I am Jackie Chan.
11  VT:         oh↑h wokay o|kay I am >Jackie Ch-< okay
12  VT:                     |((clapping))
13  Ss & JT:                |((clapping))
14                          ------(2.5)---------------------
15  S20: ((sitting in front of S1)) yes I am da yo.=
                                    It should be yes I am.
16  VT:         =yes I am. okay.
17  S1:         °yes I am° Jackie Chan=
18  VT:         =oka::y yea::h goo::d. oooh Jackie Chan
19              Hhe:::w. okay let's see now number two::.
```

In line 7, in response to the question the whole class asked ("Are you Jackie Chan?") and the signal by the JT, S1 stands up. In line 9, the JT whispers to S1 the answer that the VT has pretaught, "°(>*kotae*<) yes:° I am." However, in line 10, contrary to what was pretaught and what the JT said in the previous turn, S1 answers, "I am Jackie Chan." The form of S1's answer is not exactly the same as what the teacher instructed the students to use ("Yes, I am") but might be acceptable in conversation outside the context of the language learning classroom, as noted by the VT's final acceptance of the student's phrase in line 11 when he says, "I am >Jackie Ch-<okay." However, the teacher's acceptance of S1's answer begins with "oh↑h." The teacher's production of "oh↑h" indicates that S1's answer is something unexpected. After producing "oh↑h," the teacher then produces "wokay," but he does not start applauding at this point. Only when he starts producing "okay" the second time does he applaud. The delay of the teacher's applause relative to the verbal assessment tokens may reflect the disparity between the teacher's expectation and the student's production. The teacher continues applauding as he repeats S1's response, and then almost everyone joins him in applauding. However, S20, who is sitting in front of S1 and is not applauding, turns around to face S1 and says "Yes I am *da yo*," which means, "It should be 'Yes I am'" (line 15). In other words, S20 also

orients to the precise linguistic form, "Yes I am," that the teacher instructed the students to use at the beginning of the activity, and his lack of applause seems to treat S1's answer, "I am Jackie Chan," as somehow inappropriate. As this example illustrates, the orientation to the teacher's expectations of students' appropriate behaviors was shown not only in the teacher's behavior but also in a student's behavior.

Conclusion

In this chapter, we have paid close attention to the teachers' feedback turns through microanalysis of their verbal and nonverbal practices. Our examination of the data from the participants' perspective revealed the types of interactional assessments that allowed the interaction to move forward and how the teachers' orientations to their communicated expectations were reflected in the assessments. We have shown that the use of verbal tokens such as "good," "okay," and repetition of students' responses in the teachers' feedback turns did not always close the sequences. In contrast, when the verbal tokens were accompanied by applause, the sequence of interaction invariably moved forward to a next activity or next sequence. Thus, the applause in the classes examined has a closing-implicative function. Further, we observed that the teachers' verbal tokens such as "good," "okay," and repetition of students' responses occurred even when the answers the students provided were later corrected or accepted with delay, but the combination of applause and verbal assessments occurred only when the students' answers matched the teachers' instructed patterns of behavior. Thus, applause might be a higher level of approval than mere verbal assessment. Because applause is more of a public activity that invites everybody to join in the action of approval, teachers can demonstrate to all students the expected participation norms for classroom interaction.

Further, the data show that even when the students' contributions would have been acceptable in contexts other than the classroom, the teachers held back from applauding. In the classes we studied, it seems that the students' actions that more accurately demonstrated the teachers' communicated expectations or previously established patterns of interaction were more well received by the teachers than the students' actions that effectively communicated in the second language. When student behaviors deviated from the previously instructed patterns, the teachers displayed to the students through various techniques that the students were off course and attempted to steer the students back to the track that they had plotted. This orientation to this classroom culture was shown in both the teachers' and the students' behaviors; the students tried to design the forms of their responses to match the teachers' plans. In this way, the students were beginning to be socialized into a language classroom culture in which student responses are expected to meet the teachers' communicated expectations.

In our view, teachers may need to provide students with opportunities to experience the type of language use that does not have classroom-specific formal features. Unfortunately, the conflict remains between the need for the type of interaction found in mundane conversation and the institutional constraints of the classroom. Although teachers should not abandon verbalizing their expectations, they should remember that communicative language use is flexible and takes multiple forms. Therefore, instead of only pursuing students' adherence to teachers' instructions, teachers should allow some freedom for occasional deviation from their original expectations.

Finally, we have demonstrated that the applause in the data was a teacher-initiated action. This is understandable considering that in a teacher-fronted class, the teacher has control of when to provide positive assessments to students and when to move on to the next sequence. By constantly initiating the feedback turn, the teachers were socializing the students into the traditional interactional structure in which the teacher maintained control over turn-taking allocation. However, unlike verbal assessment, which is considered to be accomplished only by the teacher, we found that applause is a modality of assessment that actually serves to invite students to participate in the teacher's feedback turns. By receiving positive assessment not only from the teacher but also from peer students, the early second language learners in the data were likely to enjoy a sense of accomplishment, which might eventually lead to greater motivation for second language learning.[8]

Notes

1. Feedback in the third position refers to feedback that is analyzably placed next to the second pair part of a sequence, and it includes feedback occurring in third turns. Accordingly, insertion sequences can occur between the first pair part and the second pair part or between the second pair part and the feedback turn.
2. The occurrence of "okay," "yes," or "good" in negative assessment environments has also been reported in conversational contexts. In conversational interaction, it has been noted that speakers frequently produce weak agreement tokens such as "yes" or "uh huh" before producing disagreement components. This occurs even when the speakers do not agree with what the prior speakers have said (Davidson, 1984; Pomerantz, 1975, 1984; Sacks, 1987). These weak agreement tokens can be "disagreement implicative" (Pomerantz, 1975, p. 82). However, to what extent these tokens perform the same actions in institutional contexts is an empirical question for future research.
3. Under Japanese law, a certified teacher with a Japanese elementary school license must be present in the classroom during all officially scheduled classes. Therefore, the JTs always remained in the classroom with the VTs, but the degree of their participation varied.

4   Although we observed numerous examples of single claps in these data and in other classroom datasets, the analysis of single claps is beyond the scope of this chapter. However, a preliminary analysis of teachers' single clap instances indicates that as in the case of multiple clap instances, it recurrently occurred at the sequence- or activity-closing position with the verbal tokens "okay," "alright," "good," and so on.

5   The occurrence of minimal tokens such as "okay" and short assessments such as "good" in the third position is not limited to classroom contexts. In ordinary conversation, those minimal tokens and short assessments are often used as sequence-closing thirds for doing terminal work on a sequence (Goodwin, 1986; Schegloff, 2007). Moreover, "okay" and "alright" are commonly considered "change-of-activity" tokens (one type of response token), which propose shifts toward new topics, phases, or activities (Beach, 1993; Gardner, 2001).

6   In the research on applause in political speeches by Atkinson (1984a, 1984b, 1985), information on applause intensity was included. In this chapter, the timing and duration of applause manifested their importance in terms of who initiates applause and in what sequential position. In addition, the duration of applause also shows the contrast between classroom and political speech interaction.

7   The same kind of "oh" can also be observed in Excerpt 2, line 4 and Excerpt 8, line 6. In both excerpts, the teachers ask the students display questions, and the students' answers deviate from the "expected" answers.

8   Because there were two classes in which no instances of applause occurred (those classes taught by a lone JT), and the occurrence of applause has not been reported in the classes of other subjects in elementary school, there may be some other set of practices that teachers use to carry out the same action as applause. However, what practices teachers deploy other than applause in this interactional context is beyond the scope of this study and needs to be investigated in future research.

References

Aline, D., & Hosoda, Y. (2006). Team teaching participation patterns of homeroom teachers in English activities classes in Japanese public elementary schools. *JALT Journal, 28*, 5–21.

Atkinson, J. M. (1984a). *Our masters' voices. The language and body language of politics.* New York: Methuen.

Atkinson, J. M. (1984b). Public speaking and audience responses: Some techniques for inviting applause. In J. M. Atkinson & J. Heritage (Eds.), *Structures of social action: Studies in conversation analysis* (pp. 370–409). Cambridge, England: Cambridge University Press.

Atkinson, J. M. (1985). Refusing invited applause: Preliminary observations from a case study of charismatic oratory. In T. van Dijk (Ed.), *Handbook of discourse analysis: Vol. 3. Discourse and dialogue* (pp. 161–181). London: Academic Press.

Atkinson, J. M. (1986). The 1983 election and demise of live oratory. In I. Crewe & M. Harrop (Eds.), *Political communications: The general election campaign of 1983* (pp. 38–55). Cambridge, England: Cambridge University Press.

Beach, W. (1993). Transitional regularities for 'casual' "okay" usages. *Journal of Pragmatics, 19*, 325–352.

Breen, M. (1989). The evaluation cycle for language learning tasks. In R. K. Johnson (Ed.), *The second language curriculum* (pp. 187–206). Cambridge, England: Cambridge University Press.

Cook, H. M. (1999). Language socialization in Japanese elementary schools: Attentive listening and reaction turns. *Journal of Pragmatics, 31*, 1443–1465.

Coughlan, P., & Duff, P. A. (1994). Same task, different activities: Analysis of a SLA task from an activity theory perspective. In J. P. Lantolf & G. Appel (Eds.), *Vygotskian approaches to second language research* (pp. 173–193). Westport, CT: Ablex.

Davidson, J. (1984). Subsequent versions of invitations, offers, requests, and proposals dealing with potential or actual rejection. In J. M. Atkinson & J. Heritage (Eds.), *Structures of social action: Studies in conversation analysis* (pp. 102–128). Cambridge, England: Cambridge University Press.

Gardner, R. (2001). *When listeners talk*. Amsterdam: John Benjamins.

Goodwin, C. (1986). Between and within: Alternative sequential treatments of continuers and assessments. *Human Studies, 9*, 205–217.

Hellermann, J. (2003). The interactive work of prosody in the IRF exchange: Teacher repetition in feedback moves. *Language in Society, 32*, 79–104.

Heritage, J. (1984). A change-of-state token and aspects of its sequential placement. In M. J. Atkinson & J. Heritage (Eds.), *Structures of social action: Studies in conversation analysis* (pp. 299–345). Cambridge, England: Cambridge University Press.

Heritage, J. (2005). Cognition in discourse. In H. t. Molder & J. Potter (Eds.), *Conversation and cognition* (pp. 184–202). Cambridge, England: Cambridge University Press.

Heritage, J., & Greatbatch, D. (1986). Generating applause: A study of rhetoric and response at party political conferences. *American Journal of Sociology, 92*, 110–157.

Jefferson, G. (1984). On the organization of laughter in talk about troubles. In M. J. Atkinson & J. Heritage (Eds.), *Structures of social action: Studies in conversation analysis* (pp. 346–369). Cambridge, England: Cambridge University Press.

Markee, N. (2000). *Conversation analysis*. Mahwah, NJ: Lawrence Erlbaum.

McHoul, A. (1978). The organization of turns at formal talk in the classroom. *Language in Society, 7*, 349–377.

Mehan, H. (1979). *Learning lessons: Social organization in classroom talk*. Cambridge, MA: Harvard University Press.

Ministry of Education, Culture, Sports, Science and Technology. (2004). *Practical handbook for elementary school English activities*. Tokyo: Kairyuudo.

Mori, J. (2002). Task design, plan, and development of talk-in-interaction: An analysis of a small group activity in a Japanese language classroom. *Applied Linguistics, 23*, 323–347.

Ohta, A. S. (2001). *Second language acquisition processes in the classroom*. Mahwah, NJ: Lawrence Erlbaum.

Pomerantz, A. (1975). *Second assessments: A study of some features of agreements/ disagreements*. Unpublished doctoral dissertation, University of California, Irvine.

Pomerantz, A. (1984). Agreeing and disagreeing with assessments: Some features of preferred/dispreferred turn shapes. In J. M. Atkinson & J. Heritage (Eds.), *Structures of social action: Studies in conversation analysis* (pp. 57–101). Cambridge, England: Cambridge University Press.

Sacks, H. (1984). Notes on methodology. In J. M. Atkinson & J. Heritage (Eds.), *Structures of social action: Studies in conversation analysis* (pp. 21–27). Cambridge, England: Cambridge University Press.

Sacks, H. (1987). The preferences for agreement and contiguity. In G. Button & J. R. E. Lee (Eds.), *Talk and social organization* (pp. 54–69). Clevedon, England: Multilingual Matters.

Sacks, H., Schegloff, E. A., & Jefferson, G. (1974). A simplest systematics for the organization of turn-taking for conversation. *Language, 50*, 696–735.

Schegloff, E. A. (1991). Conversation analysis and socially shared cognition. In L. B. Resnick, J. M. Levine, & S. D. Teasley (Eds.), *Perspectives on socially shared cognition* (pp. 150–171). Washington, DC: American Psychological Association.

Schegloff, E. A. (2000). Overlapping talk and the organization of turn-taking for conversation. *Language in Society, 29*, 1–63.

Schegloff, E. A. (2007). *Sequence organization in interaction: A primer in conversation analysis 1*. Cambridge, England: Cambridge University Press.

Seedhouse, P. (2001). The case of missing "no": The relationship between pedagogy and interaction. In R. Ellis (Ed.), *Form-focused instruction and second language learning* (pp. 347–385). Malden, MA: Blackwell.

Seedhouse, P. (2004). *The interactional architecture of the language classroom: A conversation analysis perspective*. Malden, MA: Blackwell.

Sinclair, J. M., & Coulthard, M. (1975). *Towards an analysis of discourse: The English used by teachers and pupils*. London: Oxford University Press.

Stivers, T. (2004). "No no no" and other types of multiple sayings in social interaction. *Human Communication Research, 30*, 260–293.

Willis, J. (1987). *Spoken discourse in the ELT classroom*. Unpublished master's thesis, University of Birmingham, England.

Appendix: Transcription conventions

[	point where overlapping talk starts
(0.0)	length of silence in tenths of a second
(.)	micropause of less than 2/10 of a second
underline	emphasis
CAPS	relatively high volume
::	lengthened syllable
word-	cut-off; self-interruption
=	"latched" utterances
?/./,	rising/falling/continuing intonation
( )	unintelligible stretch
(word)	transcriber's best guess of what is said
(( ))	transcriber's descriptions of events, including nonvocal conduct
hh	audible outbreath
(hh)	laughter within a word
> <	increase in tempo, as in a rush-through
° °	passage of talk quieter than the surrounding talk
$ $	smiley voice
|	beginning of clapping
|---(number)---	duration of clapping

Other-Correction of Language Form Following a Repair Sequence

Eric Hauser

University of Electro-Communications, Tokyo, Japan

Within the framework of conversation analysis, this chapter investigates instances of other-correction of language form. The data come from 2 sources: (a) audio-recorded conversations among students and first language speakers of English at a conversation club organized by an English language school in Honolulu and (b) a video-recorded English class at a Japanese university. The term other-correction of language form *refers to a turn, or a part of a turn, that at least some of the participants orient to as accomplishing a correction of language used by a participant other than the one who performs the correction. When it occurs, other-correction of language form is often embedded in repair sequences. There are also, though, a few cases in which exposed other-correction of language form occurs following the completion of a repair sequence. Specifically, in the data for this chapter, 3 instances were found of other-correction of language form following a repair sequence. These 3 instances are the focus of this chapter. The analysis focuses on ways that these 3 instances are similar and different and on what these instances can reveal about the occurrence of other-correction of language form.*

Repair of talk during interaction, which is not unusual nor limited to correction of identifiable errors, is organized so as to avoid the necessity of other-correction, which, in contrast to self-correction, can be understood as dispreferred (Schegloff, Jefferson, & Sacks, 1977). It is unusual for a participant to interrupt another's turn-in-progress to correct or initiate a correction. Also, a participant who has just produced a turn of talk has the opportunity to self-correct during the transition space that emerges between turns, which may be lengthened as other participants delay other-correction or initiation of correction. In many cases where there is an identifiable error, and these opportunities for self-correction have been passed, the other participants also let the error pass so that neither self- nor other-correction is performed. When an error is treated as in need of correction, after these opportunities for self-correction have been passed, it is more usual for the participant who so treats the error to merely initiate the correction, rather than to actually perform it (Schegloff et al.). As a result, relative to the frequency of errors and relative to the frequency of self-correction of errors, other-correction is a rare event. This is also true of talk-in-interaction involving participants who are using a second or foreign language and of errors of language form, which can occur quite often in such talk. Such errors, when they are not self-corrected, are often allowed to pass, so that other-correction is relatively rare, and the fact that an error has occurred is not oriented to as relevant (Hauser, 2003; Hosoda, 2006; Wagner & Gardner, 2004).

Correction of an error in the talk of another can also be performed so that the correction does not become the business of the talk. This is accomplished through the embedding of a correction within a turn that accomplishes something unrelated to the work of doing correction (Jefferson, 1987). Embedded correction of errors related to language form can also be found in interaction involving participants who are using a second or foreign language (Brouwer, Rasmussen, & Wagner, 2004). On the other hand, when other-correction is not embedded, when it is exposed (Jefferson), not only is the fact that it is a correction not hidden, but other work that it accomplishes through being a correction is also exposed. In particular, exposed correction is one way to accomplish such things as disagreement (Goodwin, 1983) and instruction (Macbeth, 2004). Also, when a participant corrects an error related to language form in the talk of a participant who is using a second or foreign language, this action makes relevant a possible claim to greater expertise in the language on the part of the person doing the correction (Hosoda, 2006) and can be hearable as doing language instruction as well as, in some cases, disagreement (Takigawa, 2006). Finally, in certain institutional contexts, namely, language classrooms, if and when the focus is on accuracy, correction and the initiation of correction of language errors are resources that some teachers may use to do language instruction (Kasper, 1985; see also Schegloff's comments in Wong & Olsher, 2000, p. 122, on how, for certain activities, e.g., pedagogy, correction can be a "mainline activity").

When the connection between other-correction and such actions as disagreement and instruction is recognized, possible reasons are fairly obvious for organizing repair so as to avoid the necessity of other-correction and for often embedding correction in a turn that accomplishes unrelated work. A person who performs other-correction in an exposed manner may be seen as being, if not aggressively engaged in disagreement, in misalignment with the person he or she is correcting or as being pedantic. When a language error in the talk of a participant who is using a second or foreign language is corrected in an exposed manner, the person who performs the correction may be seen as claiming greater expertise in the language, as drawing attention to deficiencies in, and perhaps even denigrating and ridiculing, the linguistic knowledge of the person who produced the error, and as engaging in language instruction, even when he or she has no institutional mandate to act as a language teacher. In language classrooms, although correction of language errors may provide a resource for doing instruction, avoiding exposed other-correction and allowing language errors to pass may be necessary to not focus narrowly on accuracy (Kasper, 1985). Thus, there are good reasons for exposed other-correction to be relatively rare.

There are, however, two less obvious reasons that corrections are often embedded and that exposed other-correction is rare, reasons related to the sequential organization of interaction. First, when a turn of talk has been understood well enough by another to correct it, then it has also been understood well enough for that person to do a sequentially appropriate next action (Schegloff et al., 1977). In such a situation, the preferred thing to do is a sequentially appropriate next action rather than a correction. When a correction is embedded in a sequentially appropriate next action, then both are accomplished together. When exposed other-correction is performed, a sequentially appropriate next action may be noticeably absent. Second, when initial opportunities to correct are not taken and an error is allowed to pass, as the interaction progresses, further opportunities to correct the error may not become available and may become more and more difficult to claim or create.

Exposed other-correction does, however, occur. In this chapter, I look at a few instances of exposed other-correction of language form during interactions involving participants who are using English as a second or foreign language. By other-correction of language form, I refer to a turn in which participants can be seen and/or heard to orient to as accomplishing, possibly among other things, correction of something that could be considered a language error in the talk of a participant other than the one who performs the correction. This definition allows for the possibility that other-correction of language form can be either embedded or exposed. In fact, in other work (Hauser, 2006a), I have looked at how other-correction of language form can be embedded within a repair sequence. For example, a common pattern was for a participant using English as a second language to initiate repair on a candidate lexical item by indicating uncertainty with the item through such devices as elongation and rising intonation, with this candidate lexical item containing an error related to language form (e.g., a pronunciation error). Another participant, typically a first language speaker, would then complete the repair by confirming the lexical item. This could also, but not necessarily, involve other-correction of language form, but with this other-correction being embedded in the confirmation. (For work on similar repair/correction sequences, see Hosoda, 2000, and Kurhila, 2001.)

In this other work and in this chapter, I used as data several hours of audio recordings of small groups at a conversation club at an English language school in Honolulu. These groups consisted of between two and four students who participated voluntarily for the ostensible purpose of practicing English and one or two conversation partners, as they were labeled by the school, who were hired as first language speakers and paid by the school for their participation. In this interaction, language errors in the talk of the students were quite common. However, most such errors were allowed to pass without any attempt at correction. When an error was corrected, the norm was for it to be embedded within a repair sequence, such as the type of repair sequence described in the previous paragraph. However, there were also two clear cases in the data of exposed other-correction of language form. In one case, the error that was corrected was produced in a turn that was targeted for repair. In the other, the error was in a turn that initiated repair. In both cases, the other-correction was not performed until after the completion of the repair sequence. I have found one other case of exposed other-correction of language form, performed following the completion of a repair sequence, in data from a video recording of an English class at a Japanese university, in which the students, but not the teacher, are using English as a foreign language.

In this chapter, I look at these three cases of exposed other-correction of language form following a repair sequence. This is, admittedly, a very small collection, perhaps too small to really be considered a collection. However, as discussed above, this sort of exposed other-correction of language form appears, for good reasons, to be very rare. By examining closely these three cases of a rare phenomenon, it may be possible to shed light on both why this sort of correction does not occur more often and on why it occurs at all.

For all of the data, all of the participants consented verbally to being recorded. To protect the participants' anonymity, the names used in the transcripts are pseudonyms. The data excerpts are labeled "Conversation club" or "English class" to indicate their source. The transcripts follow conversation analytic transcription conventions (Jefferson, 2004, see appendix), and the data are analyzed within the framework of conversation analysis.

In the remainder of this chapter, I introduce and explicate the three instances that I have found of other-correction of language form following the completion of a repair sequence. I then discuss two striking ways in which these three instances appear to be similar as well as two striking ways that one instance differs from the other two. I then discuss the work, other than correction, which is accomplished in each instance.

Other-correction of language form following repair

As mentioned above, I have found three instances of other-correction of language form that occur following a repair sequence. Two of these were found in the data from the conversation club, and one was found in the data from the English classroom. As discussed below, the institutional setting and the participant roles relevant in that setting may be consequential for the construction of the talk.

The first instance, Excerpt 1, is from the English classroom.[1] The teacher performs other-correction of language form immediately following a repair sequence.

Excerpt 1 English class

```
1        R:    they are afraid of (.) their children.
2        T:    they're afraid of their children.
3        R:    ((nods))
4        T:    wha why are they afraid of their children.
5              (0.7)
6        R:    uh: (0.4) mixed (2.3) children of mixed
7              (1.5) marriag:e might (0.2) have a
8              difficult time.
9        T:    oh okay.=
10  →          =↑yeah.=so they're afraid for their children.
11             (0.6)
12       T:    right it might be difficult for their
13             children
14             (0.5)
15  →    T:    so they're afraid  for their children.
16             (1.2) ((camera moves off R))
17       T:    they're not afraid of their children.
18             (0.7)
19       T:    that means that (0.4) like (0.3) when
20             they see their children hahh ahh
21             (1.3)
22  →    T:    right (.) they're afraid ff for their
23  →          children (right)=
24       T:    =they're worried (0.4) about their children.
```

Repair is first initiated in this excerpt by the teacher (T) in line 2. This turn can be understood as initiating repair because, not built to display overt acceptance of what R has said, it indexes a lack of understanding. This excerpt occurs after the teacher has asked the class several questions, with R's turn in line 1 being his answer to the latest such question. As teachers often do in classrooms, the teacher has been producing third-turn responses to the students' answers, so this excerpt occurs following and as part of a series of teacher-question, student-answer, teacher-response sequences (i.e., sequences labeled IRF, Sinclair & Coulthard, 1975; IRE, Mehan, 1979; or QAC, McHoul, 1978).[2] The teacher's responses in this series of sequences (not included here) have consistently been composed of three elements: first, the word "yeah" or "okay," which marks acceptance of the student's answer; second, the word "so," which indicates that the teacher is about to offer his own formulation of the student's answer; and third, a repetition or reformulation of the student's answer (see Hauser, 2005b, 2006b). One thing that the teacher accomplishes with such responses is to display that he both understands and accepts the student's answer as adequate. However, in Excerpt 1, the teacher merely repeats word-for-word what R has said, without any indication that he accepts what R has said as an adequate answer. There is no "yeah" or "okay," nor is there anything that indicates that the teacher is about to offer his own formulation. This makes the turn hearable as a display that the teacher, although able to repeat A's answer word-for-word, does not see what R has said as a nonproblematic answer and thus as initiating repair on rather than accepting the answer. This repair initiation, though, is of fairly low strength because it does not specify the source or cause of the trouble (Schegloff et al., 1977).

In line 3, R attempts to complete the repair sequence by simply nodding. This can be understood as an attempt to complete the repair in that R treats the teacher's repetition as a candidate understanding used to initiate repair, which R attempts to complete through confirming what he takes to be a candidate understanding. However, the teacher does not orient to his own repair initiation in line 2 as a candidate understanding (which would call for either a confirmation or a correction) and so does not treat this attempted repair as adequate. Instead, he initiates repair a second time with a question in line 4. This second repair initiation is of increased strength (Schegloff et al., 1977) because it specifies how R should solve the trouble—by providing a reason. In lines 6 to 8, R completes the repair by answering this new question. Finally, T produces a third turn (within the second repair sequence) in line 9, in which he claims, through the change-of-state token (Heritage, 1984), that he now understands what R meant in line 1 and thus that he now sees how what R said in line 1 can be understood as an answer. It is important to note that "oh okay" in line 9 is produced as a complete unit. Although the teacher does not pause between "okay" and "yeah" (or between "yeah" and "so"), the intonation contour of "oh okay" is such as to render it hearably complete. In addition, there is a slight, but noticeable, resetting to a higher pitch on "yeah" so that it is heard as a new unit. The intonation contour in line 9 and the reset pitch at the start of line 10 together indicate that the repair sequence is now complete.

Following the repair sequence, the teacher performs other-correction of language form in line 10, correcting the preposition used by R in line 1, "of," to "for." This correction is not a merely incidental result of how the turn is designed. With the contrastive stress on the preposition "for," the teacher designs this turn to be heard as a correction of R's choice of preposition. It is an exposed, rather than embedded (Jefferson, 1987), correction.

In fact, in what follows, the teacher does more work to show that he is correcting R's choice of preposition. In lines 12 and 13, he explains what is meant if the preposition "for" is used. In line 15, he repeats the correction, again with contrastive stress on "for." In line 17, he rejects the formulation in which the preposition "of" is used. In lines 19 and 20, he explains what is meant if the preposition "of" is used. In lines 22 and 23, he repeats the correction again, and although this does not involve contrastive stress, it does involve the repetition of the first sound of the correct preposition. And, finally, in line 24, he once more explains what is meant if the preposition "for" is used. Overall, the error and the correction are repeated, strongly contrasted, and thoroughly explained. For his part, the student R, although he appears through his gaze to be paying attention to at least part of what the teacher is saying, does not respond, verbally or nonverbally, to the teacher's talk starting from line 9.[3]

The second instance, Excerpt 2,[4] is from the conversation club. Here, other-correction of language form also occurs after a repair sequence.

Excerpt 2 Conversation club

```
1        D:   uh- uh: I forgot you name (.) is
2             (1.8)
3        D:   hey can I (.) show (0.9) you name.
4             (0.4)
5        D:   Ally (.) hm
6        A:   [can I show y(h)our [ha ha ha
7        D:   [(xx)  (0.4)  (x)        [ye(h)ah ha ha (.)
8             Ally oh yeah yeah  [yeah
9   →    A:                             [can you
10  →         [sh(h)ow m(h)e
11       D:   [can you show .h is it ah:
12            [can you show
13       T:   [ha ha ha
14            (0.4)
15       D:   .h (.) is a can you is- I always
16            use could you. (.) yeah:=
17       T:   =yeah=
18       D:   =I use could. cou- could you show is
19            a .h
20       ?:   =(yeah)?=
21       D:   =can I: (0.3) keh could you:
22            [sometimes very (.) very confuses.=
23       A:   [yes yes yes
24       O:   =[o(h)h
25       A:   =[yeah:
26            (1.1)
27       D:   ah Ally
28            (0.6)
29       O:   °(Ally)°
30            (1.0)
31       T:   hey so are you: gonna be back in
32            Korea?
```

Unfortunately, there is no video recording of the interaction at the conversation club, so the analysis of this excerpt involves some speculation about nonverbal behavior on the part of one of the participants, the conversation partner A. However, this speculation is plausible and likely, given what can be heard in the recording and given the fact that the conversation partners wear name tags. Apparently, though, A's name tag is not visible to a student, D, who in line 1 informs A that she has forgotten her name, which can serve as an indirect request for A to tell D her name or possibly to make her name tag visible. This, though, does not get any response, resulting in the long gap in line 2. At this point, D initiates repair on the initial request. She does this by summoning A's attention ("hey") and then reformulating the request as a question, making it somewhat more direct ("can I...show...you name"). Even though she does not respond verbally, A evidently does something to make her name tag visible during the gap in line 4 because D says the name in line 5. Although this involves some speculation, what appears to be happening is that A completes the repair in line 4 through some nonverbal action, such as making her name tag visible, after which D says A's name, displaying that her request has been fulfilled.

However, even though the repair sequence is complete, A then goes on to produce other-correction of language form in lines 9 and 10. As with Excerpt 1, A's talk is designed to be heard as a correction. This is accomplished by first doing a humorous noticing (Wilkinson, 2007) of the error through repetition and laughter (line 6). A also laughs while doing the correction, in lines 9 and 10. Contrastive stress is used on the pronoun "I," displaying that it is this particular pronoun that is being repeated and treated as the source of the humor (Jefferson, 1972), in line 6 and on the pronoun "you" in the correction. This creates a contrast between the erroneous pronoun repeated from D's talk and the correct pronoun that follows the repetition, isolating D's pronoun choice as an error that is being corrected. As in Excerpt 1, the correction is exposed, rather than embedded.

Further, the laughter that accompanies the repetition and the correction highlights the error as something deviant that can be laughed at. Laughter, of course, is involved in a variety of activities, such as talking about trouble, which typically involves the person who is talking about trouble producing laughter although the recipient does not (Jefferson, 1984), or as part of the pursuit of intimacy through the use of improprieties (Jefferson, Sacks, & Schegloff, 1987). When a particular object is isolated as a laughable, and when this object can be associated with one of the current participants, such as D's formulation in line 3, then a distinction that is relevant for the participants is whether the laughter is better characterized as laughing *with* or laughing *at* (Glenn, 2003; Jefferson, 1972). In Excerpt 2, though D produces her own laughter in line 7, there are three reasons for characterizing A's laughter as laughing at D's use of language. First, as mentioned in the previous paragraph, A treats D's choice of pronoun as the source of the humor, thus treating D as the "butt" of the humor (Glenn). Second, the first laugh is by A, during the articulation of "your" in line 6. As shown by Glenn, a first laugh by the person who nominates another participant as the "butt" of the humor (or by a different participant) is a strong index of laughing at. And third, subsequent activities are also important to distinguish laughing at from laughing with (Glenn). In Excerpt 2, D engages in two activities designed to either terminate the laughter or to account for her error. On the one hand, she twice acts to return the interaction to a display that she now knows A's name and that her request has thus been fulfilled by redoing her turn at line 5. She does this first in line 8, when she says "Ally oh yeah yeah yeah." However, in lines 9 and 10, as she produces the correction, A laughs again, with D, unlike her response in line 7, not responding with more laughter. D once more displays that her request has been fulfilled by saying "ah Ally" in line 27. This time, another student, O, appears to be collaborating with this in line 29. These attempts to return the interaction to a display that she now knows A's name, a display that she first performed in line 5, can be understood as attempts by D to sequentially delete the laughter, with the second attempt, followed by a proposal for a new topic by T, a different conversation partner, being successful. On the other hand, D also accounts for her error and claims that she is concerned about using English appropriately by explaining the cause of her confusion, in lines 15–16, 18–19, and 21–22, as confusion regarding the use of "can you/I" versus "could you." For these various reasons, A's laughter is hearable as laughing at D's error, as treating her use of language as deviant, and as subjecting D's use of English, and by association D herself, to ridicule.[5] Not only is the correction exposed, but D's use of language is also exposed as deviant and humorous.

The third instance, shown in Excerpt 3, is also from the conversation club. Here, the correction follows extended repair work.

Excerpt 3 Conversation club

```
1       W:   oh I'm twenny wuh- uh- seven. seven.
2            huh heh   [heh
3       N:             [oh:   [:
4       A:                    [too young.
5            (1.2)
6       W:   I'm not young. hh  [huh huh
7       A:                      [un
8       A:   and   [(x)
9       B:         [to: get married?   [you mean?
10      A:                              [ah no no no. uh
11           [that uh twenty-seven is too young, I say,
12      B:   [(yeah)
13           (0.3)
14      A:   I'm twen- uh forty-two.
15      B:   oh: r [eally?
16      A:        [yeah
17      W:   forty-two?
```

```
18   A:  ye [s:.
19   W:     [(x)   [(thirty) (blah blah) (0.7)
20   B:          [oh
21   W:  [huh heh
22   A:  [hh   hh huh huh huh ha ha  [ha ha
23   W:                               [sorry ((smile
24       voice)) (x(h)) .h [forty-two ((smile voice))
25   A:                    [.hhh but so that I say to-
26       too young to this you have a a lot of (0.3)
27       to (kind) uh::  [to (0.6) to: (0.2) (for us)=
28   B:                  [ah:
29   A:  =(0.2) future. [to very [(griant) future
30   B:                          [ah
31   ?:                                   [mm-hm
32   A:  [also (0.5) yeah you can  [do it.
33   ?:  [mm mm
34   W:                            [thank you.
35       okay. I can do it.
36   A:  yeah
37   B:  mm hm hm
38   W:  heh heh
39       (1.1)
40   A:  also weh- Wilma have a strong power.
41   W:  mhhh
42   A:  yeah. good.
43       (1.0)
44   N:  so just a little English thing, I think she was
45       confused because you said too young? (.) which
46       mean [s like an excess?
47   W:       [(ah::/yeah::)
48   A:  oh- really=
49 → N:  =so: [maybe:       ] [(0.4) maybe very=
50   A:       [how does it ]  [un
51   N:  =young: or:,=
52   A:  =ah very youngu. yeah (0.3) very young.
```

In this excerpt, a student, W, is answering in line 1 a conversation partner's question about her age (not shown). In response to this, another student, A,[6] makes an assessment of W as "too young" (line 4). That there may be something problematic with this is indicated by the gap that follows A's assessment in line 5. What could be one problem with the assessment is that it is ambiguous whether it should be heard as a compliment or as a criticism. In addition, as either a compliment or a criticism, this assessment presents W with the difficult problem of how to respond to it. Even if it is heard more positively as a compliment, responding to compliments is a complicated matter. For example, among English speakers, this involves the balancing of two different norms, one of which favors agreement with an assessment, and the other of which involves avoidance of self-praise (Pomerantz, 1978). Responding appropriately to compliments in a second language may be especially problematic, even for very proficient speakers (Golato, 2002, 2005). Whether the assessment is taken to be a compliment or a criticism, W is not in a position within the interaction to take a neutral stance of neither agreeing nor disagreeing with it. As discussed by Bilmes (1988), when an assessment is made about a person in that person's presence, if that person does not deny the assessment, then he or she will be understood as agreeing with it. W can agree or disagree with A's assessment, and she can attempt to do this in a qualified or reluctant manner, but if she were simply not to respond, she would be understood not as being neutral but as agreeing. What W eventually does, following the long gap, is to disagree with A's assessment of her in line 6, after which she laughs, perhaps indexing the difficulty of the situation that the assessment has placed her in.

In line 9, in spite of the fact that A has started to produce more talk, a third student, B, initiates repair in the third position (Schegloff, 1992), targeting A's assessment, by proffering a candidate understanding ("to get married?") and asking if this is what A means ("you mean?"). That B proffers this particular candidate understanding is related to the fact that, prior to this excerpt, the participants have been discussing W's upcoming wedding. B apparently hears the assessment as more of a criticism, which could perhaps be glossed as, "You're too young to get married,"[7] though she leaves it to A to either confirm or correct this hearing. She also treats the trouble indexed by the gap in line 5 as a problem of understanding. After A has passed opportunities, during his turn in line 4 and the gap that follows, to initiate repair, and W, in disagreeing with A's assessment, has also passed opportunities to initiate repair, through her initiation of repair, B offers a diagnosis of the trouble, which is that what A has said is difficult to understand because he has not specified what W is "too young" to do. The three students then enter into a fairly long attempt to repair the trouble and clarify exactly what was meant with the assessment of W as "too young." This involves A self-repairing by first rejecting the candidate understanding (line 10) and perhaps also rejecting the notion that the assessment is related to W's upcoming wedding and then explaining, across several lines of transcript (lines 11, 14, 25–27, 29, 32, 40), what his assessment of W as "too young" means. Apparently, it is supposed to be a compliment because A offers his own, much higher age of 42 as a contrast (line 14), points out that W has a big future ahead of her (lines 26, 29), and seems to be saying that W has the potential to make much of this future (lines 32, 40). In addition, the repair does not treat W's upcoming marriage as relevant because A does not mention it. The repair work is extended, but it seems to be complete by, at the latest, line 40. W's and A's minimal tokens and assessment in lines 41 and 42 as well as the gap in line 43 indicate that none of these three participants have anything to add to the repair work.

Although the repair work is now complete, in lines 49 and 51, N, a conversation partner, who in fact did not participate in the repair work itself, produces other-correction of language form, correcting A's "too young" (line 4) to "very young." Again, this is done as an exposed correction. Before producing the correction, N indicates that she is going to teach A something about English (line 44), then states that A's choice of words was the cause of the confusion that made the repair necessary (lines 44, 45), and then states what "too young" means (lines 45, 46). Also, by stressing the word "too," N indicates that it is this particular word that is the cause of the trouble. The correction in lines 49 and 51 is designed as a suggestion of a different word ("very") that A could have used that probably would not have led to the confusion. This correction is also produced with stress on the word "very." The correction is delivered somewhat hesitantly and tentatively, as N first says "maybe," which she stretches, then pauses, and then says "maybe" again before providing the correction. As a result, it comes across as more of a suggestion than as a strong claim about what would have been correct. Nevertheless, a contrast is set up, as in Excerpts 1 and 2, between the error and the correct form, which, along with the accompanying explanation, makes the correction exposed, rather than embedded. Finally, N's correction and accompanying talk, although it treats the initial problem as one of understanding, offers a different diagnosis from B's of the cause of the understanding trouble.

Discussion

A striking similarity among these three excerpts, which I have already mentioned, is that in each case, the correction is designed to be heard as clearly a correction. In each case, it is an exposed correction. Whatever other work may be accomplished through the other-correction of language form, it is first and foremost a correction. This is accomplished through such devices as contrastive stress, repetition of the error, explanation (Excerpts 1 and 3), and even laughter (Excerpt 2). The exposed nature of each correction may be the result of its location relative to the error that it corrects. In each case, the correction is not adjacent to this error. In Excerpt 1, the error is in a turn that is treated as a trouble source. Between this turn and the correction, there is a repair initiation, a nonverbal repair completion, a second repair initiation, a second repair completion, and a third turn. In Excerpt 2, the error is part of the turn that initiates a repair sequence. Between the error and the correction, the repair is (apparently) completed, and the participant who initiated the repair displays that she has received the information initially requested in the trouble-source turn. And in Excerpt 3, there is extended repair work between the error and the correction that is eventually produced. Given this separation, it may be necessary for the correction to be exposed to retrieve something from prior and distant talk and target it for correction.

As part of how they are designed, these corrections do not appear by themselves but are found with other talk related to the error. This is the second striking similarity among these three excerpts. At the very least, there is in all three excerpts a repetition of the error, either before the correction (Excerpts 2 and 3) or after (Excerpt 1). There may also be some explanation of why the error was an error (Excerpts 1 and 3). The corrections form parts of larger stretches of talk about the error that are hearable as language pedagogy, talk that is supposed to teach the students something about English. Through this talk, of which the correction forms only one part, the conversation partners and the teacher not only orient to themselves as possessing relatively greater expertise in English (see Hosoda, 2006), but also as able to use this expertise to instruct the second language speakers. In addition, in Excerpt 2 (line 11) and Excerpt 3 (line 52), the participants whose use of English has been corrected respond to the correction by repeating it, displaying their own orientation to the ability of the conversation partners to use their expertise in English to instruct them.

Within the field of second language acquisition, one question that has been the focus of research and theory has been whether correction (along with instruction more generally) is, if not necessary, at least facilitative of language learning (e.g., Doughty & Varela, 1998; Gass, 2003; Long, 1996), or on the other hand, of no use, possibly even counterproductive (e.g., Krashen, 1985). Although I do not pretend to have an answer to this question, within the three excerpts presented in this chapter, the participants treat correction and language instruction as relevant activities for them to engage in. The participants do not treat the occurrence of correction or more broadly, language pedagogy, as out-of-place or otherwise problematic.

A striking difference between Excerpt 1, on the one hand, and Excerpts 2 and 3, on the other, is that in Excerpt 1, the language pedagogy is delivered by the teacher as a kind of monologue, but in Excerpts 2 and 3, it is constructed within a dialogue, involving the exchange of turns between the person whose talk is being corrected and who is being instructed and the person who is doing the correction and the instruction. This appears to reflect the different norms for taking turns of talk in the English classroom and in the conversation club as well as the participant roles that are relevant in these different institutional settings. In the English classroom, at least during the teacher-fronted teacher-student interaction from which Excerpt 1 is drawn, (as explained above) the interaction is constructed as the familiar three-part classroom routine in which a teacher asks a question, a student answers, and the teacher then comments on the answer.[8] Without violating the norms for turn-taking, the students' only opportunity to take a turn comes in the second slot, after the teacher has asked a question. Because of the extended repair work on the student's answer that precedes it, the language pedagogy in Excerpt 1 occurs in an atypical sequence in that it is not a simple three-part structure. However, because it occurs following a student's answer and the (eventual) successful repair of that answer, it can also be understood as being in the third slot of the three-part classroom routine and thus as belonging to the teacher. Unless the norms for turn-taking within this sort of teacher-fronted teacher-student interaction are violated, the next opportunity for a student to take a turn will not occur unless and until the teacher asks another question, which, as it turns out, the teacher does not do. The students, for their part, show their orientation to the turn-taking norms and the relevant participant roles by not attempting to take a turn within the teacher's monologue. However, when it comes to turn allocation in the conversation club, the conversation partners tend to act as interactional pivots (see Hauser, 2003, 2004). This seems to be part of how the conversation partners work to be what could be called perpetual primary participants. Although they do not unilaterally control such things as the allocation of turns or choice of topics, the conversation partners work to always position themselves as primary participants in the interaction. That is, as perpetual primary participants, they are either addressing talk to one or more students or are the addressee of a student's talk. In those rare instances, such as in most of Excerpt 3, in which they are not one of the primary participants, they work to reenter the interaction, which, as pointed out at the end of this section, N accomplishes with her talk starting at line 44. Even though the conversation partners work to position themselves as perpetual primary participants, the norms for turn-taking are more similar, though not identical, to what is found in mundane conversation in that the conversation partners do not exert the sort of control over opportunities to take a turn that teachers can exert when interacting with students. That is, the students in the conversation club can and do use opportunities for turns to be more active in co-constructing the language pedagogy.

A second striking difference is also related to different turn-taking norms in the English classroom and the conversation club. In Excerpts 2 and 3, the sequence that the turn containing the trouble source initiates is possibly complete. In Excerpt 2, the request for A's name has, apparently, been fulfilled by line 5. In Excerpt 3, A has made an assessment about W's age, and W has responded, with a rejection, in line 6, thus forming a first-assessment/second-assessment pair (Pomerantz, 1984). In both cases, this sequence and the repair are both possibly complete, and at the end of line 5 in Excerpt 2 and at the gap in line 43 in Excerpt 3, the interaction has reached a point where it may temporarily lull. At any rate, there is no sequentially appropriate next action that would be noticeably absent if exposed other-correction of language form were performed. In Excerpt 1, though, following a student's answer and its repair, the teacher is in a position to produce the third turn of the typical three-turn classroom sequence. Following the repair work on R's answer in line 1, which was the second turn of the three-turn sequence, it is the responsibility of the teacher to end the sequence, which places him in this position to hold the floor until he asks another question or initiates a different sort of activity and/or sequence. This provides him with the opportunity to perform exposed other-correction.

Finally, in each case, the exposed correction and the other error-relevant talk with which it is found accomplish more than language pedagogy. However, this "more" is different for each excerpt. In Excerpt 1, the correction and other error-relevant talk account for why the teacher could not understand R's original answer. It pinpoints the source of the teacher's understanding trouble as R's erroneous choice of preposition, orienting to the relevance of R's limited expertise in English. This understanding trouble has been presented as preventing the teacher from being able to accept R's answer. The first correction turn itself, however, does accomplish this acceptance in line 10. In addition, the teacher can be understood as fulfilling his institutionally mandated role as a language teacher by delivering language pedagogy. In Excerpt 2, following the correction, the participants enter into a brief discussion of the difference between using "can you/I" and using "could you." With the sequence that was initiated by D's indirect request in line 1 having been closed by line 5 (though D twice redoes this turn), the correction and other error-relevant talk launch a new sequence, within which the participants conduct a metalinguistic, or more specifically, a metapragmatic, discussion. In addition, this talk retrospectively treats D's language error as something to be laughed at. This talk not only makes relevant A's greater expertise in English, but also ridicules and denigrates D's attempt to use the language. The correction and other error-relevant talk in Excerpt 3 pinpoint the source of the understanding trouble as A's erroneous word choice, treating A's use of language as the cause of the trouble. This is similar to what happens in Excerpt 1, except that in Excerpt 1, the person who does the correction is the person who had trouble understanding, although in Excerpt 3, there is no indication that the person who does the correction shared the understanding trouble displayed by B and W. On the other hand, in diagnosing the source of the trouble, with a diagnosis that is different from the one offered previously by B (a student), N displays that she understands the trouble that these two students had and thus displays her competence to help the students not only learn English, but also communicate with one another in English. This talk also initiates a new sequence, as in Excerpt 2, and provides N with a way back into the interaction, in which she has not taken a turn since responding to W in line 3.

Concluding remarks

As mentioned above and has been observed by others (e.g., Hosoda, 2006; Wagner & Gardner, 2004), what I have called other-correction of language form is generally not something that occurs with great frequency, even when errors of language form are ubiquitous and language learning may be the ostensible purpose for participants to be interacting, as in the data presented in this chapter. In addition, when it does occur, it may be embedded, rather than exposed (Hauser, 2006a). The type of other-correction of language form that I have discussed here, occurring following a repair sequence, is even less frequent. I have been able to find only three clear instances in over 9 hours of talk in the conversation club and 3 hours of classroom talk. This type of other-correction of language form, which targets an error that is not immediately adjacent to the correction, and which may be at quite a remove, as in Excerpt 3, is nevertheless something that some participants *can* do, and when they do it, they do it as an exposed correction. This can be understood as necessary for targeting the more or less distant error for correction, an error that, like the overwhelming majority of errors, could have been allowed to pass uncorrected, especially because the correction of the error was not found by the participants to be necessary to accomplish the repair. Doing the correction as an exposed correction also makes it hearable as part of doing language pedagogy. Exactly how this language pedagogy is done, though, may depend on the participants' orientation to the institutional setting and the relevant participant roles.

As discussed in the introduction, some reasons not to correct another's error of language form, but instead to let it pass, are to avoid doing disagreement or sounding pedantic. Indeed, in Excerpt 2, as a student's English is laughed at, the potential for conflict would appear to be strongly present. In a language classroom, such as in Excerpt 1, not doing exposed correction may be a way to avoid focusing on linguistic accuracy (Kasper, 1985). Also as discussed in the introduction, though, the sequential organization of interaction may work to make the sort of exposed other-correction of language form discussed in this chapter a rare phenomenon. As discussed by Schegloff (1992), the sequential organization of interaction provides structurally for locations to initiate repair, with the fourth position, or the third turn after the turn containing a trouble source, perhaps being the final opportunity to target something for repair. After that, as the interaction moves on, any potential trouble source becomes too far removed for repair to be initiated on it. When it comes to an error of linguistic form, as the interaction moves forward, opportunities to correct it or initiate a correction quickly become more difficult to claim, perhaps necessitating extra work, as in the examples in this chapter, to do other-correction. This may be less of an obstacle to correction during interaction organized as three-part sequences between a teacher and students because the teacher may be able to hold the floor for an extended period after a student's response by simply not initiating a new sequence. This seems to be what has allowed the teacher in Excerpt 1 to other-correct more-or-less monologically. In Excerpts 2 and 3, where the conversation partners exert less control over turn allocation, it may be that the completion of a sequence and of the repair of one of the turns within the sequence, with no other pressing interactional business to return to, results in the potential for a lull in the interaction, which provides an opportunity for the conversation partners to embark on a new action, in these cases, correction.

Notes

1   I have also analyzed this excerpt in other work, such as that of Hauser (2005a). The transcript presented here has been revised slightly to show in more detail how the talk in lines 9 and 10 is produced.
2   It should be recognized that it is not inevitable that pedagogical interaction between teachers and students will be neatly organized into such three-part sequences. Rampton (2006), for example, analyzed interaction in a classroom where this sort of sequential structure appears "frayed" (p. 48). Also, in the classroom from which Excerpt 1 is drawn, most of the class time involved interaction among students, rather than between the teacher and students.
3   Unfortunately, during the gap in line 16, the camera moves off R and does not return to him, so it is unknown how long he continues to gaze at the teacher. Nor does the recording capture any verbal responses from R. Following line 24, the teacher initiates a transition to a different activity.
4   I have analyzed this excerpt in other work, namely, that of Hauser (2003, 2005c). The transcript has been revised at lines 6–8, based on repeated relistening.
5   A reviewer noted that another possible function of the laughter is to mask the delicateness involved in the correction (see Jefferson, 1984; Jefferson et al., 1987; Wilkinson, 2007).
6   This A is different from the A in Excerpt 2, who was a conversation partner.
7   Of course, this also is somewhat ambiguous in that it could be heard as a compliment, depending on the stance the speaker takes towards what is said.
8   However, most of the class time was actually devoted to small-group discussions, rather than to teacher-fronted interaction. See also note 2.

References

Bilmes, J. (1988). The concept of preference in conversation analysis. *Language in Society, 17*, 161–181.

Brouwer, C. E., Rasmussen, G., & Wagner, J. (2004). Embedded corrections in second language talk. In R. Gardner & J. Wagner (Eds.), *Second language conversations* (pp. 75–92). London: Continuum.

Doughty, C., & Varela, E. (1998). Communicative focus on form. In C. Doughty & J. Williams (Eds.), *Focus on form in classroom second language acquisition* (pp. 114–138). Cambridge, England: Cambridge University Press.

Gass, S. M. (2003). Input and interaction. In C. Doughty & M. Long (Eds.), *The handbook of second language acquisition* (pp. 224–255). Malden, MA: Blackwell.

Glenn, P. (2003). *Laughter in interaction.* Cambridge, England: Cambridge University Press.

Golato, A. (2002). German compliment responses. *Journal of Pragmatics, 34*, 547–571.

Golato, A. (2005). *Compliments and compliment responses: Grammatical structure and sequential organization.* Amsterdam: John Benjamins.

Goodwin, M. H. (1983). Aggravated correction and disagreement in children's conversations. *Journal of Pragmatics, 7*, 657–677.

Hauser, E. (2003). *'Corrective recasts' and other-correction of language form in interaction among native and non-native speakers of English: The application of conversation analysis to second language acquisition.* Unpublished doctoral dissertation, University of Hawai'i at Mānoa, Honolulu.

Hauser, E. (2004, May). Doing being an interactional pivot in interaction with language learners. Paper presented at the Conference of the American Association for Applied Linguistics, Portland, OR.

Hauser, E. (2005a). Coding 'corrective recasts': The maintenance of meaning and more fundamental problems. *Applied Linguistics, 26*, 293–316.

Hauser, E. (2005b, July). Reformulating a student's answer as a model of correct language. Paper presented at the International Pragmatics Conference, Riva del Garda, Italy.

Hauser, E. (2005c). Face-work with limited linguistic resources: Showing concern for face during language learning conversations. In D. Tatsuki (Ed.), *Pragmatics in language learning, theory, & practice* (pp. 25–42). Tokyo, Japan: Pragmatics Special Interest Group of the Japan Association for Language Teaching.

Hauser, E. (2006a, June). Positions of other-correction of language form within repair sequences. Paper presented at the International Conference of the Japanese Society for Language Sciences, Tokyo, Japan.

Hauser, E. (2006b). Teacher reformulations of students' answers during an episode of pedagogical talk. *Bulletin of the University of Electro-Communications, 19*, 93–99.

Heritage, J. (1984). A change-of-state token and aspects of its sequential placement. In J. Atkinson & J. Heritage (Eds.), *Structures of social action: Studies in conversation analysis* (pp. 299–345). Cambridge, England: Cambridge University Press.

Hosoda, Y. (2000). Other-repair in Japanese conversations between nonnative and native speakers. *Issues in Applied Linguistics, 11*, 39–65.

Hosoda, Y. (2006). Repair and relevance of differential language expertise in second language conversations. *Applied Linguistics, 27*, 25–50.

Jefferson, G. (1972). Side sequences. In D. Sudnow (Ed.), *Studies in social interaction* (pp. 294–338). New York: The Free Press.

Jefferson, G. (1984). On the organization of laughter in talk about troubles. In J. Atkinson & J. Heritage (Eds.), *Structures of social action: Studies in conversation analysis* (pp. 346–369). Cambridge, England: Cambridge University Press.

Jefferson, G. (1987). On exposed and embedded correction in conversation. In G. Button & J. R. E. Lee (Eds.), *Talk and social organisation* (pp. 86–100). Clevedon, England: Multilingual Matters.

Jefferson, G. (2004). Glossary of transcript symbols with an introduction. In G. H. Lerner (Ed.), *Conversation analysis: Studies from the first generation* (pp. 13–31). Amsterdam: John Benjamins.

Jefferson, G., Sacks, H., & Schegloff, E. (1987). Notes on laughter in the pursuit of intimacy. In G. Button & J. R. E. Lee (Eds.), *Talk and social organisation* (pp. 152–205). Clevedon, England: Multilingual Matters.

Kasper, G. (1985). Repair in foreign language teaching. *Studies in Second Language Acquisition, 7*, 200–215.

Krashen, S. (1985). *The input hypothesis: Issues and implications*. London: Longman.

Kurhila, S. (2001). Correction in talk between native and non-native speaker. *Journal of Pragmatics, 33*, 1083–1110.

Long, M. H. (1996). The role of the linguistic environment in second language acquisition. In W. C. Ritchie & T. K. Bhatia (Eds.), *Handbook of second language acquisition* (pp. 413–468). San Diego, CA: Academic Press.

Macbeth, D. (2004). The relevance of repair for classroom correction. *Language in Society, 33*, 703–732.

McHoul, A. W. (1978). The organization of turns at formal talk in the classroom. *Language and Society, 7*, 183–213.

Mehan, H. (1979). *Learning lessons: Social organization in the classroom*. Cambridge, MA: Harvard University Press.

Pomerantz, A. (1978). Compliment responses: Notes on the co-operation of multiple constraints. In J. Schenkein (Ed.), *Studies in the organization of conversational interaction* (pp. 79–112). New York: Academic Press.

Pomerantz, A. (1984). Agreeing and disagreeing with assessments: Some features of preferred/dispreferred turn shapes. In J. Atkinson & J. Heritage (Eds.), *Structures of social action: Studies in conversation analysis* (pp. 57–101). Cambridge, England: Cambridge University Press.

Rampton, B. (2006). *Language in late modernity: Interaction in an urban school*. Cambridge, England: Cambridge University Press.

Schegloff, E. A. (1992). Repair after next turn: The last structurally provided defense of intersubjectivity in conversation. *American Journal of Sociology, 97*, 1295–1345.

Schegloff, E. A., Jefferson, G., & Sacks, H. (1977). The preference for self-correction in the organization of repair in conversation, *Language, 53*, 361–382.

Sinclair, J. M., & Coulthard, R. M. (1975). *Towards an analysis of discourse: The English used by teachers and pupils*. Oxford, England: Oxford University Press.

Takigawa, Y. (2006, May). Problematic talk in Japanese among American and Japanese married couples. Paper presented at the International Conference on Conversation Analysis, Helsinki, Finland.

Wagner, J., & Gardner, R. (2004). Introduction. In R. Gardner & J. Wagner (Eds.), *Second language conversations* (pp. 1–17). London: Continuum.

Wilkinson, R. (2007). Managing linguistic incompetence as a delicate issue in aphasic talk-in-interaction: On the use of laughter in prolonged repair sequences. *Journal of Pragmatics, 39*, 542–569.

Wong, J., & Olsher, D. (2000). Reflections on conversation analysis and nonnative speaker talk: An interview with Emanuel A. Schegloff. *Issues in Applied Linguistics, 11*, 111–128.

Appendix: Transcription conventions

[	point where overlapping talk starts
(0.0)	length of silence in tenths of a second
(.)	micropause of less than 2/10 of a second
underline	emphasis
CAPS	relatively high volume
::	lengthened syllable
word-	cut-off; self-interruption
=	"latched" utterances
?/./,	rising/falling/continuing intonation
(xxx)	unintelligible stretch
(word)	transcriber's best guess of what is said
(( ))	transcriber's descriptions of events, including nonvocal conduct
hh	audible outbreath
.hh	audible inbreath
(hh)	laughter within a word
> <	increase in tempo, as in a rush-through
° °	passage of talk quieter than the surrounding talk

Agreements and Disagreements: The Small Group Discussion in a Foreign Language Classroom

Donna Fujimoto
Osaka Jogakuin College, Japan

Although small group discussions are frequently used in foreign language classrooms, there is very little research on what learners actually do during these activities. This study investigates a classroom discussion among novice learners of English, and it focuses on how the students express opinions, assessments, agreement, and disagreement. Conversation analysis is used to examine the unfolding discussion turn-by-turn as the learners display their understanding of the prior turns of other members and of the task at hand. The first part of the analysis examines a series of agreement segments that follows a basic pattern. The next part shifts to a set of disagreement sequences. One member initiates an oppositional stance that prompts the pursuit of opposition by another member. In contrast to the preference for agreement in response to assessments and opinion statements in ordinary conversation, the participants do not treat their oppositional talk as dispreferred. It is argued that the pursuit of opposition is linked to institutional goals: Making arguments enriches the discussion and provides language practice. The study also shows that although these learners have limited lexical resources in the target language, they work collaboratively to sustain the discussion with other resources.

The use of group work in the language classroom can be clearly linked to communicative language teaching (CLT), which had its beginnings in the 1970s. According to Jacobs and Farrell (2003), CLT marked a clear paradigm shift in how learning and teaching were viewed. Key changes comprised a shift from teacher-centered to learner-centered instruction, a shift from product-oriented to process-oriented instruction, and a greater focus on the social nature of learning. To allow learners more opportunities to practice and learn, teachers were encouraged to include pair and group work in their lessons. As a result, students were often placed in small groups where they were asked to carry out discussions. There has been little research on this type of discussion-for-learning activity despite the fact that it is so widespread. It thus presents a good opportunity to investigate learner behavior in the L2 classroom.

The goal of this chapter is to draw attention to the small group discussion by examining how students actually conduct this activity. The current study uses conversation analysis (CA) to understand the finer details of what occurs among a small group of novice language learners. It focuses on two aspects of student participation in the small group discussion activity: (a) how students present their opinions and (b) how they express agreement and disagreement. The analysis focuses on assessments and the succeeding sequential responses. Though these learners had limited lexical resources, they actively utilized all of the resources available to them in displaying to each other their understanding of each other's actions.

Past research on small group work

In the field of second language acquisition (SLA), there has been some research connected with group work, namely, input modification studies (Gass & Madden, 1985; Long & Porter, 1985; Pica, 1987). This body of research tested the hypothesis that negotiation of meaning leads to increased comprehensible input and output, thereby facilitating language development. The focus was on modified input, which generally contained comprehension checks, clarification requests, corrections, recasts, repetitions, restatements, and topic shifts.

Cooperative learning is an instructional approach that deliberately structures group work to produce positive interdependence, face-to-face interaction, individual and group accountability, interpersonal and small group skills, and group processing (Johnson, Johnson, & Holubec, 1993). Cooperative learning entered the language learning arena in the 1980s and became more widely known by the 1990s (Dörnyei, 1997; Jacobs, Power, & Loh, 2002). Research on this type of group work, however, was concerned mostly with learning outcomes, strategies, and motivation, rather than with the actual speech used during group work.

Conversation analysis and language classroom research

In the early years of CA studies, the focus was primarily on the naturally occurring ordinary talk of people using English (Jefferson, 1972; Sacks, 1972; Schegloff, 1980) and professional and institutional interactions, such as legal or medical discourse (Atkinson & Drew, 1979; Drew & Heritage, 1992; ten Have, 1991). Beginning in the late 1990s, there was a significant increase in CA studies where languages other than English were analyzed (Egbert, 1996; Hayashi, 1999; He, 1998; Lindstrom, 1994; Park, 1999; Sorjonen, 1996; ten Have, 1999). Although these studies uncovered some differences in how talk was realized in different languages, on the whole, this body of work provided strong and convincing evidence that the analytical tools of CA were effective no matter what language was used. The research expanded to include interactions between L1 and L2 speakers (Brouwer, 2003; Egbert, Niebecker, & Rezzara, 2004; Hauser, 2003; Hosoda, 2000; Wong, 2000) and was extended as well to the second/foreign language classroom (Gardner & Wagner, 2004; Hellermann, 2006, 2007; Koshik, 2002; Markee, 1994, 2004; Mori, 2002, 2004; Seedhouse, 2004).

Using CA to analyze interaction in pedagogical settings proved to be quite fruitful in explicating what language teachers and learners actually do on a moment-by-moment basis. Koshik (2002) noted that teachers often deliberately make incomplete utterances to elicit student responses. Markee (2004) looked at teacher question-answer sequences and ambiguous student claims that signaled to the teacher who was having difficulty. Working with Chinese language classroom interaction, He (2004) showed how the use of incomplete turn construction units (TCU, the smallest interactionally complete unit), intonation, and pausing can encourage student participation.

There are also a number of studies involving learners working together without the immediate presence of a teacher. Mori (2002) examined the talk of students in a Japanese-as-a-foreign-language classroom where the students carried out a task that did not exactly match the teacher's intention. Mondada and Pekarek Doehler (2004) worked with data from a French-as-a-second-language classroom and showed that a task is not static, but a collaborative process, where the task itself is continuously being reconfigured. Kasper (2004) demonstrated how two participants shifted between conversational and metalinguistic orientations and made their membership categories relevant. Olsher (2004) showed how EFL Japanese learners used gestures and embodied movements to complete their turns. Carroll (2000, 2005) discovered how Japanese English-as-a-foreign-language (EFL) novice learners with very limited linguistic resources were nevertheless able to precision-time their entry into the interaction using microadjustments of vocal and nonvocal behavior. Hellermann (2006, 2007) followed low-level adult English-as-a-second-language learners over a period of approximately 2 years and examined their developing interactive competence.

In most of these studies of learners interacting together, a specified task was given for the students to complete. As Seedhouse (2004) pointed out, there is a reflexive relationship between the nature of the task and the turntaking system. The type of turn, the turn order, and even the turn size are constrained by the nature of the task assigned. Tasks such as those connected with task-based language teaching are generally convergent tasks, although discussion and debate are divergent tasks (Duff, 1986; Seedhouse). The two categories of tasks are completely separate L2 classroom contexts that produce distinctly different types of interactional exchange (Seedhouse). More empirical research is clearly needed in both areas.

There are no CA studies of novice EFL learners engaged in discussion that I am aware of, and thus, the current study adds to the body of CA work involving language learner behavior. The pedagogical goal set by the instructor, that is, to discuss a topic as a means of language practice, is seemingly very simple.

However, in fact, this task is very complex and multilayered. It involves not only linguistic work, but it also contains social, interactional, and institutional demands. The fact that it is a multiparty interaction means that the participant structure is fluid, and individual learners are faced with the challenge of competing for turns.

Another pedagogical goal was that students would express opinions and agree and disagree during the discussion activity. This analysis focuses on sequences where the learners worked collaboratively on achieving this goal.

Data

A series of video recordings was made of learners of English as part of their first-year, university English communication course in Japan. These students were given a general topic one week beforehand and were told that they would participate in a group discussion just as in their usual classes except that they would be videotaped for research purposes (not for a grade). On the day of the recording, one group at a time was videotaped in an adjacent classroom to minimize the background noise. A total of 78 groups of four to six students were recorded over a period of five years. The researcher turned on the camera, signaled nonverbally to the students to begin, left the classroom, and returned to check the recording and to stop the camera after approximately 8 to 10 minutes. (This time limit was selected to ensure that all students had an opportunity to participate in a small group discussion within one class period.) The videotapes of 22 groups were transcribed, and collections were made of opinions, assessments, agreements, and disagreements. The transcription follows CA conventions as developed by Jefferson (2004) and adapted from Hutchby and Wooffitt (1998; see appendix).

The videotaped segments used for this analysis were selected because they displayed expressions of agreement and a case of very strong disagreement. Shown in Figure 1 are the 5 participants.

Figure 1. Study participants are shown sitting in a half circle from left to right: Bo (male), Li (female), Yumi (female), Kai (male), and Hiro (male).

One week before the video recording, the students had had a short in-class listening activity about a young woman who wanted to have an international marriage. For homework, they were asked to think about their opinion about international marriage and be prepared to participate in a discussion. To prevent students from preparing scripted dialogs for the discussion activity ahead of time, the students were assigned to their group immediately prior to the videotaping.

Opinion-negotiation sequences

In a discussion, it is common for participants to share not only factual information but also opinions about a topic. Mori (1999) referred to these segments as opinion-negotiation sequences in her study of discussions in casual conversations among Japanese speakers. According to her, a speaker's opinion often contains an adjective or adverb that shows the speaker's stance. Statements can be tagged with epistemic markers, such as "I think," "I wonder," or "maybe." There are many other ways that speakers can show their stance. Nonsegmental displays (such as intonation) can show a speaker's opinion, and nonvocal behaviors (such as head shakes and facial expressions) can also be used. Mori also pointed out that an utterance may be accomplishing more than one action at the same time. For example, an utterance containing an epistemic marker may also "initiate a topic, make a complaint, offer a compliment, produce an observation, provide a suggestion, and so forth" (p. 24).

There is no clear-cut definition of an opinion-negotiation sequence (see Mori, 1999). For this reason, I begin the analysis by first looking closely at student production of assessment turns. Assessments (i.e., evaluative statements made about someone or something) occur frequently and are easier to identify in the learner data than opinion-negotiation sequences. Although a single assessment can constitute an opinion, not all assessments qualify as opinions. It is my contention that an assessment is a precursor of an opinion and that an opinion can be composed of more than one assessment or of a combination of assessments and statements.

Assessments

According to Goodwin and Goodwin (1987, 1992), assessments are quite complex. The term "assessment" can refer to different events depending on the level of the organization. Goodwin and Goodwin (1987) made the following distinctions:

- An assessment can "describe a structural unit that occurs at a specific place in the stream of speech" (p. 6). For example, it could be an adjective, such as "beautiful" or "terrible." This is called an *assessment segment*.
- Involvement in an assessment can be displayed by participants through nonsegmental means, such as intonation. Involvement is also signaled through recognizable nonvocal displays. This display showing involvement is called an *assessment signal*.

- An assessment can also be a type of speech act. In contrast to the previous two items above, the emphasis here is placed more on the action and actor rather than the speech signal used to convey it. This is called an *assessment action*.
- "Assessment actions are produced by single individuals. However, assessments can be organized as an interactive activity that not only includes multiple participants, but also encompasses types of action that are not in themselves assessments. This can be called an *assessment activity*." (p. 9)
- An *assessable* is the person or entity that is being evaluated.

Assessments are "conversational events with sequential constraints" (Pomerantz, 1984, p. 58), and thus the initiation of an assessment occasions a relevant next turn. The assessment and the next turn form an adjacency pair. "Adjacency pairs are paired utterances such that on production of the first part of the pair (e.g., question) the second part of the pair (e.g., answer) becomes *conditionally relevant*" (Seedhouse, 2004, p. 16; see also Schegloff, 1968, p. 1083). In some instances of assessments, the recipient may orient to what has just been assessed and can then show a stance of agreement or disagreement.

Assessment and recipient response

After the students have been given the signal to begin, Li, Bo, and Yumi laugh, and Kai and Hiro are smiling. Hiro takes a turn in line 2 while he is still smiling.

Excerpt 1

```
1    Li, Bo, Yumi:     hehehe
2    Hiro: I think (0.2) international marriage
3          is difficult.
4    Bo:   [yes I think so too. ((nodding, smiling))]
5    Li:   [ah yes me too. ((nodding, smiling))]
6    Kai:  [((nods and smiles))]
7    Yumi: [((eye gaze to right towards Bo and Li
8          then back to Hiro with very slight
9          head nod and smiling))]
```

In Hiro's turn in lines 2–3, both the epistemic marker "I think" and the adjective "difficult" make this an *assessment segment*, following Goodwin and Goodwin's definition (1987, 1992). Hiro stresses the first syllable in "difficult," thereby drawing attention to his assessment. In response, both Bo and Li nod and smile simultaneously while gazing at Hiro, and their utterances overlap in lines 4 and 5. Kai does not vocalize, but he also nods and smiles (line 6) at the same time as Bo and Li are vocalizing their agreement. Although Kai's smile and head nod are less pronounced than those of Bo and Li, his embodied behavior nevertheless matches and aligns with theirs.

Yumi's reaction differs from the other recipients. Her eye gaze shifts towards Bo and Li just as they vocalize, then goes back to Hiro. As her head turns toward Hiro, she nods and smiles very slightly. It is unclear whether the head nod and smile are showing a stance of agreement with Hiro's statement.

The visible behavior that Bo, Li, and Kai respond with is in line with what many researchers such as C. Goodwin (1986), Hayashi (2000), Olsher (2004), and Carroll (2005), to mention merely a few, have shown to be typical, that is, both verbal and nonverbal responses work in an integrated way to display the stance of the speaker. For Goodwin and Goodwin (1987, 1992), These embodied movements can also be called assessments.

In Excerpt 2, Hiro upgrades his assessment using an intensifier, "very" (Pomerantz, 1984), and rephrases it as "very difficult problem." As Goodwin and Goodwin (1987) pointed out, unlike some other actions, assessments are repeatable. In addition, "while some repeatable actions are used to progressively operate on new material...a participant can make continuing assessments of the same assessable" (p. 34). Thus, a repeated assessment may not actually be adding more substance to the talk, but it can essentially provide an additional opportunity for others to participate, as is the case here with Hiro's repeated assessment (line 10).

Excerpt 2

```
10    Hiro:  very (0.2) uh:: (0.2) difficult problem
11    Bo:    [((nods two times))]
12    Li:    [°yes° (0.2) °yes° I (xx)]
13    Hiro:  ↓have    [(0.2)] °I think°=
14    Kai:            [((nod))]
```

In Hiro's upgraded assessment (line 10), the vocal and nonvocal responses from Bo and Li (lines 11–12) are less forceful and not as quick compared to their previous responses. Although an assessment may be repeatable, the exact same response from the recipients is unlikely. In response to an upgraded assessment, it is more likely for a recipient to

1. give a reciprocally upgraded response in keeping with the upgrade,
2. give a more muted response, or
3. not give a response at all.

Before looking more closely at Bo's and Li's responses, let us examine in detail Hiro's repeated assessment in line 10. Hiro's delivery is quite different than his initial assessment. There are pauses after almost every word in his turn, and he uses a stretched hesitation marker ("uh::"), holding the turn. Then there is a rather long 1-s pause after "very difficult problem" (line 10). During this gap, Bo nods while gazing at Hiro, and a fraction of a second later, Li, who is also gazing at Hiro, nods and inserts a soft "yes" plus "I" and a word that is not clear enough for transcription. It is clear that both Bo and Li treat the end of line 10 as a completed turn construction unit (TCU). This is an example of Goodwin and Goodwin's (1987) claim that hearers track "in rather fine detail both the emerging structure of [the] speaker's sentence, and the activity that [the] speaker is progressively entering" (p. 24).

At first glance, one might place Bo's and Li's responses in the second category given above (a more muted response) because Bo only nods this time and because Li's two minimal responses are delivered very softly. However,

1. Li shows vocally her reciprocal alignment,
2. Bo and Li show nonvocally their agreement, and
3. both show sequentially a strong display of agreement.

These actions taken together display strong congruent understanding (Goodwin & Goodwin, 1987, 1992; Jefferson, 1983). They do not display a neutral nor a muted response to Hiro's upgraded assessment. The combined turns show that Bo and Li are staying in complete alignment with Hiro.

Hiro's upgraded assessment does not follow the rules of English grammar. The structure of his statement resembles the structure of Japanese, which has "a standard SOV grammatical structure with a robust predicate-final orientation" (Tanaka, 2001, p. 564). Japanese sentences do not always require a subject, and with the verb coming at the end, they contrast greatly with the grammatical requirements of English. It is not unusual for Japanese novice speakers of English to make such direct translations as Hiro has apparently done here. He also stresses the verb, "have," and uses a downward intonation, which seems to indicate finality. In the 0.2-s pause, Kai nods, after which Hiro adds an epistemic marker, "I think," delivering it very softly.

Unlike his first response to Hiro's initial assessment, Kai's response to the repeated assessment is given without a smile, and his head nod is slighter. His gaze is in a forward-looking space, not looking directly at Hiro, as Bo and Li are. This response falls into the second category given above, a more muted response. Yumi makes no embodied movement and does not smile. She simply keeps her eye gaze on Hiro as he speaks. Her response falls into the third category, no response at all.

At this juncture, it is premature to give a definitive explanation for the different recipient responses, but Goffman's (1981) concept of *footing* may provide some plausible clues. Footing refers to the "alignment we take up to ourselves and others present as expressed in the way we manage the production or reception of an utterance" (p. 128). Within an interaction, people can display different stances or positionings, as the novice learners in this case did. We return to this idea of footing later on after the learners have progressed further in their discussion.

Expressing agreement

According to Pomerantz (1984), "assessments are produced as *products* of participation; with an assessment, a speaker claims knowledge of that which he or she is assessing" (p. 57). Pomerantz pointed out that assessments have sequential constraints. After an assessment is made, there are three possible responses: (a) agreement, (b) disagreement, or (c) declination of participating in the assessment due to a lack of access to or knowledge about what is being assessed. Even if the assessment is followed by a second assessment of the same referent, this second response can still be placed in category a or b.

There are two types of turn shapes for these assessments. One is the preferred-action turn shape of agreement, where agreement components often compose the entire turn and are delivered with a minimization of the gap after the prior turn. The other type is the dispreferred-action turn shape of disagreement, where the disagreements are often prefaced, may be composed of partial agreements or partial disagreements, contain unstated disagreement, and are delivered with gaps, delays, or hesitations (Heritage & Raymond, 2005; Levinson, 1983; Mori, 1999; Pomerantz, 1984; Sacks, 1987; Seedhouse, 2004).

In the data, the responses of Bo and Li correspond to the preferred turn shape after Hiro's initial assessment because there is an absence of a gap and their turns comprise agreement components (lines 4, 5). Kai's nonvocal response of nodding and smiling qualifies as an agreement turn (line 6), although Yumi's nonvocal response is not definite (lines 7–9) as far as showing agreement. After Hiro's upgraded assessment (lines 10, 13), Bo, Li, and Kai again deliver agreement signals (lines 11, 12, 14).

In Excerpt 3, after Hiro completes his assessment (line 13), his turn is immediately latched by Li's self-selected turn (lines 15–16).

Excerpt 3

```
13     Hiro: ↓have   [(0.2)]  °I think°=
14     Kai:          [((nod))]
15     Li:   =the biggest problem (0.2) maybe
16           is the language.
17     Hiro: language °m[m°  ] ((nod))
18     Yumi:            [°n:°]
19     Bo:              [((strong nod))]
20     Kai:             [°language°]
21     Li:   we can't communication with each
22           other very well.
23     Hiro: oh::[:   ]    [((nod))]
24     Yumi:     [°a:]:°   [((eye gaze to Hiro,]
25           then back to Li))
26     Kai:  ((nod))
```

Li has already shown her stance of strong agreement with Hiro, and she now coparticipates by adding a reason to support his assessment (line 15–16). In response, Hiro repeats the word "language," followed by a soft "mm" and a nod (line 17). Overlapping with his "mm," Yumi responds with a soft "nn" (line

18), Bo makes a strong nod (line 19), and Kai repeats "language" softly (line 20). Li self-selects the turn again (lines 21–22), adding additional support for her previous assessment. This extension of her assessment elicits nods from Kai and Hiro (lines 23, 26). Just as in her previous stance, Yumi's vocal and nonvocal responses (lines 24–25) cannot be categorized as agreement because she simply says a soft "a::," and her eye gaze shifts to the speaker on the floor. The footing of the students, which was brought up earlier, has remained the same at this point in the discussion.

Lines 15 to 26 correspond to Goodwin and Goodwin's (1987, 1992) *assessment activity*. As the discussion continues, a pattern of this type of assessment activity emerges, that is, where a member of the group offers reasons to agree with Hiro's initial assessment, and the others respond in a general display of congruent understanding and agreement.

Excerpt 4

```
27    Bo:    and the (0.2) customah (0.4)
28           is different between (0.4)
29           country ((nod))
30    Li:    yes ((nodding))
31    Hiro:  °oh:° [((2 slight nods))]
32    Kai:         [((3 nods))        ]
33    Yumi:  °h::n° ((gaze retracts from Bo
34           to forward space, head moves
35           slightly up and down))
36           (2.0)
37    Yumi:  [°u: °]
38    Li:    [the] thinking way is also different.
```

In the next assessment activity, Bo self-selects (lines 27–29) and gives another reason why international marriage is difficult: The customs of the partners are different. He prefaces his turn with the word "and," a clear indication that he is making an addition to Li's contribution. His assessment action elicits immediate responses from the others. Li (line 30) and Hiro (line 31) give both vocal and nonvocal agreement signals, but Kai (line 32) gives a nonvocal agreement response. Yumi's response is similar to that produced in the previous assessment activity: As she responds with a soft "h::n, " her gaze shifts and she nods her head slightly (lines 33–35). These actions again cannot be categorized as an agreement response. The footing of all of the participants remains the same here.

Just at the end of the 2-s gap, Yumi's says "°u:°" (line 37), and at the very same instant, Li begins a turn (line 38) in overlap. Li continues her turn and adds another reason to support the group argument by citing the difference in the couple's ways of thinking. It is notable that this time, Li's additional supporting reason does not elicit any response at all from the others.

Excerpt 5

```
38    Li:     [the] thinking way is also different.
39    Yumi:   ((gaze shifts forward as mouth opens))
40            (3.9)
41    Yumi:   they (0.8) they::y (1.4) uh their
42            chil- child dren (0.4) children.
43            (2.6) which which country's (0.6)
44            nationality?
```

Instead, there is an extended gap of 3.9 s. Although no one is taking a turn, it does not mean that nothing is happening. As Carroll (2005) pointed out, simply because talk has stopped does not mean action or interaction has stopped. In fact, silences are "spaces that continue to be occupied with material implicated in the production of the speakers' talk" (M. Goodwin, 1980, p. 314). A close look at the video recording shows indeed that Yumi is active during this gap. After Li finishes her turn (line 38), Yumi retracts her gaze slowly from Li while her mouth opens, and it is held in that position as her gaze is directed in front of her in a distant forward space. This retraction of gaze from the current speaker or potential speaker to a distant point away from participants is often an indication of a word search (Carroll; C. Goodwin, 1986). Earlier, in line 37, Yumi was in overlap with Li, and research shows that the speaker in overlap who suspends the turn often initiates a turn at a later point (Jefferson, 1986; Lerner, 2004; Sacks, 1987; Sacks, Schegloff, & Jefferson, 1974; Schegloff, 1987). There is still the possibility for her to recycle her turn beginning.

As Yumi's gaze shifts, she exhibits mouth and lip movement (line 39). Schegloff (1996), C. Goodwin (1986), Carroll (2005), and others have found that when speakers are preparing to speak, they often display behaviors, such as incipient facial expressions, gaze shifts, lip movements, preparatory gestures, body movements, coughs, and inbreaths. Yumi has already displayed such preparatory behavior in an earlier sequence in lines 33–35 and 37, but she did not take a turn at that point.

While Yumi is in word-search mode, it is notable that no one else in the group makes any vocal or nonvocal displays. Bo, Li, Kai, and Hiro do not direct their gaze to any other member, an act that can often designate the next speaker. They look to the side or towards the camera. Clearly, no one except Yumi is preparing to produce a turn, leaving her a clear opportunity to speak. Carroll (2005) demonstrated in his study of novice language learners that "being still" is an interactional resource found during forward repair or word search. According to him, "*designed-to-be-noticed stillness* on the part of co-participants...serves as a display of 'interactional abstinence'" (p. 316) that can ostensibly act as an "embedded continuer" (p. 319). Thus, this set of turns demonstrates the collaborative work of the group members, where turntaking—and refraining from turntaking—constrains each unfolding action towards an overall pattern of agreement.

When Yumi finally takes a turn (lines 41–44), her utterance contains multiple repairs, both forward and backward repairs (Carroll, 2005), and pauses. Unlike Li's and Bo's respective contributions of support for Hiro's initial assessment, Yumi poses a question, asking what the nationality of the children of an international marriage would be.

Excerpt 6

```
43    Yumi:  (2.6) which which country's
44           (0.6) nationality?
45    Hiro:  a::h ↑o:h ((head tilt left))
46    Bo:    ((2 strong nods, 2 slight nods))
47    Li:    maybe ch: ch-ehs uh:
48           decide on (0.4) where the
49           children (0.2) the child
50           (0.2) uh was born.
51           (0.7)
52    Yumi:  m:: ((nodding 2 times)) ((3 nods))
53    Li:    uh if I: uh get married with Japanese
54    Yumi:  ((slight nod))
55    Li:    uh is a child (1.9) born in Japan maybe
56    Yumi:  ((nod))
57    Li:    uh (0.4) he is Japanese
58    Yumi:  m: ((nodding)) ((gaze shift forward
59           then towards Hiro, then to upper left
60           to distant point, head tilted))
```

In Excerpt 6, after Yumi's question, Li responds to Yumi's turn as a request for information, so she answers (lines 47–50) that the nationality would depend on where the child was born. This contrasts with the previous two exchanges in the group's interaction because here Yumi poses a question, rather than declaring a reason in support of Hiro's initial assessment. As a result, the others do not respond to her utterance with the same pattern of clear agreement. Bo's nods here are not the same as his nods in lines 4 and 19, which showed clear agreement. Instead, these nods function more as receipt tokens, while Hiro responds with vocal receipt tokens (line 45). Bo and Hiro may be orienting to an "as-yet-unstated reason" for the difficulty of international marriage. Yumi's turn, although in question format, follows and adds to the general position previously made by Hiro, Bo, and Li.

After Li responds to Yumi's question (lines 47–50), there is a gap of 0.7 s. Yumi's lack of immediate uptake may be a delay signaling an upcoming dispreferred response or be indicative of a lack of understanding. Yumi finally responds with a receipt token, "m:," as she nods and then continues to nod slightly three times, keeping her gaze on Li. Li, upon hearing no immediate response from Yumi, expands her response by giving an example about a child's nationality (lines 53 and 57). Yumi's nods in lines 54 and 56 display that she is attending to Li, but not necessarily that she is understanding her. The timing of her listener responses is consistent with the Japanese discourse practice of producing *aizuchi* while another is speaking (S. Maynard, 1986; Ohta, 2001; Szatrowski, 2002; Tanaka, 2000). After Li's expansion, Yumi responds immediately with no gap, saying "m::" and retracting her gaze from Li while still nodding. She settles back in her chair with her gaze forward. Her gaze shifts to Hiro, and then, as her head tilts to the left, her gaze moves upward to a distant point. She begins a solitary word search, which is then interrupted by Bo self-selecting a turn (lines 61–63). This turn terminates the sequences about children's nationality, leaving no opportunity for anyone in the group to display agreement or disagreement.

Excerpt 7

```
61    Bo:     but then i- if we can (1.6)
62            uh:: love the k- (0.2) the
63            foreigner (0.2) ↓foreigner
64            (2.0)
65    Yumi:   °n::° ((gaze up))
66            (1.0)
```

In Excerpt 7, Bo begins his turn with "but," a lexical item that usually indicates that there will be a contrast with what has gone on before. He posits a hypothetical by using an if clause, but does not complete the latter part of the hypothetical. There is a long gap of 2 s, after which Yumi says "n::" softly and gazes upward (line 65). This is followed by a 1-s gap.

It is not clear whether Bo is attempting to make a contrast with Yumi's contribution to the argument, which is immediately previous, or if he is making a contrast with the collective reasons presented thus far. Considering that he is bringing up two previously unmentioned terms, "love" and "foreigner," it is plausible that he is attempting to make a shift from the pattern of already stated reasons for the difficulty of international marriage; however, he does not complete his thought.

Excerpt 8

```
67    Li:     ah: ((head dips)) .hh
68            (questioning face towards Bo))
69            [but]
70    Kai:    [sense] of value,
71            (0.4)
72    Li:     ((leans forward, gazes at Kai))
```

```
73      Kai:    sense of value sense of value
74              (0.2) is difficult.
75      Bo:     [((2 nods))]
76      Li:     [°ah yes° ((slightly nodding))]
77      Kai:    between [(0.8)] uh A and A
78      Li:                     [mhm]
79      Kai:    and A and B like that.
80              (0.8)
81      Li:     [°o: °] ((3 nods))
82      Yumi:   [°n: °]((very slight nod))
83              ((mouth opens slightly))
84              (1.0)
```

In Excerpt 8, after a 1-s gap, Li responds with a receipt token, "ah:" (line 67). Her head movement (head dips, line 67) looks as if she is starting to nod, but suddenly, she produces an inbreath and switches to a questioning gaze back towards Bo. The inbreath occurs right at the switch to the questioning gaze. Directly after this she says "but," and because it is in overlap with Kai, she stops, leans forward as she gazes at Kai, and allows him to take the turn.

When we examine Li's and Kai's overlapped turns more closely, it is clear that Li is oriented to Bo's incomplete turn. Kai, on the other hand, is not attempting to clarify Bo's meaning. Instead, he is intent on making his own contribution to the discussion. He brings up the idea that the values of the couple can make international marriage difficult. When he offers this additional reason, Li gives both vocal and nonvocal agreement signals (lines 76, 78, 81), and Bo gives a nonvocal agreement (line 75). Yumi gives a reactive token and a very slight nod (line 82) with her mouth opening slightly (line 83), but these signals still cannot be categorized as expressing clear agreement. Hiro does not show agreement or disagreement; he simply has his gaze directed towards Kai.

This sequence with Kai offering another reason to support Hiro's initial assessment fits the general pattern of the previous displays where one member offers a reason, and the others respond, usually with clear agreement signals. Yumi and Kai took longer to produce such initial assessment turns, but with the occurrence of long gaps between rounds of assessment activity, these two were able to fit their turns into the overall pattern that had been set by Li. By line 77, all members of the group have been able to initiate a round of assessment activity as a means of making a contribution to the discussion.

Expressing disagreement

Levinson (1983), Pomerantz (1984), and Sacks (1987) have demonstrated that interlocutors in affiliative interaction delay and/or mitigate their delivery of disagreement. Disagreement turns are often delayed and prefaced with hesitation markers such as "uh" or "well" (Pomerantz, p. 70). The delay may be due to a lack of understanding, or it also may be due to a constraint against disaffiliation. There are often hesitations, hedges, requests for clarification, partial repeats, and other repair initiators (p. 72). There can be prefaces to disagreement in the form of asserted agreements, weak agreements, same evaluation agreements, and qualified agreements (p. 72). "Co-occurring with agreements, the disagreement components are formed as partial agreements/partial disagreements; as qualification, exceptions, additions, and the like" (p. 74). It is also common for speakers to give an account for their stance.

Timing is crucial here. As Mori (1999) stated, "the timing of delivery exhibits a systematic difference between agreeing turns and disagreeing turns....Thus facing the lack of immediate uptake, the initial speakers are likely to anticipate a forthcoming disagreement" (p. 85). As Goodwin and Goodwin (1987) stated, the placement of strong agreement is "almost a mirror image" of the way disagreement is displayed sequentially (p. 30).

Disagreement in the data

In the data up to now, there has been a general pattern of agreement; however, later in this discussion, disagreement sequences also occur. Hiro, who initiated the discussion at the outset, now moves the discussion in a different direction.

Excerpt 9

```
85    Hiro:  BUT (0.6) uh:: (0.2) some
86           cou pul
87    Bo:    [((nod))]
88    Li:    [°mhm° ((slightly nodding))
89    Hiro:  uh: (0.2) uh successful their
90           (0.4) life.
91    Bo:    [((nod))]
92    Li:    [°yeh° ((nodding))]
93    Yumi:  [°m: ° ((2 slight nods))]
94    Kai:   [o:: ((nodding 4 times, smiling))]
95           (0.4)
96    Hiro:  thuh:: reason (0.4) why.
97           (0.7)
98    Bo:    ((head tilts back and to right))
99           o:: ((smiling))
100   Yumi:  ah:: ((leaning back, smiling)) hehe
101          [hehe]
102   Bo:    [hehe]
103   Kai:   [huhu]((gaze shift toward Bo))
```

In Excerpt 9, after a 1-s gap in line 84, Hiro begins his turn with "BUT," a contrastive connector that he delivers at a noticeably higher volume. This serves to heighten the attention to what is to follow. His turn contains several pauses and hesitations, yet he succeeds in making a statement saying that some couples are successful. The "BUT" at a higher volume contrasts with all the sequences of agreement made so far, and it also contrasts with his own initial assessment made in line 1. He has added a qualification to this initial assessment and makes a different statement about some couples who have an international marriage. His statement elicits immediate agreement from all of the others (lines 91–94). It is interesting to note that this agreement sequence is different from the other sequences in that the recipients, including Yumi, unanimously display agreement signals at the same moment in the interaction. It is also notable that Hiro is actually leading the others to a point that is essentially in opposition to the main argument that they have been collectively making.

In line 96, Hiro turns his statement into a question. The structure he uses here does not follow the rules of English grammar, and he may have been translating literally as he did back in lines 10 and 13. In Japanese, the topic can be followed by an interrogative marker to form a question, but the interrogative is usually delivered with a rising intonation. In Hiro's case, his intonation goes down. Bo's (line 98) and Yumi's (line 100) nonverbal reactions to his uninflected question show that they understand his turn as a question and are considering it; and after their minimal tokens, they laugh, with Kai joining in (line 102). According to Jefferson, Sacks, and Schegloff (1987), laughter is a socially organized phenomenon, and its achievement conforms to an underlying order. Sequentially, laughter may be produced in response to a prior utterance, and it exerts an effect on what is to follow. It is not possible to analyze in detail the joint laughter here other than to point to the possibility that the laughter may have been in response to the fact that no one could readily answer Hiro's question.

Li is the only one who does not laugh in response to Hiro's question. Her gaze stays on Hiro and she self-selects the next turn.

Excerpt 10

```
104    Li:      but in fact uh you don't know
105             (0.2) if they (0.6) if they
106             are successful or not (0.4) you
107             only see the TV (0.6) don't you?
108             (0.4)
109    Hiro:    o::h:: so-
110    Li:      but what the real things (0.2)
111             you don't know. °in fact.°
112             (1.6)
```

In Excerpt 10 (lines 103–107), Li makes a direct counter to Hiro's previous assessment (lines 85, 89–90). She begins with the contrastive marker, "but," and follows it with a strong statement, stressing "don't know." She directly challenges his knowledge, claiming that his information is not sufficient because it is only from television. The tag question, "don't you?" (line 106), serves to sharpen and strengthen her challenge even more. Li has clearly allocated the next turn to Hiro, and after a 0.4-s gap, Hiro responds with "o::h:: so-," which is a receipt token, and before he can make a response, Li continues with her challenge, saying, "but what the real things (0.2) you don't know. in fact" (lines 109–110). Here, Li is intensifying her challenge (lines 103–106), and she accomplishes this in several ways. First, she uses the contrastive marker, "but," which signals that what will follow is in contrast to a prior turn. Second, this TCU has the same basic structure as her previous turn, "but" + challenge. This TCU does not add a different challenge because it is qualifying her previous turn. In essence, then, it is a restatement, and it thus serves to add emphasis to her stance. Third, Li uses "real things" to suggest that what Hiro sees on TV is not factual and believable. Fourth, she makes a direct challenge by stating, "you don't know." This is delivered without any mitigation. Fifth, the "in fact" added after her completed TCU acts as an intensifier, adding more strength to her challenge despite the fact that this phrase is delivered so softly. Hiro is still being designated the next speaker; however, he does not take the turn, and there is a long 1.6-s gap. Because Hiro still has not given his response, Bo self-selects.

Excerpt 11

```
113    Bo:    but in our (0.2) university
114           (0.7)
115    Li:    °m:°
116           (0.9)
117    Bo:    um (1.8) th- coup- uh
118           there are many coupul (0.8)
119           °couple °
120           (0.2)
121    Li:    °mhm°
122    Yumi:  [((3 nods))]
123    Hiro:  [((2 slight nods))]
124    Kai:   [((2 very slight nods))]
125    Bo:    ((2 nods in general direction
126           of Yumi, Kai, and Hiro))
127    Bo:    ((gaze shift to Li))
128           (0.4)
129    Li:    but they are (1.0) uh: not (0.8)
130           uh they are not married yet (1.0)
131           a- aren't they? (0.4) if they are
132           married, (0.2) uh: there will be a
133           lot of problems.
```

```
134              (1.4)
135   Bo:        it's in front of thih marriage (0.2)
136              isn't it?
137              (1.0)
138   Li:        in front of marriage?
139              (0.6)
140   Bo:        °marriaji° ((head nod down))
141              (0.6)
142   Li:        ((eye blink, lateral head shake,
143              with questioning gaze at Bo))
144              [°I don't understand°]
145   Bo:        [((presses lips together,
146              head tilts left, smiling))]
147   Bo:        [((head tilts to right and upward,
148              eyes squinted, smiling broadly))]
149   Yumi:      [HEHEHE]
150   Hiro:      [HUHUHU]
151   Kai:       [hehe]
```

Thus, lines 104–107 mark a sharp shift in the discussion. Where previously, there has been a series of agreement sequences in which all members participated, here, there is an adversarial challenge brought on by one member directly against another member. There is an absence of pauses, delays, hesitations, and mitigations (Levinson, 1983; Mori, 1999; Pomerantz, 1984; Sacks, 1987), as might be expected from this group that has been working collaboratively up to this point.

To understand what is happening here, it is important to look closely at the next turns to determine how lines 104–107 are being received by the others. After the designated next speaker does not take a turn in line 112, Bo provides a counter to Li's direct challenge by stating that there are some successful couples at their university (lines 113, 117–119), thus countering Li's claim that Hiro does not have any real facts. Bo begins his turn with "but," indicating that his statement is in contrast to Li's challenge. It is clear that Bo is providing the preferred next turn that has been set up by Li's challenge (lines 104–107, 110–111). It is also notable that back in lines 61–63, Bo had given an indication that there is another side to the issue of the difficulty of international marriage (when he brings up "love" and "foreigner"), so his turn may not have been used simply to help Hiro out, but he may have taken the opportunity provided by Hiro's nonresponse to show more of his own stance.

In Bo's response to Li (lines 113, 117–119), there are frequent long pauses and multiple repairs, and Yumi, Hiro, and Kai display their understanding with head nods. Li also shows that she has understood by responding quickly, making a counterclaim where she completely invalidates Bo's stance by saying that because these couples are not married, they are not part of the argument.

After a 1.4-s gap, Bo responds by saying, "it's in front of thih marriage (0.2) isn't it?" (lines 134–135). Li's rising intonation when she repeats "in front of marriage?" invites Bo to explain this phrase. Bo answers with a soft "marriaji," and his downward head nod is delivered at the same time as the last syllable, "ji," as if indicating that this is what he has to offer. Li indicates with her lateral head shake and "I don't understand" that she does not accept this as an explanation. Bo then presses his lips together, tilts his head to the left, and displays a "thinking face" (Carroll, 2000; C. Goodwin, 1986). He then tilts his head to the right and upward, his eyes squinted, and smiles broadly. At the second head tilt, Yumi, Kai, and Hiro laugh. This laughter may have been in response to Bo's inability to provide an answer in the same way that everyone laughed in lines 101 and 102 when no one could answer Hiro's question about why there are some successful couples. In both instances, the laughter effectively terminates the topic on the floor.

Disagreement and arguing

The interaction in lines 85 to 150 is similar to conversational arguing (Muntigl & Turnbull, 1998), disputing (Kotthoff, 1993), and oppositional argument (Schiffrin, 1985). There are three basic turn exchanges (Antaki, 1994; D. Maynard, 1985; Muntigl & Turnbull) in an argument exchange: (a) Turn 1, where a claim is made by Speaker A; (b) Turn 2, where Speaker B disputes Turn 1; and (c) Turn 3, where Speaker A either directly defends the claim in Turn 1 or directly disagrees with Turn 2. In the data, lines 85–86 and 89–90 would correspond to Turn 1, and lines 103–106 and 109–110 would compose Turn 2. In this particular instance, Turn 3 was not delivered by Speaker A but by a different speaker altogether (Bo in lines 112, 116–118). Bo's act of stepping in to provide Turn 3 allows the argument sequence to continue.

Saft (2000, 2004), in his study of arguing in the institutional context, showed that arguing is a productive interactional activity that is realized through a basic two-party participation structure, but the interactants are not limited to two. An argument consists of an initiation of opposition, the pursuit of opposition, and finally, the termination of opposition. In both conversational and institutional discourse, the absence of the pursuit of opposition has negative consequences. The speaker who fails to take the turn loses the argument. In the data, Bo demonstrates that he understands that the opposition initiated by Li demands a response. Although Hiro was the designated next speaker, his failure to pursue the opposition, either because of his lack of understanding of the interaction required or his lack of language skills, provided an opportunity space for Bo to pursue the opposition.

Muntigl and Turnbull (1998) suggested that there are four types of disagreement: (a) irrelevancy claims, (b) challenges, (c) contradictions, and

(d) counterclaims. In lines 104–107, Li presents type b, a challenge, when she says that Hiro does not know because his information is only from television. In lines 113 and 117–119, Bo responds with type c, a contradiction, when he says that Hiro does indeed have facts because there are successful couples on campus. In lines 129–133, Li disputes this with type a, an irrelevancy claim, saying that those couples are not married yet, so they do not count. It appears, then, that these novice learners have sufficient tools for pursuing opposition and expressing disagreement.

However, what stands out in this arguing exchange is the fact that there is an absence of politeness markers. Li's sudden challenge in lines 104–107 is a potentially face-threatening act (Brown & Levinson, 1987; Goffman, 1967). The expected dispreferred turn shape with delays and mitigating prefaces (Pomerantz, 1984) does not occur. In fact, according to Muntigl and Turnbull's (1998) analysis of the four types of disagreements, the ranking from most to least face aggravating is

1. irrelevancy claim,
2. challenge,
3. contradiction,
4. a combination of contradiction and a counterclaim, and finally,
5. the counterclaim.

Based on this, the students use the most face-threatening structures and do not use the least face-threatening, the counterclaim, at all.

It would be unfair to conclude that the students do not have enough proficiency to accomplish this facework, so I would like to offer an alternative explanation. Although in conversation, agreement is the preferred turn shape after an assessment (Levinson, 1983; Mori, 1999; Pomerantz, 1984; Sacks, 1987), there are a number of other contexts where disagreement is, in fact, preferred and expected. As Pomerantz pointed out, in the case of self-deprecation, disagreement is preferred. In focus groups (Myers, 1998), disagreements are seen as "allowable and encouraged" (p. 96). Atkinson and Drew (1979) showed that in the courtroom after an accusation, a contradiction is preferred; otherwise, the accused is assumed to be guilty. Tannen (1981) and Schiffrin (1984) wrote about communities where disputes are expected, and they are seen as a form of sociable practice. M. Goodwin and C. Goodwin (1987) have found that opposition moves are highlighted and unmitigated in children's arguments. Among adults, Kotthoff (1993) found that even in friendly conversations, once an argument begins, that is, after the first dissent-turn sequence occurs, there are fewer and fewer mitigations and hesitations; disagreement becomes more and more explicit, and agreement is no longer preferred. Participants are expected to defend their positions and not to concede.

It is my contention that the classroom is another context where disagreement is preferred, that is, particularly in a debate or a discussion. A discussion can draw to an end rather quickly if everyone agrees with each other on every point, but if there are differences of opinion, the discussion can be expanded or be pursued in greater depth. Disagreements can be a good resource for students to display their knowledge. Argumentation can also help students explore the subject matter. In addition, the ability to disagree can sharpen students' social skills as they interact with their classmates. Li and Bo may have taken this stance, and they may very well have been displaying their behavior of "doing being a student."

If this is the case, however, there was no discernible indication to the group that Li was moving to the challenge mode ("but in fact you don't know" in lines 104–107). This may account for the fact that Hiro is still in receipt mode ("o::h:: so-" in line 109), and he is about to say something when Li cuts in and delivers an addition to her challenge. Perhaps it is because there is no expectation by the others that Li would be making a frame shift (Goffman, 1981; M. Goodwin, 1996; Tannen, 1993) that there is a long gap of 1.6 s (line 82) where no one responds. Bo finally responds, and once he enters the interaction, the argument-like sequence ensues.

We must also not forget that this discussion takes place within an institutional context. Many CA researchers (Drew & Heritage, 1992; Seedhouse, 2004; ten Have, 1999) have demonstrated that institutional discourse is qualitatively different from conversational discourse. How the talk in institutional settings is organized is closely connected to the institution. It is through participants interacting that the institution is invoked and maintained. In other words, the institution should not be conceptualized as a stable container (Goodwin & Heritage, 1990; Hutchby & Wooffitt, 1998) where the interaction takes place. Instead, evidence of the institution and how it is structured can be found through the analysis of the interactions of the participants who display in their speech their understanding of the institution's goals and tasks. As Seedhouse (2004) put it, the institutional context and institutional identities are "talked into and out of being" by the members themselves (pp. 199–204). Thus, in this study, the learners are demonstrating their interpretations of the pedagogical focus, for example, using only their L2, staying on one main topic, expressing opinions, and so on. Bo and Li display their institutional understanding by initiating and pursuing opposition.

Collaborative work

In this group discussion, the first section is made up of a series of agreement segments that follow a basic pattern. All of the members orient to the initial assessment made at the opening of the discussion. The individual members also seem to keep to a basic pattern throughout the series. Bo and Li display strong vocal and nonvocal agreement; Kai shows a more muted agreement, but Yumi does not always show clear alignment. The second part of the discussion shifts to a series of disagreement sequences. After several rounds of agreement, moving to a different stance created an opportunity space for the discussion to continue. Perhaps because all of the members were able to add reasons for the difficulty of international marriage, Hiro may have been influenced to make a qualification of his own initial assessment that some couples are successful (lines 85-86, 89-90). Li responds to this qualification, lodging a strong and direct disagreement calling Hiro's knowledge into question (lines 104-107, 110-109). It is possible that Li is standing by the first position taken up by all of the members, so she is essentially supporting Hiro because he is the one who made the first statement. Li's direct challenge transforms the interaction into an arguing exchange. When Hiro fails to take up the third turn (line 112) either because he has not yet adjusted to the shift to the argumentative frame, or he is experiencing language difficulties (or both), Bo takes up the third turn. This kind of collaborative work helps the discussion continue smoothly.

Although there are several indications of language difficulties (i.e., ungrammatical word order, incomplete utterances, disfluent production, etc.), this does not deter the members from making responses that display their understanding of the prior turns of the group members. They wait until they can understand what the person is saying, and they give vocal and nonvocal signals to show that they understand. Although one might conclude that the frequent occurrence of long gaps between turns is evidence that these novice learners lack linguistic skills, this overlooks the real possibility that some gaps may have been the result of intentionally refraining from taking a turn. Close examination of the timing indicates that the speakers may have been cooperating to allow greater participation of the other members.

Expressing an opinion in another language is not easy. As Myers (1998) wrote, "The small moves of turntaking—adding an example, giving a gist, disagreeing or attributing—are part of what defines a statement as an opinion about an issue" (p. 106). Although the novice learners in this study may have struggled with their utterances, with each member responding to the others' turns, the group succeeds in the formation of opinions. These were opinions not made by single individuals in single turns, but reached through their collaborative work.

Conclusion

This study examined closely how novice language learners in Japan participated in a classroom discussion. Even with learners with less-than-perfect linguistic abilities, it was possible for them to carry out a discussion. The members made use of many conversational resources that may have compensated for their difficulties with grammar and vocabulary. For example, they used embodied movements, gaze shifts, the contrastive lexical marker "but," receipt tokens, and laughter. They were able to make assessments and to respond with agreement and disagreement. The first part of the discussion had a pattern of similar agreement sequences, and this was followed by a series of disagreements. Two members were able to participate in this argument-like exchange, and they utilized a number of common disagreement types: challenge, contradiction, and the irrelevancy claim. Clearly, the novice learners were well equipped to deliver both disagreements and agreements.

The novice learners also showed a high degree of collaboration. This analysis revealed that particular actions provided more opportunities for others to participate. For example, a repeated assessment is an invitation for further responses from other participants. Keeping eye gaze averted from other members means that a next turn is not being allocated to anyone in particular; and this simple action allows time for a speaker to self-select. Refraining from taking a turn also allows more opportunities for others to speak. Cooperation was also shown through the members' clear displays of understanding. Some learners seemed to rely heavily on the understanding of the others when they left their turns uncompleted. In all but one case, the subsequent turns showed that the message had been communicated.

This study suggests that assessments are important building blocks for the formation of opinions. For novice learners, it is easier to make a simple assessment that invites agreement or disagreement than to express a well-formed opinion. Each of the novice learners in the data contributed responses, and the group was able to build a more substantive opinion collaboratively.

Although opinions are important for a discussion, it is also apparent that points of disagreement help to expand and deepen the interaction. This chapter contends that within the context of the classroom discussion or debate, disagreement should be the preferred and expected response. Rather than avoiding disagreements, it is far more beneficial for our language learners to sharpen their skills of argumentation. M. Goodwin and C. Goodwin (1987) found in their analysis of children's arguments that "rather than being disorderly, arguing provides children with a rich arena for the development of proficiency in language, syntax, and social organization" (p. 200). In the same vein, the classroom discussion that values disagreement and the defense of one's position should prove to be an extremely important site for effective language learning.

References

Antaki, C. (1994). *Explaining and arguing: The social organization of accounts.* London: Sage.

Atkinson, J., & Drew, P. (1979). *Order in court: The organization of verbal interaction in judicial settings.* London: Macmillan.

Brouwer, C. (2003). Word searches in NNS-NS interaction: Opportunities for language learning? *The Modern Language Journal, 87,* 534–545.

Brown, P., & Levinson, S. (1987). *Politeness: Some universals in language usage.* Cambridge, England: Cambridge University Press.

Carroll, D. (2000). Precision timing in novice-to-novice L2 conversations. *Issues in Applied Linguistics, 11,* 67–110.

Carroll, D. (2005). *Co-constructing competence: Turn construction and repair in novice-to-novice second language interaction.* Unpublished doctoral dissertation, University of York, York, England.

Dörnyei, Z. (1997). Psychological processes in cooperative language learning: Group dynamics and motivation. *The Modern Language Journal, 81,* 482–493.

Drew, P., & Heritage, J. (1992). *Talk at work: Interactions in institutional settings.* Cambridge, England: Cambridge University Press.

Duff, P. (1986). Another look at interlanguage talk: Taking task to task. In R. Day (Ed.), *Talking to learn: Conversation in second language acquisition.* Rowley, MA: Newbury House.

Egbert, M. (1996). Context-sensitivity in conversation: Eye gaze and the German repair initiator *bitte? Language in Society, 25,* 587–612.

Egbert, M., Niebecker, L., & Rezzara, S. (2004). Inside first and second language speakers' trouble in understanding. In R. Gardner & J. Wagner (Eds.), *Second language conversations* (pp. 178–200). London: Continuum.

Gardner, R., & Wagner, J. (2004). *Second language conversations.* London & New York: Continuum.

Gass, S., & Madden, C. (Eds.). (1985). *Input and second language acquisition.* Rowley, MA: Newbury House.

Goffman, E. (1967). On facework: An analysis of ritual elements in social interaction. In A. Jaworski & N. Coupland (Eds.), *The discourse reader* (pp. 306–321). London: Routledge.

Goffman, E. (1981). *Forms of talk.* Philadelphia: University of Pennsylvania Press.

Goodwin, C. (1986). Gesture as a resource for the organization of mutual orientation. *Semiotica, 62,* 29–49.

Goodwin, C., & Goodwin, M. (1987). Concurrent operations of talk: Notes on the interactive organization of assessments. *IPrA Papers in Pragmatics, 1,* 1–54.

Goodwin, C., & Goodwin, M. (1992). Assessment and the construction of context. In A. Duranti & C. Goodwin (Eds.), *Rethinking context: Language as an interactive phenomenon* (pp. 151–189). Cambridge, England: Cambridge University Press.

Goodwin, C., & Heritage, J. (1990). Conversation analysis. *Annual Review of Anthropology, 19,* 283–307.

Goodwin, M. (1980). *He-said-she-said: Talk as social organization among black children.* Bloomington: Indiana University Press.

Goodwin, M. (1996). Shifting frame. In D. Slobin, J. Gerhardt, A. Kyratzis, & J. Guo (Eds.), *Social interaction, social context, and language* (pp. 71–82). Mahwah, NJ: Lawrence Erlbaum.

Goodwin, M., & Goodwin, C. (1987). Children's arguing. In S. Philips, S. Steele, & C. Tanz (Eds.), *Language, gender, and sex in comparative perspective* (pp. 200–248). Cambridge, England: Cambridge University Press.

Hauser, E. (2003). 'Corrective recasts' and other-correction of language form in interaction among native and nonnative speakers of English. Unpublished doctoral dissertation, University of Hawaiʻi at Mānoa, Honolulu.

Hayashi, M. (1999). Where grammar and interaction meet: A study of co-participant completion in a Japanese conversation. *Human Studies, 22,* 475–499.

Hayashi, M. (2000). *Practices in joint utterance construction in Japanese conversation.* Unpublished doctoral dissertation, University of Colorado, Boulder.

He, A. (1998). Answering questions in language proficiency interviews. In R. Young & A. He (Eds.), *Talking and testing: Discourse approaches to the assessment of oral proficiency* (pp. 101–115). Amsterdam: John Benjamins.

Hellermann, J. (2006). Classroom interactive practices for developing L2 literacy: A microethnographic study of two beginning adult learners of English. *Applied Linguistics, 27,* 377–404.

Hellermann, J. (2007). The development of practices for action in classroom dyadic-interaction: Focus on task openings. *The Modern Language Journal, 91,* 83–96.

Heritage, J., & Raymond, G. (2005). The terms of agreement: Indexing epistemic authority and subordination in talk-in-interaction. *Social Psychology Quarterly, 68,* 15–38.

Hosoda, Y. (2000). Other-repair in Japanese conversations between non-native and native speakers. *Issues in Applied Linguistics, 11,* 39–65.

Hutchby, I., & Wooffitt, R. (1998). *Conversation analysis: Principles, practices and applications.* Cambridge, England: Polity Press.

Jacobs, G., & Farrell, T. (2003). Understanding and implementing the communicative language teaching paradigm. *RELC Journal, 34,* 5–30.

Jacobs, G. M., Power, M. A., & Loh, W. I. (2002). *The teacher's sourcebook for cooperative learning: Practical techniques, basic principles, and frequently asked questions.* Thousand Oaks, CA: Corwin Press.

Jefferson, G. (1972). Side sequences. In D. Sudnow (Ed.), *Studies in social interaction* (pp. 294–338). New York: Free Press.

Jefferson, G. (1983). Caveat speaker: Preliminary notes on recipient topic-shift implicature. *Tilburg Papers in Language and Literature, 30,* 1–25.

Jefferson, G. (1986). Notes on 'latency' in overlap onset. *Human Studies, 9,* 153–183.

Jefferson, G. (2004). Glossary of transcription symbols with an introduction. In G. Lerner (Ed.), *Conversation analysis: Studies from the first generation* (pp. 13–31). Amsterdam: John Benjamins.

Jefferson, G., Sacks, H., & Schegloff, E. (1987). Notes on laughter in the pursuit of intimacy. In G. Button & J. Lee (Eds.), *Talk and social organization* (pp. 152–205). Clevedon, England: Multilingual Matters.

Johnson, D., Johnson, R., & Holubec, E. (1993). *Cooperation in the classroom.* Edina, MN: Interaction Book Company.

Kasper, G. (2004). Participant orientations in German conversation-for-learning, *The Modern Language Journal, 88,* 551–567.

Koshik, I. (2002). Designedly incomplete utterances: A pedagogical practice for eliciting knowledge displays in error correction sequences. *Research on Language and Social Interaction, 35*, 277–309.

Kotthoff, H. (1993). Disagreement and concession in disputes: On the context sensitivity of preference structures. *Language in Society, 22*, 193–216.

Lerner, G. (Ed.). (2004). *Conversation analysis: Studies from the first generation.* Amsterdam: John Benjamins.

Levinson, S. (1983). *Pragmatics.* Cambridge, England: Cambridge University Press.

Lindstrom, A. (1994). Identification and recognition in Swedish telephone conversation openings. *Language in Society, 23*, 231–252.

Long, M., & Porter, P. (1985). Group work, interlanguage talk and second language acquisition. *TESOL Quarterly, 19*, 207–228.

Markee, N. (1994). Toward an ethnomethodological respecification of second language acquisition studies. In E. Tarone, S. Gass, & A. Cohen (Eds.), *Research methodology in second language acquisition* (pp. 89–116). Hillsdale, NJ: Lawrence Erlbaum.

Markee, N. (2004). Zones of interactional transition in ESL classes. *The Modern Language Journal, 88*, 583–596.

Maynard, D. (1985). How children start arguments. *Language in Society, 14*, 1–30.

Maynard, S. (1986). On back-channel behavior in Japanese and English casual conversation. *Linguistics, 24*, 1070–1108.

Mondada, L., & Pekarek Doehler, S. (2004). Second language acquisition as situated practice: Task accomplishment in the French second language classroom. *The Modern Language Journal, 88*, 501–518.

Mori, J. (1999). *Negotiating agreement and disagreement in Japanese: Connective expressions and turn construction.* Amsterdam: John Benjamins.

Mori, J. (2002). Task, design, plan, and development of talk-in-interaction: An analysis of a small group activity in a Japanese language classroom. *The Modern Language Journal, 23*, 323–347.

Mori, J. (2004). Negotiating sequential boundaries and learning opportunities: A case from a Japanese language classroom. *The Modern Language Journal, 88*, 536–550.

Muntigl, P., & Turnbull, W. (1998). Conversational structure and facework in arguing. *Journal of Pragmatics, 29*, 225–256.

Myers, G. (1998). Displaying opinions: Topics and disagreement in focus groups. *Language in Society, 27*, 85–111.

Ohta, A. (2001). *Second language acquisition processes in the classroom: Learning Japanese.* Mahwah, NJ: Lawrence Erlbaum.

Olsher, D. (2004). Talk and gesture: The embodied completion of sequential actions in spoken interactions. In R. Gardner & J. Wagner (Eds.), *Second language conversations* (pp. 221–245). London and New York: Continuum.

Park, Y. (1999). The Korean connective *nuntey* in conversational discourse. *Journal of Pragmatics, 31*, 191–218.

Pica, T. (1987). Second language acquisition, social interaction and the classroom. *Applied Linguistics, 8*, 3–21.

Pomerantz, A. (1984). Agreeing and disagreeing with assessments: Some features of preferred/dispreferred turn shapes. In M. Atkinson & J. Heritage (Eds.), *Structures of social action: Studies in conversation analysis* (pp. 57–101). Cambridge, England: Cambridge University Press.

Sacks, H. (1972). An initial investigation of the usability of conversational materials for doing sociology. In D. N. Sudnow (Ed.), *Studies in social interaction* (pp. 31–74). New York: Free Press.

Sacks, H. (1987). On the preferences for agreement and contiguity in sequences in conversation. In G. Button & J. Lee (Eds.), *Talk and social organization* (pp. 54–69). Clevedon, England: Multilingual Matters.

Sacks, H., Schegloff, E., & Jefferson, G. (1974). A simplest systematics for the organization of turntaking in conversation. *Language, 50*, 696–735.

Saft, S. (2000). *Arguing in the institution: Context, culture and conversation analysis in a set of Japanese university faculty meetings.* Unpublished doctoral dissertation, University of Hawai'i at Mānoa, Honolulu.

Saft, S. (2004). Conflict as interactional accomplishment in Japanese: Arguments in university faculty meetings. *Language in Society, 33*, 549–584.

Schegloff, E. (1968). Sequencing in conversational openings, *American Anthropologist, 70*, 1075–1095.

Schegloff, E. (1980). Preliminaries to preliminaries: 'Can I ask you a question?' *Sociological Inquiry, 50*, 104–152.

Schegloff, E. (1987). Recycled turn beginnings: A precise repair mechanism in conversation's turn-taking organization. In G. Button & J. Lee (Eds.), *Talk and social interaction* (pp. 70–85). Clevedon, England: Multilingual Matters.

Schegloff, E. (1996). Turn organization: One intersection of grammar and interaction. In E. Ochs, E. Schegloff, & S. Thompson (Eds.), *Interaction and grammar* (pp. 51–133). Cambridge, England: Cambridge University Press.

Schiffrin, D. (1984). Jewish argument as sociability. *Language in Society, 13*, 311–335.

Schiffrin, D. (1985). Everyday argument: The organization of diversity in talk. In T. A. van Dijk (Ed.), *Handbook of discourse analysis* (pp. 35–46). London: Academic Press.

Seedhouse, P. (2004). The interactional architecture of the language classrooms: A conversation analysis perspective. *Language Learning, 54*, 1–300.

Sorjonen, M. (1996). On repeats and responses in Finnish conversation. In E. Ochs, E. Schegloff, & S. Thompson (Eds.), *Interaction and grammar* (pp. 277–327). Cambridge, England: Cambridge University Press.

Szatrowski, P. (2002). Gaze, head nodding, and *aizuchi* in information presenting activities. *Japanese/Korean Linguistics, 11*, 119–132.

Tanaka, H. (2000). Turn projection in Japanese talk-in-interaction. *Research on Language and Social Interaction, 33*, 1–38.

Tanaka, H. (2001). Adverbials for turn projection in Japanese: Toward a demystification of the "telepathic" mode of communication. *Language in Society, 30*, 559–587.

Tannen, D. (1981). New York Jewish conversational style. *International Journal of the Sociology of Language* 30, 133–149.

Tannen, D. (1993). *Framing in discourse.* Oxford, England: Oxford University Press.

ten Have, P. (1991). Talk and institution: A reconsideration of the 'asymmetry' of doctor-patient interaction. In D. Boden & D. Zimmerman (Eds.), *Talk and social structure: Studies in ethnomethodology and conversation analysis* (pp. 138–165). Berkeley: University of California Press.

ten Have, P. (1999). *Doing conversation analysis: A practical guide.* London: Sage.

Wong, J. (2000). Delayed next turn repair initiation in native/non-native speaker English conversation. *Applied Linguistics, 21*, 244–267.

Appendix: Transcription symbols

(0.5)	The number in brackets indicates a time gap in tenths of a second.
(.)	A dot enclosed in a bracket indicates a pause of less than 2/10 of a second.
=	An 'equal' sign indicates 'latching' between utterances.
[ ]	Square brackets between adjacent lines of concurrent speech indicate the onset and end of a spate of overlapping talk.
.hh	A dot before an 'h' indicates a speaker in-breath. The more h's, the longer the in-breath.
hh	An 'h' indicates an outbreath. The more h's, the longer the breath.
(( ))	A description enclosed in double parentheses indicates a nonverbal activity.
–	A dash indicates the sharp cut-off of the prior word or sound.
:	A colon indicates that the speaker has stretched the preceding sound or letter. The more colons, the greater the extent of the stretching.
(xxx)	Parentheses indicate the presence of an unclear fragment. The words within single parentheses indicate the transcriber's best guess at an unclear utterance.
.	A period indicates a full stop, falling in tone. It does not necessarily indicate the end of a sentence.
,	A comma indicates a 'continuing' intonation.
?	A question mark indicates a rising inflection. It does not necessarily indicate a question.
↑↓	Pointed arrows indicate a marked falling or rising intonational shift. They are placed immediately before the onset of the shift.
underline	Underlined fragments indicate speaker emphasis.
CAPS	Words in capitals mark a section of speech noticeably louder than that surrounding it.
º º	Degree signs are used to indicate that the talk they encompass is spoken noticeably quieter than the surrounding talk.
> <	'Greater than' and 'less than' signs indicate that the talk they encompass was produced noticeably quicker than the surrounding talk.
< >	'Less than' and 'greater than' signs indicate that the talk they encompass was produced noticeably slower than the surrounding talk.

Transcription developed by Gail Jefferson, adapted from Hutchby & Wooffitt (1998).

"I Can Be With!"
A Novice Kindergartner's Successes and Challenges in Play Participation and the Development of Communicative Skills

Martha Sif Karrebæk

University of Copenhagen, Denmark

This chapter presents a longitudinal study of a 3-year-old kindergartener's participation in peer-group activities. The kindergartner had a minority language background and was a novice in the kindergarten community. The objective is to investigate this novice's competence as demonstrated by his use of resources, his possibilities for participation within activities, and his position in the peer-group community of practice. I illustrate the child's development through microanalysis of three examples within a 6-month period. I focus particularly on his strategies in the negotiation of play entry and play position, and I compare the outcomes of these negotiations. On the basis of the analyses, I conclude that the use of increased and more varied resources does not necessarily lead to greater access to central positions in the peer-group activities. As these positions constitute a part of the basis on which participation status within the community of practice (Lave & Wenger, 1991) is formed, they are to a large extent controlled by the oldtimers. Consequently, participation may depend on the opportunities offered by the oldtimers.

It is a widely held assumption that children learn language easily, effortlessly, and inevitably (Lightbown & Spada, 2003; Tabors, 1993; Wong-Fillmore, 1976). Also, it is believed that the linguistic and social development of children is best supported in peer groups in institutional settings. In Denmark, this viewpoint resulted in new legislation during the 1990s that aimed to ensure that linguistic minority children attend public kindergartens similar to those of the mainstream children (*The Folkeskole Act*, n.d.).[1] This legislation is highly controversial, however. We know very little about the linguistic environment in kindergartens and preschools (but see Aukrust, 2004; Ladegaard, 2004; Ladegaard & Bleses, 2003; Rydland & Aukrust, 2005), less about their sociolinguistic environment (but see Björk-Willén, 2007; Danby & Baker, 1998; Pallotti, 1996, 2001; Palludan, 2005), and particularly little about the sociolinguistic processes in the "classroom underlife" (Corsaro, 1990; Goffman, 1961) in kindergartens, that is, the so-called secondary adjustments performed by the children outside the attention of caretakers and teachers (but see Björk-Willén; Corsaro, 1979, 1988, 1990; Corsaro & Rizzo, 1990; Lerner & Zimmerman, 2003; Maynard, 1985, 1986). The following analyses are based on a longitudinal study of the communicative skill development and peer-group participation of a 3-year-old boy in this classroom underlife context. By "communicative skill development," I mean changes in linguistic as well as nonlinguistic socially directed actions and orientations, and by "peer-group participation," I mean the positions that the boy occupies in the participation framework (Goffman, 1981) of different play activities. This chapter primarily focuses on three exemplary episodes, but the particular cases are contextualized through ethnographic descriptions.

The peer-group-oriented approach adopted in this chapter does not suggest that adult-child interaction is considered less important. On the contrary, this study should help improve situations when adult caretakers have to intervene in counterproductive socialization processes within the peer group (cf. Toohey, 2000, 2001). However, the Danish kindergarten is regarded as a noneducational institution where free play is encouraged, and there is little explicit focus on teaching. Also, because there are many children per kindergarten teacher, the children spend much more time engaged in peer-group activities than with teachers. Because adult-child-interaction is often the more well-described type of child socialization (see also Kidwell, 2005; Kidwell & Zimmerman, 2006; Schegloff, 1989; Wootton, 1997), I have concentrated on the peer-group aspect of kindergarten life—with a complementary neglect of teacher-child interaction (see Blum-Kulka & Snow, 2004, and Hutchby, 2005, for additional references regarding studies on peer-group interaction).

In this chapter, I assume that the primary goal for a newcomer to the kindergarten is to play with the other children and ultimately to become a member of the community of practice (Lave & Wenger, 1991). For this to happen, the child needs to become a competent communicator, which represents a huge challenge for children, especially for those with fewer linguistic resources available in the dominant language such as second language learners (see Čekaite, 2007; Pallotti, 1996, 2001). My analyses of communicative skill development and participation substantiate the claim that for a newcomer to become a full member of the (kindergarten) community, he or she needs to acquire something other than linguistic structures (e.g., Brouwer & Wagner, 2004; Čekaite; Hellermann, 2007; Nguyen, 2006, 2008). Analyses of situated participation are necessary to determine the success of a particular course of development or socialization. He (2003) remarked that the process of socialization is often characterized as smooth and seamless, and the novices are presumed to be passive and ready recipients of socialization. However, she added that successful socialization cannot be accomplished without the co-construction of the novice, and, based on the data to be presented here, I argue that this includes the novice and experts or oldtimers agreeing on the possibilities and constraints for the novice status (see also Garrett & Baquedano-López, 2002; Kulick & Schieffelin, 2004). Furthermore, the oldtimers represent an important source of knowledge of what constitutes adequate participation—they are expert members—and in that position, they also are powerful gatekeepers to activities and to the entire community of practice. Thereby, generally inspired by the language socialization framework (Garrett & Baquedano-López; Kulick & Schieffelin; Ochs & Schieffelin, 1995; Schieffelin & Ochs, 1986; Watson-Gegeo & Nielsen, 2003), this chapter aligns itself with the few discourse studies on problematic socialization processes (e.g., Čekaite, 2007; M. Goodwin, 2006a; Toohey, 2000, 2001; Willett, 1995; Wong-Fillmore, 1976).

Participation, development, and learning

As mentioned above, I assume that a new kindergartner such as the child in this study normally wishes to become part of the social activities with the other children within the class community. To accomplish this, he or she needs to recognize, understand, and gain competence in both linguistic and nonlinguistic practices that are socially embedded. Also, he needs to (co-)construct the social reality that he is a part of and at the same time struggle to find a satisfactory position within it (cf. Garfinkel's 1984/1967 study on Agnes). This is the *double bind* of the second language learner (Tabors, 1993). Within the continuous stream of complex information, the novice must disentangle the essential from the coincidental on the background of discrete hints on what is appropriate, adequate, relevant, and so on. These hints come in the form of other participants' acknowledgments, recyclings, elaborations, or ignorance of the novice's initiatives, but they can only be interpreted with a certain amount of experience. In short, through participation, a child needs to learn the norms of participation.

Participation, however, is a complex phenomenon empirically, theoretically, and analytically. First, the communicative space in a kindergarten contains different types of relations between action, activity, and individuals. Activities are interwoven, and to orient in social space, kindergarteners need to draw on much more than physical proximity or linguistic signals. Notions such as *speaker* and *listener* are unfruitful reductions (Björk-Willén, 2007; Goffman, 1981; C. Goodwin, 1981; Goodwin & Goodwin, 2004) because social interaction incorporates signals in many modalities. Goffman's *participation framework* is a useful starting point, but at the same time, it is important to bear in mind that participant status is flexible and negotiable and that work done by participants other than the producer is also cognitively and interpretively complex (C. Goodwin, 2007; Goodwin & Goodwin).

Goodwin and Goodwin (2004) defined participation as "actions demonstrating forms of involvement performed by parties within evolving structures of talk" (p. 222). Further, C. Goodwin (2007) pointed out that "participants demonstrate their understanding of what each other is doing and the events they are engaged in together by building both vocal and nonvocal actions that help to further constitute those very same events" (p. 38), emphasizing the importance of nonverbal actions as well as the reflexive relationship between a recipient's conduct and the shape of the unfolding talk. Participation in this sense can be understood as also involving the more general, or abstract, social relations between individuals involved in communities. Competencies and practices, meanings and knowledge that the individual wishes to understand and acquire, are defined with respect to these communities, not only with respect to activities. Thus, learning and development are bound in and driven by social interaction and participation. In other words, learning and development themselves are social rather than individual phenomena (cf. Firth & Wagner, 1997; Ochs & Schieffelin, 1995; Rogoff, Paradise, Mejía Arauz, Correa-Chávez, & Angelillo, 2003; Wenger, 1998).

Insight from language socialization studies that suggests that one learns about the world within it and through participation (Schieffelin & Ochs, 1986) also constitutes the basis for the notion of *legitimate peripheral participation* (Lave & Wenger, 1991). Here, participation is regarded as happening within *communities of practice*, and membership is seen as an on-going process from the peripheral membership of the novice/newcomer to the full membership of the oldtimers/ experts. Peripheral members only participate in a subset of the community's entire repertoire; they master practices and skills to a lesser degree, and they are not seen as fully responsible for the final products. Yet, the novice is a member of the community of practice to the same degree as the expert (Wenger, 1998), and peripheral participation is socially accepted—or *legitimate*.

Learning takes place within communities, and it is about the gradually increasing access to different possibilities of participation (Wenger, 1998, p. 226*f*), which, in my view, can be reinterpreted as different positions within the community of practice. The process of learning or development of the novice depends on his access to the necessary and sufficient material and immaterial resources as well as his legitimate participation alongside the experts. It is important that the individual's development within the community (from peripheral to full participation) implies changes in relationships to all community members; newcomers become oldtimers with respect to other newcomers, who will probably become oldtimers eventually, and so on. This process of change is inevitable, and it is potentially destabilizing to the community. New members have to accept the premises of the community, and they need to understand the existing practices. In return, they can expect increasing access to the repertoire of and positions within the community. The demands and expectancies of the not-so-new novice will grow; he can expect more influence, and he can challenge the privileged positions of the oldtimers as experts and consequently, the existing shared repertoire of the community (Wenger). In that way, a community's reproductive processes can introduce tension between oldtimers and newcomers. However, if the knowledge of the newcomer never gets accepted as relevant, he may be marginalized, and he can even develop a nonparticipation identity (Wenger), which may make it harder for him to learn in that community of practice at all (Wenger). The presence of a community of practice, such as the group of kindergarteners in this study, should not be considered a warrant for successful learning or participation.

An important part of gaining increased participation in a community of practice is to be able to enter into ongoing activities of the community's members. In the next sections, I discuss the notion of entry negotiation in general and in child play in particular.

Entry negotiations

Becoming a ratified participant within a play activity is not a secured right. It is a privilege that may be obtained through strategic positioning and skilled interactional negotiations. Similarly to adults, children routinely protect their social activities from intruders, and this may result in extended and complex *entry negotiations* (Cromdal, 2001). The structure of entry negotiations is often rather rigid, fixed, and conventional, which enhances the impression of them as a sort of ritual practice as in Corsaro's (1979) *access rituals* (see also Goffman, 1981, 1982/1967; Rampton, 2009). Entry negotiations may even function as more general ways of negotiating social positions and relations.

Corsaro (1979) described 15 such ritual strategies that (American) preschoolers (2;10 to 4;10 years) used to obtain participation in social play activities. He also showed that some of these strategies were more efficient in enhancing the chances for getting accepted as a ratified participant. For instance, one strategy was the so-called *disruptive entry*, which refers to when a child enters into an area where other children are already engaged in interaction and then produces behaviour that disrupts the ongoing activity (Corsaro, p. 321). This was generally much less successful than if the child produced variants of ongoing behaviour (Corsaro, pp. 321, 324). Furthermore, the relative placement of strategies could also account for the degree of success. Initial attempts were, thus, often turned down, which then led to elaborate sequences of negotiations (see also, e.g., Björk-Willén, 2007; Corsaro & Rizzo, 1990; M. Goodwin, 2006a). With data from slightly older children (6 to 8;6 years) in a multilingual context, Cromdal (2001), in a conversation analytic study, nuanced Corsaro's conclusion by showing that the interactional process of entry negotiation is very much a "joint accomplishment between the party seeking entry and the party striving to protect the ongoing activity" (Cromdal, p. 517). The entire trajectory, as well as its outcome, is *co-constructed* (Jacoby & Ochs, 1995; see also Sawyer, 1997). Consequently, it is not only a question of the (relative) appropriateness or adequacy of the strategies used by the individual but just as much of what the child wishes to obtain, how the child makes this wish accessible to other children, and how it is received by the other children. Furthermore, all of this depends on the particular contextual circumstances. For instance, as Cromdal pointed out, if you want to play chess, and there are already two players, it is not easy to join the game, but if you want to participate in jump rope, you can much more easily obtain a position by the end of the twirling rope (see also Evaldsson & Corsaro, 1998; cf. M. Goodwin). Thus, in general, some activities are inherently easier to gain access to, and the same goes for some positions and play roles (Cromdal, p. 521*f*).

There is also a developmental reason for looking at entry negotiation. Recurrence of activities has been argued to help the newcomer factor out important communicative routines and practices, and the recurrence of entry negotiations may thus make it salient to the newcomer. Furthermore, entry negotiations often have a conventional or routinized structure, and routines are argued to provide a scaffold on which to build active contributions (cf. Ervin-Tripp, 1986; Kanagy, 1999; Wong-Fillmore, 1976). Because entry negotiation is essential to master in order to be made a participant, Cromdal (2001, p. 518) suggested that basic skills in this interactional sequence are acquired early in SLA, and although this is still an open question, we would at least expect entry negotiation to be an activity in which the kindergartner engages from early on and to the end of his kindergarten career. As such, entry negotiation is both a resource and a goal for language acquisition (Cromdal, p. 518) and an opportunity for learning that leads to other learning opportunities. In this chapter, I investigate how a kindergartener engaged in entry negotiation over time.

'To be with'

In the kindergarten class under study and in Danish play language in general, an important notion that needs some explanation is the expression *at være med* ('to be with'; see also Cromdal, 2001, on bilingual Swedish-English practices). This is the children's own idiomatic expression for participation, but it is an expression with significantly different content than the theoretical concept of participation. Theoretically, participation can be a question of degree. Goffman (1981) treated all individuals within hearing (or visual) range as participants, and for Lave and Wenger (1991), both more and less active members, both newcomers and oldtimers, are participants. However, when the children talk about 'being with,' it is only a matter of legitimate, ratified participation, and moreover, it is an either-or question. Explicit and verbal entry negotiation constitutes a high-risk activity, the result of which could have immense consequences for the immediate social situation. Explicit negotiation, therefore, does not necessarily constitute the strategically best way to gain access to peer-group activities, and there are, of course, also other ways to negotiate entry and to participate (cf. Corsaro, 1979; Cromdal). 'Being with' functions as a means of differentiation, delimiting ratified participants from nonratified participants, 'us' from 'them,' and player from nonplayer (Bateson, 2000). Because the categorizations of 'being with' or 'not being with' have implications for the child's rights and obligations with respect to an activity, they are of great moral as well as practical significance. For instance, once considered 'being with,' the child cannot be expelled from an activity without an explicit reason. I return to the subject of entry negotiation in a later section (for further discussion on these play-related aspects, see, e.g., Cromdal; Danby & Baker, 1998; M. Goodwin, 2006a; Sheldon, 1996).

In light of the discussion above, in this chapter, I follow C. Goodwin (2007) and define participation as *individuals' mutual positioning* within and across activities. Participation thus involves active social engagement—or interaction—as well as silent observation. It also involves individuals' engagement and positions within a particular activity as well as their overall type of membership in the community of practice. As for development, I adopt the following tripartite definition. Development is a general change in the *positions* available to an individual in the participation framework (cf. Čekaite, 2007; de Léon, 2000; Pallotti, 2001). A kindergartner may start out by watching the other children engaged in a board game, and then some time later, he gets to move the pawns as a ratified participant performing the actions within the activity. Also, development is a change in the *rights* that the individual is able to obtain within the activity (cf. Danby & Baker, 1998). The newcomer may be the baby in the family roleplay and later, as an expert, rise to become the father (this implies that the father position is more valued than that of the baby, which is often the case in children's play). Such changes are accompanied by increased obligations of living up to the community's norms and standards. Lastly, development concerns changes in the *resources* utilized by the individual (cf. Brouwer & Wagner, 2004; Lave & Wenger, 1991). It includes, for example, the appropriation of new resources to accomplish well-known tasks, as when the newcomer one day suddenly asks the playing peers if he "can be with" instead of merely watching their playing. It also refers to the use of old resources in new ways, as when the same newcomer refuses access to another newcomer by saying "you can't be with." Accordingly, I do not regard development as an individual, teleologic, unidirectional, and inevitable process. Rather, I look at how social order in play entry is co-constructed, how positions within play get assigned, and whether patterns of communicative behaviour in negotiation emerge and change over time.

Methodology

The data were collected over a 9-month period. The ethnographic part of my work took place in the kindergarten Around the World, which was located in a former working-class neighbourhood of Copenhagen, now inhabited by an ethnically mixed population. The 30+ kindergartners between 3 and 6 years came from a variety of ethnic and linguistic backgrounds. Only about half of them were ethnic Danes, and at least 10 different first languages were represented.

I video recorded the children in peer-group activities (primarily) during free playtime with a handheld digital video camera. Selected sequences of the approximately 33 hours of recordings were transcribed, a great deal of them in a broad CA standard (Schegloff, 2007), and the transcript of the verbally transmitted phenomena was enriched with relevant information on contextual and kinaesthetic details. The representations, however, still have a clear linguistic and verbal bias, primarily for reasons of accessibility and space.[2] Intervening turns that are not integrated in the interactions are omitted, no matter the degree of relevance and topic sharing with the interaction in focus. This is only done to ensure readability.

In contrast to similar studies such as those of Pallotti (1996, 2001), my focus was child-child interaction in free playtime. It turned out that the children engaged in a plethora of peer-group activities, from social roleplay to dancing, from drawing to playing board games, and few (if any) of the activities appear in all of the months. Also, the number of participants in the activities varied. The children played in groups, in dyads, or alone, and they frequently changed play partners. This diversity represents a challenge to the analyst with regard to the (lack of) comparability of data, and, to circumvent the issue, I have selected a number of episodes that are unmistakably socially oriented, child-centred, and focused. The examples in the following analysis are drawn from this selection.

Background: Around the world with Suliman

Suliman[3] was the only new child in the kindergarten Around the World in the spring when I started my field work (he had just entered the class 1 week before I came). He was 3 years and 4 months old, by far the youngest boy in the kindergarten. Suliman had a contagious smile, and he was well liked. His charming appearance surely secured him a good deal of positive attention (see Toohey, 2000, and Wong-Fillmore, 1976, on the relation between physical appearance and social position), and I felt very comfortable with him. His competence in Danish at that point was unclear,[4] but at least, I know that his entrance in Around the World was his debut in the official Danish educational system; he had not attended daycare or other child institutions before. Suliman's first language was Somali, although his mother said regretfully that none of her four children had a good command of it. Suliman was her youngest child. I never heard Suliman speak Somali during the recording period, although several other children in the class also had Somali as a mother tongue. In fact, in the beginning, he did not speak much at all, and when he did, it was usually in a very low voice; his turns were short and mostly composed of what appeared to be prefabricated chunks. In sum, Suliman was a novice regarding kindergarten life, and although he surely had some knowledge of Danish, he was also a novice regarding the use of Danish in an institutional setting.

Suliman had an older brother, Ibrahim, who also attended Around the World. At first, Suliman mostly followed Ibrahim around, recycling and shadowing (Björk-Willén, 2007) his movements in space, but after some time, Suliman got less reserved towards the other children. In particular, a group of older boys began to attract him. This group constituted a (sub) community of practice. The boys preferred to spend time with each other, they shared a set of (preferred) play practices, they adopted particular ways of speaking and acting, and they were particular about who could and who could not participate in their common activities. In this way, they kept other children at a physical and social distance. Ibrahim was not a (full) member of this community, and he rarely played with these boys, which had the consequence that at a point, Suliman had to choose between Ibrahim's company and that of the other boys. Suliman's choice fell on the boys' group, and consequently, he spent less and less time with his brother. The boys' community consisted of at least seven full members: Slavko, Abdo, Villads, Søren, Klaus, Yusuf, and Musse, who were between 4;4 and 5;7 years of age and thereby all considerably older than Suliman. The community had a clear social hierarchy. Abdo was the dominant boy whenever he was around. However, he often arrived much later than the other children or he spent time outside with one or two selected children[5] on the playground, and this occasioned power struggles between some of the other group members. Slavko positioned himself as the next in the power line, and during the frequent challenges, Villads would normally back him up. Although in the beginning, Suliman did not seem to have any playmate preference other than his brother, after his 3rd month, I never saw him seek to initiate or enter play activities with any children other than these boys. If he did engage in activities with other children, it would be a coincidence, a result of teacher-orchestrated play organization or of a particularly stubborn initiative of the other child.

Analysis

An emerging participant?

When entering kindergarten, a child becomes a kindergartner. This is merely an institutional predicate, though, and the newcomer has yet to find out how to impersonate the kindergartner persona appropriately. This includes finding out how adequate active participation is done. The first experiences are often acquired through active observation either from a distance (Saville-Troike, 1988; Tabors, 1993) or as a directly implied but noncentral participant in a shared endeavour by *intent participation* (Rogoff et al., 2003). A typical case is that the newcomer keeps silent (Lantolf & Thorne, 2006; Saville-Troike; Tabors & Snow, 1994), but silent participation in the form of 'active observation' is, of course, also participation.

Suliman was indeed silent during his first weeks in kindergarten. Often physically situated in the periphery of the other children's activities, he observed their engagement intensively. Suliman would sit at the table and watch two children play "memory." He would stay behind while a group gathered in front of the computer. With a short but noticeable delay, he would follow in the footsteps of the other children when they were chasing each other, often using the same movements, the same gestures. His unobtrusive behaviour had a linguistic parallel in that he rarely offered any linguistically performed bids that elaborated or substantiated the activities. In fact, Suliman spoke very little, and when he did (as judged by the movements of his lips), he was often not in the company of the other children, and his voice tended to be so low that it almost cannot be heard in the recordings. Nobody responded or reacted to these verbalizations. Nevertheless, Suliman seemed content and curious, and he was surely intensely focused on the other children. The first excerpt illustrates how Suliman discretely and indirectly suggested his engagement in a computer game. Aicha was in charge of the mouse, Canan and Ibrahim were sitting on either side of her, and behind them was Suliman. Seated at a table behind the computer group were Maimouna and Jette, the aide, who were primarily engaged in a drawing activity.

Excerpt 1 Computer game doodles (1st month). Participants: Ibrahim (5;1), Aicha (5;0), Suliman (3;2), Canan (5;4), Maimouna (6;3), Computer, Jette (adult aide)

```
01     ((Long silence. Only the computer voice and children
       elsewhere are heard. Aicha is playing, the others watch.))
02     Jet:   Canan¿ (.) du ka øve dig til skolen.
              Canan¿ (.) you can practice for school.
03     Aic:   ¹en to tre fire fem og seks. ((¹points on the screen,
              one beat for each number.))
              ¹one two three four five and six.
04            (1)
```

```
05  Mai:  det er dem der.
          it is them that.
06  Mai:  det er dem der skal hjem hvis man xxx.
          it is them that are going home if you xxx.
07  Can:  ²en to tre fire fem s:eks. ((²points on the screen,
          similar to Aicha; at the same time Suliman crawls up on the chair
          and down again.))
          ²one two three four five si:x.
08  Jet:  der ska hjem ⁄til dig, hvornår skal xx hjem
          til dig?
          that are going home ⁄to you, when are xx going
          home to you?
09         (4) ((only speech from the computer.))
10  Sul:  °mmmmm[mmmmmmmmmmm°. ((plaintive sound.))
11  Jet:        [når du har haft fødselsdag?
                [when it has been your birthday?
12  Sul:  ³j kan i:k se:. ((plaintive voice; ³turns around to the
                               table behind.))
          ³I ca:n't see:.
13  Jet:  ≈nå.
          ≈oh.
14  Com:  godt.
          good.
15  Com:  og nu hvor du har klaret seks spørgsmål (.)
          er tiden inde til at ↑gæ:[t↓te.
          and now when you have done six questions (.)
          time has come to      ↑gu:[↓es.
16  Jet:                              [hukhr. ((laughing))
17  Jet:  VED DU NOGET OM ANETTE HUN ER GÅET?
          DO YOU KNOW IF ANETTE SHE HAS LEFT?
18  Com:  [ved du hvad der er på billedet?
          [do you know what there is on the picture?
19  Jet:  [ER ANETTE GÅET MED TIL RYTMIK?
          [HAS ANETTE LEFT FOR EURYTHMICS WITH
          THE OTHERS?
20  Ibr:  ⁻nej. ((then takes his finger to the screen.))
          ⁻no.
21  Com:  det var svært.
          that was hard.
22         (1)
23  ((Ibrahim slowly takes his hand from the screen.))
24  Ibr:  tryk der.
          push there.
25  Ibr:  du sku trykke på øh [hunden].
          you needed to push on the eh [dog].
```

In the beginning of this excerpt, Maimouna and the adult aide, Jette, are sitting at a table behind the others. Maimouna is drawing; what Jette is doing is unknown. The rest of the children concentrate on the screen. Then, two parallel activities occur. First, Jette encourages Canan to "practice" (line 2), probably meaning to practice counting. This topic continues over a few turns. Aicha then responds on behalf of Canan (line 3), and a few seconds later, Canan follows as well (line 7). In the meantime, Jette asks Maimouna about something (line 8), and then everybody becomes silent again. Suliman does not demonstrate his engagement in the computer game until line 10, when, in a period of silence, he starts emitting a plaintive sound that seems to signal his dissatisfaction. In overlap with Suliman, Jette proposes a candidate answer to her question to Maimouna (line 11). When she reaches a possible completion point (Sacks, Schegloff, & Jefferson, 1974), Suliman turns around to face her (he is standing in front of the table where Jette and Maimouna are sitting) and says that he cannot see (line 12). Jette's next turn, "oh," (line 13) is not followed by any further action addressed toward Suliman (she then turns to another teacher in lines 17, 19) and on this account, Suliman did not succeed in getting Jette's attention. The other children also ignore Suliman and continue playing, all with active participation bids, illustrated by Ibrahim's advice to Aicha: "you needed to push on the eh dog" (line 25), and so on.

This excerpt shows, first, how these participants coordinate and adjust their turns at talk so that they fit both into the activity in which they are primarily engaged and into activities where they may be secondary participants. For instance, although there are two parallel activities in the excerpt, there are few overlaps. Both Maimouna, Canan, and Suliman seem to place their turns so that they have the best chance at getting attention, that is, at possible completion points or in conversationally dead (i.e., silent) periods. Second, the excerpt shows how computer games are often social activities, no matter how many participants the game is designed to accommodate. The primary player is, of course, the child in charge of the mouse (Aicha). The other children, however, may demonstrate their engagement actively. In the segment above, Jette selects Canan as a ratified participant, and Ibrahim gives advice to Aicha, the primary player. Further, children can demonstrate their involvement through physical positioning such as standing next to or very close to the primary player in charge of the mouse.

In this excerpt, Suliman is obviously interested in what the other children are doing. However, he fails to position himself as a ratified participant. Both Jette and the other children ignore his nonlinguistic complaint as well as the indirect speech act by means of which Suliman requests assistance to see the screen. Regarding his physical positioning, Suliman actually places his body in a very similar way as the other computer-game participants. His face is turned towards the screen, and he is only placed slightly further back in the room than some of the other participants. And yet, the other children (and the aide) treat these signs of engagement (physical positioning and sensitivity to turn-taking mechanism) as inadequate bids, and consequently, Suliman is positioned as an unratified spectator—or bystander. In this way, the example demonstrates that it actually takes experience and skills to position oneself as a ratified spectator in such activities as computer games.

I suggest that this has to do with both the focus and addressee of Suliman's only active linguistic turn. This turn did not contribute to or comment on the social centre of attention, that is, on the content of or action in the computer game, nor was it addressed to the other children. Suliman requested help from the adult aide, and by doing this, he actually treated the computer activity as organized and controlled by her rather than by the children themselves. Suliman did not negotiate entry to the activity, he did not contest the fact that he was ignored by the children, and he did not treat their ignoring as a moral injustice that a ratified participant would have every reason to do. Also, by not orienting towards the other children, Suliman did not give *them* reason to treat him as a ratified participant in the activity that they themselves treated primarily as child-directed and adult-independent.

On a broader level, I suggest that Excerpt 1 illustrates how, at this point, Suliman was not even a peripheral member of the community of practice. According to Wenger (1998), the newcomer or peripheral member does not have to live up to the standards of competent engagement, and he or she may stumble and violate norms without sanctions. However, my data suggest that even a newcomer, to be acknowledged by the community of practice, has to demonstrate knowledge and acceptance of certain norms, and not all bids for participation may therefore be successful. To ignore is to delete sequentially (He, 2003), and it is clearly a social act that indicates power and group alignment (cf. M. Goodwin, 2006a). Thus, by ignoring Suliman, the other children showed that he was not demonstrating the appropriate form of alignment to be positioned as a participant in their kindergarten community of practice.

Entry negotiation: How and why you can (or can't) get to 'be with'

For Suliman, the silent period phased out by the end of his 2nd month in the kindergarten. By then, he gradually sought more contact with the other kindergartners, and he did it more explicitly. He also clearly oriented towards the other children rather than towards the kindergarten teachers, and by doing that, he positioned himself as a potential participant. As the other children openly recognized his attempts to get accepted as a co-player, entry negotiation became an analytically relevant focus, and we now look at how Suliman engaged in entry negotiation. In the previous section, I described how Suliman was not necessarily orientated towards the peer-group activities with the agenda of becoming a ratified participant in the peer community, at least not from his first day. He was also ignored, and thereby positioned as a marginal member or an outsider. In the following excerpt, it is clear that Suliman's attitude has changed, although he has yet to gain confidence and competence in a more varied repertoire of practices relevant for negotiating entry. In Excerpt 2, three older boys, Villads, Slavko and Søren, have been engaged in a social activity for some time. In the beginning of the excerpt, they are playing "dentist." At the particular moment when Suliman arrives, Slavko and Villads are positioned on the floor, while Søren is standing by a shelf to their left.

Excerpt 2 Hood man (3rd month). Participants: Slavko (5;3), Søren (4;11), Villads (4;11), Suliman (3;4)

```
01   Sla:  SNART får du (0.5) en (0.5) tand¹pasta
           og noget andet. ((¹Suliman arrives, looks at Slavko and Villads.
           His hands are over his head on his hood.))
           SOON you are going to get (0.5) a (0.5)tooth¹paste
           and something else.
02   Sla:  ²og en parfume. ((²bends down over Villads.))
           ²and a perfume.
03   Sul:  [jeg har hue på.] ((to Søren; pointing to his hood.))
           [I have cap on.]
04   Vil:  [adv (.) mande]parfume. ((to Slavko.))
           [yuf (.) men's] perfume.
05   Sla:  [ja (.)] en mandeparfume. ((to Villads.))
           [yeah (.)] a men's perfume.
06   Sul:  [³jeg har hue på] °jeg har hue på°. ((³Suliman turns
           around and speaks to Søren who is walking towards Villads and Slavko.))
           [³I have cap on] °I have cap on°.
07   ((Søren is looking at Suliman, walks around him since Suliman is standing
       in his way. Suliman looks after Søren, then he follows.))
08   Vil:  ja (.) [°ik dameparfume°.] ((to Slavko.))
           yes (.) not women's perfume.
09   Sla:         [og og så] får du oss en.
           [and and then] you will get one as well.
10   ((Suliman walks directly towards Slavko, pads him slightly on his head.))
11   Sul:  jeg har en hue på hoved. ((touches his own head.))
           I have a cap on head.
12   ((Slavko lifts his head to look at Suliman, makes a fast but discrete movement
       with his left hand that waves Suliman away. Then his gaze turns back to Villads.))
```

When entering the room, Suliman fumbles with his hood. He gazes at Villads and Slavko on the floor; they are obviously deeply engaged in a shared endeavour. Then he turns around and sees Søren, whom he approaches with no further hesitation. Suliman says, "I have cap on" (line 3), but apparently, Søren does not respond. (He is not in focus of the camera, though.) Søren is going back to Slavko and Villads, and Suliman is in his way. When Søren gets closer, Suliman tries once more to catch his attention by repeating: "I have cap on" (line 6). The second attempt is probably provoked by Søren's initial lack of response, but it is only slightly more successful. Søren looks at Suliman but pushes him out of the way and then continues towards Slavko and Villads. Suliman gazes after Søren and follows after a slight delay, now with a new target: Slavko. Suliman integrates a supplementary resource in the attempt of getting Slavko's attention. He pats Slavko softly on the head, and when Slavko turns around to look, Suliman (partly) repeats for the third time, "I have a cap on head" (line 11). Slavko's response, however, is also in the negative. With his left hand, he briefly waves Suliman away while simultaneously changing his gaze back to Villads to resume their joint activity (lines 12).

In this excerpt, Suliman wants to engage in interaction. His strategies for getting attention are insistence (as when he uses repetition) and nonlinguistic acts such as patting Slavko's head and standing in Søren's way. These strategies do not prove to be successful, however. I suggest that this is because Suliman does not demonstrate any orientation towards the other children's meaning-making practices (cf. Cromdal, 2001). He does not compose his turns so that they build on prior ones and create coherence. He simply focuses on his own agenda. Because he does not take a starting point in the other children's interactive space (Corsaro, 1985), his turns are not interpreted as valid bids for entry. Furthermore, because his reason for interrupting is not sufficiently interesting for the other boys to give up their own project, he is treated as a nuisance, and they do not even give him linguistic replies or explicit accounts for their refusal. Consequently, Suliman is not positioned as a potential participant in the play activity.

After the final rejection in Excerpt 2, Suliman withdraws, but he stays in the periphery of the play arena from where he closely observes Slavko, Villads, and Søren. This strategy proves to be much more successful, and Suliman gets assigned the role of patient in the dentist activity. Villads is still a patient, lying on the floor, while the dentists (Søren and Slavko) sit on either side of him.

Excerpt 3 Medicine man (3rd month). Participants: Slavko (5;3), Søren (4;11); Villads (4;11); Suliman (3;4)

```
01      ((Suliman stands with his back against the wall and observes.))
02 Sla: n:u ska du ha me (.) ²memi⁻stin. ((²leans over Villads.))
        no:w you are going to have me (.) ²memi⁻stine.
                                                      ((= medicine.))
03 Vil: [adv] den prutter ma(ha)nd. ((giggling.))
        [yuf] it farts ma(ha)n.
04 Sla: [xx].
05 Sør: AHAH. ((=no.))
06 Sla: ne:j den prutter ik. ((sulkingly))
        no: it doesn't fart.
07 Vil: hehe.
08 Sla: ³hva for noget? ((³bends forward over Villads.))
        ³what?
```

```
09          (2.5)
10  Sør:    den gør sådan så du bliver rask.
            it does so that you will get well.
11  Sla:   SÅDAN HER [⁴Villads (.)] årh.  ((⁴takes his head back.))
           LIKE THIS [⁴Villads (.)] orh.
12  Sør:                [nu er du rask].
                        [now] you are well].
13  Sør:   nu er du rask.
           now you are well.
14         ((Villads gets up.))
15  Sla:   ⁵DU SKA DU SKA HA ⁶sådan [her].  ((⁵grabs Villads' arm; ⁶takes
                                              his head back, face up.))
           ⁵YOU ARE YOU ARE GOING TO HAVE ⁶like [this].
16  Sør:                               [Suliman] vil du være med?
                                       [Suliman] do you want
                                                      to be with?
17         ((Suliman takes his head back in a movement similar to the one Slavko did l. 11,15.))
18  Sul:   orh.  ((guttural sound.))
19         ((The boys start playing two by two: Suliman (patient) and Søren (dentist),
           Villads (patient) and Slavko (dentist).))
```

Søren and Slavko are working on Villads' teeth. Slavko is feeding Villads medicine through a plastic figurine that farts according to Villads (line 3). This move constitutes a threat to Slavko's (medical) authority because it implies that Slavko does not know serious matters (i.e., medication) from nonsense toys (i.e., a farting figurine), and Slavko responds accordingly when, in a sulking voice, he contradicts Villads (line 6). Søren aligns with Slavko as he explains that the medicine will make Villads well again (line 10), and then he announces twice, "now you are well" (lines 12, 13). But Søren's turn is sequentially deleted because Slavko is demonstrating to Villads how to hold his head when being given medicine (lines 11, 15). Søren is now a disposable participant, and to make himself relevant again, he has to find a new patient. He quickly tunes in on an obvious candidate player: Suliman. Suliman has been circling on tiptoe around the group after having been rejected several minutes earlier, doing what Corsaro (1979) calls *encirclement*. By this, Suliman demonstrates both that he is so eager to join that he can wait, and also, that in spite of his physical placement in the middle of the other children's play arena, he is competent enough not to disturb them. He can wait, and he can wait in silence. The efficacy of this strategy becomes visible when finally Søren invites Suliman to join (line 16). As a third indication of his play potential, Suliman produces his answer to Søren as an embodied recycling (or *shadowing*, according to Björk-Willén, 2007), that is, as a close variant of the head gesture that Slavko used earlier (lines 17). Producing variants of participants' actions is a well-recognized and efficient way of demonstrating alignment (Björk-Willén; Corsaro; Cromdal, 2001). Of course, Slavko did the head gesture to demonstrate appropriate patient behaviour to Villads, whereas in Suliman's interpretation, it resembles an exaggerated nod. We do not know if Suliman actually recognizes and exploits this ambiguity, but in the present context, his reply is clearly treated as meaningful; it creates coherence, and it demonstrates that he has been watching the activity closely.

In conclusion, in Excerpt 3, as Søren invites Suliman into the activity, he seems to consider Suliman's tenacity (i.e., that he remains in the vicinity) and his signs of interest (i.e., that he watches closely). Thus, by means of indirect although socially interpretable strategies, Suliman has managed to render probable his own play potential so that he finally gets to "be with."

Positions available for adequate bids (and appropriate kids!)

Not all negotiations are difficult. Activities may comprise positions that are relatively easy to obtain because they are considered less desirable. In jump rope, for instance, the newcomer normally gets to hold the twirling rope (Cromdal, 2001; Evaldsson & Corsaro, 1998), and similarly, in the excerpt above, Suliman was offered the position of patient, not that of doctor. Also, activities are not difficult to gain access to at all times. The child may even get invited to join one if there is considered to be an empty position. This was the case in Excerpt 3, when Søren found himself in need of a patient: He asked Suliman to join and become the patient. At other times, entry negotiation may be more difficult and interactionally complex. If a child wants to play chess, he or she naturally faces a more difficult task if there are already two players. Nevertheless, it is not impossible to get to touch the pawns even if others are already playing because all activities constrain but do not determine the participation structure and number of positions within a specific activity. This point was illustrated by Sheldon (1996) in an analysis of a family roleplay where a girl designated "the baby brother" fights for her right to be born and through this gets to materialize her play position. The size and composition of a family is negotiable and varies with the needs and wants of the participants, and often, it is as part of an entry negotiation that "roles" and positions get defined, assigned, and given content. In this way, entry negotiation may evolve into a negotiation of relative social positions in general (Sheldon). How the applicant is regarded by the other players is also of significance to the outcome of an entry negotiation. When Søren asked Suliman to become the patient, he demonstrated confidence in Suliman's play potential with regard to this position. I claimed this to be due to a felicitous entry negotiation on the part of Suliman. However, taking into account that Suliman was a verbally and interactionally inexperienced child and that he made use of simple and a limited number of resources, it is clearly also important that it requires relatively little to impersonate a patient, such as opening one's mouth and not biting the dentist.

These observations suggest that participation in social activities and ultimately in the community of practice depends on several factors. Skills isolated from social context do not provide a sufficient account. The observations regarding the degree of desirability of the position, the default interpretation of the activity, the number of empty slots, and the will to negotiate all point in that direction. Therefore, I claim that a competent entry negotiation at least implies that the child makes him- or herself stand out as an asset and a resource to the other children's activity. This normally requires demonstrating interest in and understanding of the social endeavour, and on seeing this, the other children can negotiate an interpretation of the activity in question that may make the entry applicant compatible. Also, there is at least one more aspect to consider. A bystanding child may not be allowed to be a father, a patient, or even a baby brother if this is at odds with other plans, including if the child is considered to be a danger to the interactive space or the social order in general. For a newcomer like Suliman, the social order comprises norms of legitimate peripheral participation. The special constraints to which the novice is subjected are not transparent, inherent, and fixed. However, oldtimers defend their powerful positions as experts, while newcomer-novices strive for increasing possibilities of participation. Disagreements about what it implies to be a novice may therefore emerge as may disagreements on whether a child is actually still a legitimate *peripheral* participant. Suliman's expectations of his own participation grew as he got more (kindergarten) experience. His expectations, though, did not grow at the same rate as the oldtimers' willingness to give him increasing access to positions. Suliman probably accepted the dominance of the oldtimers because he wanted to become a full member of the community, and the oldtimers, for their part, were also normally interested in his participation. Sometimes, there were simply no other children around to play with, but more importantly, the mere presence of Suliman confirmed their status as experts. The dilemma was, of course, that the transfer of powers to Suliman would mean a reduction of their own. In the following example from Suliman's 7th month, the resources he made use of were clearly more sophisticated and varied than before, and yet he was challenged by Slavko, one of the oldtimers. This challenge both regarded his participation status as ratified participant and also what this status implied. In other words, a conflict regarding possibilities for and constraints on participation emerged.

Suliman, Slavko, and Villads have been playing inside the playhouse. Slavko and Villads leave and ask Suliman to look after the house. Suliman understands this as an explicit ratification of his participation. Nevertheless, when Slavko returns, Suliman feels his status challenged. Suliman objects and asks for explicit acknowledgement.

Excerpt 4 "I can be with!" (7th month). Participants: Slavko (5;7), Suliman (3;8), MSK (researcher)

```
01  Sla:  wa::::har (.) Su:li:ma:n. ((talks in a scary voice,
           with increasing and decreasing intensity; enters the playhouse.))
02  Sla:  weduweduwaad. ((walks towards the kitchenette.))
03  Sla:  gi mig gi mi:g (.) gi mig den der.
           give me give me (.) give me that one.
04  Sla:  og gi mig gi mig (.) og læg den der.
           and give me give me (.) and put it over there.
05         ((something falls on the floor, Suliman covers his ears with his hands.))
06  Sla:  DET ER DIG DER xx. ((bends down and
                              talks directly into Suliman's face.))
           it is you that xx.
07  Sul:  jeg må være [med! ((takes his arms down.))
           I can be    [with!
08  Sla:              [nej. ((shakes his head once.))
                      [no
09  Sul:  nrrr. ((whining.))
10  Sla:  jo du må.
           yes you may.
11  Sul:  JO JEG MÅ. ((walks towards the door where there is more
                       kitchenware.))
           yes I may.
12  Sla:  du er (ik?) [min mor.
           you are (not?) [my mother.
13  Sul:               [godt!
                       [good!
14        ((Suliman, who is handing MSK a pan, turns to face Slavko.))
15  Sul:  JO.
           YES.
16  Sla:  nej.
           no.
17        ((Suliman turns back to MSK.))
18  Sla:  ne::j. ((whining.))
           no::.
19        ((Suliman turns around to Slavko again.))
20  Sul:  [du selv.
           [you self.
21  Sla:  [kra kra ((non-linguistic, unconventional, aggressive play sounds.))
22  Sul:  du sagde
           you said
23  Sla:  kra
24  Sul:  du sagde ne:j jo!
           you said no: yes!
25  Sla:  jo du gjorde.
           yes you did.
```

```
26    Sul:   du sagde ja jo.
             you said yes yes.
27    Sla:   hihi jah jo jo jo.  ((Slavko giggles, tickles Suliman
                                               under the chin.))
             hihi yeah yes yes yes.
28    Sla:   ihihihihi.
29    Sul:   jeg må være med!  ((looks at Slavko, lifts his one hand and
                                               touches him with it.))
             I can be with!
30           ((1.4))
31    Sla:   [°ne:j xx°.
             [°no: xx°.
32    Sul:   [jeg m[å JO  ((walks away from Slavko and slaps him with his hand))
             [I    c[an YES
33    Sla:          [°nej°.
                    [°no°.
34    Sul:   ≈JO!  ((slaps Slavko))
             ≈YES!
35    Sla:   nej.
             no.
36           ((0.9))
37           ((Suliman is leaving.))
38    Sla:   ↗JO DU MÅ JO DU MÅ JO DU MÅ (.) °kom° (0.9)
             sæt dig ned så.
             ↗YES YOU MAY YES YOU MAY YES YOU MAY (.) °come°
             (0.9) sit down then.
39           ((Slavko gets hold of Suliman on the first part, nods lightly; Suliman returns.))
```

The entry negotiation demonstrated in Excerpt 4 is atypical in that the first child on the play arena, Suliman, is the one who feels in need of negotiating his play legitimacy. Slavko, who enters last, is behaving provocatively and aggressively. He issues orders (lines 3, 4), talks in a scary voice (lines 1–6, 21, 23), issues incomprehensible threats or accusations (line 6), answers linguistically performed actions with nonsense (lines 21, 23, 25, 27), and by that he simulates noncomprehension of Suliman. In that way, Slavko makes Suliman's actions appear irrelevant and ridiculous. Suliman, for his part, does not accept this as acceptable behaviour. He opposes Slavko by referring to the fact that originally it was Slavko who ratified Suliman's participation (lines 20, 22, 24); it is against kindergarten morals to grant access and then deny it without any explanation. The rather rudimentary oppositional routines, or *argument recycling* (M. Goodwin, 2006b), in lines 7–10, 15–18, and 24–38, illustrate Suliman's tenacity as well as his competence within this culturally prevalent practice. Finally, Suliman gives up and is about to leave when suddenly Slavko exclaims: "yes you may yes you may yes you may (.) come" (line 38). Suliman complies and returns.

In this excerpt, Suliman has obviously changed from an inexperienced and reserved newcomer into a more confident child with a more varied repertoire. He demonstrates his competence by engaging in oppositional sequences, and he can now both insist and elaborate on his own point of view. With respect to kindergarten norms and values, the insistence on his right 'to be with' orients to the norm that even oldtimers cannot expel anybody from an activity in which he is a legitimate participant—at least not without giving an account. Furthermore, it makes it worse and even immoral when the opposing child was the one who originally ratified the other's 'being with,' as indicated by Suliman's use of the second-person singular pronoun "you" and the emphasized "self." However, Slavko's behaviour is not easily interpreted. On the one hand, he is aggressive, insisting, and even apparently about to cry (line 18), which signals that this is serious business. On the other hand, he changes footing (Goffman, 1981) by giggling (line 27), making funny noises (lines 1, 2, 21, 23), and having a cooperative playful attitude, for example, tickling Suliman (line 27), which signals "this is play" (Bateson, 2000). Furthermore, Slavko apparently shifts his stance between refusing (lines 8, 16, 18, 31, 33, 35) and granting Suliman access (lines 10, 27, 38). Whether Slavko does or does not see his actions as immoral, he seems to strive for Suliman's acknowledgment of him as an authority. This, however, Suliman continues to challenge. It is first when Suliman finally complies and turns around to leave that Slavko provides Suliman with an explicit acknowledgment token and an invitation to "come and sit down," perhaps as a way of asserting his authority.

In the above excerpt, Suliman's play participation was (finally) ratified and with that, his position among the ratified participants of the activity. However, the power hierarchy within the activity as well as outside it became demarcated; Suliman was clearly inferior to Slavko. By accepting to leave, Suliman established Slavko's right to decide who was and who was not a ratified participant, and when he returned, Suliman once more validated Slavko's authority as the one who was in charge of defining the play activity, the play roles of the participants, and what counted as legitimate actions. This observation is confirmed in the following excerpt, which occurs shortly after the previous one. Suliman is sitting on the bench as Slavko has told him to do while Slavko is walking around in the playhouse, talking to himself (at least, he does not wait for any responses). Suliman has been following Slavko with his eyes, but he does not take any initiatives, and thereby, he gives the impression that he is waiting for Slavko to include him more actively in the activity. Right before the excerpt, he has risen from the bench, but no invitation to participate came, and he is now seated again. Then, Slavko brings some plates to the table.

Excerpt 5 "It is really hot" (7th month). Participants: Suliman, Slavko, Villads, Uni=Unidentified

```
01  Sla:  se her.
          look here.
02  ((Slavko puts a plate on the table and pushes it past Suliman.))
03  Sul:  det er min ¹tal[lerken,  ((¹gets up and grabs the plate.))
          this is my ¹pla[te.
04  Sla:                [NE²J.  ((²takes the plate away.))
                        [N²O.
05  ((Suliman sits down, and Slavko puts plate back on table.))
06  Sla:  ³jeg laver ↑lige (.) ↓tallerkenerne klar. ((³laying th
          table with the rest of the plates, and continues for the next
          couple of turns.))
          ³I am just ↑going to make (.) ↓the plates ready.
07        (1)
08  Sla:  væk (.) det er xxs, (.) ↗det er din.
          away/gone (.) this is xxs, (.) ↗this is yours.
09  Sul:  det her [det er min.
          this one is [this is mine.
10  Sla:          [og den er Villads.
                  [and this is Villads'.
11  Uni:  nej.
          no.
12  ((Slavko puts the plate back under the stack.))
13  Sla:  her ta.
          here take.
14  Sla:  ⁴du har fået den her. ((⁴continuing laying the table.))
          ⁴you have got this one.
15  Sla:  °her°.
          °here°.
16        (11)
17  ((Slavko walks around inside the house, apparently he has finished putting the
    plates on the table; Suliman is sitting waiting on the bench.))
18  Sla:  ⁵VILLADS VI LAVER MAD. ((⁵walking around the house, Suliman
                                       still on the bench.))
          ⁵VILLADS WE ARE COOKING.
19  Vil:  OKAY.
20  Sul:  NU ER DEN ⁶VARM NU ER DET RIGTIG VARME. ((⁶gets up,
                                       walks towards Slavko.))
          NOW IT IS ⁶HO:T NOW IT IS REALLY HOT.
21  Sul:  ⁷DEN ER ⁸RIGTIG VARM. ((⁷stands on Slavko's right side;
          ⁸Slavko puts a fried egg on the pan, he doesn't look at Suliman.))
          ⁷IT IS ⁸REALLY HOT.
22  Sul:  den er rigtig ⁹varm. ((⁹one beat with his left hand.))
          it is really hot.
23  Sul:  den er rigtig va:rm?
          it is really ho:t?
```

"I can be with!" A novice kindergartner's successes and challenges 349

```
24     ((Slavko makes a beat with his left hand as to wave Suliman away, he is still
       looking at the pan.))
25 Sul: DEN ER RIGTIG VARM (.) denne her.
           ((points to the fried egg.))
           IT IS REALLY HOT (.) this one.
26     ((Suliman takes the pan of the kitchenette.))
27 Sla: NEJ SULIMAN. ((turns shortly towards Suliman and then continues
       towards the corner where he remains.))
       NO SULIMAN.
28     ((Suliman starts putting back the pan on the kitchenette.))
29 Sla: det er mig der laver mad.
       it is me who is cooking.
```

When this excerpt begins, Slavko is laying the table and cooking. He talks to himself while Suliman observes from the bench. Suliman is not integrated into the activity at all. After a while, Slavko brings some plates to the table and accompanies this nonlinguistic action with a linguistic directive: "look here" (line 1). Suliman responds to this as an invitation to participate more actively in that he gets up, takes a plate, and exclaims that it is his (line 3). Slavko, however, shouts "no" (line 4), demonstrating that he did not seem to have envisaged anything else for Suliman to do besides "looking." Suliman sits down again and waits with an impatient look. Again he uses a plate as an entrance ticket when he for a second time grabs one and says that it is his (line 9). This plate can be seen as a reification of the play activity, and it has a metonymic relation to active participation. Ownership of a plate equals ownership of a more central play role or position. However, linguistically, Suliman seems to be ignored, and nonlinguistically, Slavko refuses his attempt by taking the plate and putting it back in the stack. Suliman waits for a while, but Slavko does not issue any invitations to him. In contrast, he shouts to his friend Villads, who is engaged in a similar activity just outside the house. After a while, Suliman gets up, this time equipped with a new idea: he walks towards the kitchenette while repeating "now it is hot," with variations in wording and pronunciation (lines 20–25). This sounds like a competent move. The theme that something is hot is semantically connected to the cooking situation. The information is also pragmatically relevant in that if something is hot, you need to be careful, and if you do not know that it is hot, you need to be told. As such, it can be understood as a warning to Slavko. Sequentially, a warning can appear anywhere and does not need an introduction or a first pair part. In this way, Suliman contributes with new content to the activity at the same time as he establishes cohesive links within the activity. Linguistically, *"den er varm"* ("it is hot") is a formula that Suliman is likely to know from kitchen and eating situations in the kindergarten. In this way, Suliman deploys what may be a prefabricated linguistic chunk to assume a more active role. The chunk helps him to express semantically and pragmatically relevant information in a sequentially relevant way, and he has good reason to believe that his contribution is adequate. Slavko reacts differently, though. He ignores Suliman until after the fifth repetition where he finally shouts: "no Suliman" (line 27). Suliman puts back the pan and sits down.

This excerpt illustrates some of the many types of ratified participation. The differences between the rights Slavko and Suliman can claim are striking, and this has consequences. It also illustrates the eternal conflict between the child's expectations of his own opportunities for participation, on the one hand, and on the other, the possibilities that are ratified by the other children. Slavko was not orienting towards the activity as co-constructed, and in spite of several attempts, Suliman never got to participate in the active practice and development of the roleplay activity, and his attempts were turned down in an unmitigated way. Suliman actually did not get to participate in a constructive and active way; his attempts were refused very directly. This makes a stark contrast to the former, excerpt where Suliman reacted rather aggressively upon the questioning of his legitimacy and position. Thus, the question is, what is the difference between the two situations? One possible difference is that in the first episode, Suliman felt morally offended. Slavko and Villads had given him reason to consider himself a legitimate and ratified participant, and there was no reason for this legitimacy to be withdrawn. Slavko's questioning therefore appeared to be a principal injustice. At the same time, Suliman did not demonstrate an understanding that ratified participation may also include active interpretation, elaboration, and negotiation of the play activity. Suliman did not challenge the fact that Slavko refused his (Suliman's) apparently relevant and adequate bids with no justification or account, which suggests that Suliman actually regarded Slavko as being entitled to define Suliman's rights and possibilities of action. There may be various reasons for this. It could be because Slavko was more active in the making and initiation of play activities, but it could also be because Suliman was the newest member of the kindergarten community of practice.

To sum up, Excerpts 4 and 5 illustrate only partly successful entry negotiation. Although the child finally obtained explicitly ratified participation, it was unsuccessful in that he never fulfilled his expectations to be a member with more rights. The lack of success stands out on the background of the child's increased potential in play, judged on the basis of a social orientation and communicative flexibility, his social orientation, and his communicative flexibility.

The complex processes of development among kindergartners (and other human beings)

Children participate in play activities in very different ways. Some of these mean that they actively and cooperatively create, develop, and consolidate the activities and that their interpretations of the frame are treated as legitimate. For others, 'to be with' is essentially about submitting to a social and interactional order that is mostly defined and developed by other children. These children need to demonstrate competence on the others' premises with little influence on frame or content. As remarked by Norton (1995), it is not so that "language learners can choose under what conditions they will interact with members of the target language community and that the language learner's access to the target language community is a function of the language learner's motivation" (p. 12). Suliman was subjected to an apparently predefined power hierarchy, and despite his motivation and investment in the community of practice, he never obtained a central position in this, at least during the time of data collection of this study.

I propose that we include the following angles in our understanding of participation in the kindergarten. First of all, participation is about obtaining status as ratified participants within activities. The ease with which such status is obtained depends on several factors. First, it depends on the activity type and its current interpretation by players. Suliman was only asked to join the dentist activity in Excerpts 2 (Hood man) and 3 (Medicine man) when an empty position emerged—that of the patient. This, of course, only occurred after his engagement in extended entry negotiation, but I suggest that this entry negotiation actually became possible only after he had been positioned as a potential participant, that is, as a novice. The bids of a mere newcomer, not yet anchored or positioned with respect to the community of practice, would not necessarily be interpreted as a bid for entrance (contrast Excerpt 1, where Suliman did not become a participant, with Excerpt 3, where he did), and his attempts at communicating needs, wants, ideas, and so on would not be considered relevant but be ignored (e.g., Excerpt 1, where Suliman did not even succeed in getting a better view).

A different angle on participation concerns the rights to engage actively in the creation, elaboration, and consolidation of a social activity. As illustrated in Excerpt 5 ("It is really hot"), ratified participant status does not guarantee having such rights, although it constitutes a precondition for it. Active participation is a continuous negotiation and a practical achievement (Cromdal, 2001) in social interaction, but the difference between participants' possibilities of action (their "play rights") and opportunities of success when negotiating is not coincidental. It is, on the contrary, related to the expectations that members of a community of practice may have regarding their own and others' positions. In Excerpts 4 ("I can be with!") and 5 ("It is really hot"), Slavko's actions indicated that he expected to be the dominant part in relation to Suliman and that he expected Suliman to be submissive. After an initial struggle to emphasize his legitimacy within the activity and his attempts at materializing his play potential, Suliman actually validated Slavko's expectations regarding the distribution of power and submitted to the social order by accepting the position pointed out by Slavko. And thus, the two boys continued to co-construct their unequal power relations.

As for the other main focus of this study, Suliman's development, I have shown that his competence within entry negotiation surely increased over the months. In the beginning, he mostly focused on his own agenda, and when he overcame that perspective, he also entered into genuine negotiations. His initial communicative strategies were mostly nonverbal, indirect, and unobtrusive, and he left the initiative to the other children. In the latter recordings, however, Suliman demonstrated a social orientation and sensitivity from the beginning. His repertoire of communicative resources had increased, and now it comprised a variety of linguistic and nonlinguistic resources that he used flexibly to try to position himself as a competent kindergartner and co-player.

In the few illustrative examples presented here, we saw that Suliman apparently became more communicatively confident and competent over the course of the months, but in terms of integration within the community, the development was not equally successful. He changed his status from nonintegrated to peripheral member to more central member, but then back to peripheral member again. Although Suliman was never a talkative child, he did at some point start to talk more (seen in the contrast between Excerpts 1–3 and Excerpts 4–5). However, this did not give him access to more positions or to more powerful positions within the peer community, as illustrated in Excerpt 5. This picture got even clearer in the months following the excerpts presented. Suliman talked less and less, and when he spoke, his linguistic contributions were simple and chunk-like. He also gradually approached the other boys less. He did not enter into complex rounds of negotiations, but withdrew from the boys' community of practice. His attempts on initiating social contact with peers consisted of yanking the girls' hair and so on, which got him into numerous conflicts. When I finished my recordings, Suliman was less, rather than more, centrally placed in the group of kindergarten boys. It seems evident that there existed a relation between Suliman's lack of success within the peer group and his gradually more sparse use of language. This case suggests that different expectations from participants involved in a process of language socialization can bring about frustration (cf. He, 2003). This in turn may have negative consequences for the novice. This is one more reason that language socialization is not a unidirectional process (see Garrett & Baquedano-López, 2002; Kulick & Schieffelin, 2004). Although we cannot be certain about all the reasons behind it, we do know from the excerpts shown in this chapter that to percolate from peripheral member to central member within a community of practice, it is not sufficient to get acquainted with and master the interactional structures and socioculturally important activities. Obviously, increased communicative resources are not necessarily followed by increased possibilities of participation.

My admittedly partial description of Suliman's development thus suggests that his course of development was not entirely successful during the period of my observation. If I had collected further data, the picture might have been different, of course, and Suliman might finally have become a successful kindergartner. But development is a never-ending process, and the possible picture of Suliman as a successful kindergartner could also be replaced later by one of Suliman as an unsuccessful 1st grader, 5th grader, or high school drop-out. This study shows that even in kindergarten, complex social processes heavily influence the life of the individual, and once more, we have seen that language acquisition and communicative skill development are complex processes. There is no guarantee that development goes from periphery to centre, from bystander to ratified participant, from incompetent and unintegrated to competent and integrated. This becomes very obvious when we consider situated development rather than isolated skills. When we talk about peer-group play activities as a potential space for development and learning, it is important to consider the mutual expectations and positions of the children and how they handle them. Inspired by Norton (1995), I conclude that we cannot take for granted that those who speak regard those who listen as worthy to do anything but listen. The oldtimers and experts may actually represent an obstacle to the learning and development of the newcomer, novice, and language learner. When Suliman did not want to be the passive patient or mere observer of the other boys anymore, they did not seem to have room for him in the play activities. Ratified participant or not, there was no position available in this case. Suliman's position could not change any further, probably because this would imply that the relative positions of the others might also change. If Suliman's rights increased, by the same token, the rights of the others might decrease. As demonstrated, Slavko did not seem to be interested in that (see also, e.g., Myers, 2005).

Some of the findings presented in this chapter may appear particular to children. This is accentuated by the focus on play. However, a new kindergartner faces challenges comparable to those of newcomers to other kinds of communities of practice such as getting acquainted with culturally valued practices and relevant and necessary skills, gaining experience with and confidence in them, and finding a way to be positioned as a competent and full member of the community. Suliman is, I believe, in several respects, not different from the minority women described by Norton (1995). I show that it demands much more than linguistic competence for a child to engage in interaction with other children, an observation paralleled by findings in other areas (e.g., Čekaite, 2007; C. Goodwin & M. Goodwin, 2004; Hellermann, 2007; Mondada & Pekarek Doehler, 2004). Finally, there is reason to believe that some forms of negotiation remain relatively invariant across age (cf. Maynard, 1986). Thus, this study offers general insight into possible processes of socialization and development. Suliman's increasing difficulties with successful participation represent a possible course of events. It demonstrates that it is not enough for the newcomer to acquire certain skills and structurally defined phenomena to become a full member of the (kindergarten) community. One more important precondition for this to take place is that the oldtimers of the community of practice have the incentive to accept the newcomer. Language use and socialization processes among preschoolers can be anything but simple, unidirectional, and inevitably successful.

Notes

1. An alternative possibility is that the linguistic minority child, if found in need of it, receives extensive 'language stimulation' outside kindergarten.
2. The issue of representation, representation of child interaction, and not the least, representation of second language child interaction, is an important subject that I cannot develop here; for further discussion, see, for example, the work of Bucholtz (2000, 2007), Fine (1984), Hamo & Blum-Kulka (2004), Mishler (1991), and Ochs (1979).
3. Suliman is, as are all participant names, a pseudonym.
4. I did not subject him to any formal language test because I suspected that it would complicate his relations both to me and to the other children.
5. The oldest children could obtain permission to go outside, without adult supervision, alone or in small groups of two or three. At times, the kindergarten teachers even encouraged the more physically active and challenging children to do that. Abdo could be considered such a challenging child.

References

Aukrust, V. G. (2004). Explanatory discourse in young second language learners' peer play. *Discourse Studies, 6*, 393–412.

Bateson, G. (2000). *Steps to an ecology of mind: Collected essays in anthropology, psychiatry, evolution and epistemology*. Chicago: University of Chicago Press. (Original work published 1972)

Björk-Willén, P. (2007). Participation in multilingual preschool play: Shadowing and crossing as interactional resources. *Journal of Pragmatics, 39*, 2133–2158.

Blum-Kulka, S., & Snow, C. (2004). Introduction: The potential of peer talk. *Discourse Studies, 6*, 291–306.

Brouwer, C. E., & Wagner, J. (2004). Developmental issues in second language conversation. *Journal of Applied Linguistics, 1*, 29–47.

Bucholtz, M. (2000). The politics of transcription. *Journal of Pragmatics, 32*, 1439–1465.

Bucholtz, M. (2007). Variation in transcription. *Discourse Studies, 9*, 784–808.

Čekaite, A. (2007). A child's development of interactional competence in a Swedish L2 classroom. *The Modern Language Journal, 91*, 45–62.

Corsaro, W. (1979). "We're friends, right?" Children's use of access rituals in a nursery school. *Language in Society, 8*, 315–336.

Corsaro, W. (1985). *Friendship and peer culture in the early years*. Norwood, NJ: Ablex.

Corsaro, W. (1988). Routines in the peer culture of American and Italian nursery school children. *Sociology of Education, 61*, 1–14.

Corsaro, W. (1990). The underlife of nursery school: Young children's social representations of adult rules. In G. Duveen & B. Lloyd (Eds.), *Social representations and the development of knowledge* (pp. 11–26). Cambridge, England: Cambridge University Press.

Corsaro, W., & Rizzo, T. (1990). Disputes in the peer culture of American and Italian nursery school children. In A. Grimshaw (Ed.), *Conflict talk* (pp. 21–66). New York: Cambridge University Press.

Cromdal, J. (2001). Can I be with?: Negotiating play entry in a bilingual school. *Journal of Pragmatics, 33*, 515–543.

Danby, S., & Baker, C. (1998). How to be masculine in the block area. *Childhood, 5*, 151–175.

de Léon, L. (2000). The emergent participant: Interactive patterns in the socialization of Tzotzil (Mayan) infants. *Journal of Linguistic Anthropology, 8*, 131–161.

Ervin-Tripp, S. (1986). Activity structure as scaffolding for children's second language learning. In J. Cook-Gumperz, W. Corsaro, & J. Streeck (Eds.), *Children's worlds and children's language* (pp. 337–366). Berlin: Mouton de Gruyter.

Evaldsson, A. C., & Corsaro, W. (1998). Play and games in the peer cultures of preschool and preadolescent children: An interpretative approach. *Childhood, 5*, 377–402.

Fine, E. (1984). *The folklore text: From performance to print*. Bloomington & Indianapolis: Indiana University Press.

Firth, A. & Wagner, J. (1997). On discourse, communication, and (some) fundamental concepts in SLA research. *The Modern Language Journal, 81*, 285–296.

Garfinkel, H. (1984/1967). *Studies in ethnomethodology*. Malden, MA: Polity Press/ Blackwell Publishing.

Garrett, P., & Baquedano-López, P. (2002). Language socialization: Reproduction and continuity, transformation and change. *Annual Review of Anthropology, 31*, 339–361.

Goffman, E. (1961). *Asylums: Essays on the social situation of mental patients and other inmates*. New York: Anchor Books.

Goffman, E. (1981). *Forms of talk*. Philadelphia: University of Pennsylvania Press.

Goffman, E. (1982). *Interaction ritual: Essays on face-to-face behavior*. New York: Pantheon. (Original work published 1967)

Goodwin, C. (1981). *Conversational organization: Interaction between speakers and hearers*. New York: Academic Press.

Goodwin, C. (2007). Interactive footing. In E. Holt & R. Clift (Eds.), *Reporting talk: Reported speech in interaction* (pp. 16–46). Cambridge, England: Cambridge University Press.

Goodwin, C., & Goodwin, M. H. (2004). Participation. In A. Duranti (Ed.), *A companion to linguistic anthropology* (pp. 222–244). Cambridge, England: Blackwell.

Goodwin, M. H. (2006a). *The hidden life of girls: Games of stance, status, and exclusion*. Malden, MA: Blackwell.

Goodwin, M. H. (2006b). Participation, affect, and trajectory in family directive/response sequences. *Text & Talk, 26*, 513–541.
Hamo, M., & Blum-Kulka, S. (2004). From observation to transcription and back: Theory, practice, and interpretation in the analysis of children's naturally occurring discourse. *Research on Language and Social Interaction, 37*, 71–92.
He, A. W. (2003). Novices and their speech roles in Chinese heritage language classes. In In R. Bayley & S. Schecter (Eds.), *Language socialization in bilingual and multilingual societies* (pp. 128–146). Clevedon, England: Multilingual Matters.
Hellermann, J. (2007). The development of practices for action in classroom dyadic interaction: Focus on task openings. *The Modern Language Journal, 91*, 83–96.
Hutchby, I. (2005). Children's talk and social competence. *Children & Society, 19*, 66–73.
Jacoby, S., & Ochs, E. (1995). Co-construction: An introduction. *Research on Language and Social Interaction, 28*, 171–183.
Kanagy, R. (1999). Interactional routines as a mechanism for L2 acquisition and socialization in an immersion context. *Journal of Pragmatics, 31*, 1467–1492.
Kidwell, M. (2005). Gaze as social control: How very young children differentiate "the look" from a "mere look" by their adult caregivers. *Research on Language and Social Interaction, 38*, 417–449.
Kidwell, M., & Zimmerman, D. (2006). "Observability" in the interactions of very young children. *Communication Monographs, 73*, 1–28.
Kulick, D., & Schieffelin, B. (2004). Language socialization. In A. Duranti (Ed.), *A companion to linguistic anthropology* (pp. 349–368). Malden, MA: Blackwell.
Ladegaard, H. J. (2004). Politeness in young children's speech: Context, peer group influence and pragmatic competence. *Journal of Pragmatics, 36*, 2003–2022.
Ladegaard, H. J., & Bleses, D. (2003). Gender differences in young children's speech: The acquisition of sociolinguistic competence. *International Journal of Applied Linguistics, 13*, 222–233.
Lantolf, J. P., & Thorne, S. L. (2006). *Sociocultural theory and the genesis of second language*. Oxford, England: Oxford University Press.
Lave, J., & Wenger, E. (1991). *Situated learning: Legitimate peripheral participation*. Cambridge, England: Cambridge University Press.
Lerner, G., & Zimmerman, D. (2003). Action and the appearance of action in the conduct of very young children. In P. Glenn, C. LeBaron, & J. Mandelbaum (Eds.), *Studies in language and social interaction* (pp. 441–457). Mahwah, NJ: Lawrence Erlbaum.
Lightbown, P. M., & Spada, N. (2003). *How languages are learned* (2nd ed.). Oxford, England: Oxford University Press.
Maynard, D. (1985). On the functions of social conflict among children. *American Sociological Review, 50*, 207–223.
Maynard, D. (1986). Offering and soliciting collaboration in multi-party disputes among children (and other humans). *Human Studies, 9*, 261–285.
Mishler, E. G. (1991). Representing discourse: The rhetoric of transcription. *Journal of Narrative and Life History, 1*, 255–280.

Mondada, L., & Pekarek Doehler, S. (2004). Second language acquisition as situated practice: Task accomplishment in the French second language classroom. *The Modern Language Journal, 88*, 501–518.

Myers, G. (2005). Communities of practice, risk, and Sellafield. In D. Barton & K. Tusting (Eds.), *Beyond communities of practice: Language, power, and social context* (pp. 198–213). Cambridge, England: Cambridge University Press.

Nguyen, H. t. (2006). Constructing 'expertness': A novice pharmacist's development of interactional competence in patient consultations. *Communication & Medicine, 3*, 147–160.

Nguyen, H. t. (2008). Sequence organization as local and longitudinal achievement. *Text & Talk, 28*, 501–528.

Norton Peirce, B. (1995). Social identity, investment, and language learning. *TESOL Quarterly, 29*, 9–31.

Ochs, E. (1979). Transcription as theory. In E. Ochs & B. Schieffelin (Eds.), *Developmental pragmatics* (pp. 43–72). New York: Academic Press.

Ochs, E., & Schieffelin, B. (1995). The impact of language socialization on grammatical development. In P. Fletcher & B. MacWhinney (Eds.), *The handbook of child language* (pp. 73–94). Maldon, England: Blackwell.

Pallotti, G. (1996). Towards an ecology of second language acquisition: SLA as a socialization process. *EUROSLA, 2*, 121–134.

Pallotti, G. (2001). External appropriations as a strategy for participating in intercultural multi-party conversations. In A. Di Luzio, S. Günther, & F. Orletti (Eds.), *Culture in communication* (pp. 297–334). Amsterdam: Benjamins.

Palludan, C. (2005). *Børnehaven gør en forskel: Et pædagogisk-antropologisk perspektiv på sproglige differentieringsprocesser* [Kindergarten makes a difference: A pedagogical-anthropological perspective on linguistic differentiation processes]. Unpublished doctoral dissertation, København, Denmark: Danmarks Pædagogiske Universitet.

Rampton, B. (2009). Interaction ritual and not just artful performance in crossing and stylization. *Language in Society, 38*, 149–176.

Rogoff, B., Paradise, R., Mejía Arauz, R., Correa-Chávez, M., & Angelillo, C. (2003). Firsthand learning through intent participation. *Annual Review of Psychology, 54*, 175–203.

Rydland, V., & Aukrust, V. G. (2005). Lexical repetition in second language learners' peer play interaction. *Language Learning, 54*, 229–274.

Sacks, H., Schegloff, E., & Jefferson, G. (1974). A simplest systematics for the organization of turn-taking for conversation. *Language, 50*, 696–735.

Saville-Troike, M. (1988). Private speech: Evidence for second language learning strategies during the 'silent period.' *Journal of Child Language, 15*, 567–590.

Sawyer, R. K. (1997). *Pretend play as improvisation: Conversations in the preschool classroom.* Mahwah, NJ: Lawrence Erlbaum.

Schegloff, E. A. (1989). Reflections on language, development, and the interactional character of talk-in-interaction. In M. H. Bornstein & J. S. Bruner (Eds.), *Interaction in human development* (pp. 139–153). Hillsdale, NJ: Lawrence Erlbaum.

Schegloff, E. A. (2007). *Sequence organization in interaction.* Cambridge, England: Cambridge University Press.

Schieffelin, B., & Ochs, E. (1986). *Language socialization across cultures.* Cambridge, England: Cambridge University Press.

Sheldon, A. (1996). You can be the baby brother but you aren't born yet: Preschool girls' negotiation for power and access in pretend play. *Research on Language and Social Interaction, 29,* 57–80.

Tabors, P. O. (1993). *One child, two languages: A guide for early childhood educators of children learning English as a second language.* Baltimore, MD: Paul H. Brookes.

Tabors, P. O., & Snow, C. E. (1994). English as a second language in preschools. In F. Genesee (Ed.), *Educating second language children: The whole child, the whole curriculum, the whole community* (pp. 103–125). New York: Cambridge University Press.

The Folkeskole Act. (n.d.). Retrieved November 30, 2006, from http://eng.uvm.dk/publications/laws/folkeskole.htm?menuid=2010

Toohey, K. (2000). *Learning English at school: Identity, social relations and classroom practice.* Clevedon, England: Multilingual Matters.

Toohey, K. (2001). Disputes in child L2 learning. *TESOL Quarterly, 35,* 257–278.

Watson-Gegeo, K., & Nielsen, S. (2003). Language socialization in SLA. In C. J. Doughty & M. H. Long (Eds.), *The handbook of second language acquisition* (pp. 155–177). Oxford, England: Blackwell.

Wenger, E. (1998). *Communities of practice: Learning, meaning, and identity.* Cambridge, England: Cambridge University Press.

Willett, J. (1995). Becoming first graders in an L2: An ethnographic study of L2 socialization. *TESOL Quarterly, 29,* 473–503.

Wootton, A. (1997). *Interaction and the development of mind.* Cambridge, England: Cambridge University Press.

Wong-Fillmore, L. (1976). *The second time around: Cognitive and social strategies in second language acquisition.* Unpublished doctoral dissertation, Stanford University, Palo Alto, CA.

Appendix: Transcription conventions

[	point where overlapping talk starts
(0.0)	length of silence in tenths of a second
(.)	micropause of less than 2/10 of a second
underline	emphasis
CAPS	relatively high volume
::	lengthened syllable
-	cut-off; self-interruption
?/./,	rising/falling/continuing intonation
!	animated tone, not necessarily an exclamation
xxxxx	unintelligible stretch
(word)	transcriber's best guess of what is being said
° °	passage of talk quieter than the surrounding talk
/xx	faster speech than in the previous (part of the) turn
¹xxxx. ((¹xxxx.))	activity occurring simultaneously with the turn or part of the turn
‾xx	high pitch
(not?)	probable but unsure hearing
hihi	laughter

about the contributors

David Aline (EdD, Temple University) is a professor at Kanagawa University, Yokohama, Faculty of Foreign Languages, Department of Cross-Cultural Studies, and teaches psycholinguistics in the Graduate School of Foreign Languages. His research examines second language acquisition and use in university, elementary school, lingua franca, and tutorial settings through a conversation analytic perspective. He has published in the *Canadian Journal of Applied Linguistics* and *JALT Journal*, among others, and is coauthor of *Psycholinguistics: Language, Mind and World* (D. Steinberg, H. Nagata, & D. Aline, 2001).

Kathleen Bardovi-Harlig, Professor of Second Language Studies at Indiana University Bloomington, has presented at Pragmatics and Language Learning since 1987. Her work on second language pragmatics has appeared in *Pragmatics and Language Learning*, *Studies in Second Language Acquisition*, and *Language Learning*. Her current work in L2 pragmatics focuses on the development of pragmalinguistic resources.

Maria-Thereza X. Bastos is a PhD candidate in the Literacy, Culture and Language Education Department at Indiana University Bloomington. She holds an MA in TESL from the University of Illinois at Urbana-Champaign. Her research interests include methods of teaching foreign and second languages, teacher education, interlanguage pragmatics, sociolinguistics, critical literacy, and pedagogical drama applied to the teaching of foreign/second languages.

Beatrix Burghardt is a PhD candidate in the Department of Second Language Studies at Indiana University Bloomington. Her research interests include foreign language classroom discourse, child language acquisition, and the role of the syntax-semantics interface in L2 acquisition. Currently, her work focuses on the development of spatial language and the emergence of the aspectual system in adult L2 learners of Hungarian.

Eric Chappetto is a PhD student in the department of Spanish and Portuguese at Indiana University Bloomington whose interests are discourse analysis, pragmatics, and sociolinguistics.

Margaret Ann DuFon is an associate professor in the English Department at California State University-Chico where she teaches courses in second language acquisition, reading pedagogy, Asian-American literature, and academic writing. Her main research areas are interlanguage pragmatics and second language socialization, particularly as they apply to the acquisition of Indonesian language by study abroad learners. Her publications include the book *Language Learners in Study Abroad Contexts*, coedited with Eton Churchill, and articles on the acquisition of language and culture such as the socialization of taste during study abroad in Indonesia and gift giving in Indonesia.

Donna T. Fujimoto is Associate Professor at Osaka Jogakuin College in Osaka, Japan, where she teaches English and comparative culture studies. She received her MA from the University of Hawaiʻi at Mānoa and is a doctoral candidate at Temple University, Japan, Osaka campus. She has published articles related to the areas of classroom research, narrative studies, and intercultural communication. She is currently focusing on multiparty interaction of novice language learners in the EFL classroom.

Toshiaki Furukawa is a PhD candidate in the Department of Linguistics at the University of Hawaiʻi at Mānoa. His current research focuses on the discursive construction of multilingual and multiracial identities in densely semiotized spaces. He has published articles on stylization in Local stand-up comedy shows as culturally specific activities in Hawaiʻi.

Tim Greer is an associate professor in the School of Languages and Communication at Kobe University. His research focuses on bilingual interaction and second language talk, using ethnography and conversation analysis to examine discursive displays of identity. He is also researching a variety of interactional practices in naturally occurring talk between novice and expert speakers of English. He is the editor of the *Japan Journal of Multilingualism and Multiculturalism* and has recently published work in *Multilingua*, the *Journal of Applied Linguistics*, and *JALT Journal*.

Eric Hauser is an associate professor of English at the University of Electro-Communications in Tokyo. His research focuses on conversational interaction, in particular, interaction that occurs within English language classrooms and similar settings. This research has involved such matters as the organization of language correction, turn-taking during student discussions, the use of categories in constructing an argument, and participant orientation to and construction of classroom context.

Yuri Hosoda (EdD, Temple University) is an associate professor in the Faculty of Foreign Languages, Department of Cross-Cultural Studies, and the Graduate School of Foreign Languages at Kanagawa University, Yokohama. Her research interests include the investigation of second language use and learning in Japanese and English at universities, elementary schools, and work places and in mundane conversation through a conversation analytic perspective. She has published in *Applied Linguistics*, the *Canadian Journal of Applied Linguistics*, and *Issues in Applied Linguistics*, among others.

Martha Sif Karrebæk (PhD, University of Copenhagen) is a postdoctoral fellow at the Center of Danish as a Second Language, University of Copenhagen. Her work focuses on the communicative opportunities and constraints of linguistic minority children in mainstream kindergartens and early school grades. Her research interests include language socialization, peer-group socialization, interactional sociolinguistics, language acquisition, and child language.

Junko Mori is Professor of Japanese language and linguistics at the University of Wisconsin-Madison. Her research interests center on the application of conversation analysis to the study of talk-in-interaction involving first and second language speakers of Japanese. Her publications have appeared in journals such as *Applied Linguistics*, *International Review of Applied Linguistics in Language Teaching*, *The Modern Language Journal*, and *Research on Language and Social Interaction* as well as in various edited volumes. She is currently working on a book-length monograph that explores how to integrate the development of current research in interactional linguistics and sociolinguistics into language education.

Edelmira L. Nickels is a PhD candidate in the Department of Second Language Studies, Indiana University Bloomington, and works with career-military English learners from around the world. Her research interests include pragmatics and second language acquisition, pragmatic awareness in the classroom, discourse pragmatics of nonnative speakers, Puerto Rican political discourse in the United States, English in Puerto Rico, and issues in world Englishes.

Carsten Roever is Senior Lecturer in Applied Linguistics at the University of Melbourne. His research interests are interlanguage pragmatics, language testing, and second language acquisition. He holds a PhD in second language acquisition from the University of Hawai'i at Mānoa and has published several book chapters, journal articles, and books, most recently, *Language Testing: The Social Dimension* with Tim McNamara.

Marda Rose is a PhD student in Hispanic Linguistics at Indiana University Bloomington. She currently teaches Spanish as a foreign language in the Department of Spanish and Portuguese and English as a second language in the Department of Second Language Studies. Her research interests include interlanguage pragmatics, L2 phonology, and the use of theater in research and teaching. She also directs Grupo de Teatro VIDA, a Spanish-language performance group.

Steven Talmy is an assistant professor in the Department of Language & Literacy Education at the University of British Columbia. His work on "oldtimer" ESL student resistance to schooling has appeared in such journals as *Applied Linguistics*, *Linguistics and Education*, and *Journal of Language, Identity, and Education*, in addition to several edited anthologies. His academic interests include critical analyses of discourse, K–12 ESL, the sociology of ESL education, teacher education, and (critical) qualitative research methods.

Lynda Yates is currently Associate Professor in Linguistics at Macquarie University, Sydney. After earning a degree in languages (Russian and French), Lynda taught English to adult speakers of other languages in the UK, France, Armenia, and Egypt in a range of settings. Lynda's research interests include adult language learning and use, settlement issues for immigrants, cross-cultural and interlanguage pragmatics, pronunciation teaching and learning, and TESOL teacher professional development.

NATIONAL FOREIGN LANGUAGE RESOURCE CENTER
University of Hawai'i at Mānoa

ordering information at nflrc.hawaii.edu

Pragmatics & Interaction
Gabriele Kasper, series editor

Pragmatics & Interaction ("P&I"), a refereed series sponsored by the University of Hawai'i National Foreign Language Resource Center, publishes research on topics in pragmatics and discourse as social interaction from a wide variety of theoretical and methodological perspectives. P&I welcomes particularly studies on languages spoken in the Asian-Pacific region.

TALK-IN-INTERACTION: MULTILINGUAL PERSPECTIVES
HANH THI NGUYEN & GABRIELE KASPER (EDITORS), 2009

This volume offers original studies of interaction in a range of languages and language varieties, including Chinese, English, Japanese, Korean, Spanish, Swahili, Thai, and Vietnamese; monolingual and bilingual interactions, and activities designed for second or foreign language learning. Conducted from the perspectives of conversation analysis and membership categorization analysis, the chapters examine ordinary conversation and institutional activities in face-to-face, telephone, and computer-mediated environments.

430 pp., ISBN 978–0–8248–3137–0 $30.

Pragmatics & Language Learning
Gabriele Kasper, series editor

Pragmatics & Language Learning ("PLL"), a refereed series sponsored by the National Foreign Language Resource Center, publishes selected papers from the biannual International Pragmatics & Language Learning conference under the editorship of the conference hosts and the series editor. Check the NFLRC website for upcoming PLL conferences and PLL volumes.

PRAGMATICS AND LANGUAGE LEARNING VOLUME 11
KATHLEEN BARDOVI-HARLIG, CÉSAR FÉLIX-BRASDEFER, & ALWIYA S. OMAR (EDITORS), 2006

This volume features cutting-edge theoretical and empirical research on pragmatics and language learning among a wide-variety of learners in diverse learning contexts from a variety of language backgrounds and target languages (English, German, Japanese, Kiswahili, Persian, and Spanish). This collection of papers from researchers around the world includes critical appraisals on the role of formulas in interlanguage pragmatics and speech-act research from a conversation analytic perspective. Empirical studies examine learner data using innovative methods of analysis and investigate issues in pragmatic development and the instruction of pragmatics.

430 pp., ISBN 978-0-8248-3137-0 $30.

NFLRC Monographs
Richard Schmidt, series editor

Monographs of the National Foreign Language Resource Center present the findings of recent work in applied linguistics that is of relevance to language teaching and learning (with a focus on the less commonly taught languages of Asia and the Pacific) and are of particular interest to foreign language educators, applied linguists, and researchers. Prior to 2006, these monographs were published as "SLTCC Technical Reports."

RESEARCH AMONG LEARNERS OF CHINESE AS A FOREIGN LANGUAGE
MICHAEL E. EVERSON & HELEN H. SHEN (EDITORS), 2010

Cutting-edge in its approach and international in its authorship, this fourth monograph in a series sponsored by the Chinese Language Teachers Association features eight research studies that explore a variety of themes, topics, and perspectives important to a variety of stakeholders in the Chinese language learning community. Employing a wide range of research methodologies, the volume provides data from actual Chinese language learners and will be of value to both theoreticians and practitioners alike. *[in English & Chinese]*

180pp.; 978-0-9800459-4-9 $20

MANCHU: A TEXTBOOK FOR READING DOCUMENTS (SECOND EDITION)
GERTRAUDE ROTH LI, 2010

This book offers students a tool to gain a basic grounding in the Manchu language. The reading selections provided in this volume represent various types of documents, ranging from examples of the very earliest Manchu writing (17th century) to samples of contemporary Sibe (Xibo), a language that maybe considered a modern version of Manchu. Since Manchu courses are only rarely taught at universities anywhere, this second edition includes audio recordings to assist students with the pronunciation of the texts.

418pp.; ISBN 978-0-9800459-5-6 $36.

TOWARD USEFUL PROGRAM EVALUATION IN COLLEGE FOREIGN LANGUAGE EDUCATION
JOHN M. NORRIS, JOHN McE. DAVIS, CASTLE SINICROPE, & YUKIKO WATANABE (EDITORS), 2009

This volume reports on innovative, useful evaluation work conducted within U.S. college foreign language programs. An introductory chapter scopes out the territory, reporting key findings from research into the concerns, impetuses, and uses for evaluation that FL educators identify. Seven chapters then highlight examples of evaluations conducted in diverse language programs and institutional contexts. Each case is reported by program-internal educators, who walk readers through critical steps, from identifying evaluation uses, users, and questions, to designing methods, interpreting findings, and taking actions. A concluding chapter reflects on the emerging roles for FL program evaluation and articulates an agenda for integrating evaluation into language education practice.

240pp., ISBN 978-0-9800459-3-2 $30.

SECOND LANGUAGE TEACHING AND LEARNING IN THE NET GENERATION
RAQUEL OXFORD & JEFFREY OXFORD (EDITORS), 2009

Today's young people—the Net Generation—have grown up with technology all around them. However, teachers cannot assume that students' familiarity with technology in general transfers successfully to pedagogical settings. This volume examines various technologies and offers concrete advice on how each can be successfully implemented in the second language curriculum.

240pp., ISBN 978-0-9800459-2-5 $30.

CASE STUDIES IN FOREIGN LANGUAGE PLACEMENT: PRACTICES AND POSSIBILITIES
THOM HUDSON & MARTYN CLARK (EDITORS), 2008

Although most language programs make placement decisions on the basis of placement tests, there is surprisingly little published about different contexts and systems of placement testing. The present volume contains case studies of placement programs in foreign language programs at the tertiary level across the United States. The different programs span the spectrum from large programs servicing hundreds of students annually to small language programs with very few students. The contributions to this volume address such issues as how the size of the program, presence or absence of heritage learners, and population changes affect language placement decisions.

201pp., ISBN 0-9800459-0-8 $40.

CHINESE AS A HERITAGE LANGUAGE: FOSTERING ROOTED WORLD CITIZENRY
Agnes Weiyun He & Yun Xiao (Editors), 2008

Thirty-two scholars examine the socio-cultural, cognitive-linguistic, and educational-institutional trajectories along which Chinese as a Heritage Language may be acquired, maintained and developed. They draw upon developmental psychology, functional linguistics, linguistic and cultural anthropology, discourse analysis, orthography analysis, reading research, second language acquisition, and bilingualism. This volume aims to lay a foundation for theories, models, and master scripts to be discussed, debated, and developed, and to stimulate research and enhance teaching both within and beyond Chinese language education.

280pp., ISBN 978-0-8248-3286-5 $40.

PERSPECTIVES ON TEACHING CONNECTED SPEECH TO SECOND LANGUAGE SPEAKERS
James Dean Brown & Kimi Kondo-Brown (Editors), 2006

This book is a collection of fourteen articles on connected speech of interest to teachers, researchers, and materials developers in both ESL/EFL (ten chapters focus on connected speech in English) and Japanese (four chapters focus on Japanese connected speech). The fourteen chapters are divided up into five sections:

- What do we know so far about teaching connected speech?
- Does connected speech instruction work?
- How should connected speech be taught in English?
- How should connected speech be taught in Japanese?
- How should connected speech be tested?

290 pp., ISBN 978-0-8248-3136-3 $38.

CORPUS LINGUISTICS FOR KOREAN LANGUAGE LEARNING AND TEACHING
Robert Bley-Vroman & Hyunsook Ko (Editors), 2006

Dramatic advances in personal-computer technology have given language teachers access to vast quantities of machine-readable text, which can be analyzed with a view toward improving the basis of language instruction. Corpus linguistics provides analytic techniques and practical tools for studying language in use. This volume provides both an introductory framework for the use of corpus linguistics for language teaching and examples of its application for Korean teaching and learning. The collected papers cover topics in Korean syntax, lexicon, and discourse, and second language acquisition research, always with a focus on application in the classroom. An overview of Korean corpus linguistics tools and available Korean corpora are also included.

265 pp., ISBN 0-8248-3062-8 $25.

NEW TECHNOLOGIES AND LANGUAGE LEARNING: CASES IN THE LESS COMMONLY TAUGHT LANGUAGES
Carol Anne Spreen (Editor), 2002

In recent years, the National Security Education Program (NSEP) has supported an increasing number of programs for teaching languages using different technological media. This compilation of case study initiatives funded through the NSEP Institutional Grants Program presents a range of technology-based options for language programming that will help universities make more informed decisions about teaching less commonly taught languages. The eight chapters describe how different types of technologies are used to support language programs (i.e., Web, ITV, and audio- or video-based materials), discuss identifiable trends in elanguage learning, and explore how technology addresses issues of equity, diversity, and opportunity. This book offers many lessons learned and decisions made as technology changes and learning needs become more complex.

188 pp., ISBN 0-8248-2634-5 $25.

AN INVESTIGATION OF SECOND LANGUAGE TASK-BASED PERFORMANCE ASSESSMENTS
James Dean Brown, Thom Hudson, John M. Norris, & William Bonk, 2002

This volume describes the creation of performance assessment instruments and their validation (based on work started in a previous monograph). It begins by explaining the test and rating scale development processes and the administration of the resulting three seven-task tests to 90 university level EFL and ESL students. The results are examined in terms of (a) the effects of test revision; (b) comparisons among the task-dependent, task-independent, and self-rating scales; and (c) reliability and validity issues.

240 pp., ISBN 0-8248-2633-7 $25.

MOTIVATION AND SECOND LANGUAGE ACQUISITION
Zoltán Dörnyei & Richard Schmidt (Editors), 2001

This volume—the second in this series concerned with motivation and foreign language learning—includes papers presented in a state-of-the-art colloquium on L2 motivation at the American Association for Applied Linguistics (Vancouver, 2000) and a number of specially commissioned studies. The 20 chapters, written by some of the best known researchers in the field, cover a wide range of theoretical and research methodological issues, and also offer empirical results (both qualitative and quantitative) concerning the learning of many different languages (Arabic, Chinese, English, Filipino, French, German, Hindi, Italian, Japanese, Russian, and Spanish) in a broad range of learning contexts (Bahrain, Brazil, Canada, Egypt, Finland, Hungary, Ireland, Israel, Japan, Spain, and the US).

520 pp., ISBN 0-8248-2458-X $25.

A FOCUS ON LANGUAGE TEST DEVELOPMENT: EXPANDING THE LANGUAGE PROFICIENCY CONSTRUCT ACROSS A VARIETY OF TESTS
THOM HUDSON & JAMES DEAN BROWN (EDITORS), 2001

This volume presents eight research studies that introduce a variety of novel, non-traditional forms of second and foreign language assessment. To the extent possible, the studies also show the entire test development process, warts and all. These language testing projects not only demonstrate many of the types of problems that test developers run into in the real world but also afford the reader unique insights into the language test development process.

230 pp., ISBN 0–8248–2351–6 $20.

STUDIES ON KOREAN IN COMMUNITY SCHOOLS
DONG-JAE LEE, SOOKEUN CHO, MISEON LEE, MINSUN SONG, & WILLIAM O'GRADY (EDITORS), 2000

The papers in this volume focus on language teaching and learning in Korean community schools. Drawing on innovative experimental work and research in linguistics, education, and psychology, the contributors address issues of importance to teachers, administrators, and parents. Topics covered include childhood bilingualism, Korean grammar, language acquisition, children's literature, and language teaching methodology. [in Korean]

256 pp., ISBN 0–8248–2352–4 $20.

A COMMUNICATIVE FRAMEWORK FOR INTRODUCTORY JAPANESE LANGUAGE CURRICULA
WASHINGTON STATE JAPANESE LANGUAGE CURRICULUM GUIDELINES COMMITTEE, 2000

In recent years the number of schools offering Japanese nationwide has increased dramatically. Because of the tremendous popularity of the Japanese language and the shortage of teachers, quite a few untrained, non-native and native teachers are in the classrooms and are expected to teach several levels of Japanese. These guidelines are intended to assist individual teachers and professional associations throughout the United States in designing Japanese language curricula. They are meant to serve as a framework from which language teaching can be expanded and are intended to allow teachers to enhance and strengthen the quality of Japanese language instruction.

168 pp., ISBN 0–8248–2350–8 $20.

FOREIGN LANGUAGE TEACHING AND MINORITY LANGUAGE EDUCATION
KATHRYN A. DAVIS (EDITOR), 1999

This volume seeks to examine the potential for building relationships among foreign language, bilingual, and ESL programs towards fostering bilingualism. Part I of the volume examines the sociopolitical contexts for language partnerships, including:

- obstacles to developing bilingualism
- implications of acculturation, identity, and language issues for

linguistic minorities.
- the potential for developing partnerships across primary, secondary, and tertiary institutions

Part II of the volume provides research findings on the Foreign language partnership project designed to capitalize on the resources of immigrant students to enhance foreign language learning.

152 pp., ISBN 0–8248–2067–3 $20.

DESIGNING SECOND LANGUAGE PERFORMANCE ASSESSMENTS
John M. Norris, James Dean Brown, Thom Hudson, & Jim Yoshioka, 1998, 2000

This technical report focuses on the decision-making potential provided by second language performance assessments. The authors first situate performance assessment within a broader discussion of alternatives in language assessment and in educational assessment in general. They then discuss issues in performance assessment design, implementation, reliability, and validity. Finally, they present a prototype framework for second language performance assessment based on the integration of theoretical underpinnings and research findings from the task-based language teaching literature, the language testing literature, and the educational measurement literature. The authors outline test and item specifications, and they present numerous examples of prototypical language tasks. They also propose a research agenda focusing on the operationalization of second language performance assessments.

248 pp., ISBN 0–8248–2109–2 $20.

SECOND LANGUAGE DEVELOPMENT IN WRITING: MEASURES OF FLUENCY, ACCURACY, AND COMPLEXITY
Kate Wolfe-Quintero, Shunji Inagaki, & Hae-Young Kim, 1998, 2002

In this book, the authors analyze and compare the ways that fluency, accuracy, grammatical complexity, and lexical complexity have been measured in studies of language development in second language writing. More than 100 developmental measures are examined, with detailed comparisons of the results across the studies that have used each measure. The authors discuss the theoretical foundations for each type of developmental measure, and they consider the relationship between developmental measures and various types of proficiency measures. They also examine criteria for determining which developmental measures are the most successful and suggest which measures are the most promising for continuing work on language development.

208 pp., ISBN 0–8248–2069–X $20.

THE DEVELOPMENT OF A LEXICAL TONE PHONOLOGY IN AMERICAN ADULT LEARNERS OF STANDARD MANDARIN CHINESE
Sylvia Henel Sun, 1998

The study reported is based on an assessment of three decades of research on the SLA of Mandarin tone. It investigates whether differences in learners' tone perception and production are related to differences in the effects of certain linguistic, task, and learner factors. The learners of focus are American students of Mandarin in Beijing, China. Their performances on two perception and three production tasks are analyzed through a host of variables and methods of quantification.

328 pp., ISBN 0–8248–2068–1 $20.

NEW TRENDS AND ISSUES IN TEACHING JAPANESE LANGUAGE AND CULTURE
HARUKO M. COOK, KYOKO HIJIRIDA, & MILDRED TAHARA (EDITORS), 1997

In recent years, Japanese has become the fourth most commonly taught foreign language at the college level in the United States. As the number of students who study Japanese has increased, the teaching of Japanese as a foreign language has been established as an important academic field of study. This technical report includes nine contributions to the advancement of this field, encompassing the following five important issues:

- Literature and literature teaching
- Technology in the language classroom
- Orthography
- Testing
- Grammatical versus pragmatic approaches to language teaching

164 pp., ISBN 0–8248–2067–3 $20.

SIX MEASURES OF JSL PRAGMATICS
SAYOKO OKADA YAMASHITA, 1996

This book investigates differences among tests that can be used to measure the cross-cultural pragmatic ability of English-speaking learners of Japanese. Building on the work of Hudson, Detmer, and Brown (Technical Reports #2 and #7 in this series), the author modified six test types that she used to gather data from North American learners of Japanese. She found numerous problems with the multiple-choice discourse completion test but reported that the other five tests all proved highly reliable and reasonably valid. Practical issues involved in creating and using such language tests are discussed from a variety of perspectives.

213 pp., ISBN 0–8248–1914–4 $15.

LANGUAGE LEARNING STRATEGIES AROUND THE WORLD: CROSS-CULTURAL PERSPECTIVES
REBECCA L. OXFORD (EDITOR), 1996, 1997, 2002

Language learning strategies are the specific steps students take to improve their progress in learning a second or foreign language. Optimizing learning strategies improves language performance. This groundbreaking book presents new information about cultural influences on the use of language learning strategies. It also shows innovative ways to assess students' strategy use and remarkable techniques for helping students improve their choice of strategies, with the goal of peak language learning.

166 pp., ISBN 0–8248–1910–1 $20.

TELECOLLABORATION IN FOREIGN LANGUAGE LEARNING: PROCEEDINGS OF THE HAWAI'I SYMPOSIUM
Mark Warschauer (Editor), 1996

The Symposium on Local & Global Electronic Networking in Foreign Language Learning & Research, part of the National Foreign Language Resource Center's 1995 Summer Institute on Technology & the Human Factor in Foreign Language Education, included presentations of papers and hands-on workshops conducted by Symposium participants to facilitate the sharing of resources, ideas, and information about all aspects of electronic networking for foreign language teaching and research, including electronic discussion and conferencing, international cultural exchanges, real-time communication and simulations, research and resource retrieval via the Internet, and research using networks. This collection presents a sampling of those presentations.

252 pp., ISBN 0–8248–1867–9 $20.

LANGUAGE LEARNING MOTIVATION: PATHWAYS TO THE NEW CENTURY
Rebecca L. Oxford (Editor), 1996

This volume chronicles a revolution in our thinking about what makes students want to learn languages and what causes them to persist in that difficult and rewarding adventure. Topics in this book include the internal structures of and external connections with foreign language motivation; exploring adult language learning motivation, self-efficacy, and anxiety; comparing the motivations and learning strategies of students of Japanese and Spanish; and enhancing the theory of language learning motivation from many psychological and social perspectives.

218 pp., ISBN 0–8248–1849–0 $20.

LINGUISTICS & LANGUAGE TEACHING: PROCEEDINGS OF THE SIXTH JOINT LSH-HATESL CONFERENCE
Cynthia Reves, Caroline Steele, & Cathy S. P. Wong (Editors), 1996

Technical Report #10 contains 18 articles revolving around the following three topics:

- Linguistic issues—These six papers discuss various linguistic issues: ideophones, syllabic nasals, linguistic areas, computation, tonal melody classification, and wh-words.
- Sociolinguistics—Sociolinguistic phenomena in Swahili, signing, Hawaiian, and Japanese are discussed in four of the papers.
- Language teaching and learning—These eight papers cover prosodic modification, note taking, planning in oral production, oral testing, language policy, L2 essay organization, access to dative alternation rules, and child noun phrase structure development.

364 pp., ISBN 0–8248–1851–2 $20.

ATTENTION & AWARENESS IN FOREIGN LANGUAGE LEARNING
Richard Schmidt (Editor), 1996

Issues related to the role of attention and awareness in learning lie at the heart of many theoretical and practical controversies in the foreign language field. This collection of papers presents research into the learning of Spanish, Japanese, Finnish, Hawaiian, and English as a second language (with additional comments and examples from French, German, and miniature artificial languages) that bear on these crucial questions for foreign language pedagogy.

394 pp., ISBN 0–8248–1794–X $20.

VIRTUAL CONNECTIONS: ONLINE ACTIVITIES AND PROJECTS FOR NETWORKING LANGUAGE LEARNERS
Mark Warschauer (Editor), 1995, 1996

Computer networking has created dramatic new possibilities for connecting language learners in a single classroom or across the globe. This collection of activities and projects makes use of email, the internet, computer conferencing, and other forms of computer-mediated communication for the foreign and second language classroom at any level of instruction. Teachers from around the world submitted the activities compiled in this volume—activities that they have used successfully in their own classrooms.

417 pp., ISBN 0–8248–1793–1 $30.

DEVELOPING PROTOTYPIC MEASURES OF CROSS-CULTURAL PRAGMATICS
Thom Hudson, Emily Detmer, & J. D. Brown, 1995

Although the study of cross-cultural pragmatics has gained importance in applied linguistics, there are no standard forms of assessment that might make research comparable across studies and languages. The present volume describes the process through which six forms of cross-cultural assessment were developed for second language learners of English. The models may be used for second language learners of other languages. The six forms of assessment involve two forms each of indirect discourse completion tests, oral language production, and self-assessment. The procedures involve the assessment of requests, apologies, and refusals.

198 pp., ISBN 0–8248–1763–X $15.

THE ROLE OF PHONOLOGICAL CODING IN READING KANJI
Sachiko Matsunaga, 1995

In this technical report, the author reports the results of a study that she conducted on phonological coding in reading kanji using an eye-movement monitor and draws some pedagogical implications. In addition, she reviews current literature on the different schools of thought regarding instruction in reading kanji and its role in the teaching of non-alphabetic written languages like Japanese.

64 pp., ISBN 0–8248–1734–6 $10.

PRAGMATICS OF CHINESE AS NATIVE AND TARGET LANGUAGE
Gabriele Kasper (Editor), 1995

This technical report includes six contributions to the study of the pragmatics of Mandarin Chinese:

- A report of an interview study conducted with nonnative speakers of Chinese; and
- Five data-based studies on the performance of different speech acts by native speakers of Mandarin—requesting, refusing, complaining, giving bad news, disagreeing, and complimenting.

312 pp., ISBN 0–8248–1733–8 $15.

A BIBLIOGRAPHY OF PEDAGOGY AND RESEARCH IN INTERPRETATION AND TRANSLATION
Etilvia Arjona, 1993

This technical report includes four types of bibliographic information on translation and interpretation studies:

- Research efforts across disciplinary boundaries—cognitive psychology, neurolinguistics, psycholinguistics, sociolinguistics, computational linguistics, measurement, aptitude testing, language policy, decision-making, theses, dissertations;
- Training information covering program design, curriculum studies, instruction, school administration;
- Instruction information detailing course syllabi, methodology, models, available textbooks; and
- Testing information about aptitude, selection, diagnostic tests.

115 pp., ISBN 0–8248–1572–6 $10.

PRAGMATICS OF JAPANESE AS NATIVE AND TARGET LANGUAGE
Gabriele Kasper (Editor), 1992, 1996

This technical report includes three contributions to the study of the pragmatics of Japanese:

- A bibliography on speech act performance, discourse management, and other pragmatic and sociolinguistic features of Japanese;
- A study on introspective methods in examining Japanese learners' performance of refusals; and
- A longitudinal investigation of the acquisition of the particle ne by nonnative speakers of Japanese.

125 pp., ISBN 0–8248–1462–2 $10.

A FRAMEWORK FOR TESTING CROSS-CULTURAL PRAGMATICS
Thom Hudson, Emily Detmer, & J. D. Brown, 1992

This technical report presents a framework for developing methods that assess cross-cultural pragmatic ability. Although the framework has been designed for Japanese and American cross-cultural contrasts, it can serve as a generic approach that can be applied to other language contrasts. The focus is on the variables of social distance, relative power, and the degree of imposition within the speech acts of requests, refusals, and apologies. Evaluation of performance is based on recognition of the speech act, amount of speech, forms or formulæ used, directness, formality, and politeness.

51 pp., ISBN 0–8248–1463–0 $10.

RESEARCH METHODS IN INTERLANGUAGE PRAGMATICS
GABRIELE KASPER & MERETE DAHL, 1991

This technical report reviews the methods of data collection employed in 39 studies of interlanguage pragmatics, defined narrowly as the investigation of nonnative speakers' comprehension and production of speech acts, and the acquisition of L2-related speech act knowledge. Data collection instruments are distinguished according to the degree to which they constrain informants' responses, and whether they tap speech act perception/comprehension or production. A main focus of discussion is the validity of different types of data, in particular their adequacy to approximate authentic performance of linguistic action.

51 pp., ISBN 0–8248–1419–3 $10.